Thank you for purchasing volume 27!
In these turbulent times, I'm once again
reminded of the joy of knowing that people are
reading my series.

KOHEI HORIKOSHI

27

SHONEN JUMP Manga Edition

STORY & ART KOHEI HORIKOSHI

TRANSLATION & ENGLISH ADAPTATION Caleb Cook
TOUCH-UP ART & LETTERING John Hunt
DESIGNER Julian [JR] Robinson
SHONEN JUMP SERIES EDITOR John Bae
GRAPHIC NOVEL EDITOR Mike Montesa

BOKU NO HERO ACADEMIA © 2014 by Kohei Horikoshi
All rights reserved.
First published in Japan in 2014 by SHUEISHA Inc., Tokyo.
English translation rights arranged by SHUEISHA Inc.

The stories, characters and incidents mentioned in this publication are entirely fictional.

Printed in the U.S.A.

Published by VIZ Media, LLC
P.O. Box 77010
San Francisco, CA 94107

10 9 8 7 6 5 4 3 2 1
First printing, April 2021

PARENTAL ADVISORY
MY HERO ACADEMIA is rated T for Teen
and is recommended for ages 13 and up.
This volume contains fantasy violence.

MY HERO ACADEMIA vol.27

One's Justice

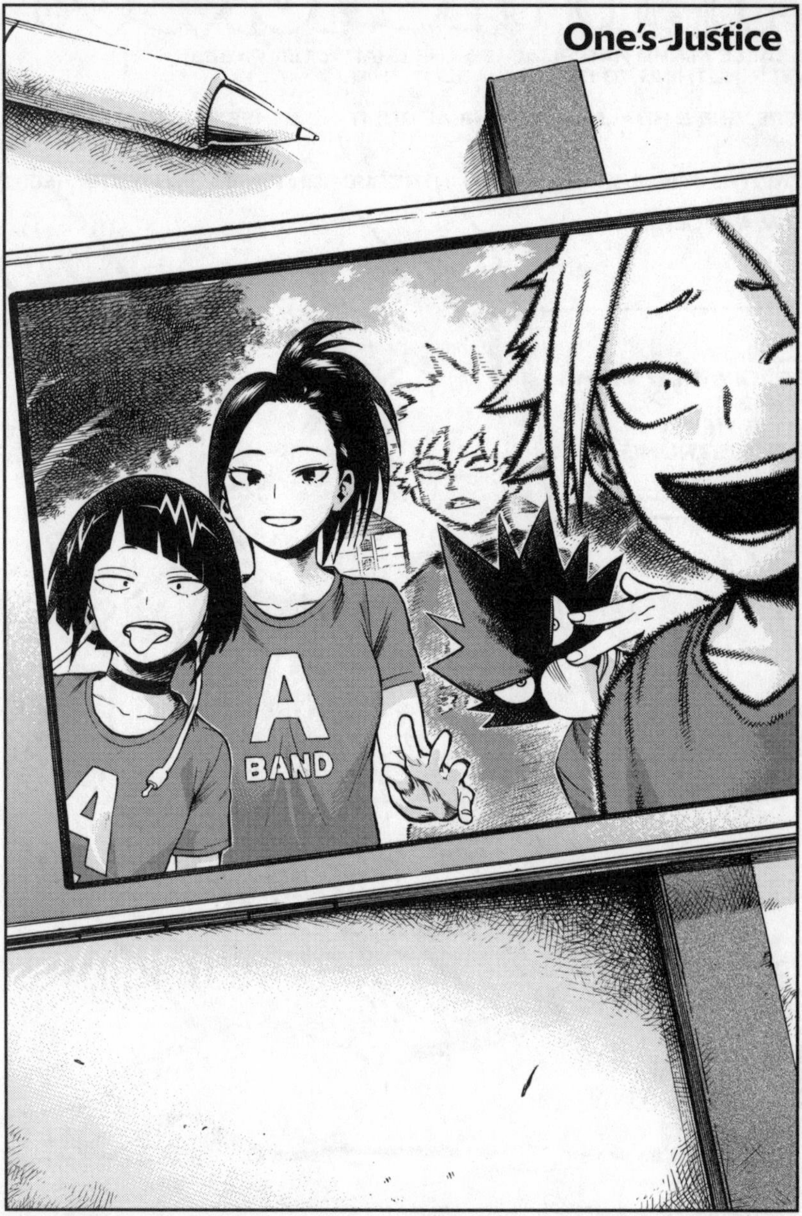
A
BAND

KOHEI HORIKOSHI

AHH! HIJACKED!

MIRACLE MIRKO HAS HIJACKED THE CHARACTER PAGES!
WELP, NOTHING TO BE DONE ABOUT THAT.

NOPE. SHE'S HIJACKED THEM REAL GOOD. NO SENSE FIGHTING IT AT THIS POINT.

NOW THEY'RE JUST THE MIRKO INTRODUCTION PAGES! WHAT THE HECK!

HOW AWFUL!

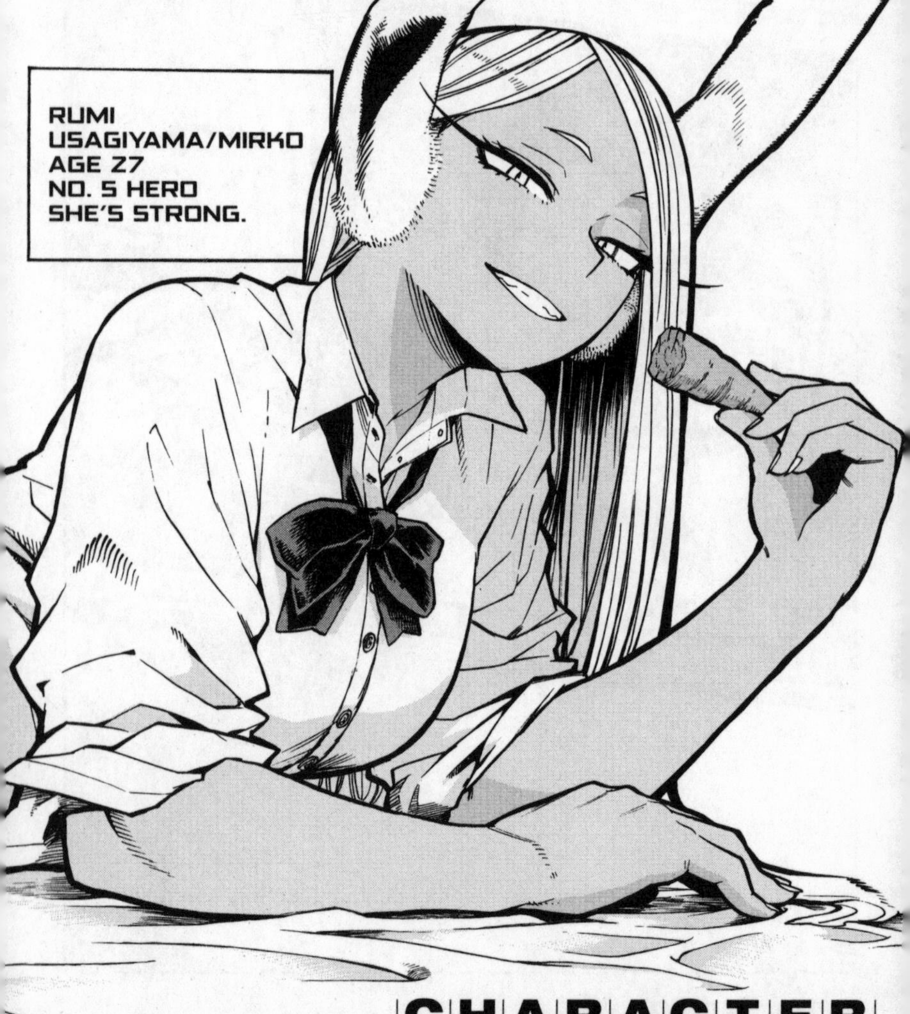
RUMI USAGIYAMA/MIRKO
AGE 27
NO. 5 HERO
SHE'S STRONG.

CHARACTER

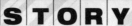

STORY

ONE DAY, PEOPLE BEGAN MANIFESTING SPECIAL ABILITIES THAT CAME TO BE KNOWN AS "QUIRKS," AND BEFORE LONG, THE WORLD WAS FULL OF SUPERPOWERED HUMANS. BUT WITH THE ADVENT OF THESE EXCEPTIONAL INDIVIDUALS CAME AN INCREASE IN CRIME, AND GOVERNMENTS ALONE WERE UNABLE TO DEAL WITH THE SITUATION. AT THE SAME TIME, OTHERS EMERGED TO OPPOSE THE SPREAD OF EVIL! AS IF STRAIGHT FROM THE COMIC BOOKS, THESE HEROES KEEP THE PEACE AND ARE EVEN OFFICIALLY AUTHORIZED TO FIGHT CRIME. OUR STORY BEGINS WHEN A CERTAIN QUIRKLESS BOY AND LIFELONG HERO FAN MEETS THE WORLD'S NUMBER ONE HERO, STARTING HIM ON HIS PATH TO BECOMING THE GREATEST HERO EVER!

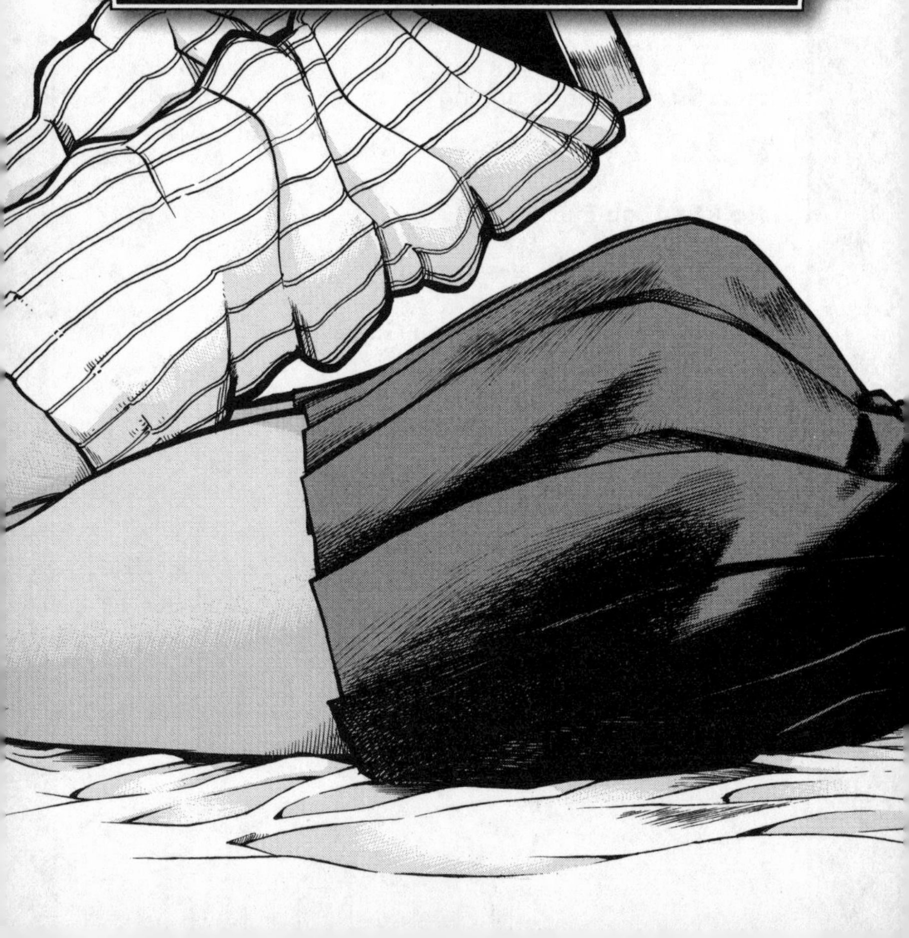

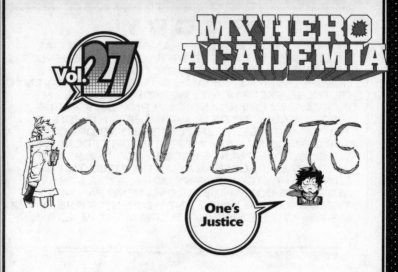

MY HERO ACADEMIA

Vol. 27

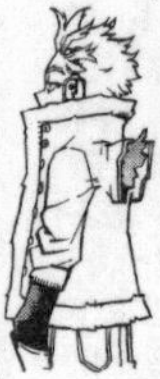

CONTENTS

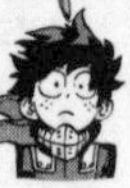

One's Justice

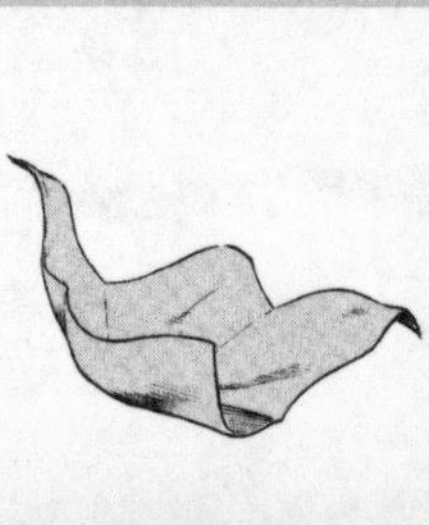

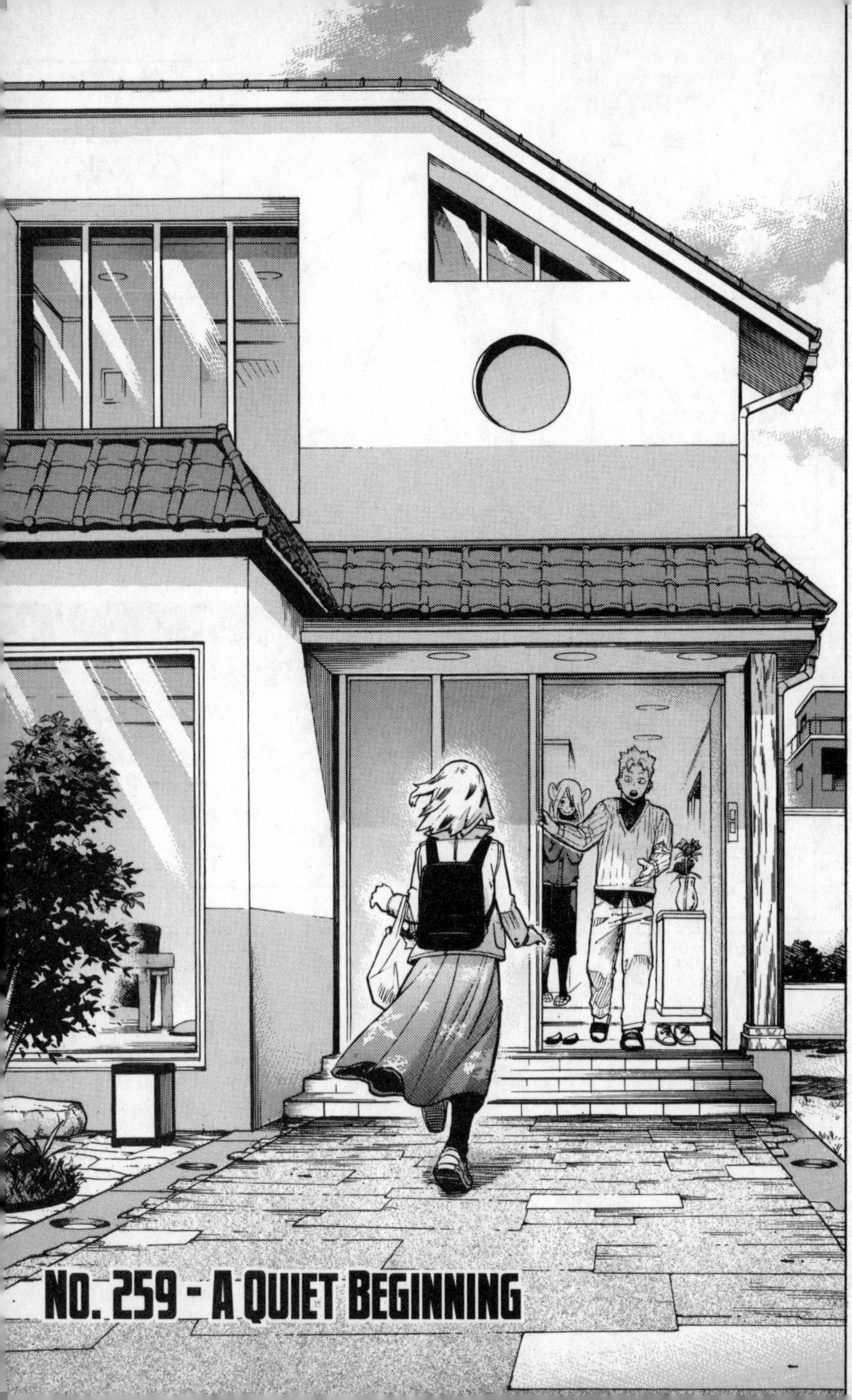
No. 259 - A Quiet Beginning

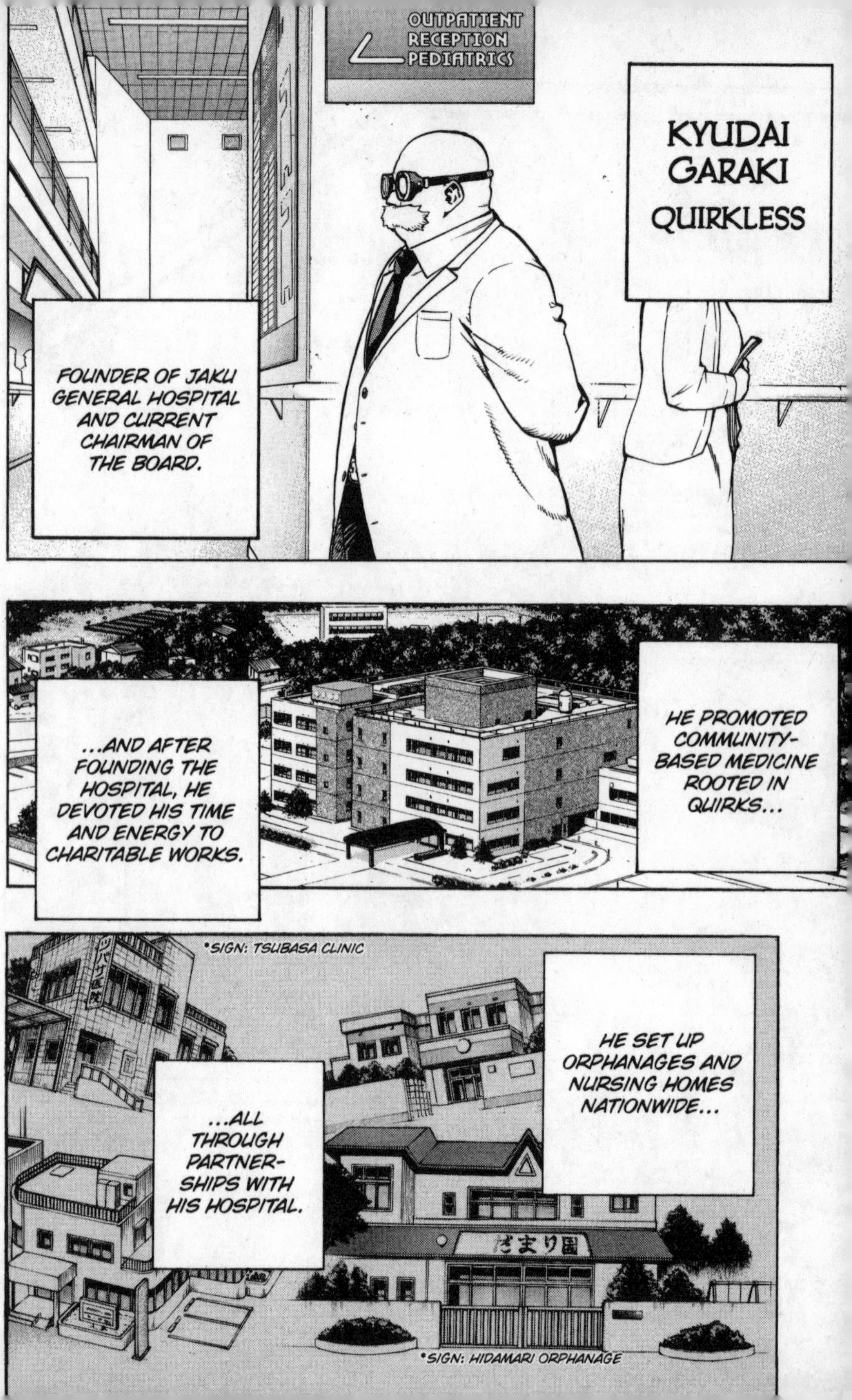
OUTPATIENT RECEPTION PEDIATRICS
KYUDAI GARAKI QUIRKLESS
FOUNDER OF JAKU GENERAL HOSPITAL AND CURRENT CHAIRMAN OF THE BOARD.
HE PROMOTED COMMUNITY-BASED MEDICINE ROOTED IN QUIRKS...
...AND AFTER FOUNDING THE HOSPITAL, HE DEVOTED HIS TIME AND ENERGY TO CHARITABLE WORKS.
*SIGN: TSUBASA CLINIC
HE SET UP ORPHANAGES AND NURSING HOMES NATIONWIDE...
...ALL THROUGH PARTNER-SHIPS WITH HIS HOSPITAL.
*SIGN: HIDAMARI ORPHANAGE

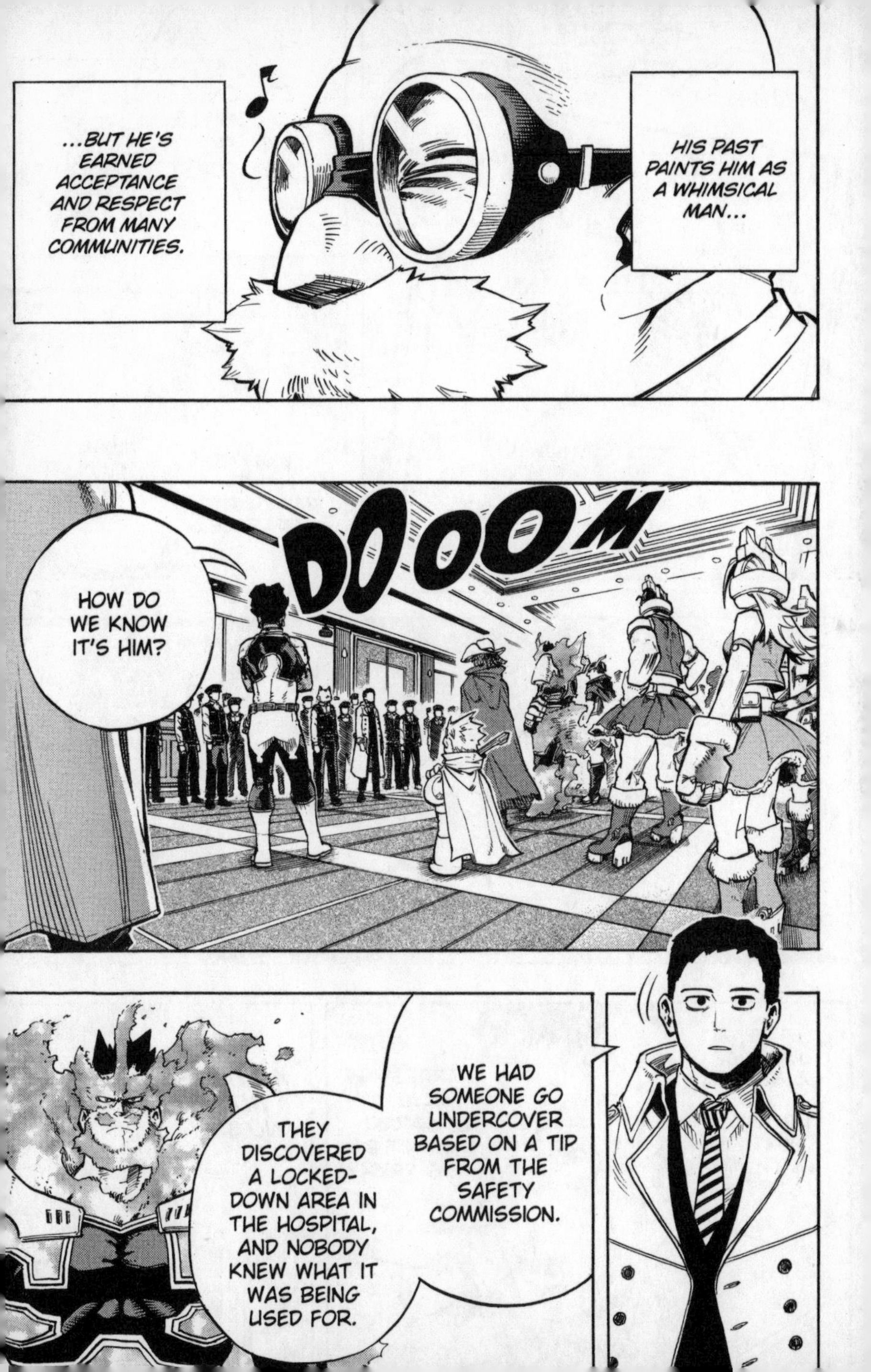
HIS PAST PAINTS HIM AS A WHIMSICAL MAN...
...BUT HE'S EARNED ACCEPTANCE AND RESPECT FROM MANY COMMUNITIES.
DOOOM
HOW DO WE KNOW IT'S HIM?
WE HAD SOMEONE GO UNDERCOVER BASED ON A TIP FROM THE SAFETY COMMISSION.
THEY DISCOVERED A LOCKED-DOWN AREA IN THE HOSPITAL, AND NOBODY KNEW WHAT IT WAS BEING USED FOR.

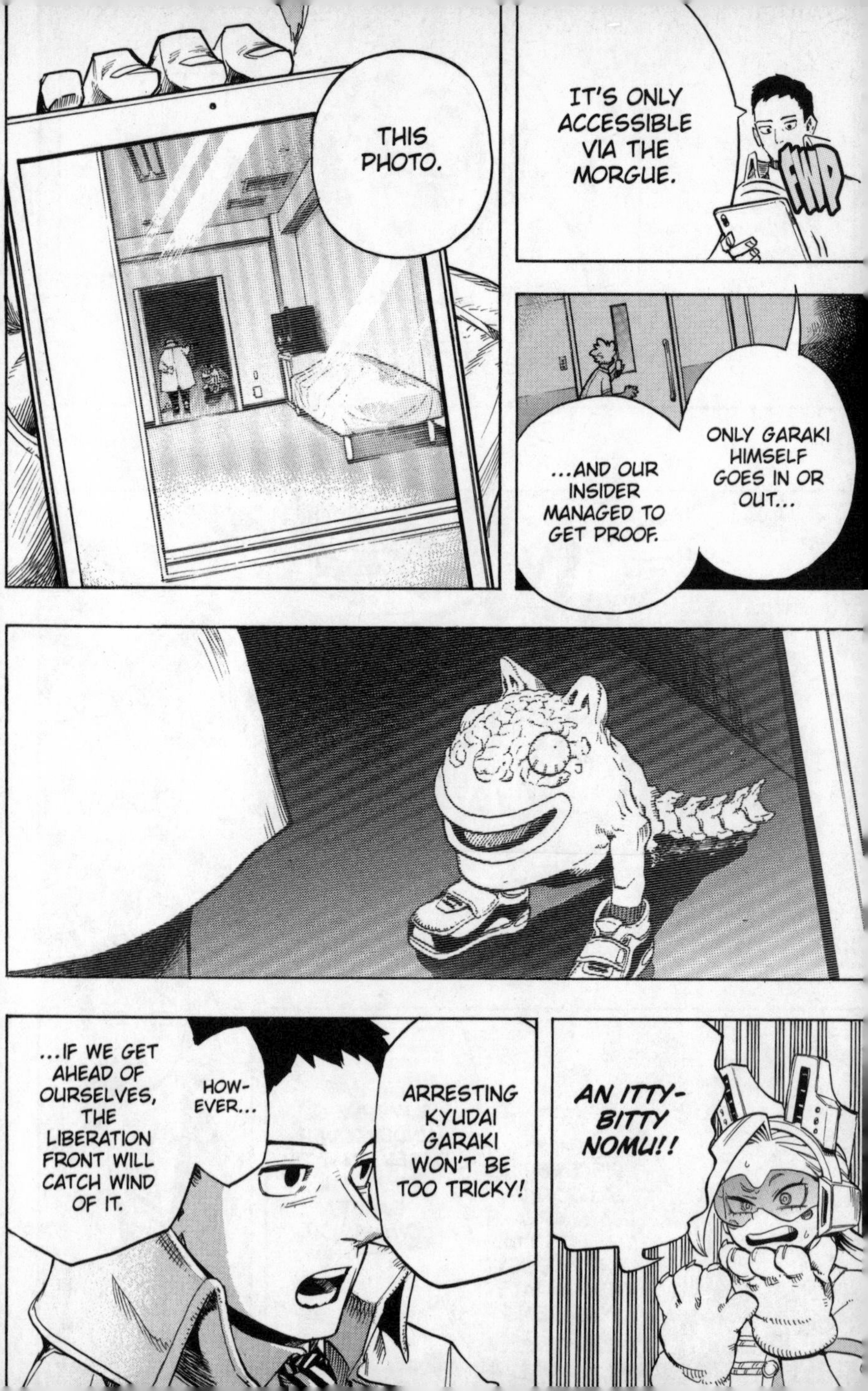
IT'S ONLY ACCESSIBLE VIA THE MORGUE.
ONLY GARAKI HIMSELF GOES IN OR OUT...
...AND OUR INSIDER MANAGED TO GET PROOF.
THIS PHOTO.
AN ITTY-BITTY NOMU!!
ARRESTING KYUDAI GARAKI WON'T BE TOO TRICKY!
HOW-EVER...
...IF WE GET AHEAD OF OURSELVES, THE LIBERATION FRONT WILL CATCH WIND OF IT.

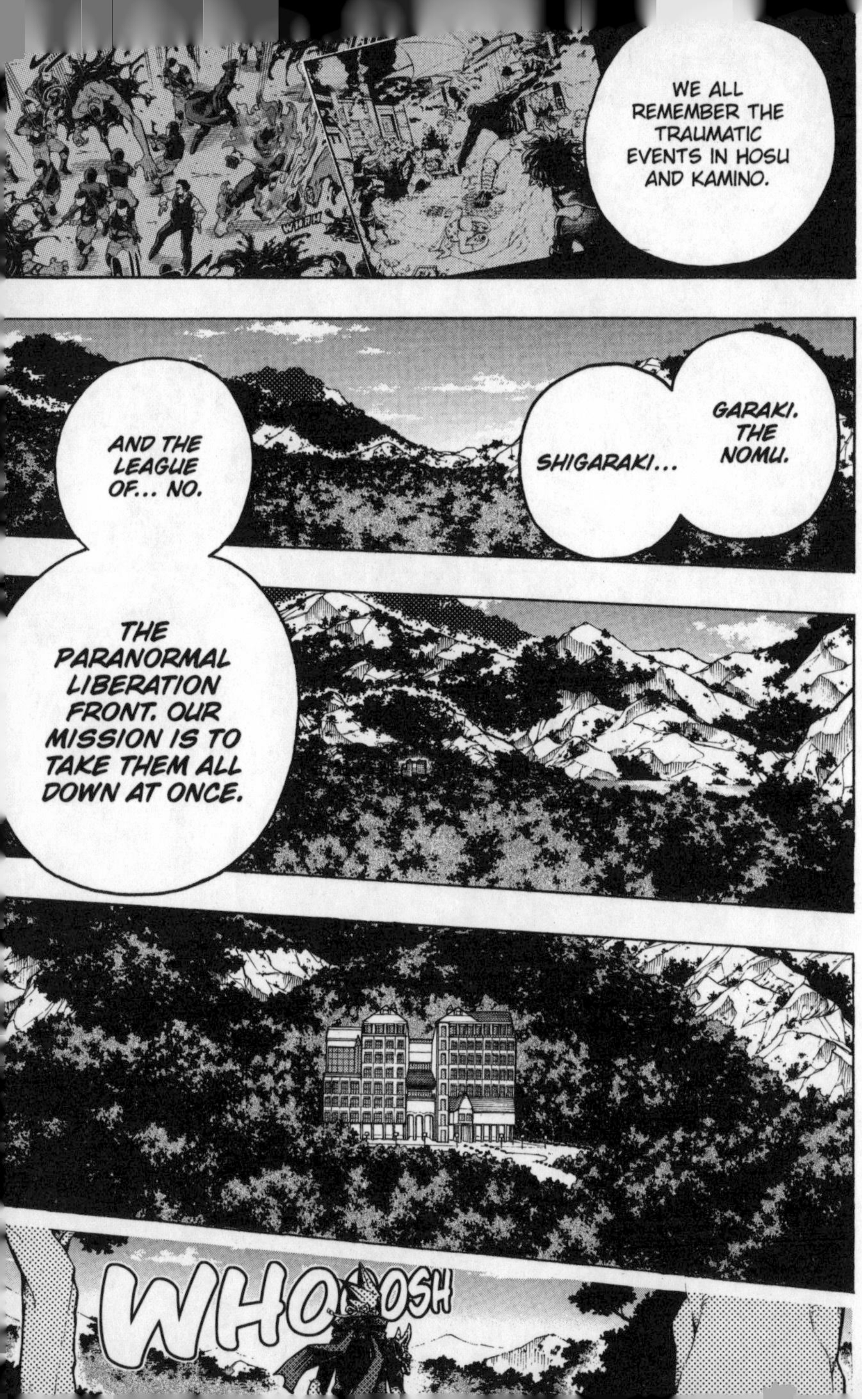
WE ALL REMEMBER THE TRAUMATIC EVENTS IN HOSU AND KAMINO.
SHIGARAKI...
GARAKI. THE NOMU.
AND THE LEAGUE OF... NO.
THE PARANORMAL LIBERATION FRONT. OUR MISSION IS TO TAKE THEM ALL DOWN AT ONCE.
WHOOOSH

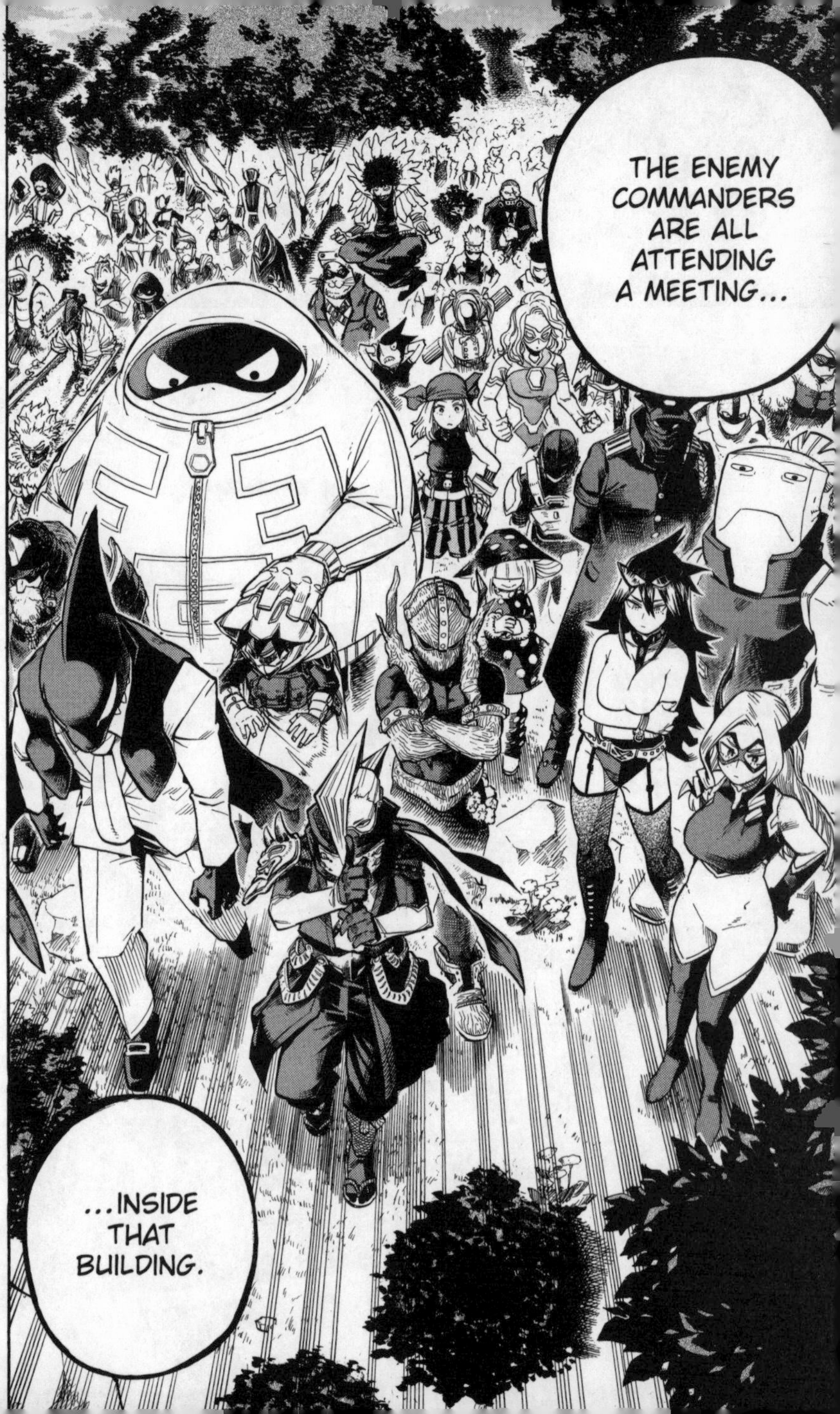
THE ENEMY COMMANDERS ARE ALL ATTENDING A MEETING...
...INSIDE THAT BUILDING.

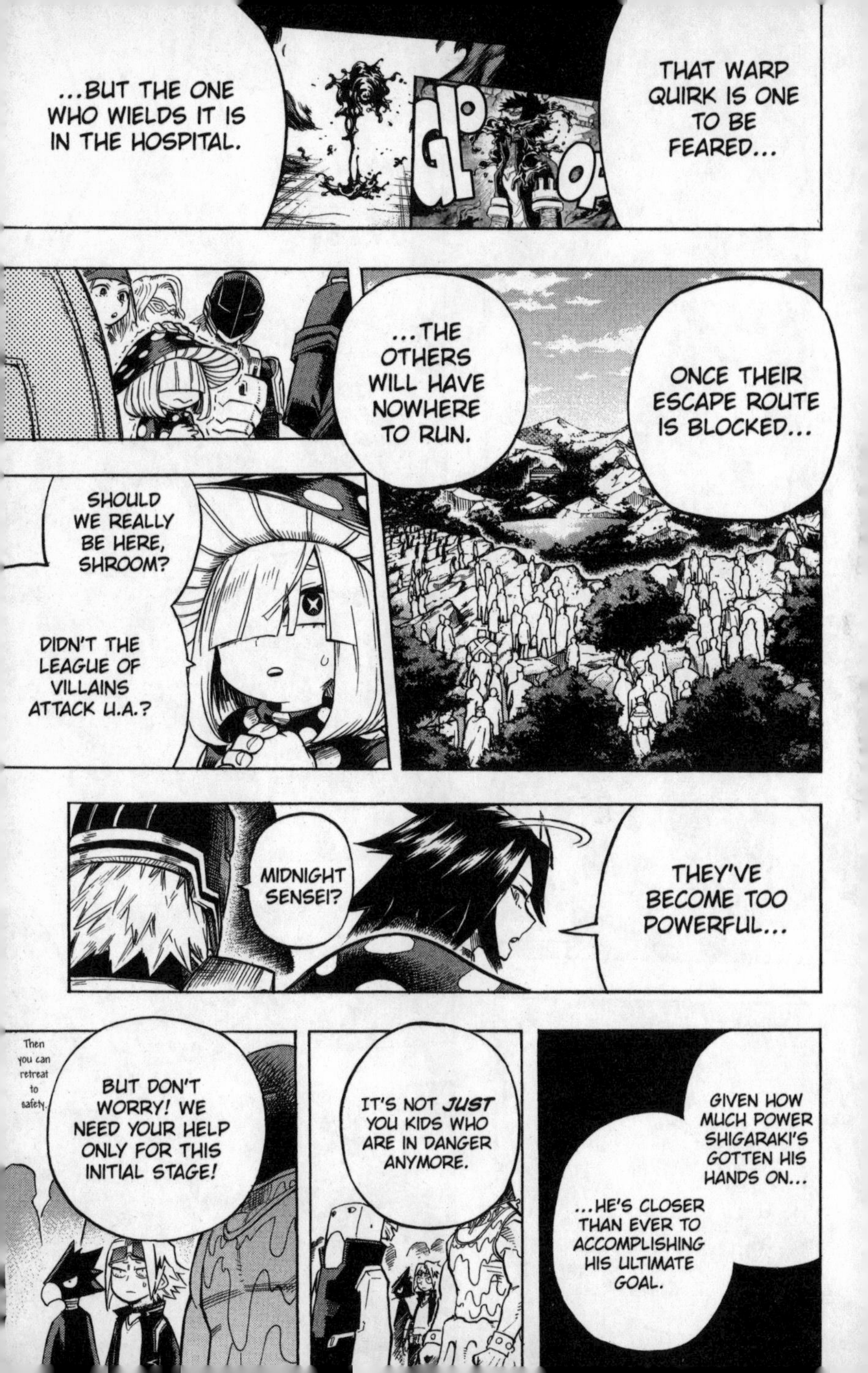
THAT WARP QUIRK IS ONE TO BE FEARED...
...BUT THE ONE WHO WIELDS IT IS IN THE HOSPITAL.
ONCE THEIR ESCAPE ROUTE IS BLOCKED...
...THE OTHERS WILL HAVE NOWHERE TO RUN.
SHOULD WE REALLY BE HERE, SHROOM?
DIDN'T THE LEAGUE OF VILLAINS ATTACK U.A.?
THEY'VE BECOME TOO POWERFUL...
MIDNIGHT SENSEI?
GIVEN HOW MUCH POWER SHIGARAKI'S GOTTEN HIS HANDS ON...
...HE'S CLOSER THAN EVER TO ACCOMPLISHING HIS ULTIMATE GOAL.
IT'S NOT *JUST* YOU KIDS WHO ARE IN DANGER ANYMORE.
BUT DON'T WORRY! WE NEED YOUR HELP ONLY FOR THIS INITIAL STAGE!
Then you can retreat to safety.

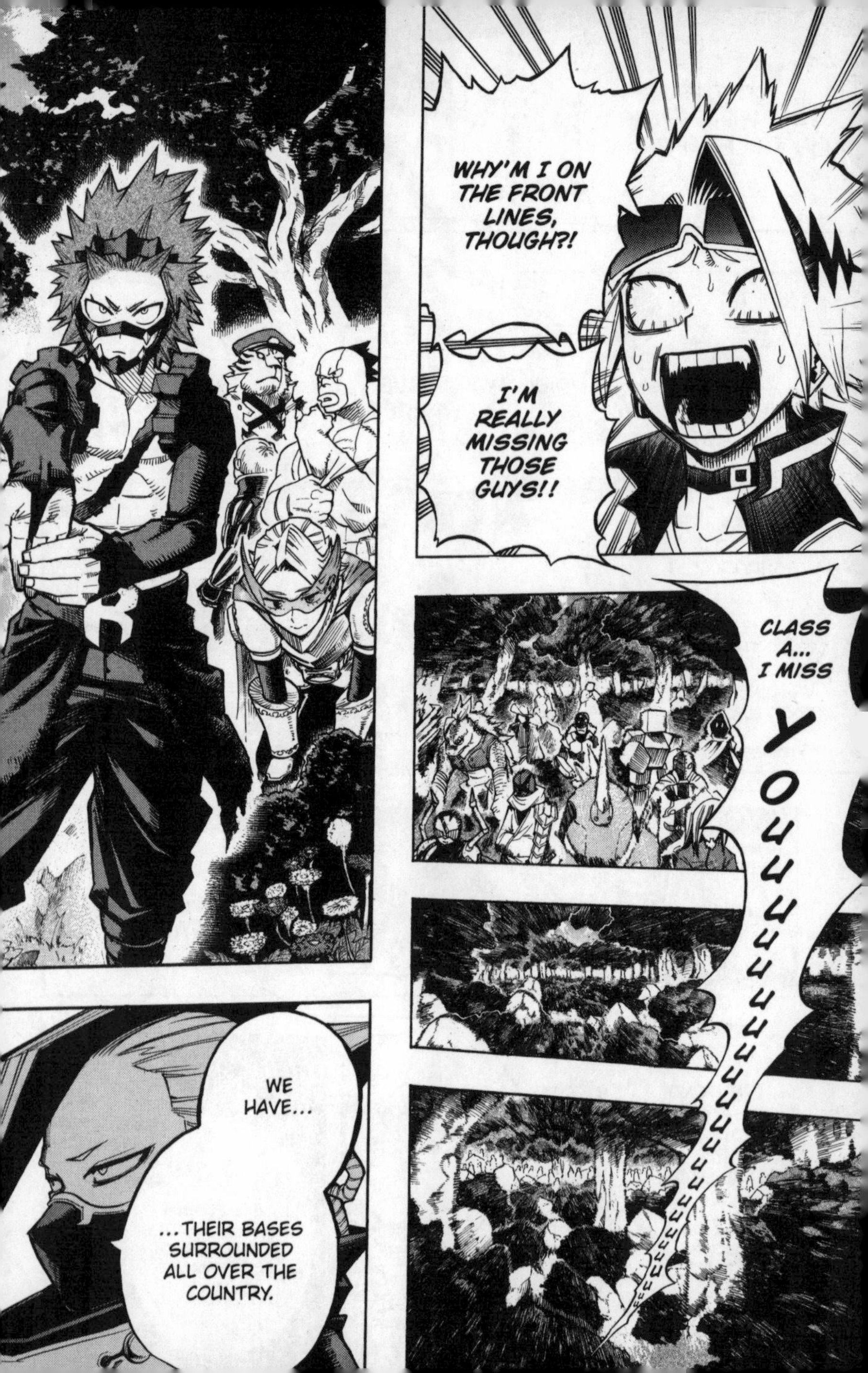
WHY'M I ON THE FRONT LINES, THOUGH?!
I'M REALLY MISSING THOSE GUYS!!
CLASS A... I MISS
YOUUUUUUUUUUUUUUUUUUUUU
WE HAVE...
...THEIR BASES SURROUNDED ALL OVER THE COUNTRY.

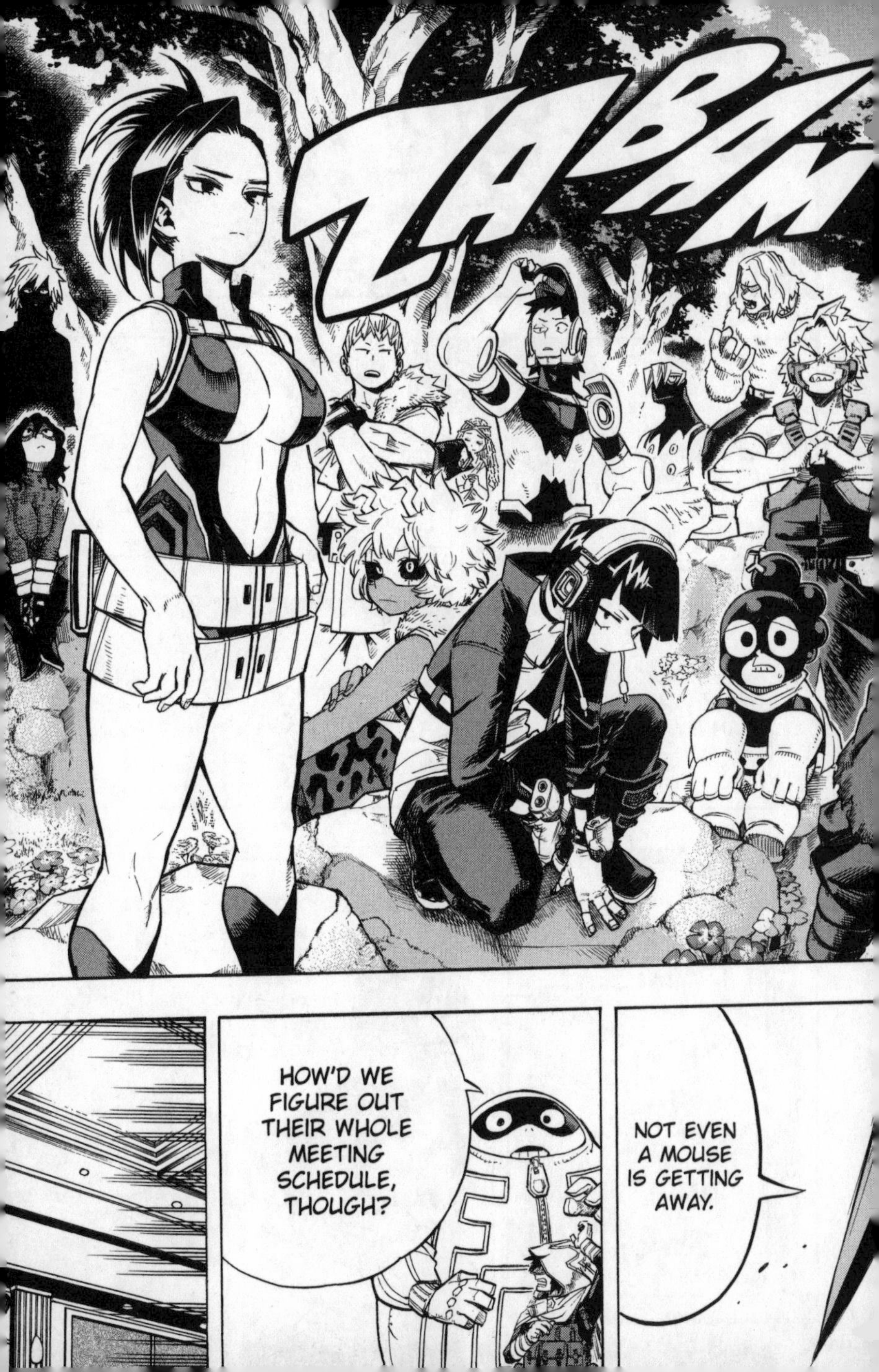
ZABAM
NOT EVEN A MOUSE IS GETTING AWAY.
HOW'D WE FIGURE OUT THEIR WHOLE MEETING SCHEDULE, THOUGH?

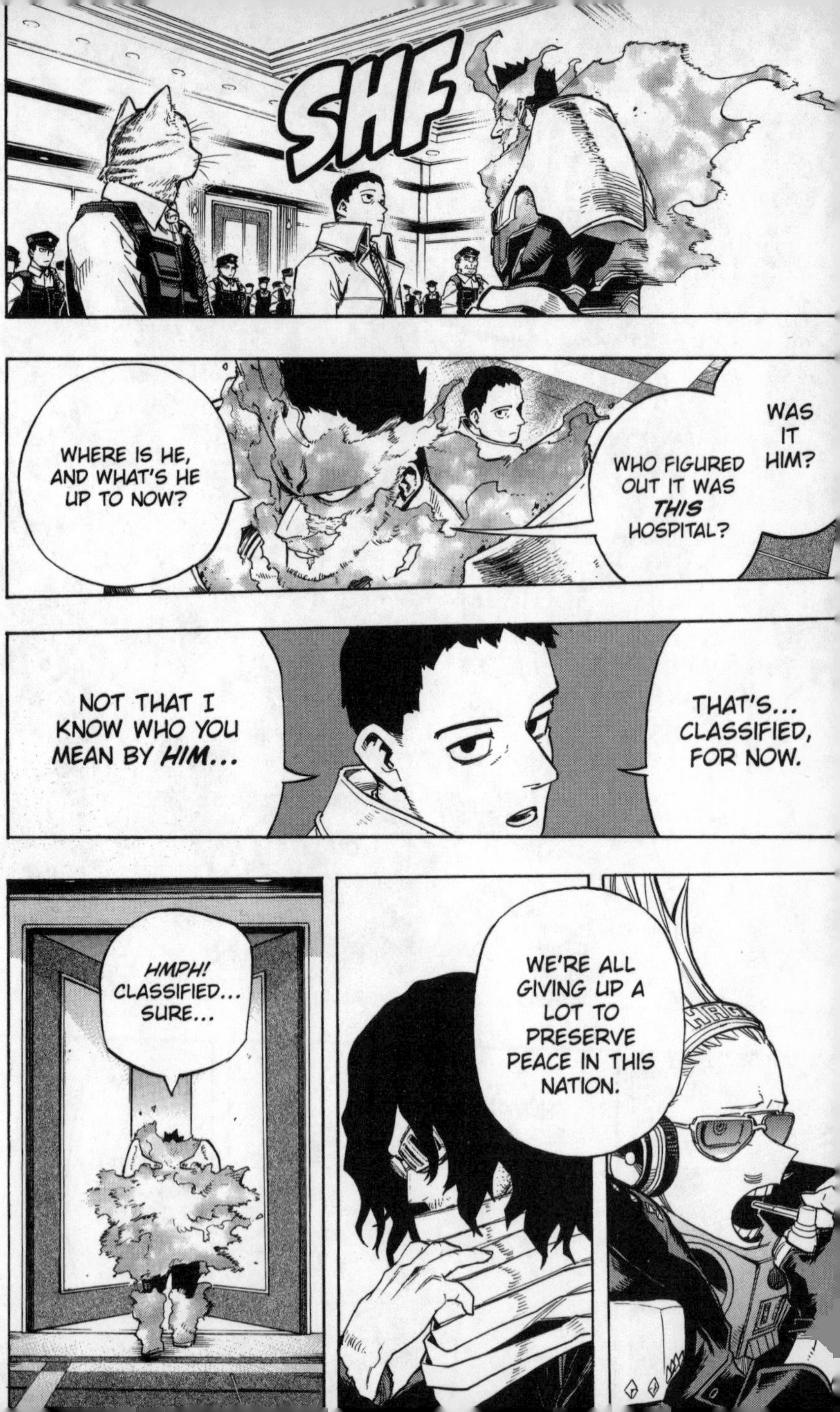
SHF
WAS IT HIM?
WHO FIGURED OUT IT WAS *THIS* HOSPITAL?
WHERE IS HE, AND WHAT'S HE UP TO NOW?
THAT'S... CLASSIFIED, FOR NOW.
NOT THAT I KNOW WHO YOU MEAN BY *HIM*...
WE'RE ALL GIVING UP A LOT TO PRESERVE PEACE IN THIS NATION.
HMPH! CLASSIFIED... SURE...

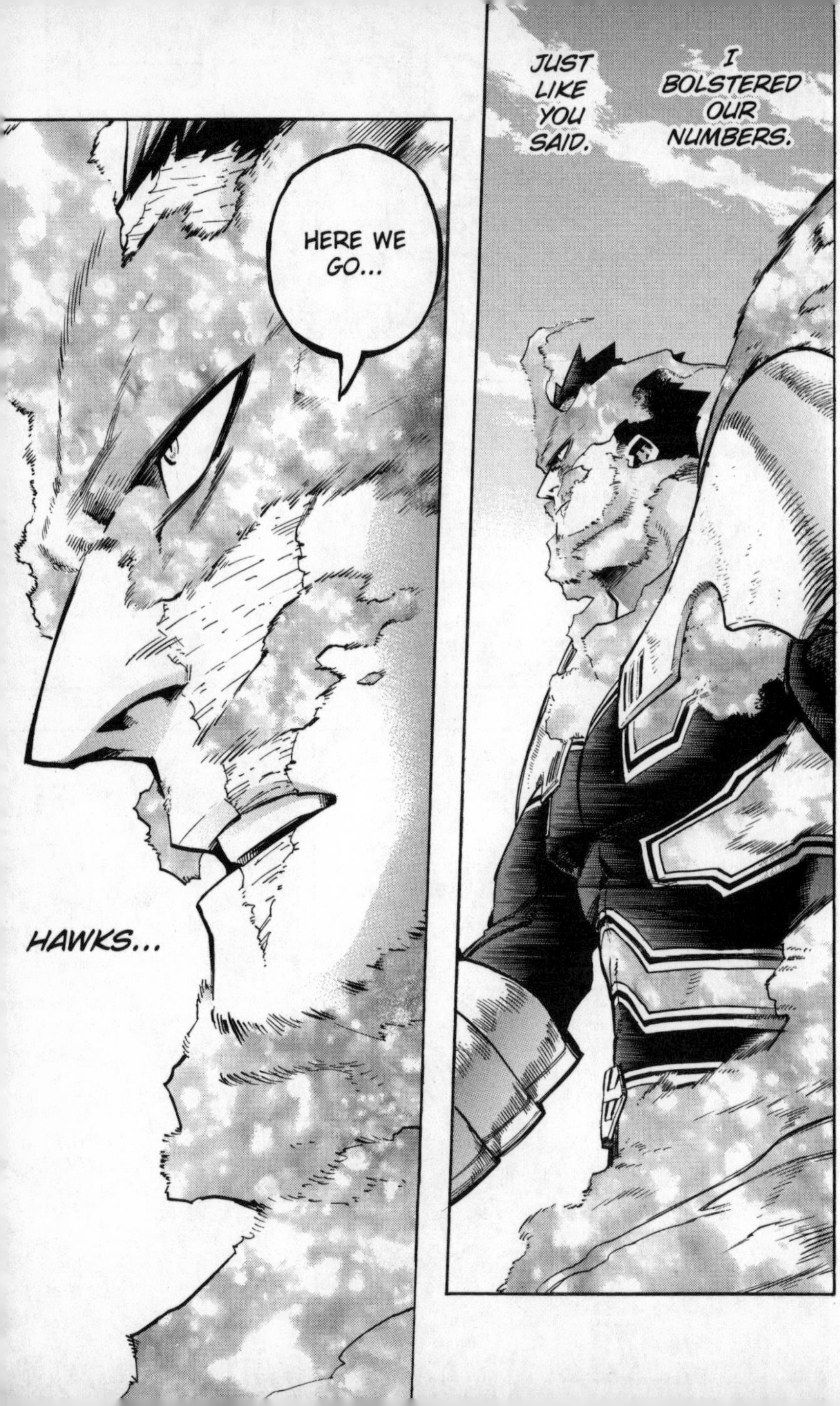
I BOLSTERED OUR NUMBERS.
JUST LIKE YOU SAID.
HERE WE GO...
HAWKS...

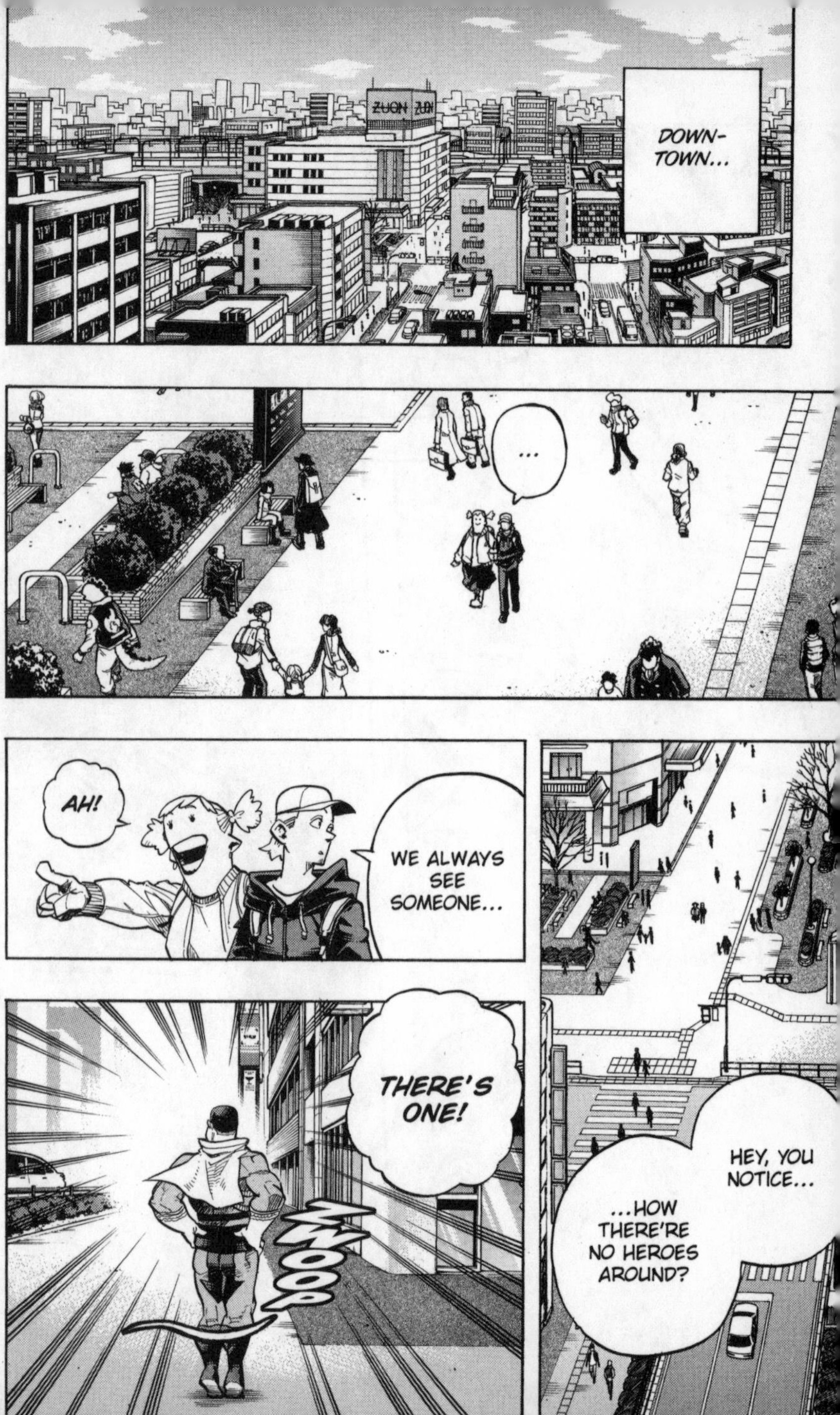
DOWN-TOWN...
...
HEY, YOU NOTICE...
...HOW THERE'RE NO HEROES AROUND?
AH!
WE ALWAYS SEE SOMEONE...
THERE'S ONE!
WWOOP

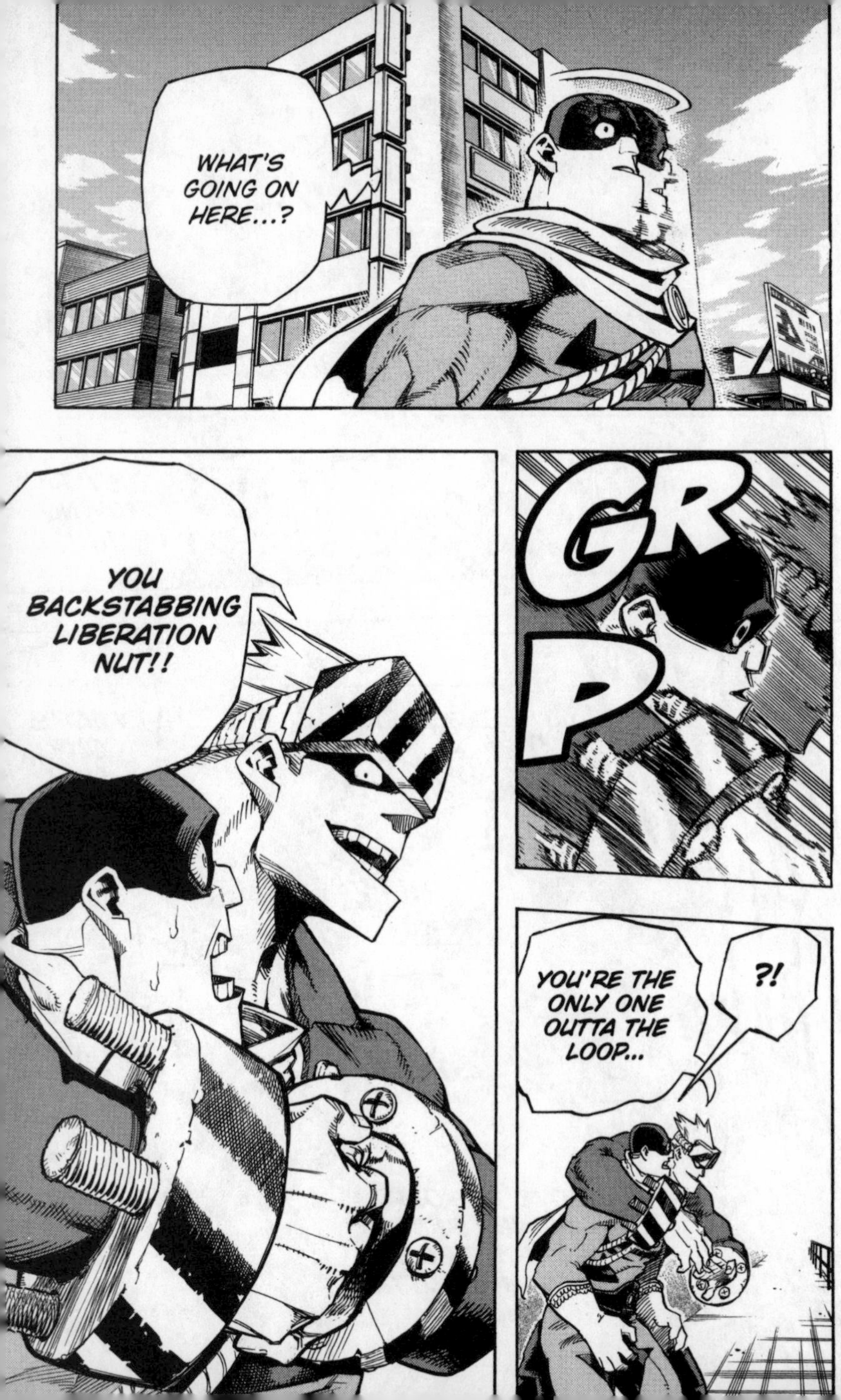
WHAT'S GOING ON HERE...?
GRP
?!
YOU'RE THE ONLY ONE OUTTA THE LOOP...
YOU BACKSTABBING LIBERATION NUT!!

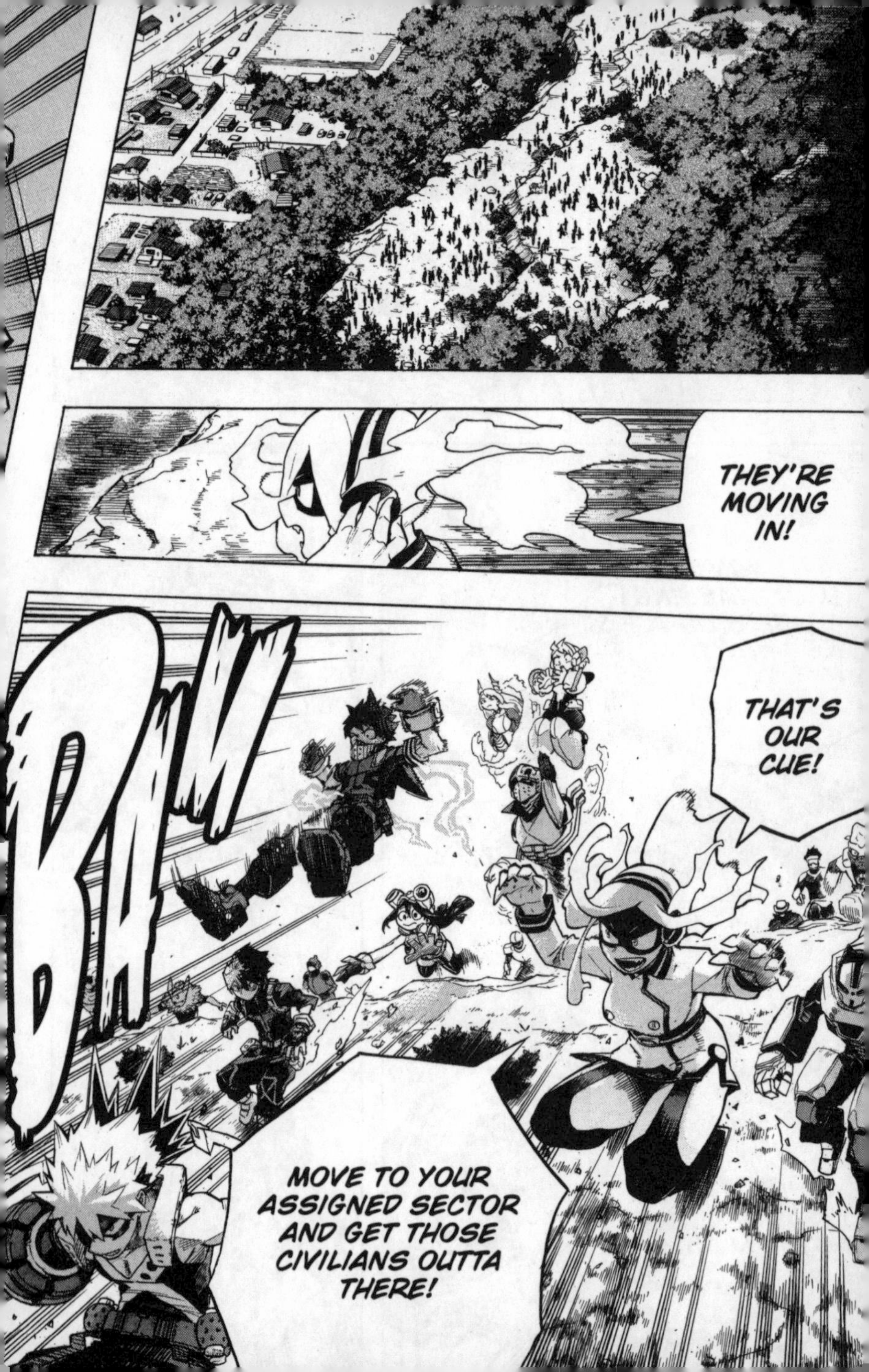
THEY'RE MOVING IN!
THAT'S OUR CUE!
BAM
MOVE TO YOUR ASSIGNED SECTOR AND GET THOSE CIVILIANS OUTTA THERE!

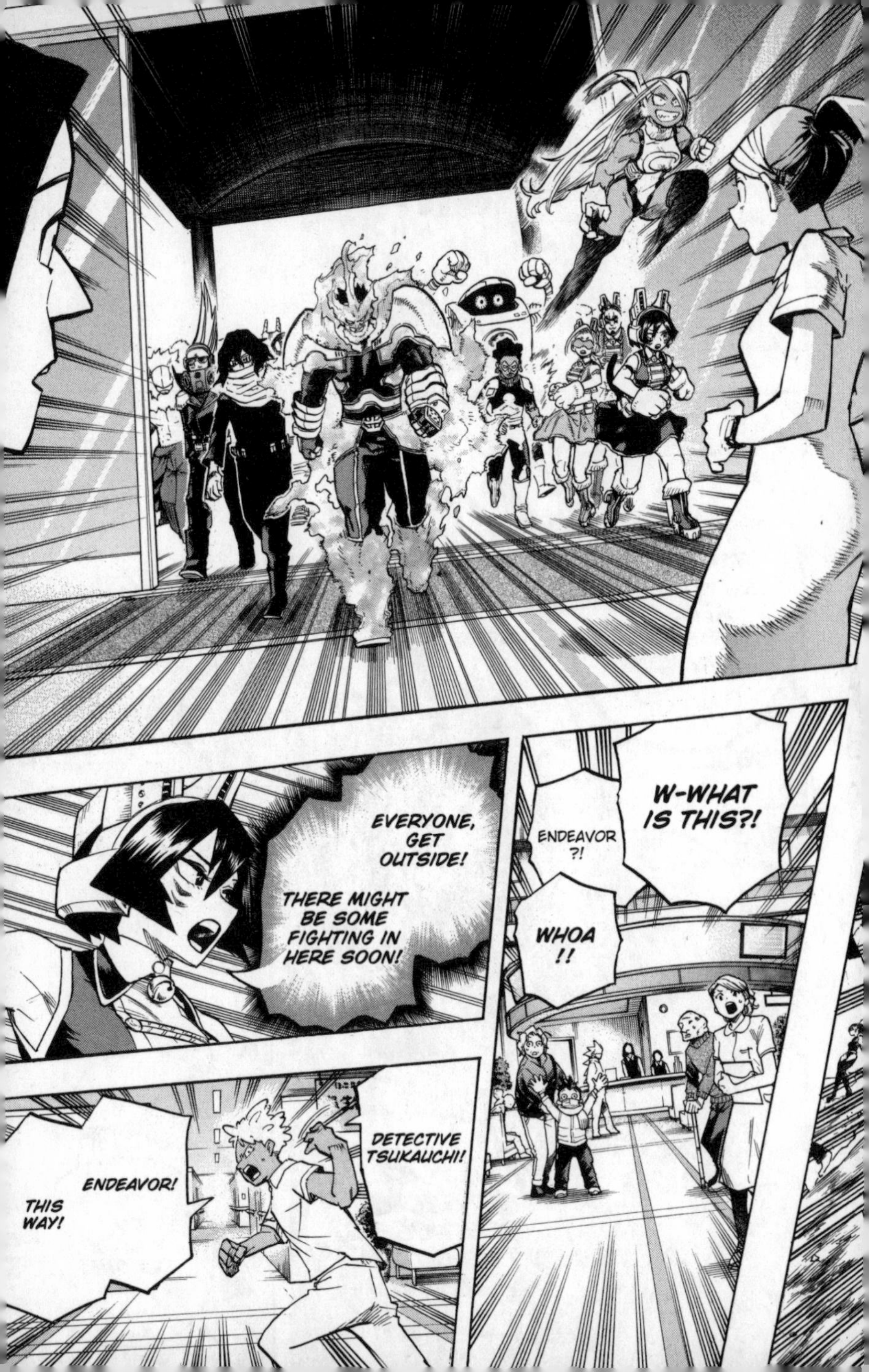
W-WHAT IS THIS?!
ENDEAVOR ?!
WHOA !!
EVERYONE, GET OUTSIDE!
THERE MIGHT BE SOME FIGHTING IN HERE SOON!
DETECTIVE TSUKAUCHI!
ENDEAVOR!
THIS WAY!

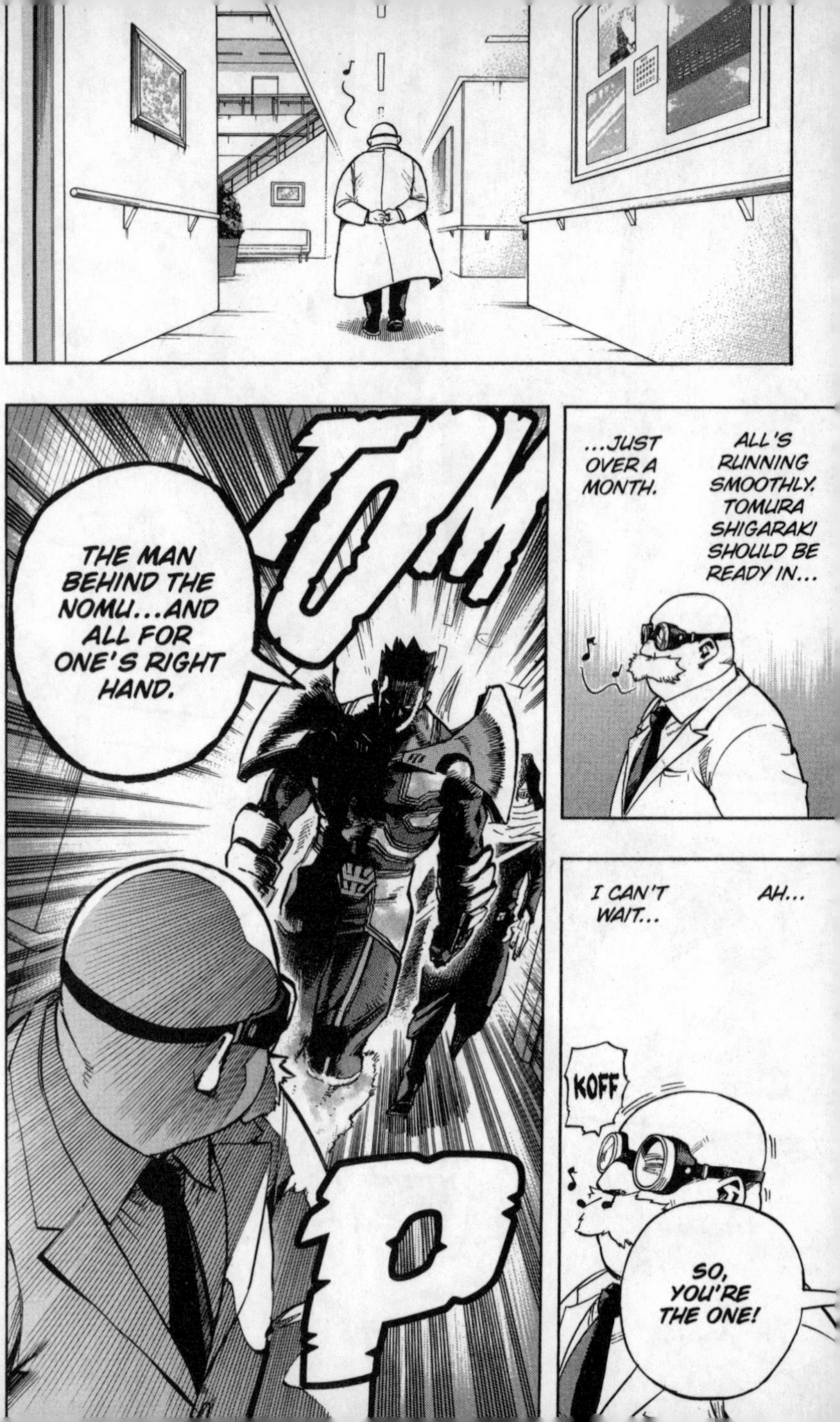
ALL'S RUNNING SMOOTHLY. TOMURA SHIGARAKI SHOULD BE READY IN...
...JUST OVER A MONTH.
AH...
I CAN'T WAIT...
KOFF
SO, YOU'RE THE ONE!
TOMP
THE MAN BEHIND THE NOMU...AND ALL FOR ONE'S RIGHT HAND.

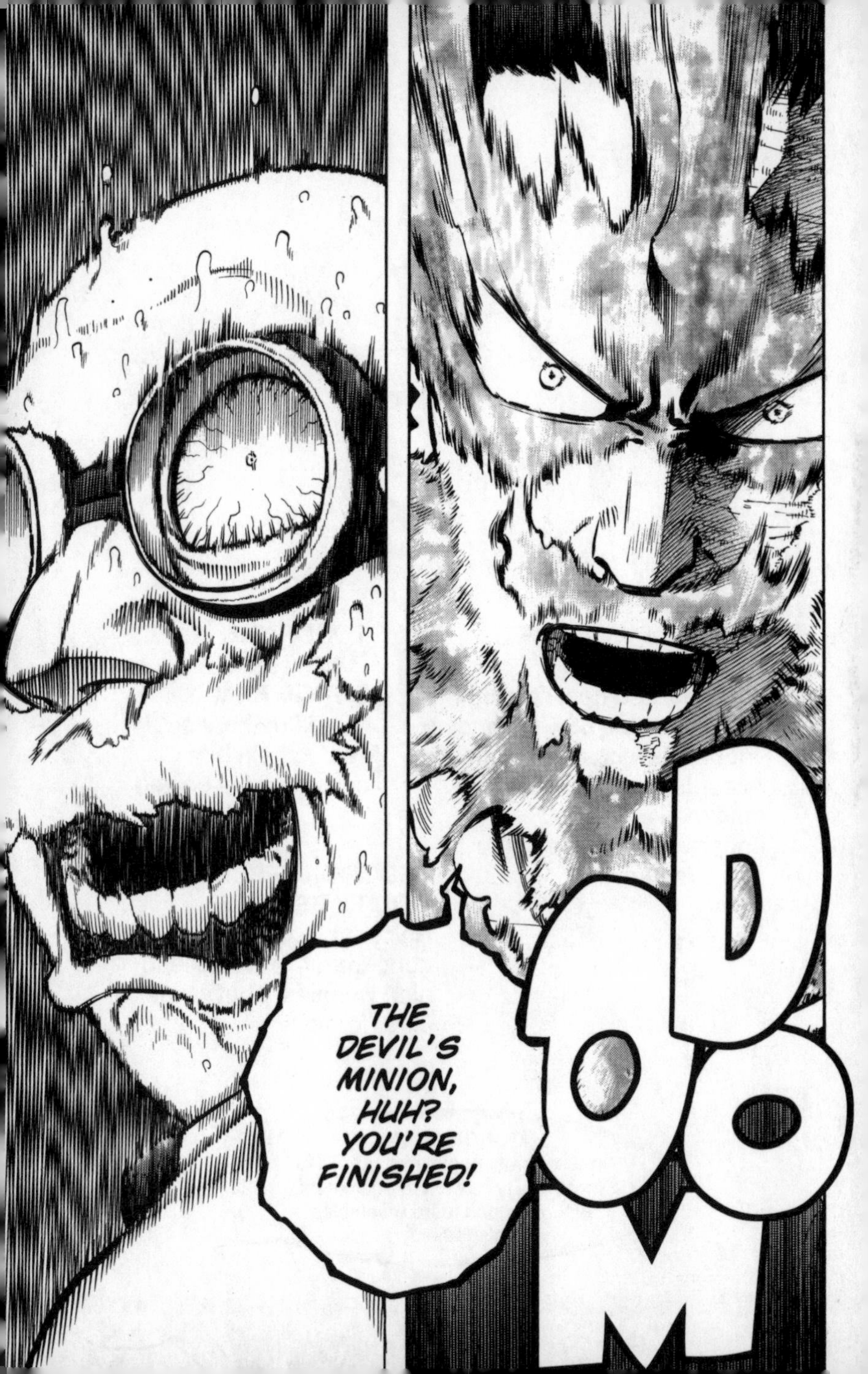
THE DEVIL'S MINION, HUH? YOU'RE FINISHED!
DOOM

SHOTO TODOROKI'S COSTUME GAMMA

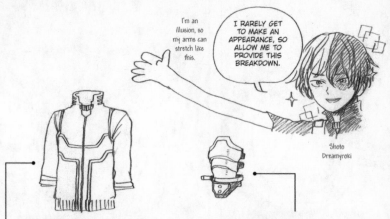

I'm an illusion, so my arms can stretch like this.

I RARELY GET TO MAKE AN APPEARANCE, SO ALLOW ME TO PROVIDE THIS BREAKDOWN.

Shoto Dreamyroki

TODOROKI'S JACKET:
HEAT RESISTANT

A specialized heat resistant jacket capable of withstanding Todoroki's increased firepower. According to him, it's stiffer than the last model! His underwear is made of the same material.

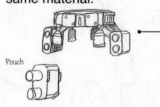

Pouch

TODOROKI'S GAUNTLET:
SURGE ARM

Stores up heat and cold to help him condense his power!

TODOROKI'S BELT:
UTILITY BELT

Holds more than ever! He's gone from five weenies to nine weenies! That's plus ultra, for you!

CONCLUSION:
In a sad twist of fate, the pursuit of functionality has led to equipment that more and more resembles his father's.

No. 260 - Life's Work

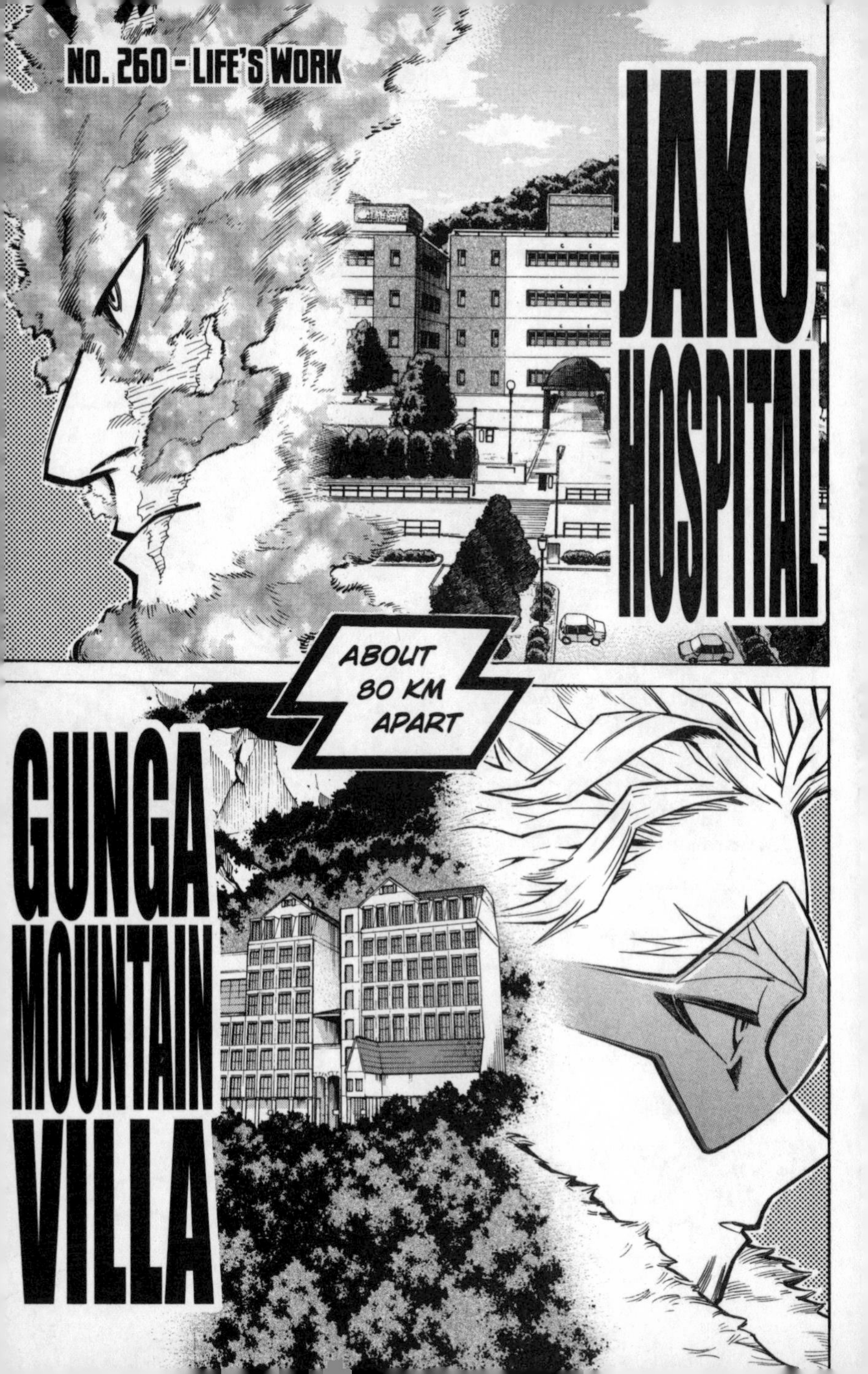
JAKU HOSPITAL
ABOUT 80 KM APART
GUNGA MOUNTAIN VILLA

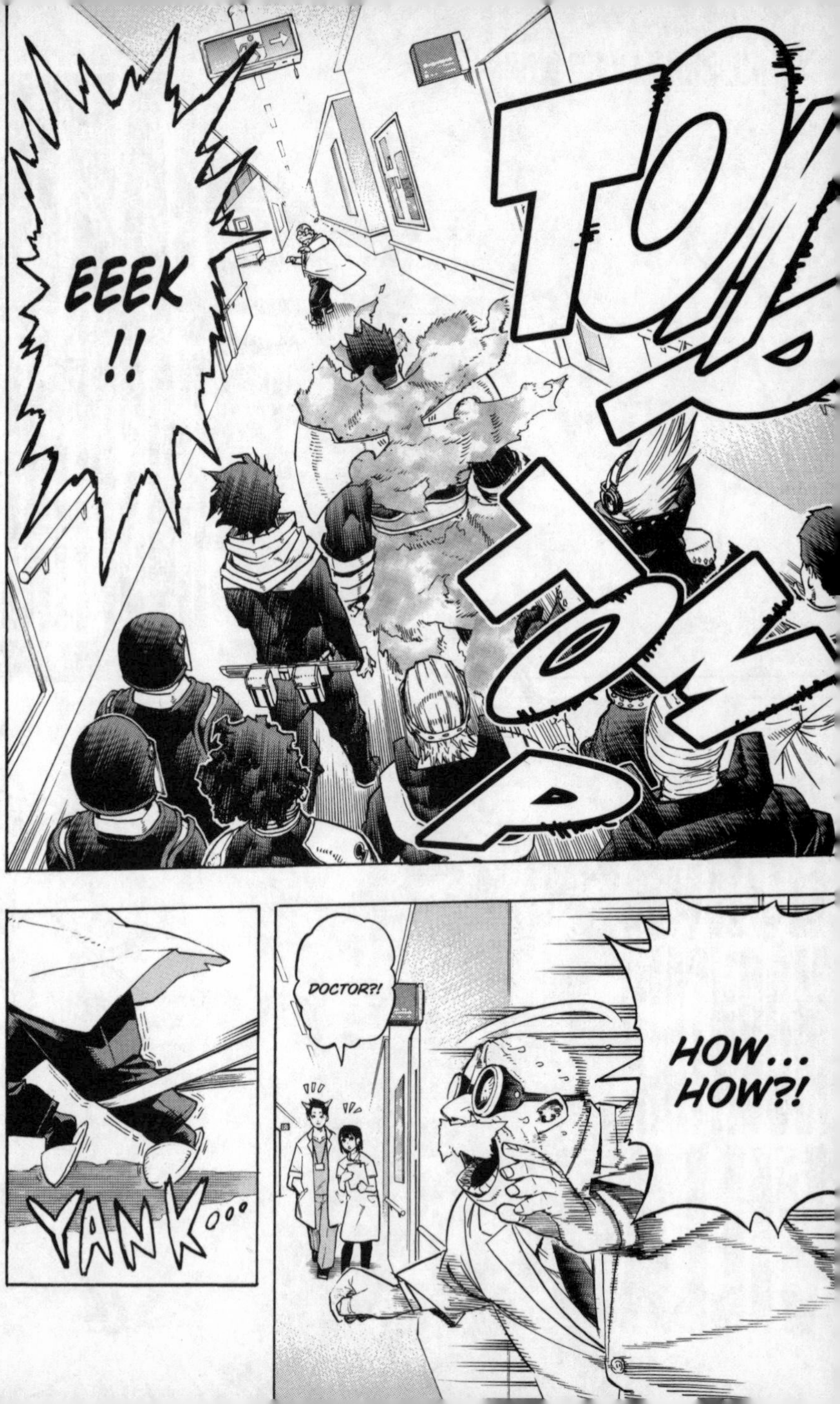
TO
EEEK!!
TOMP
HOW... HOW?!
DOCTOR?!
YANK

WHEEZ WHEEZ

KOFF!

SKF

THUD

WORMP

HFF...

HFF...

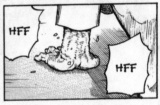

HFF

HFF

LOOKS LIKE...

TP

...THE REGISTRY WAS WRONG.

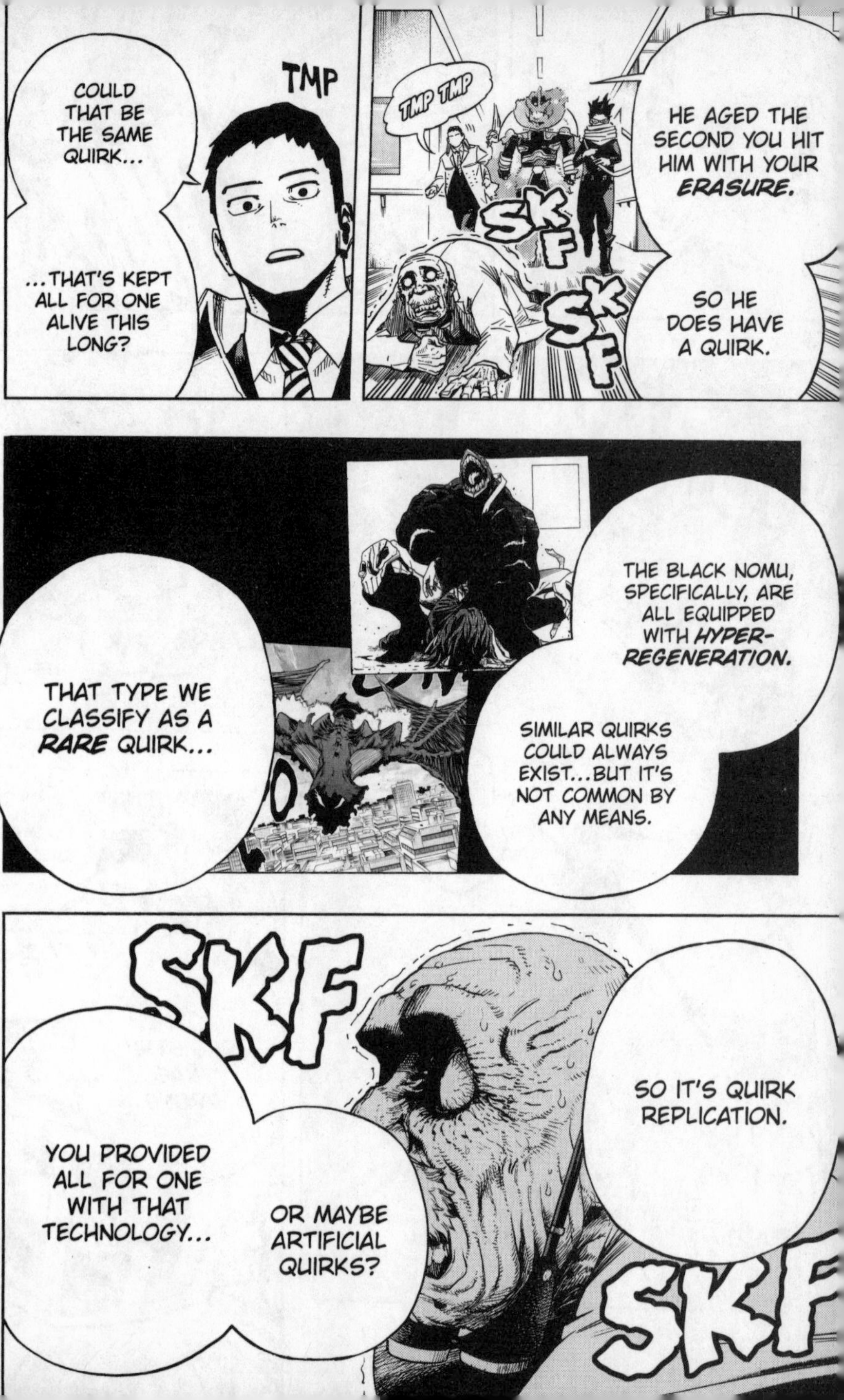
TMP TMP
HE AGED THE SECOND YOU HIT HIM WITH YOUR ERASURE.
SO HE DOES HAVE A QUIRK.
SKF
SKF
TMP
COULD THAT BE THE SAME QUIRK...
...THAT'S KEPT ALL FOR ONE ALIVE THIS LONG?
THE BLACK NOMU, SPECIFICALLY, ARE ALL EQUIPPED WITH HYPER-REGENERATION.
SIMILAR QUIRKS COULD ALWAYS EXIST...BUT IT'S NOT COMMON BY ANY MEANS.
THAT TYPE WE CLASSIFY AS A RARE QUIRK...
SO IT'S QUIRK REPLICATION.
SKF
OR MAYBE ARTIFICIAL QUIRKS?
YOU PROVIDED ALL FOR ONE WITH THAT TECHNOLOGY...
SKF

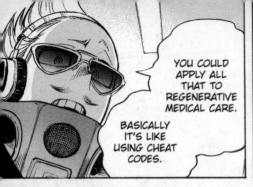

YOU COULD APPLY ALL THAT TO REGENERATIVE MEDICAL CARE.

BASICALLY IT'S LIKE USING CHEAT CODES.

WOW... NEAT.

YANK

WHY USE IT THE WAY YOU DID?!

EEP!

ROLL

YET...

FWP

KKK

WHY'D YOU DO IT, YOU OLD PIECE OF TRASH?!

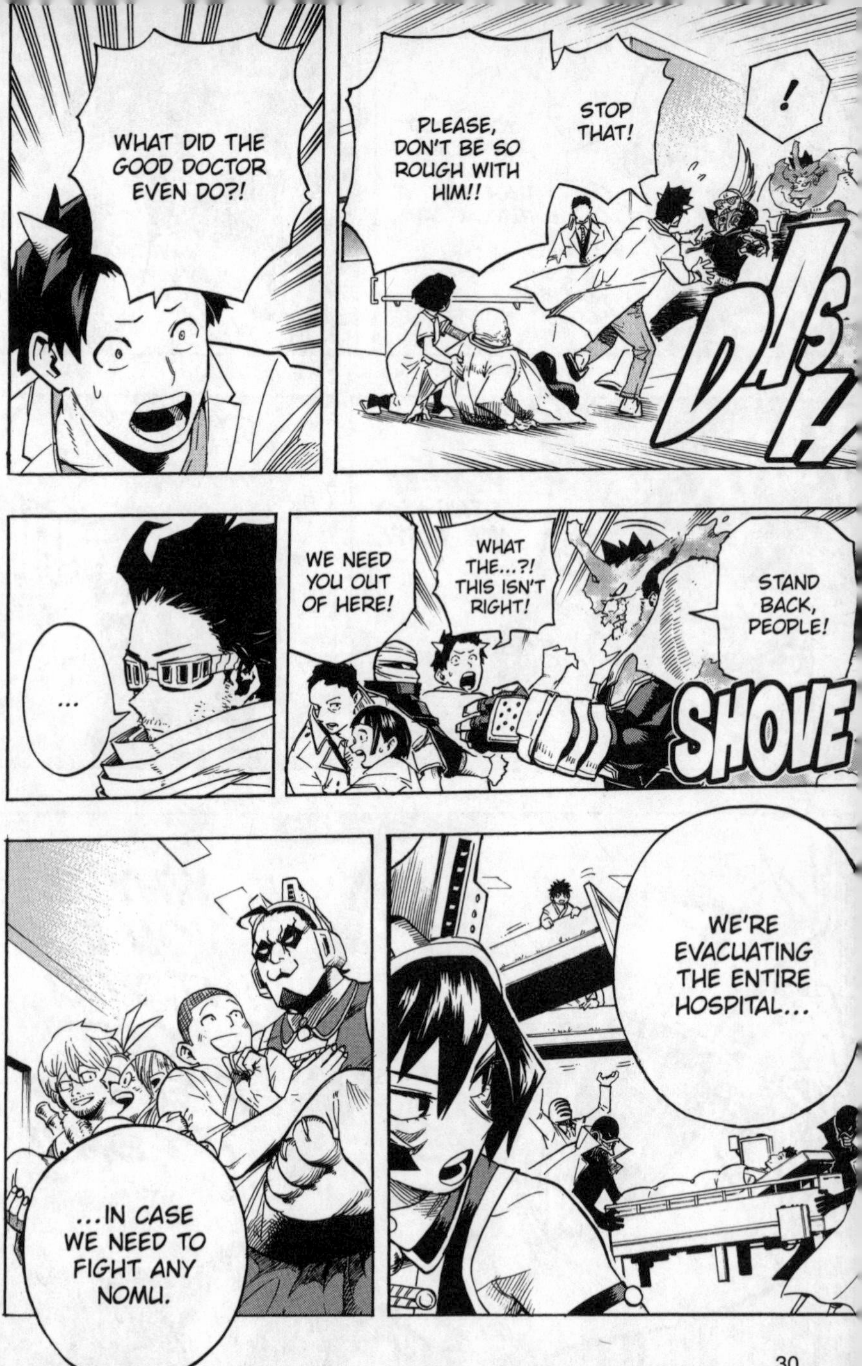
!
STOP THAT!
PLEASE, DON'T BE SO ROUGH WITH HIM!!
DASH
WHAT DID THE GOOD DOCTOR EVEN DO?!
STAND BACK, PEOPLE!
SHOVE
WHAT THE...?! THIS ISN'T RIGHT!
WE NEED YOU OUT OF HERE!
...
WE'RE EVACUATING THE ENTIRE HOSPITAL...
...IN CASE WE NEED TO FIGHT ANY NOMU.

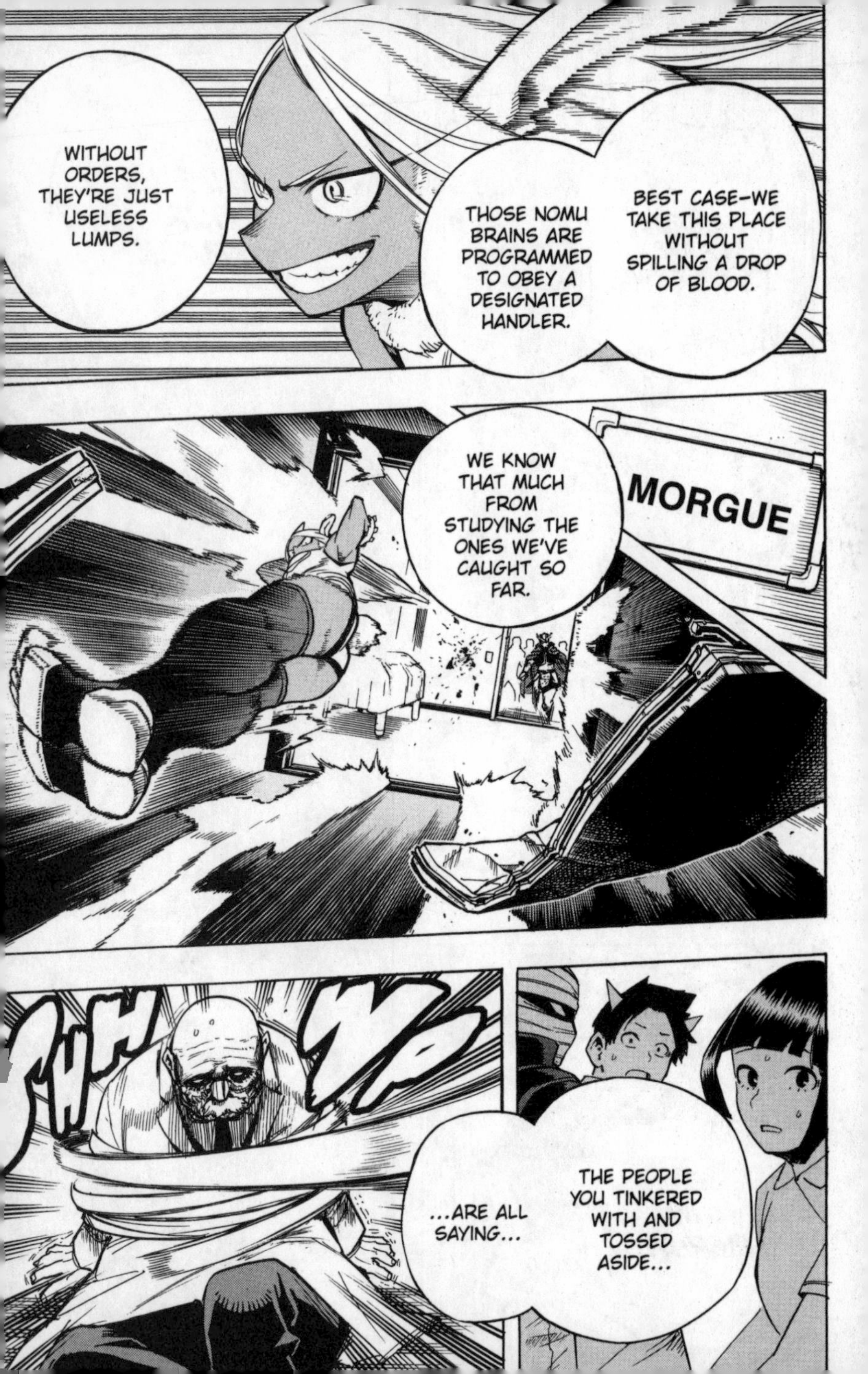
BEST CASE—WE TAKE THIS PLACE WITHOUT SPILLING A DROP OF BLOOD.
THOSE NOMU BRAINS ARE PROGRAMMED TO OBEY A DESIGNATED HANDLER.
WITHOUT ORDERS, THEY'RE JUST USELESS LUMPS.
WE KNOW THAT MUCH FROM STUDYING THE ONES WE'VE CAUGHT SO FAR.
MORGUE
THE PEOPLE YOU TINKERED WITH AND TOSSED ASIDE...
...ARE ALL SAYING...

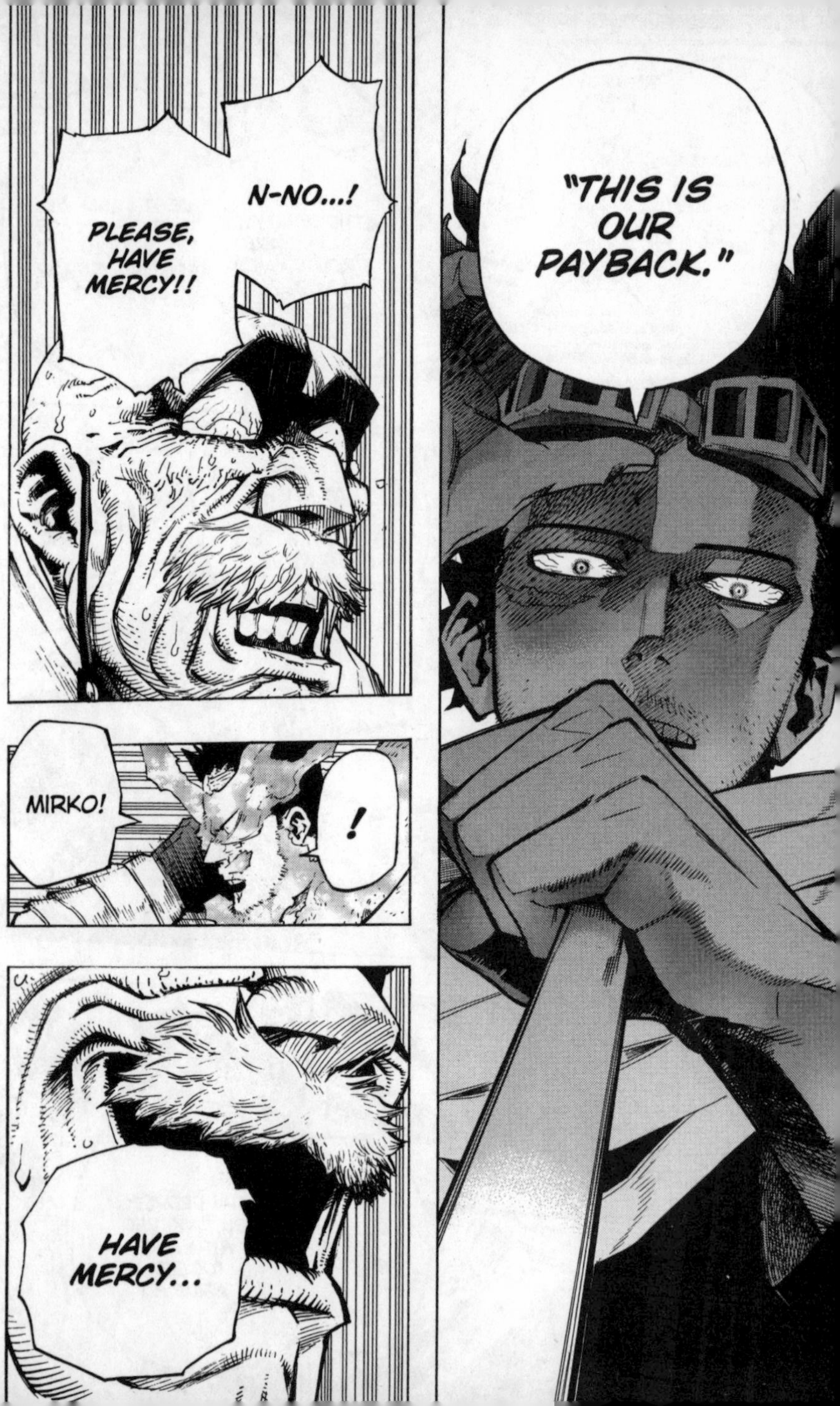
"THIS IS OUR PAYBACK."
N-NO...!
PLEASE, HAVE MERCY!!
!
MIRKO!
HAVE MERCY...

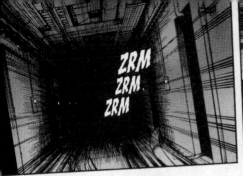

ZRM
ZRM
ZRM

HEH H

ENDEAVOR
!!

WE GOT
COMPANY
!!

ZRM

ZRM

ZRM

ZRM

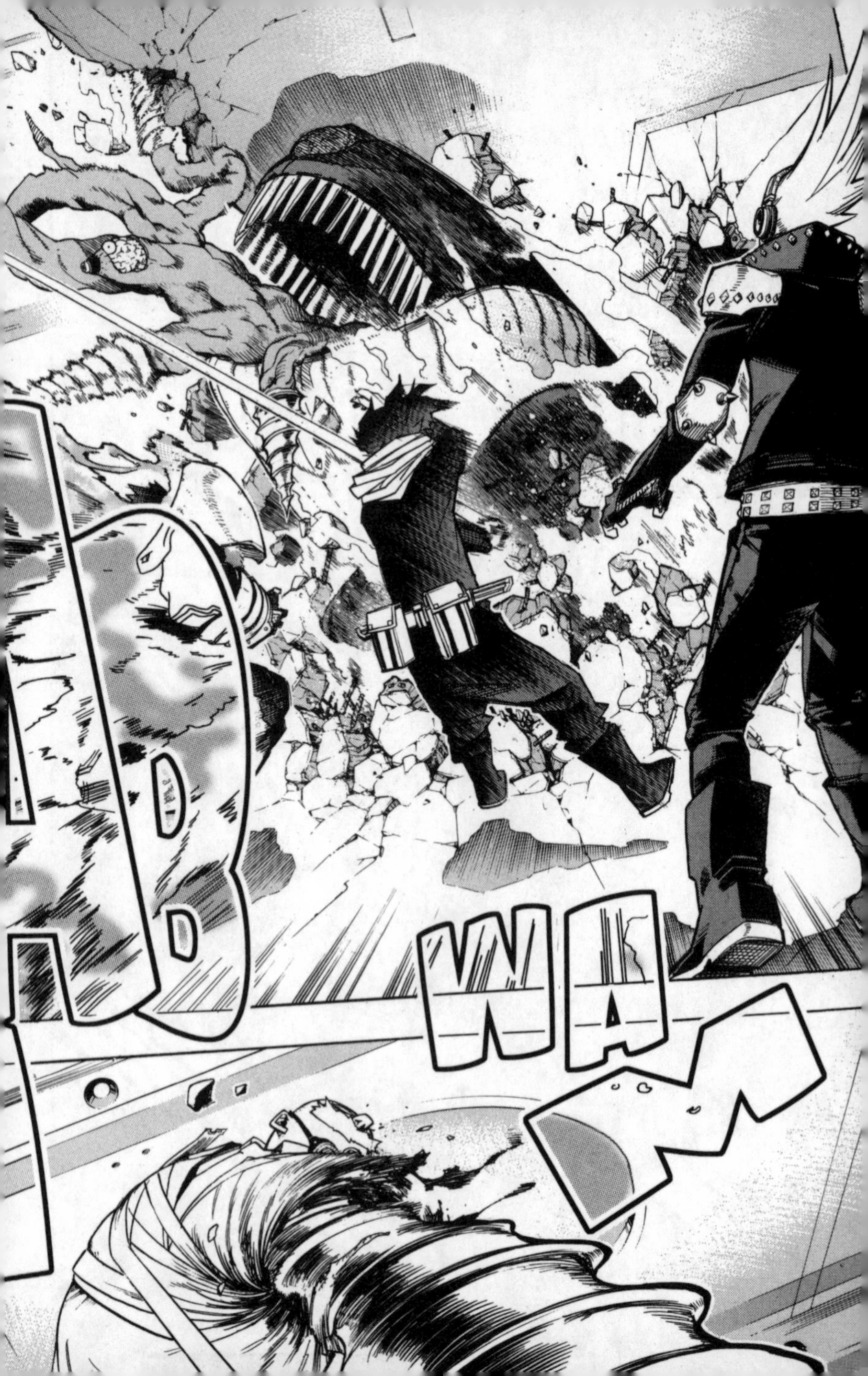
WAM

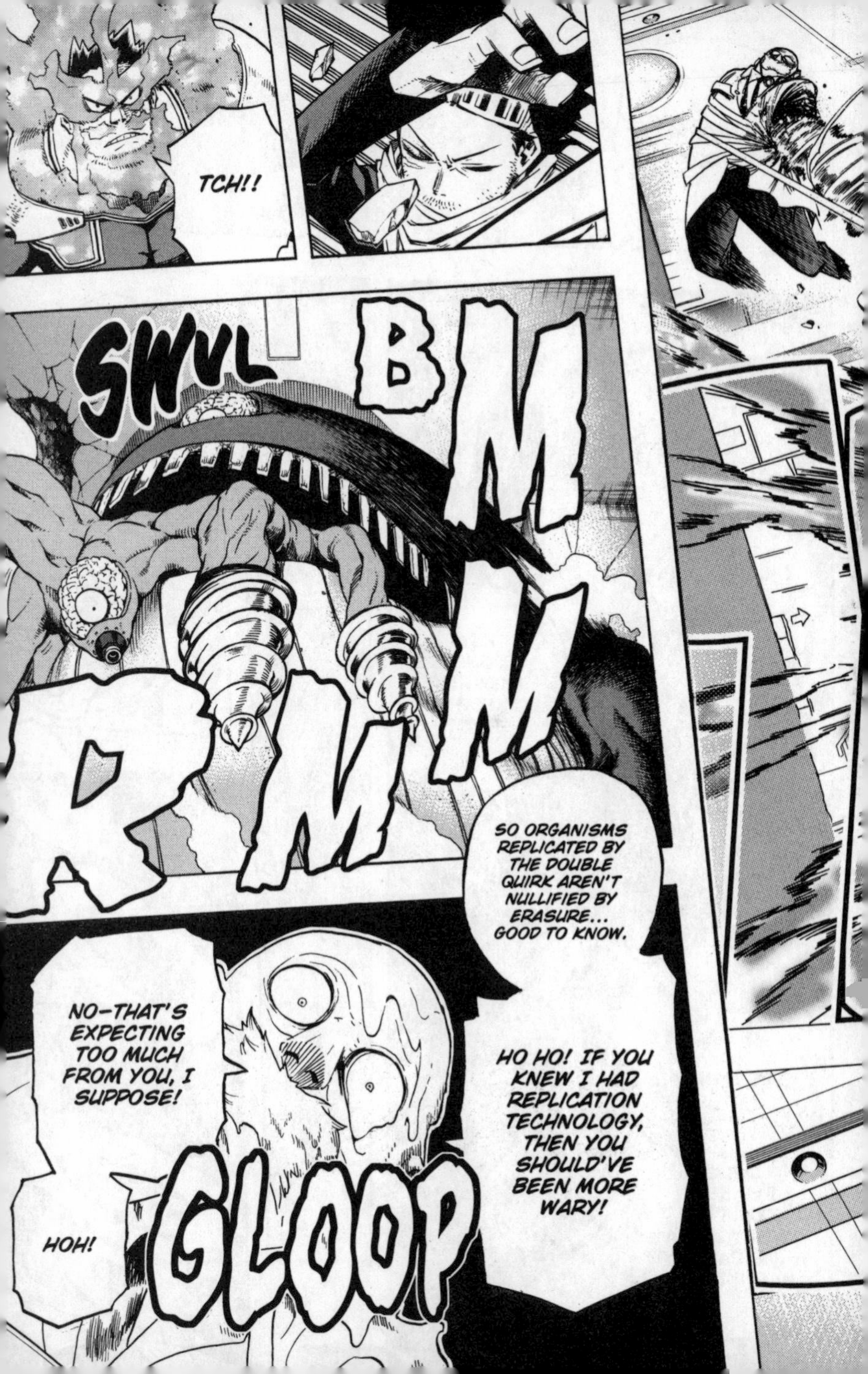

TCH!!
SWVL
BMM
SO ORGANISMS REPLICATED BY THE DOUBLE QUIRK AREN'T NULLIFIED BY ERASURE... GOOD TO KNOW.
HO HO! IF YOU KNEW I HAD REPLICATION TECHNOLOGY, THEN YOU SHOULD'VE BEEN MORE WARY!
NO—THAT'S EXPECTING TOO MUCH FROM YOU, I SUPPOSE!
HOH!
GLOOP

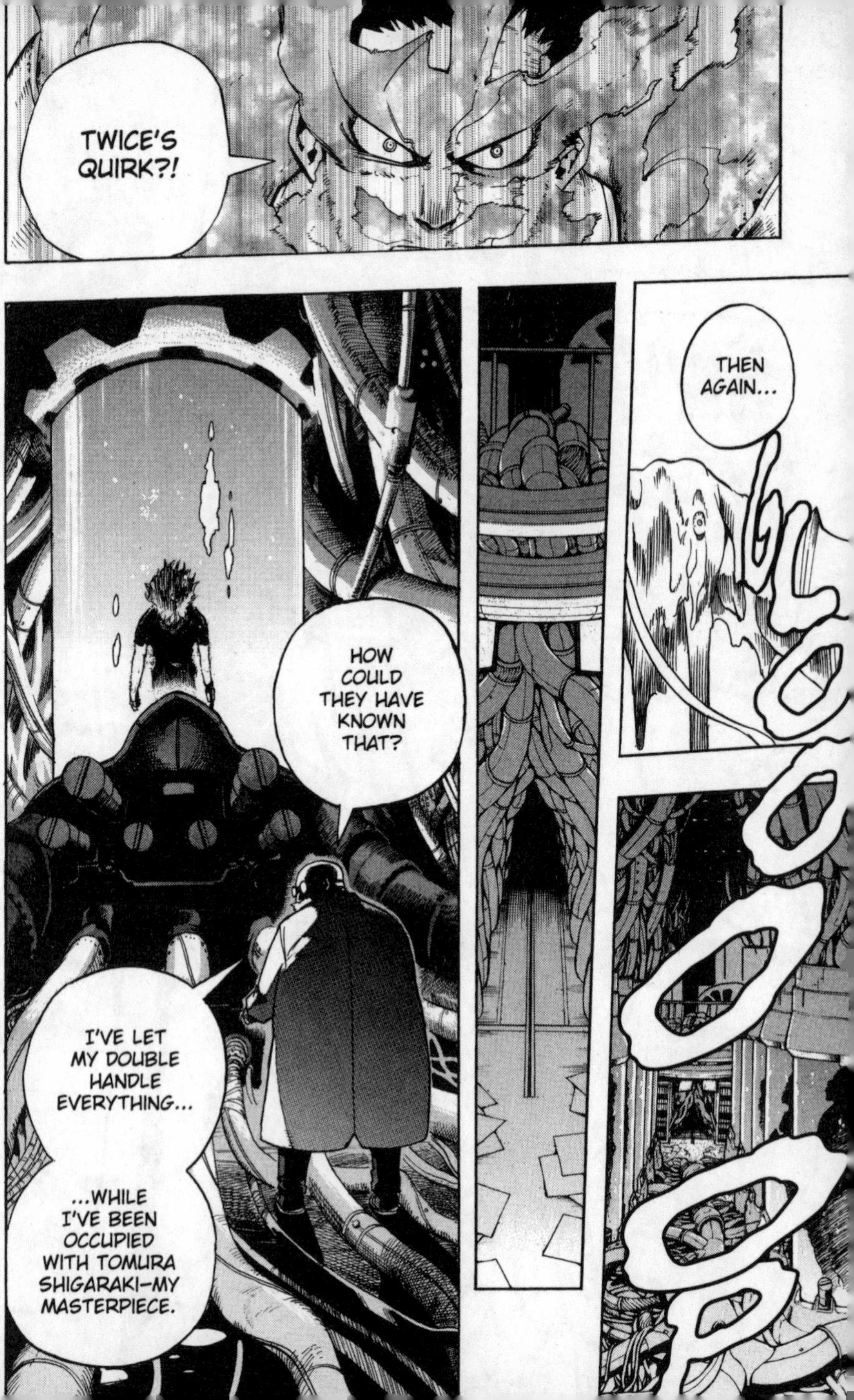
TWICE'S QUIRK?!
THEN AGAIN...
HOW COULD THEY HAVE KNOWN THAT?
I'VE LET MY DOUBLE HANDLE EVERYTHING...
...WHILE I'VE BEEN OCCUPIED WITH TOMURA SHIGARAKI—MY MASTERPIECE.

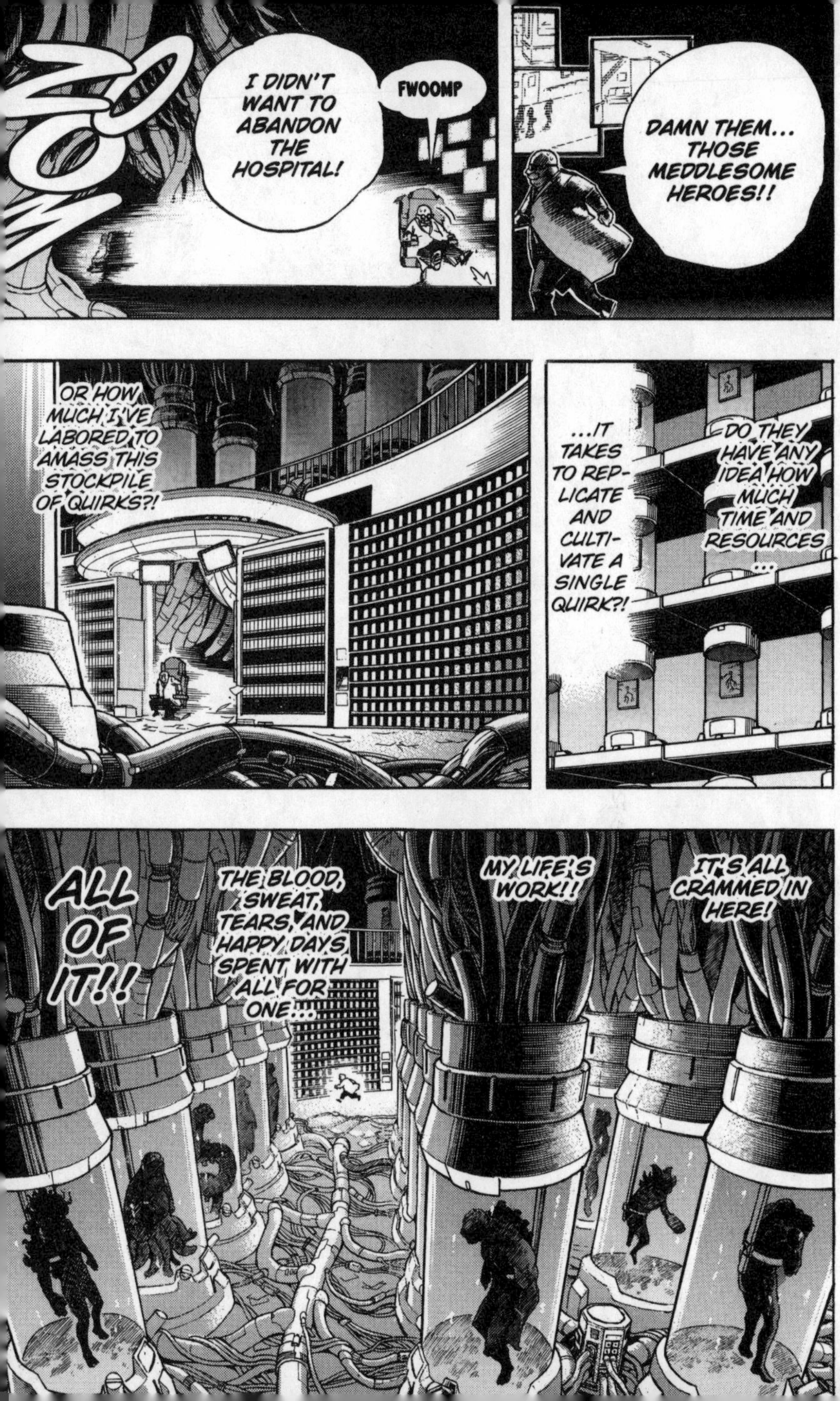
DAMN THEM... THOSE MEDDLESOME HEROES!!
I DIDN'T WANT TO ABANDON THE HOSPITAL!
FWOOMP
DO THEY HAVE ANY IDEA HOW MUCH TIME AND RESOURCES...
...IT TAKES TO REPLICATE AND CULTIVATE A SINGLE QUIRK?!
OR HOW MUCH I'VE LABORED TO AMASS THIS STOCKPILE OF QUIRKS?!
IT'S ALL CRAMMED IN HERE!
MY LIFE'S WORK!!
THE BLOOD, SWEAT, TEARS, AND HAPPY DAYS SPENT WITH ALL FOR ONE...
ALL OF IT!!

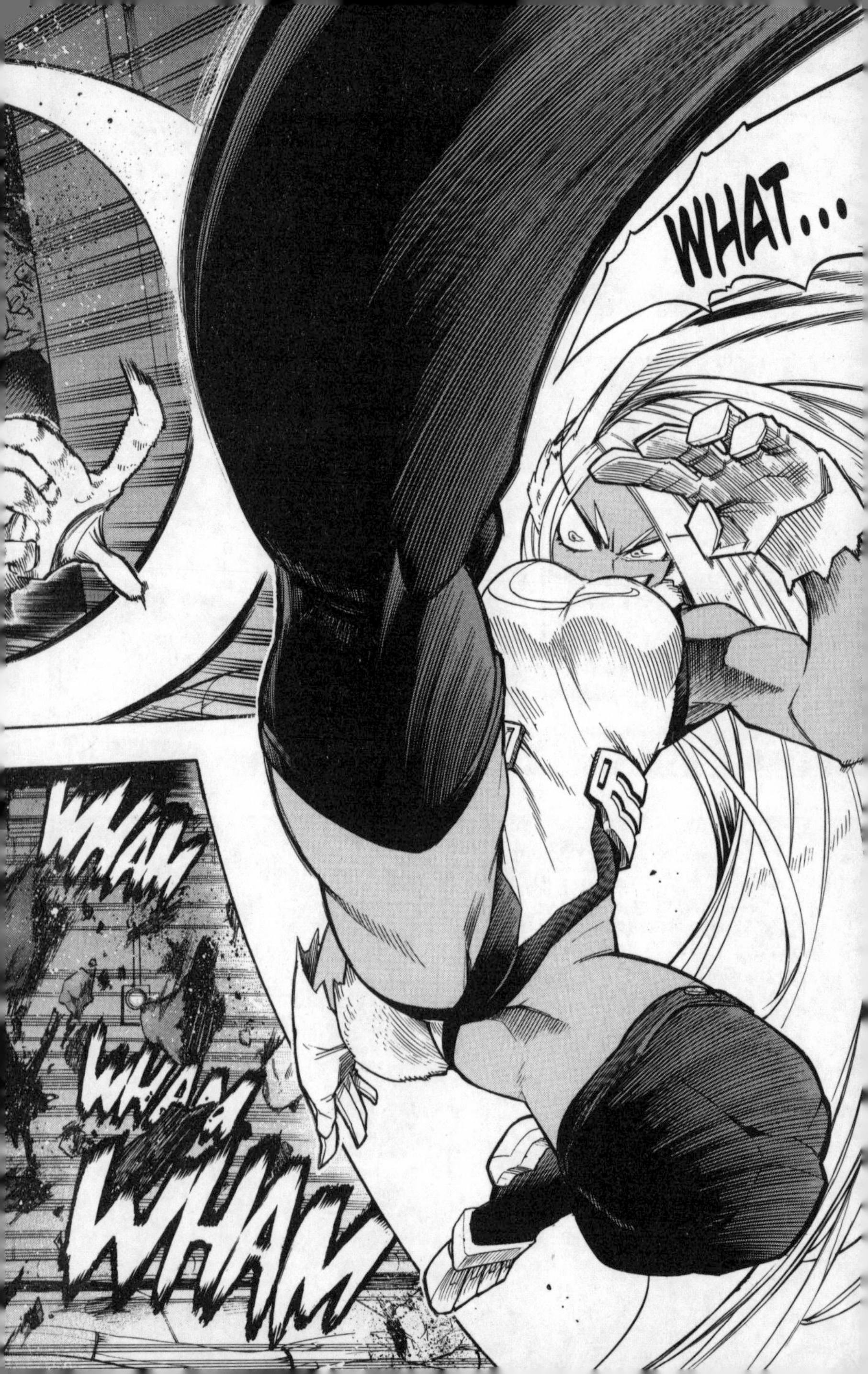
WHAT...
WHAM
WHAM
WHAM

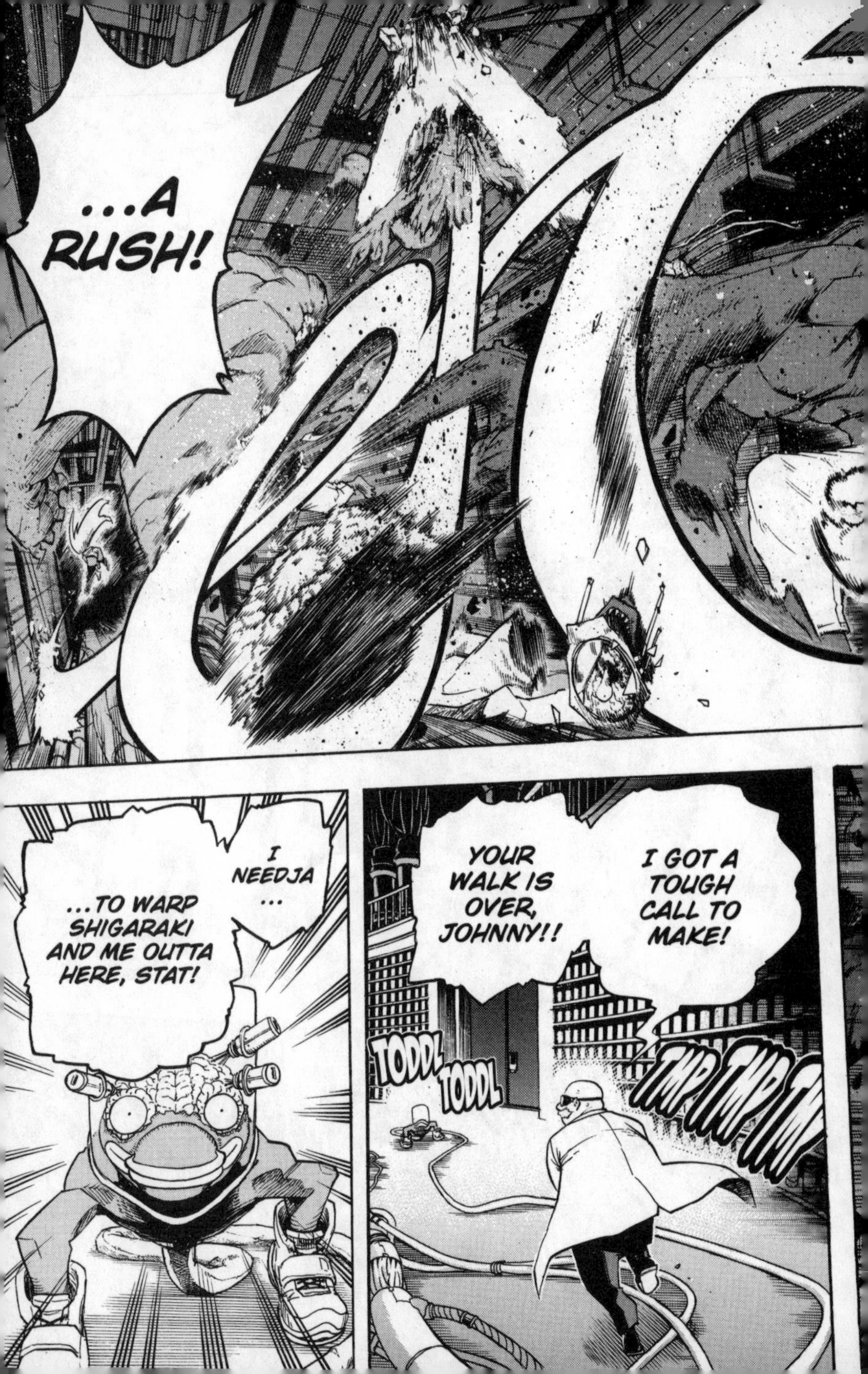
...A RUSH!
I GOT A TOUGH CALL TO MAKE!
YOUR WALK IS OVER, JOHNNY!!
TMP TMP
TODDL TODDL
I NEEDJA...
...TO WARP SHIGARAKI AND ME OUTTA HERE, STAT!

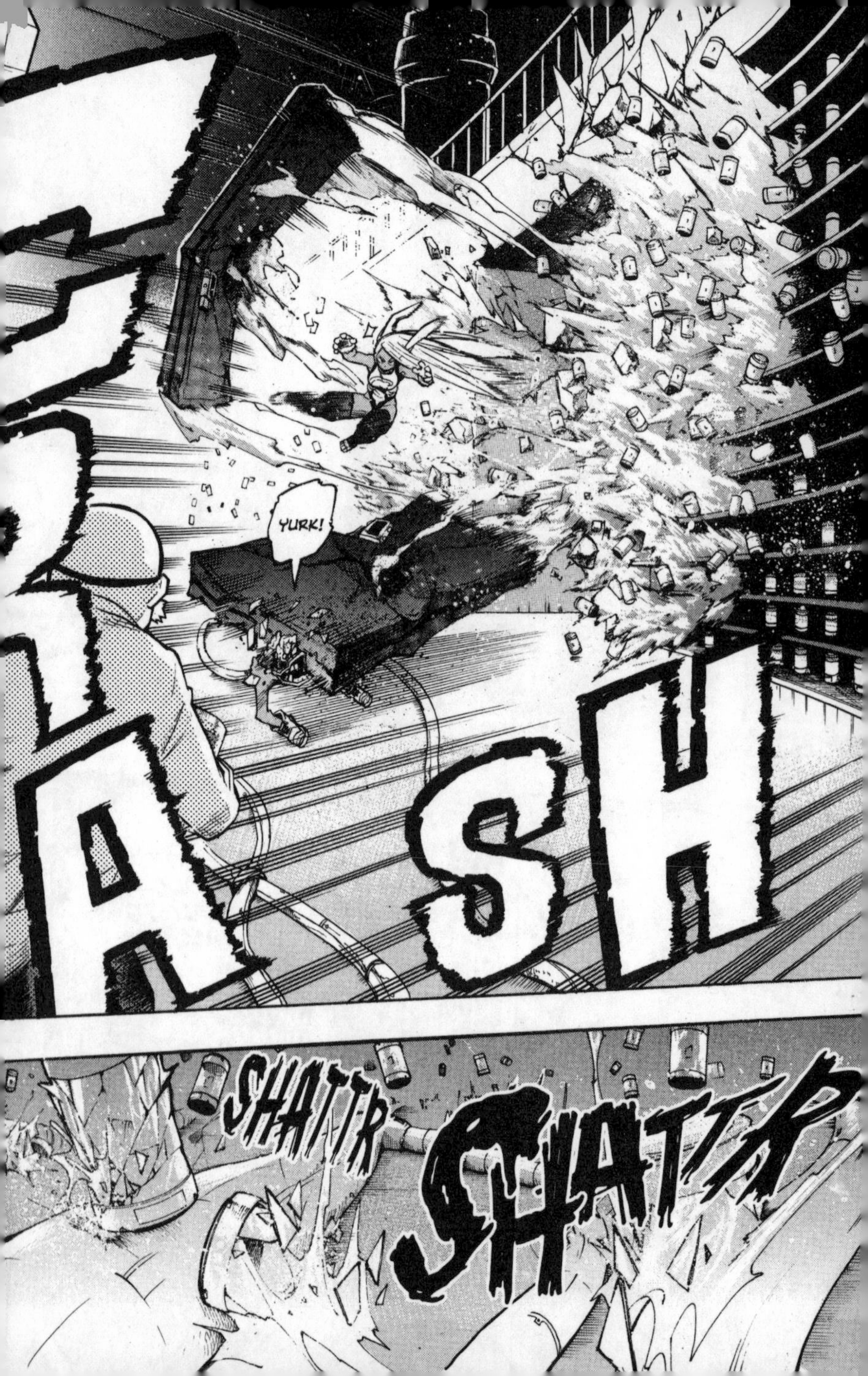
YURK!
SHATTR
SHATTR

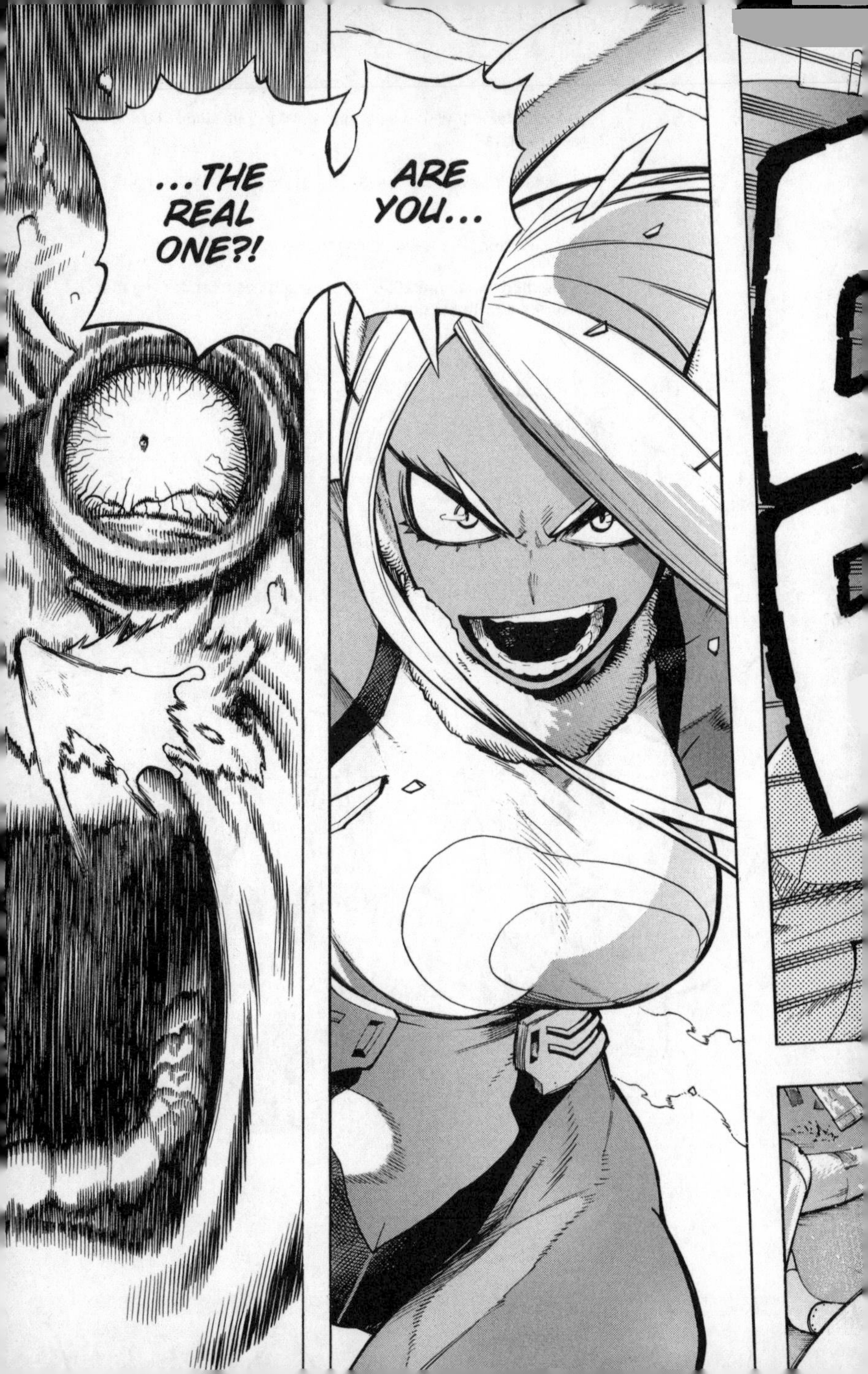
ARE YOU...
...THE REAL ONE?!

Raise your hand if you're wondering, "Who's this lady starring in these chapters?"

Well, take a look at volumes 20 and 21 again. She's the no. 5 hero.

Ever since then, I've been itching to use her in the story.

She debuted in volume 20, so that means I've been feeling that itch for seven whole books.

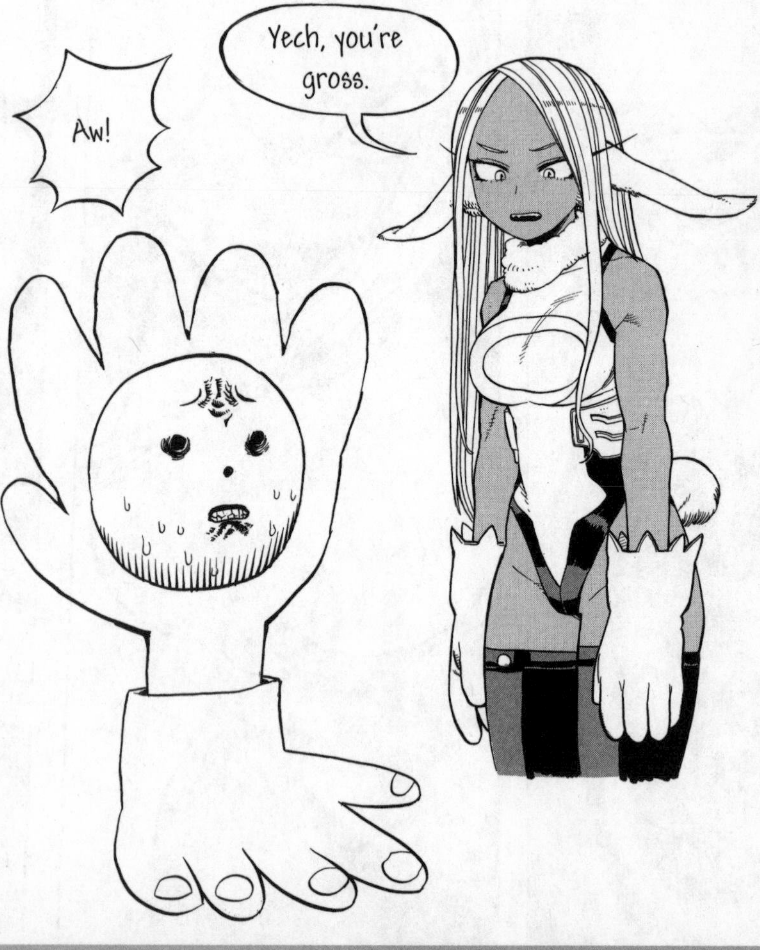
Yech, you're gross.
Aw!

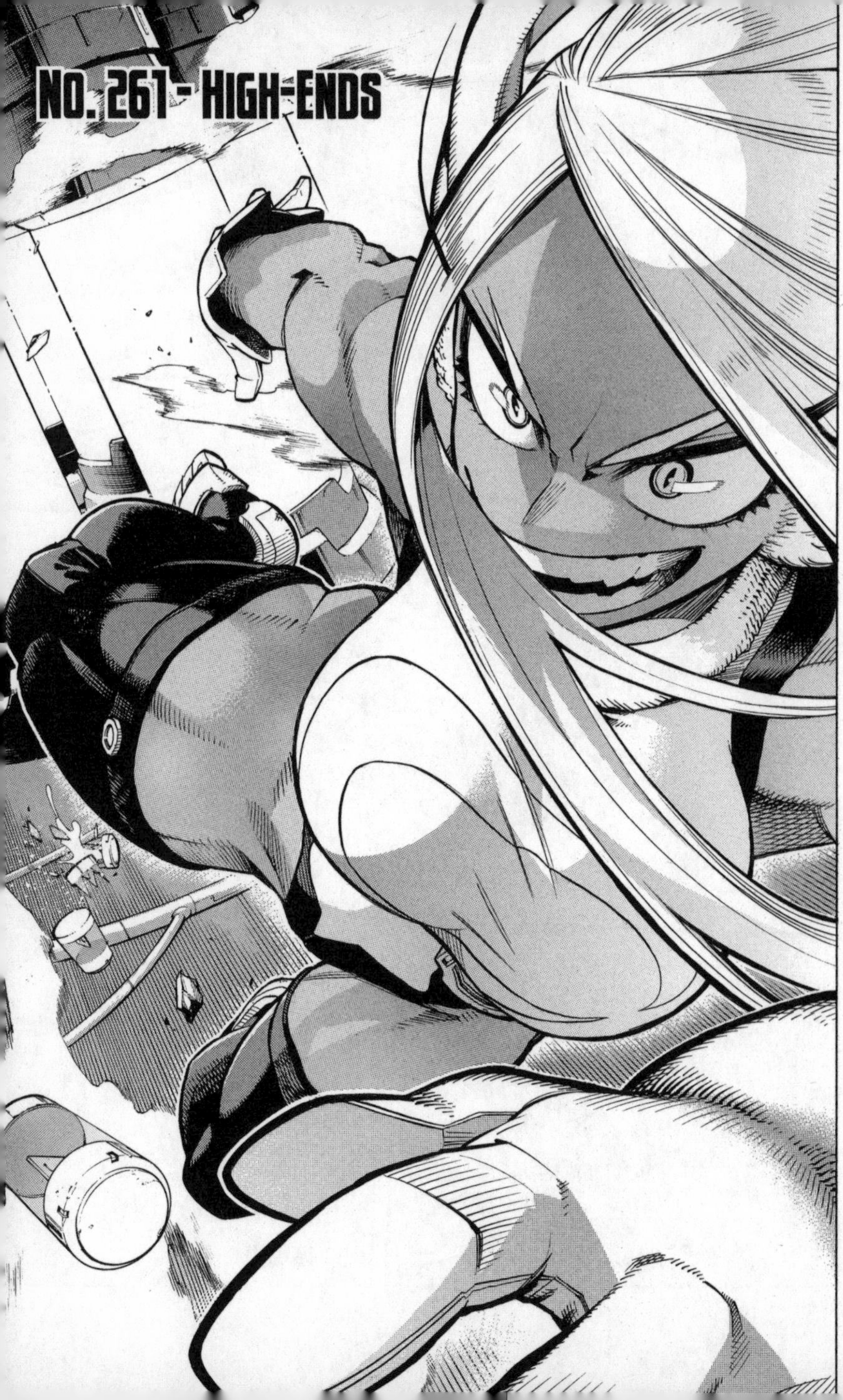
No. 261 - High-Ends

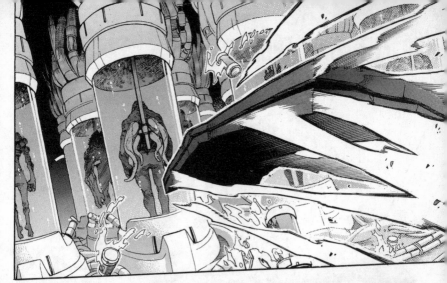

...JOHNNY.

GOOD BOY. WELL DONE...

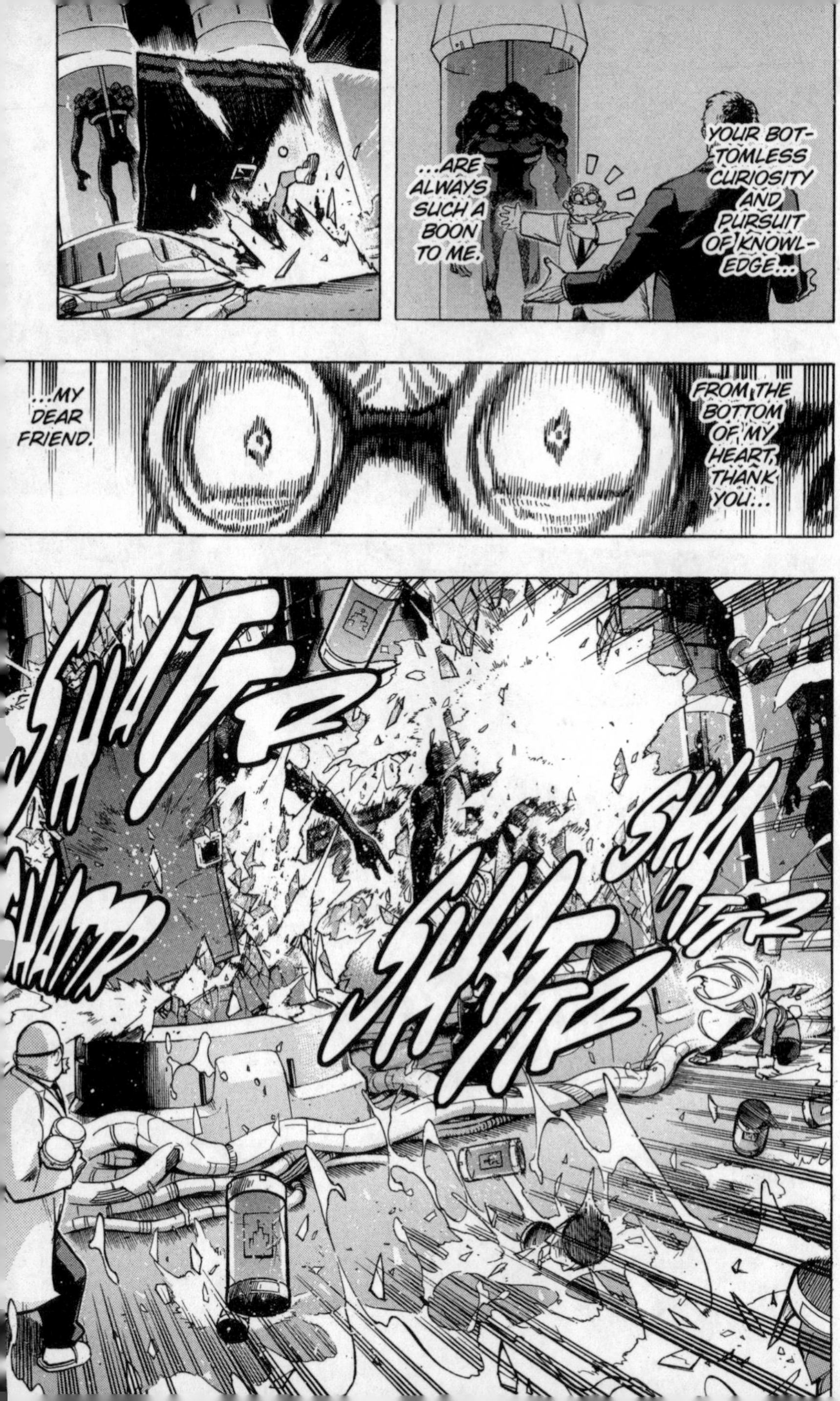
YOUR BOT-TOMLESS CURIOSITY AND PURSUIT OF KNOWL-EDGE...
...ARE ALWAYS SUCH A BOON TO ME.
FROM THE BOTTOM OF MY HEART, THANK YOU...
...MY DEAR FRIEND.
SHATTER
SHATTER
SHATTER
SHATTER

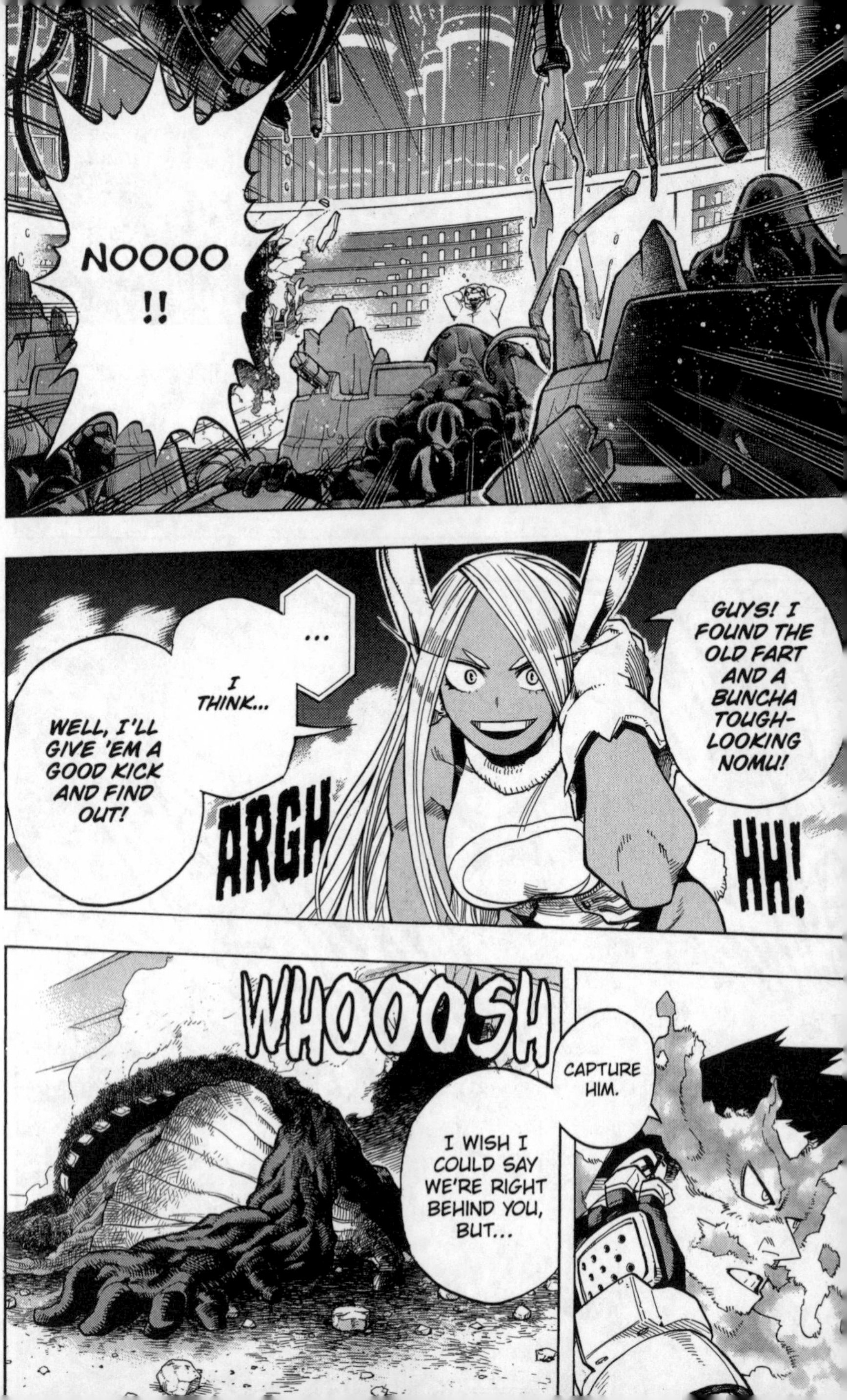
NOOOO !!
GUYS! I FOUND THE OLD FART AND A BUNCHA TOUGH-LOOKING NOMU!
ARGHHH!
...
I THINK...
WELL, I'LL GIVE 'EM A GOOD KICK AND FIND OUT!
CAPTURE HIM.
I WISH I COULD SAY WE'RE RIGHT BEHIND YOU, BUT...
WHOOOSH

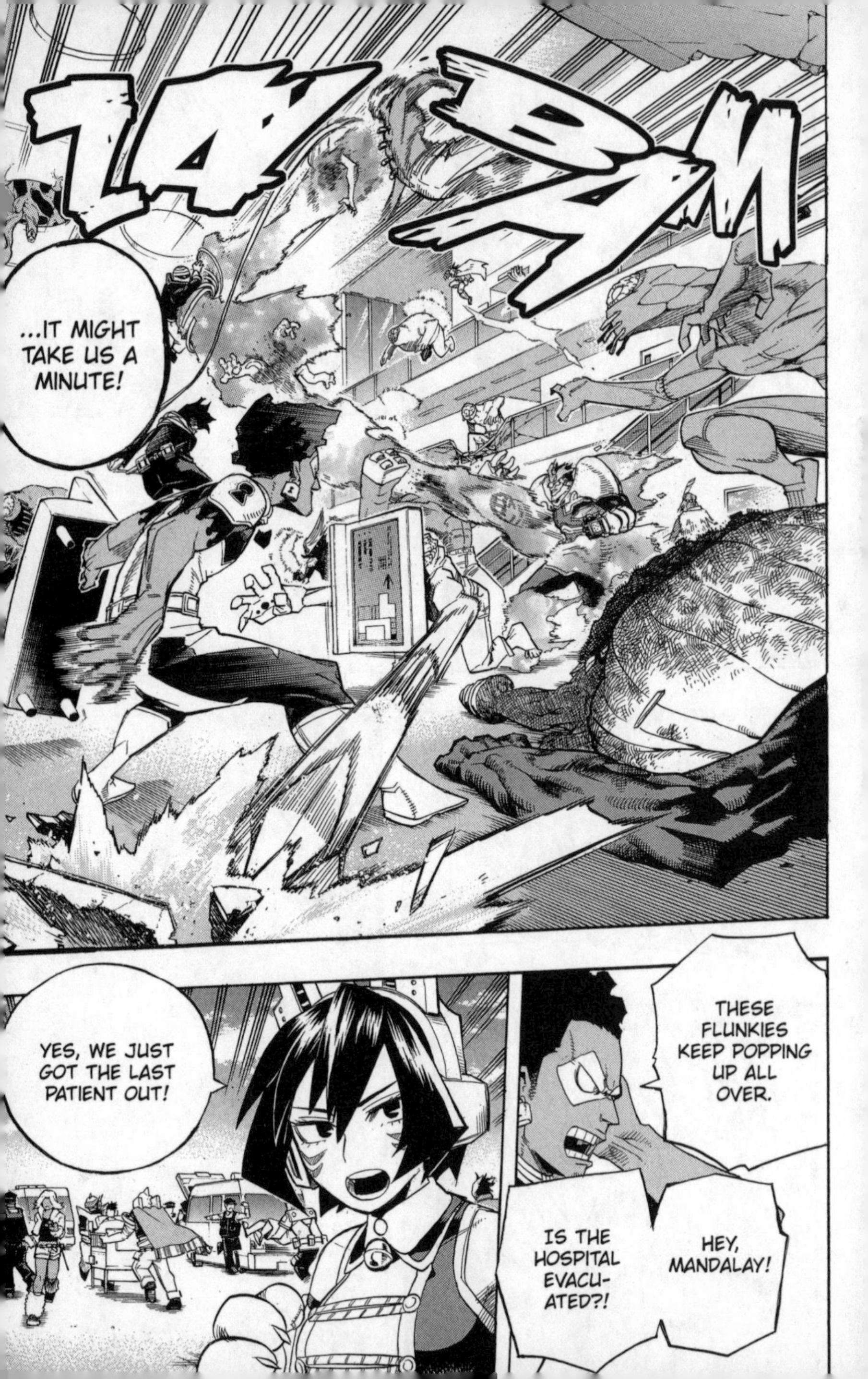
...IT MIGHT TAKE US A MINUTE!
THESE FLUNKIES KEEP POPPING UP ALL OVER.
HEY, MANDALAY!
IS THE HOSPITAL EVACU-ATED?!
YES, WE JUST GOT THE LAST PATIENT OUT!

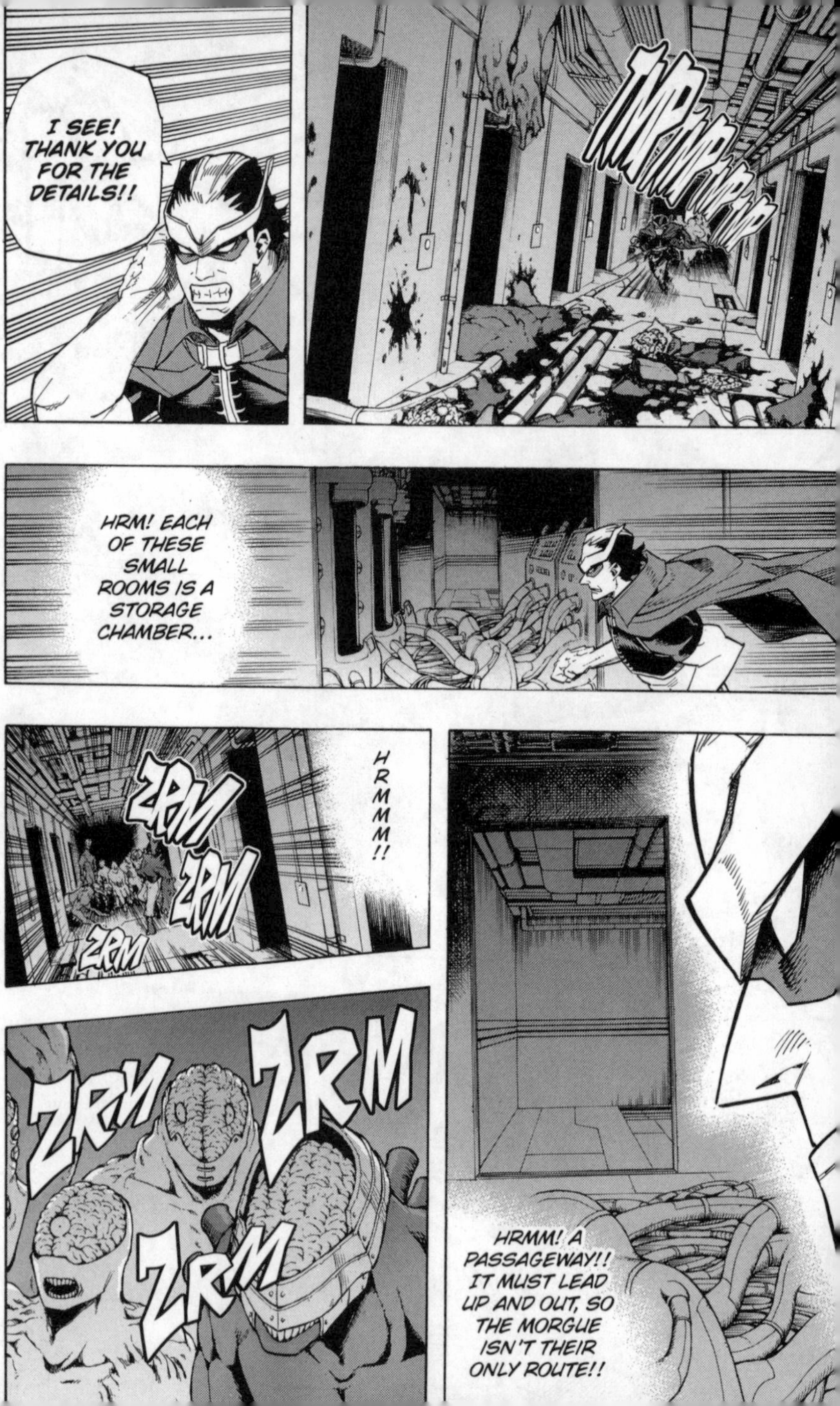
TMP TMP TMP
I SEE! THANK YOU FOR THE DETAILS!!
HRM! EACH OF THESE SMALL ROOMS IS A STORAGE CHAMBER...
HRMM! A PASSAGEWAY!! IT MUST LEAD UP AND OUT, SO THE MORGUE ISN'T THEIR ONLY ROUTE!!
HRMMM!!
ZRM ZRM ZRM
ZRM ZRM ZRM

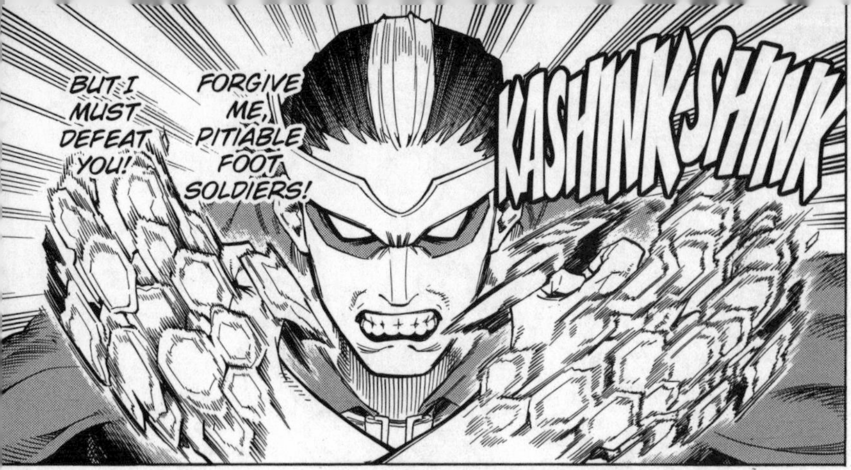
KASHINK-SHINK
FORGIVE ME, PITIABLE FOOT SOLDIERS!
BUT I MUST DEFEAT YOU!
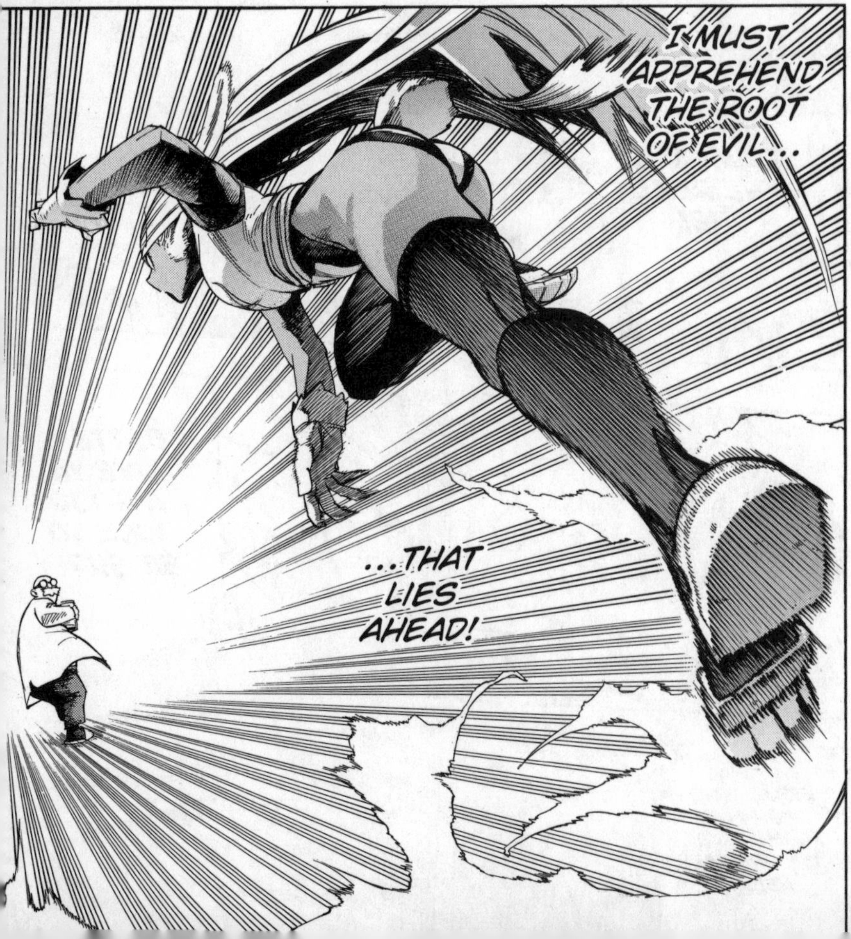
I MUST APPREHEND THE ROOT OF EVIL...
...THAT LIES AHEAD!

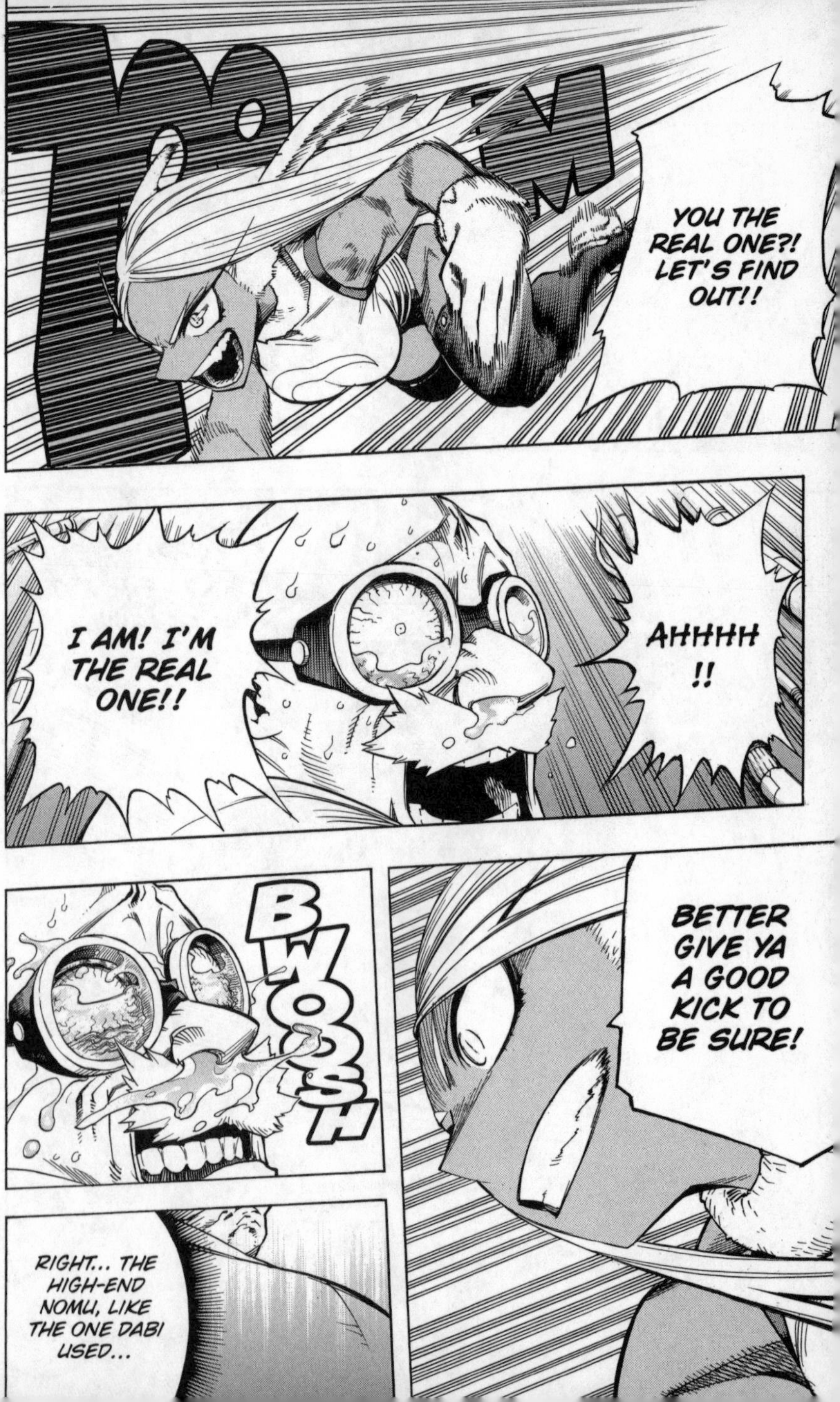
YOU THE REAL ONE?! LET'S FIND OUT!!
AHHHH !!
I AM! I'M THE REAL ONE!!
BETTER GIVE YA A GOOD KICK TO BE SURE!
BWOOSH
RIGHT... THE HIGH-END NOMU, LIKE THE ONE DABI USED...

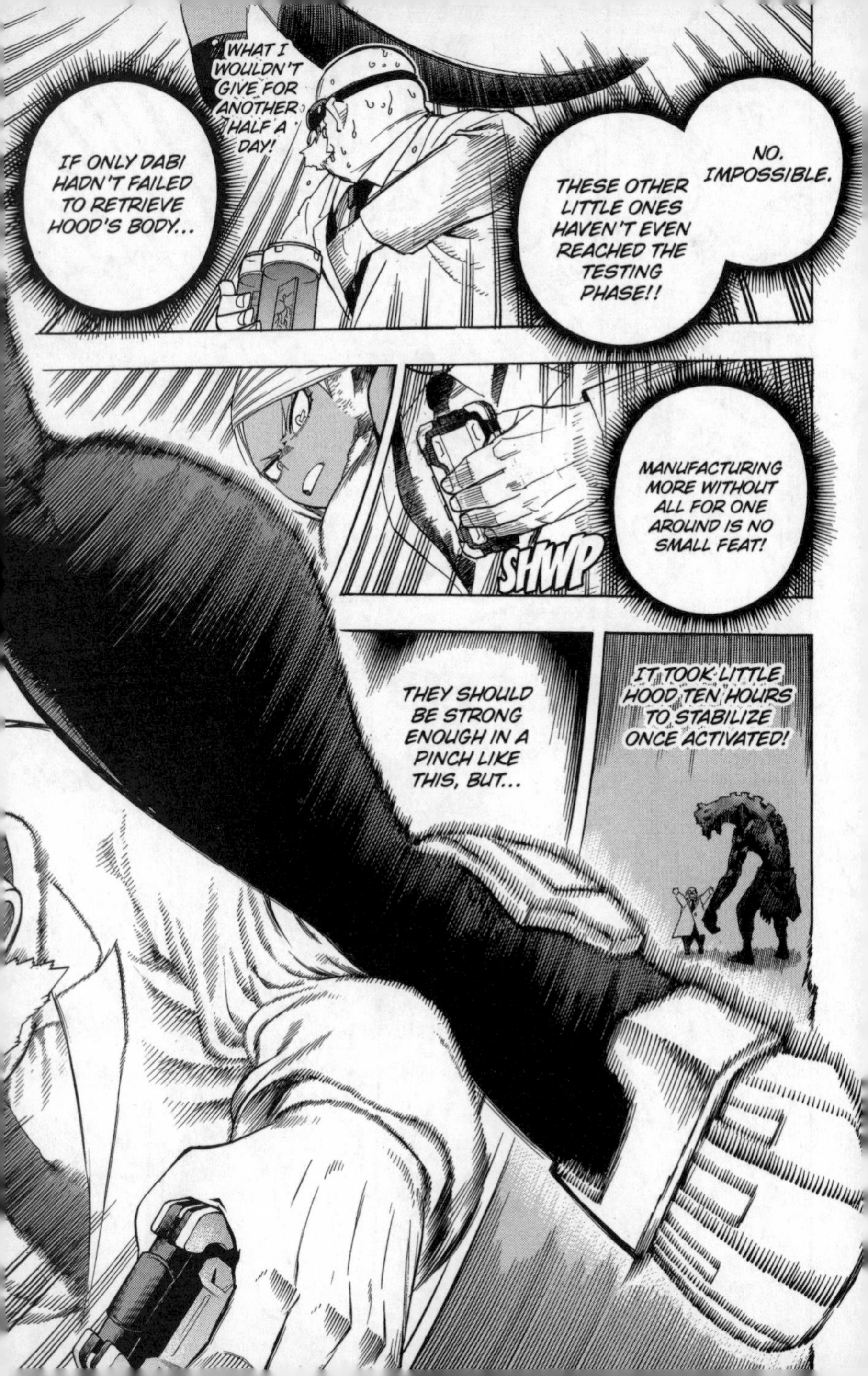
NO. IMPOSSIBLE.
THESE OTHER LITTLE ONES HAVEN'T EVEN REACHED THE TESTING PHASE!!
WHAT I WOULDN'T GIVE FOR ANOTHER HALF A DAY!
IF ONLY DABI HADN'T FAILED TO RETRIEVE HOOD'S BODY...
MANUFACTURING MORE WITHOUT ALL FOR ONE AROUND IS NO SMALL FEAT!
SHWP
IT TOOK LITTLE HOOD TEN HOURS TO STABILIZE ONCE ACTIVATED!
THEY SHOULD BE STRONG ENOUGH IN A PINCH LIKE THIS, BUT...

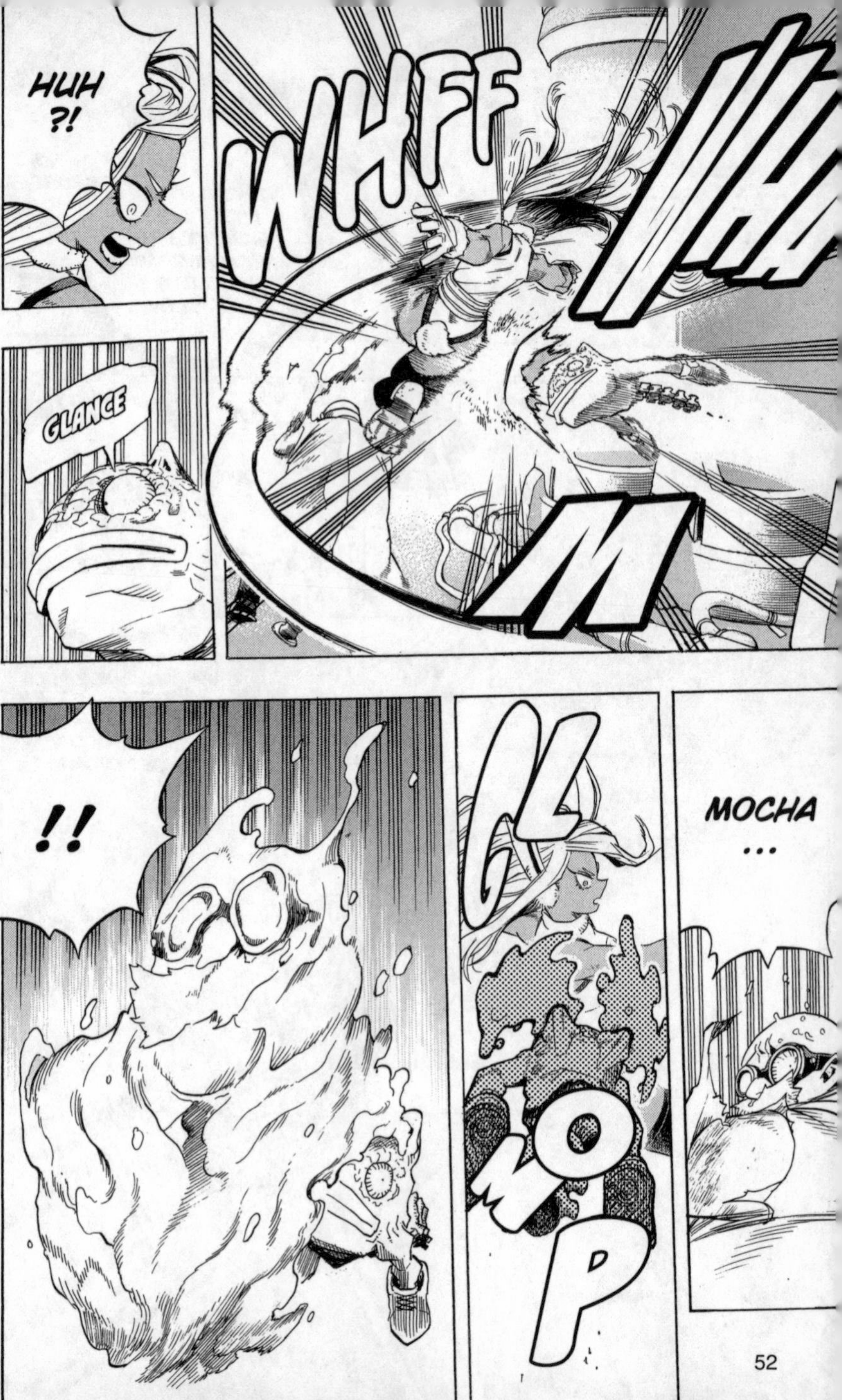

WHAM
WHFF
HUH ?!
GLANCE
MOCHA ...
GLOMP
!!

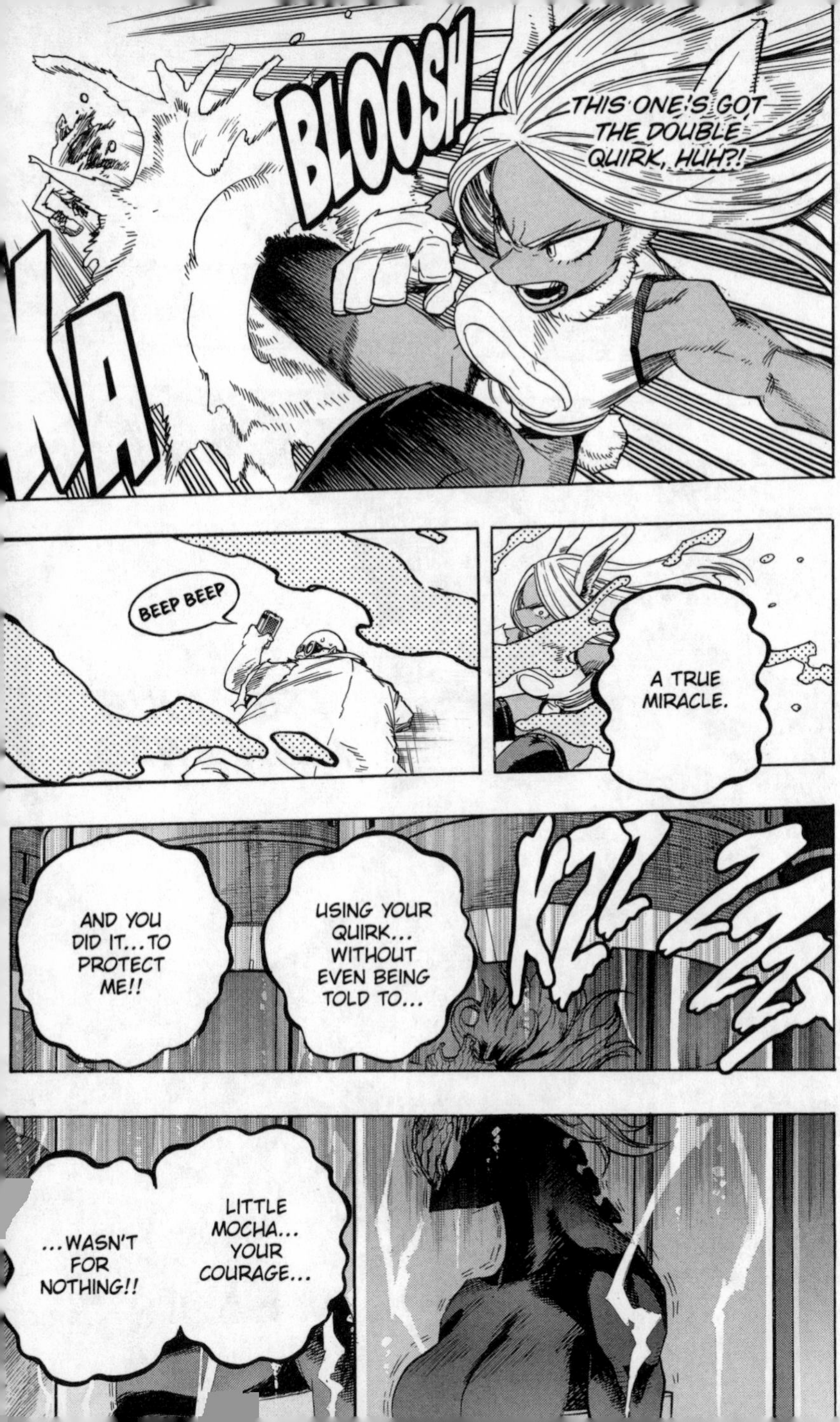
THIS ONE'S GOT THE DOUBLE QUIRK, HUH?!
BLOOSH
A TRUE MIRACLE.
BEEP BEEP
KZZ ZZZ
USING YOUR QUIRK... WITHOUT EVEN BEING TOLD TO...
AND YOU DID IT...TO PROTECT ME!!
LITTLE MOCHA... YOUR COURAGE...
...WASN'T FOR NOTHING!!

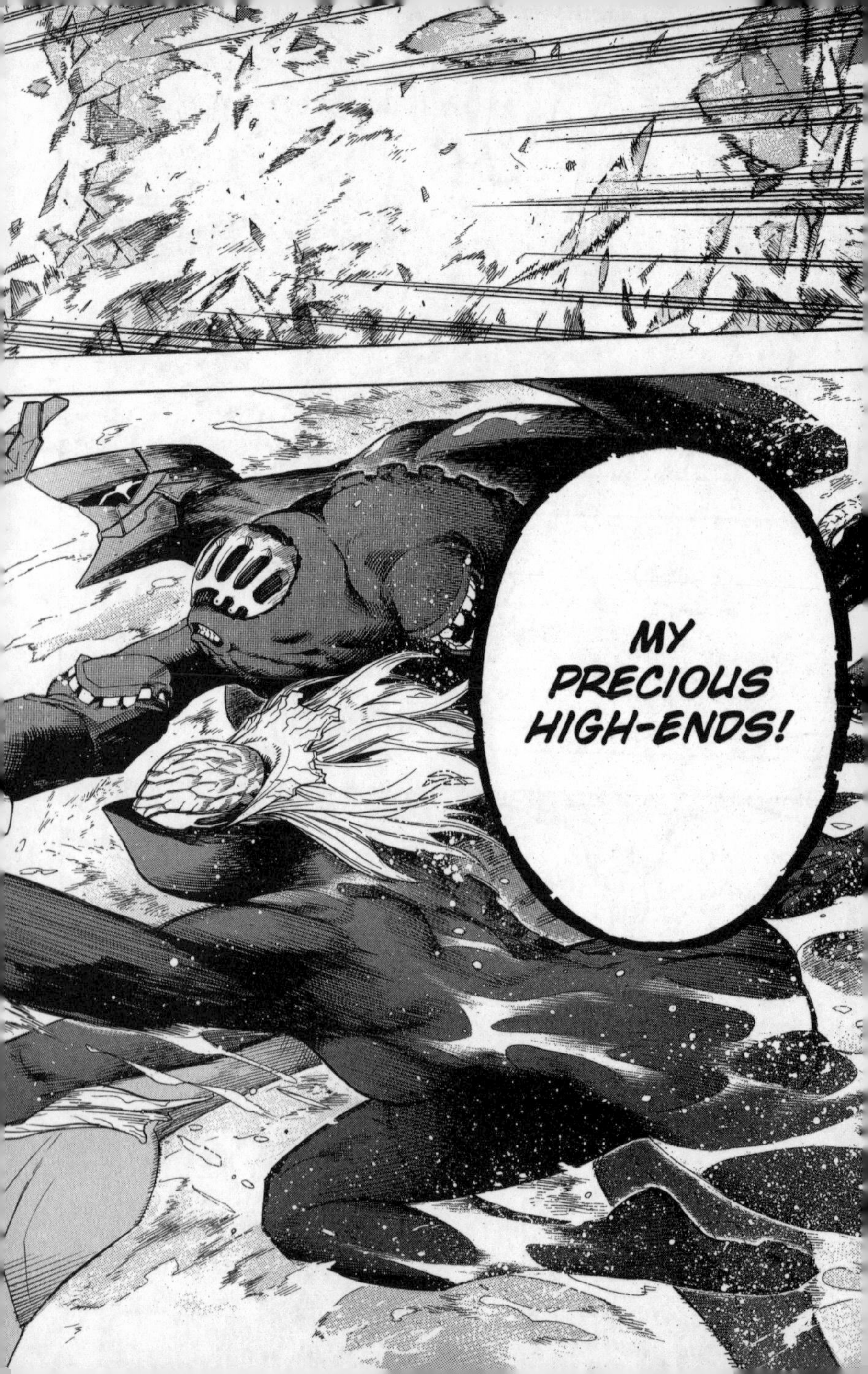
MY PRECIOUS HIGH-ENDS!

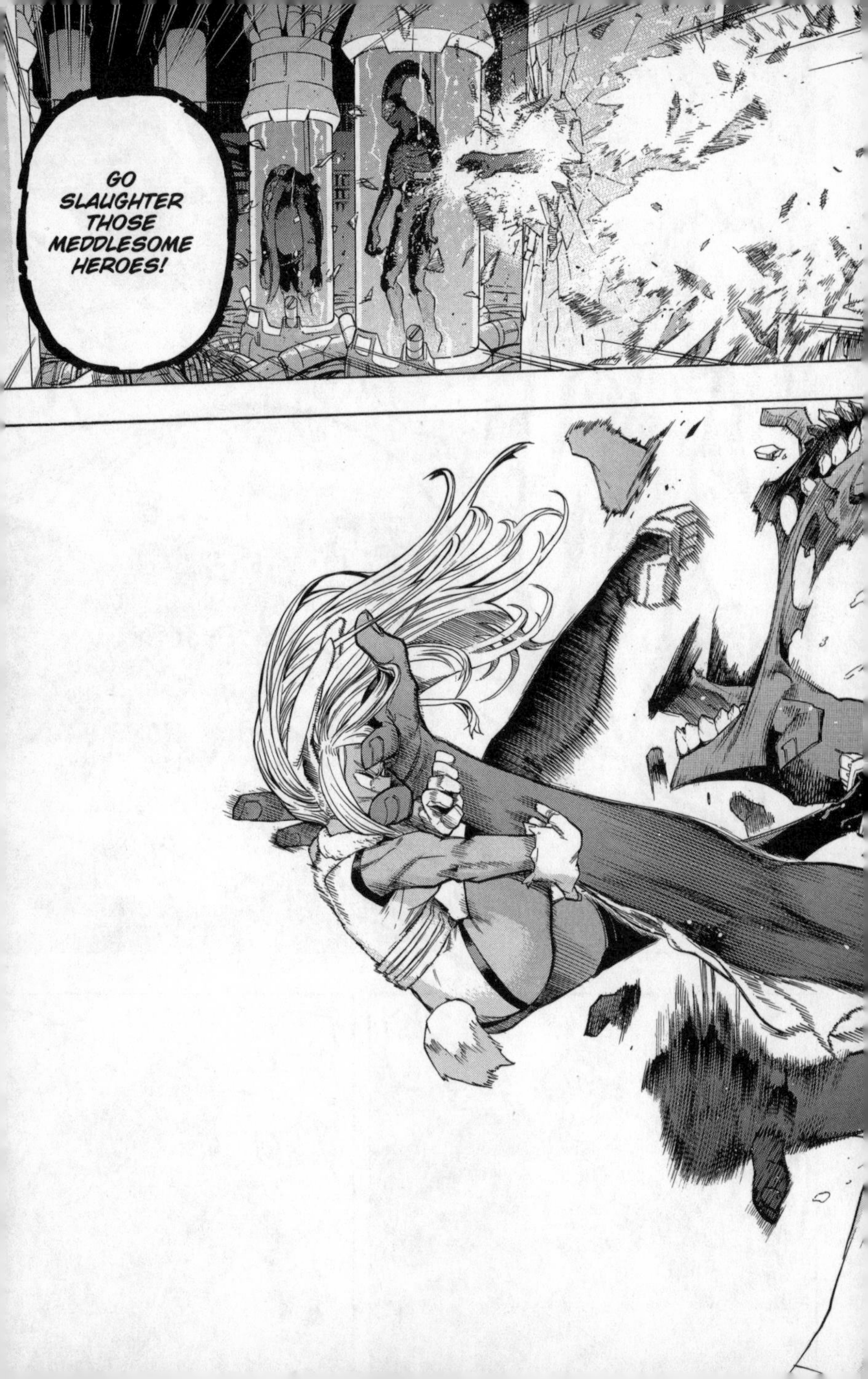
GO SLAUGHTER THOSE MEDDLESOME HEROES!

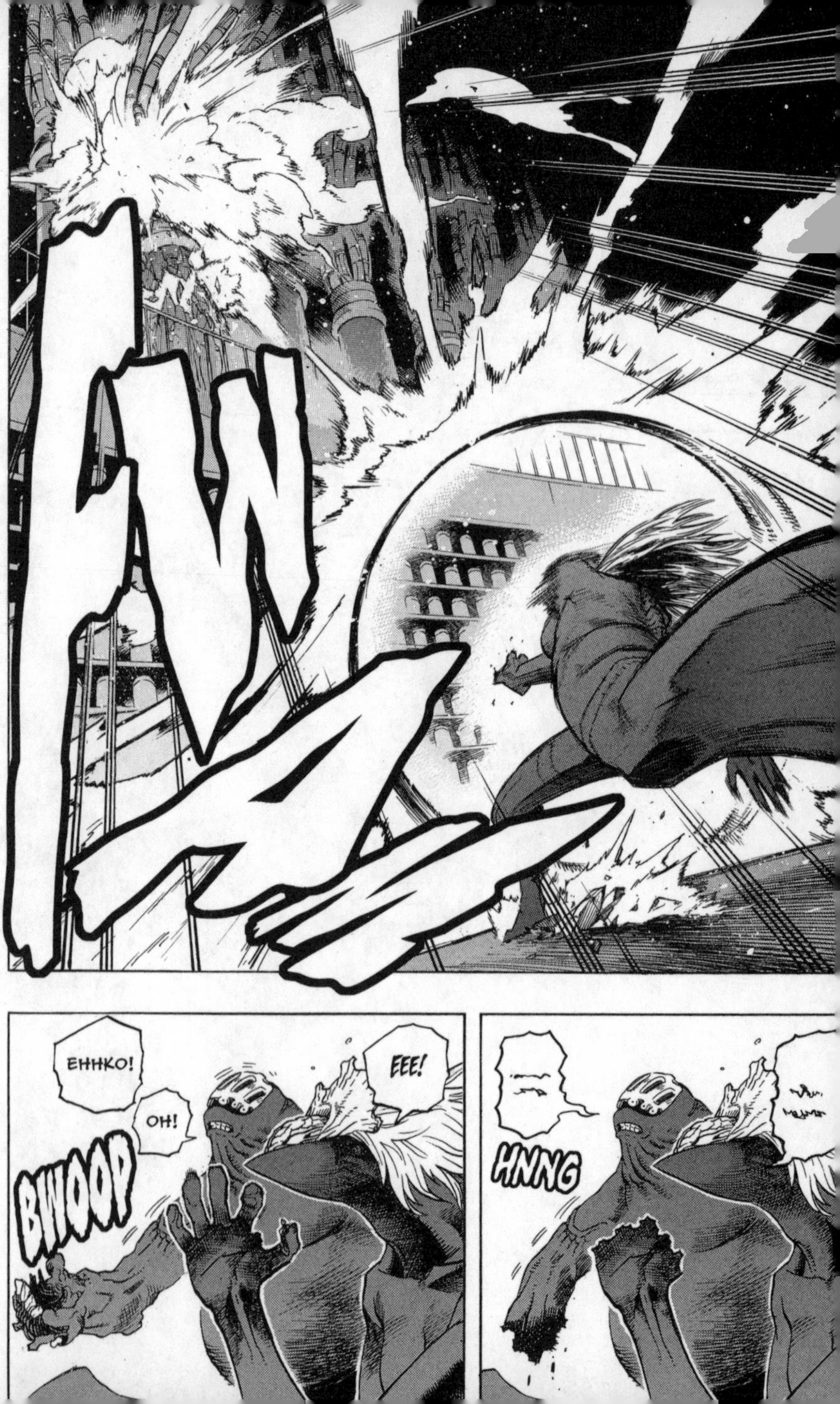
HNNG
EEE!
EHHKO!
OH!
BWOOP

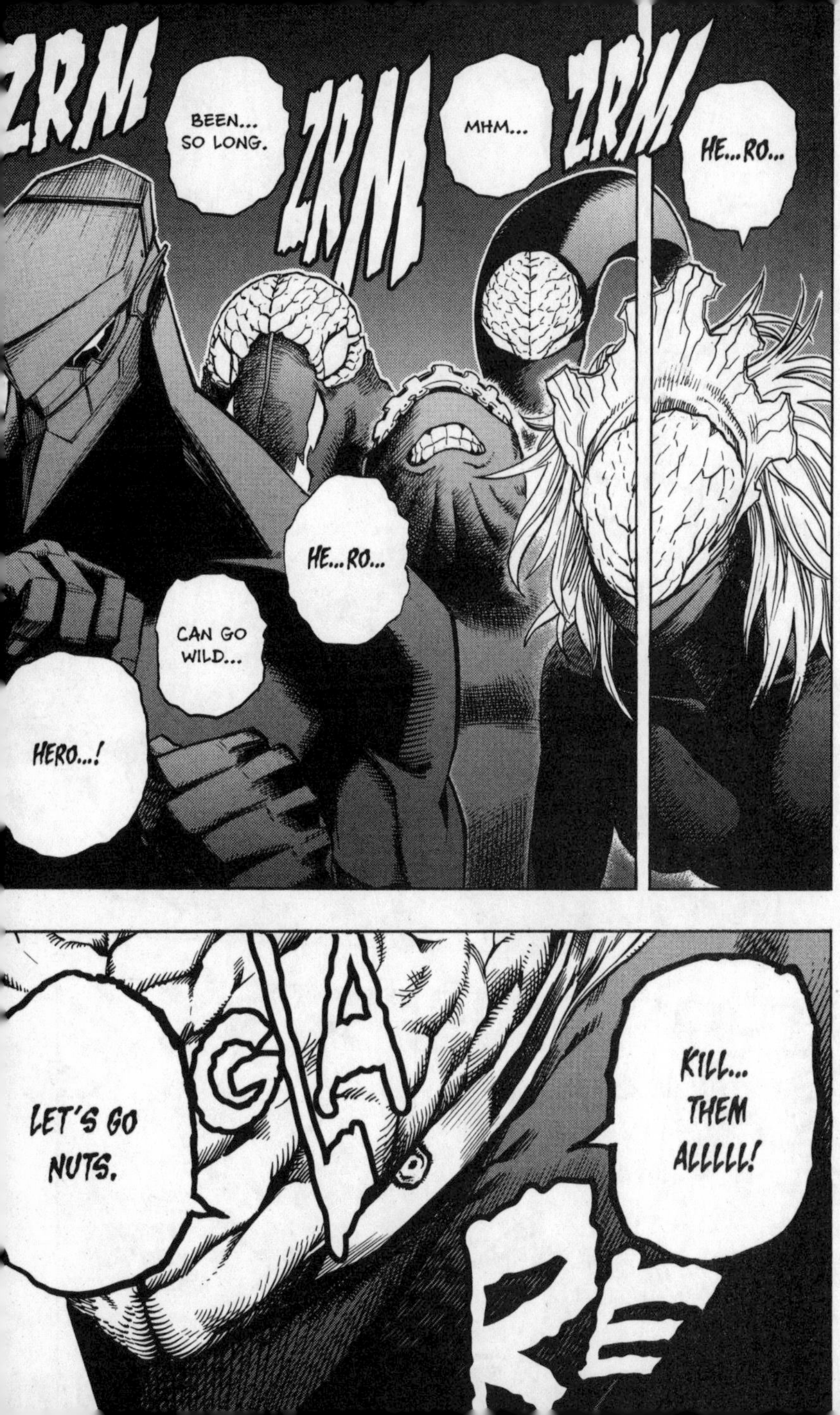
HE...RO...
ZRM
MHM...
ZRM
BEEN... SO LONG.
ZRM
ZRM
HE...RO...
CAN GO WILD...
HERO...!
KILL... THEM ALLLLL!
LET'S GO NUTS.

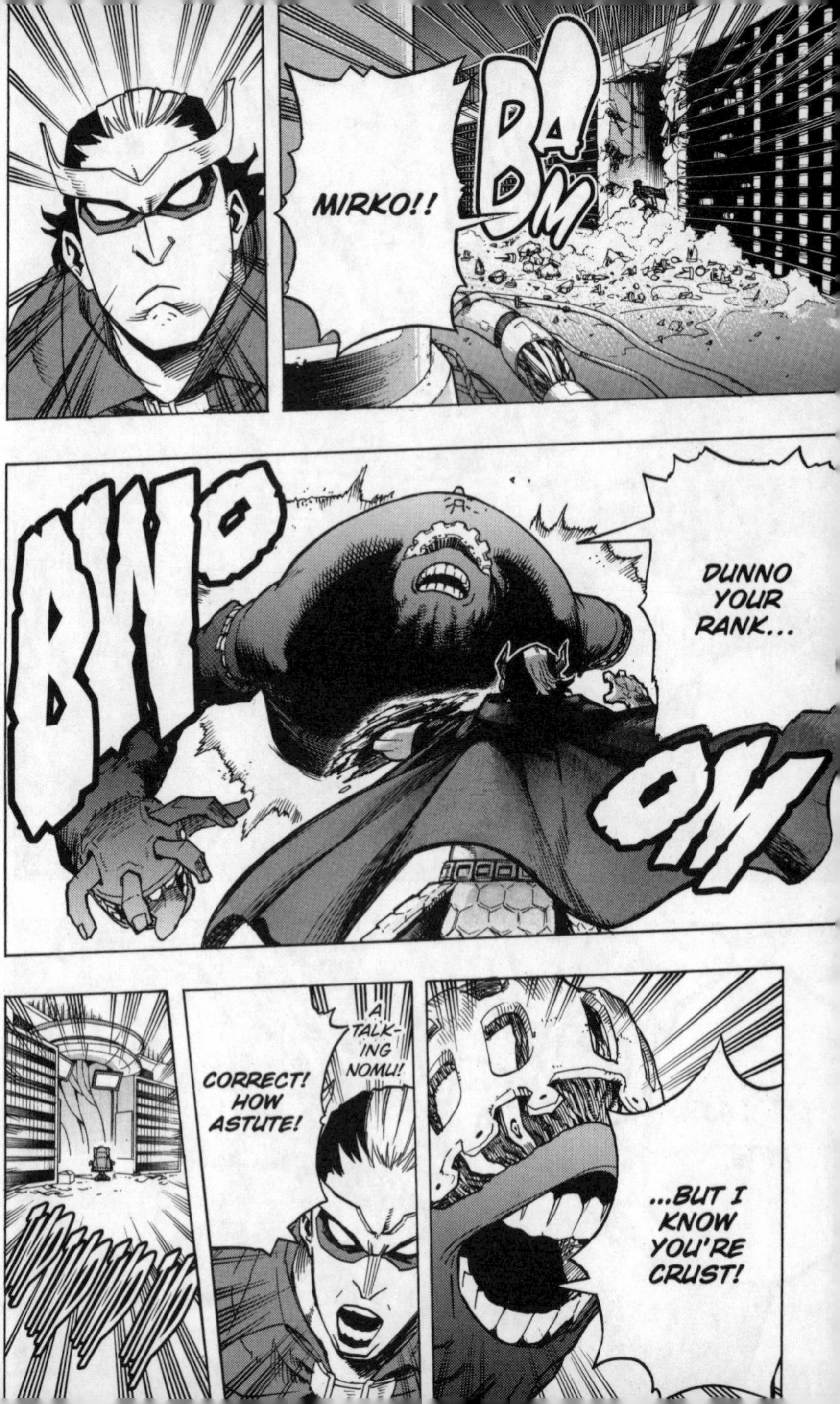
MIRKO!!
DUNNO YOUR RANK...
...BUT I KNOW YOU'RE CRUST!
A TALK-ING NOMU!
CORRECT! HOW ASTUTE!

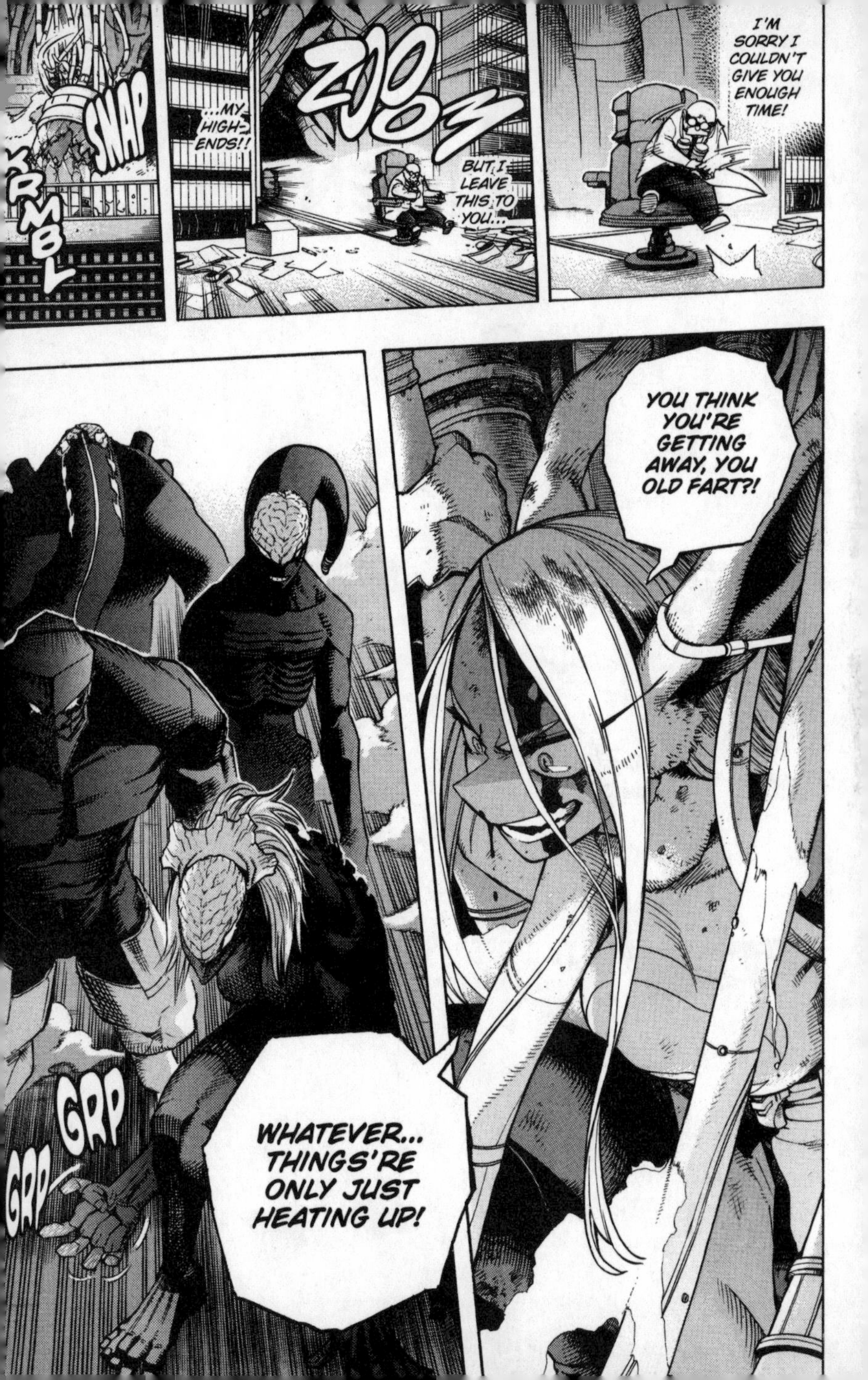
I'M SORRY I COULDN'T GIVE YOU ENOUGH TIME!
ZOOOM
...MY HIGH-ENDS!!
BUT I LEAVE THIS TO YOU...
SNAP
KRMBL
YOU THINK YOU'RE GETTING AWAY, YOU OLD FART?!
WHATEVER... THINGS'RE ONLY JUST HEATING UP!
GRP
GRP

THE HIGH-ENDS

WOMAN — Calm and levelheaded

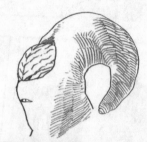

RIBBY — Made from the body of a psycho killer.

ROBOT — Equipped with armor, because the brain is only loosely attached.

CHUBS — Made from the body of a glutton.

ELEPH — Specialized for pure power.

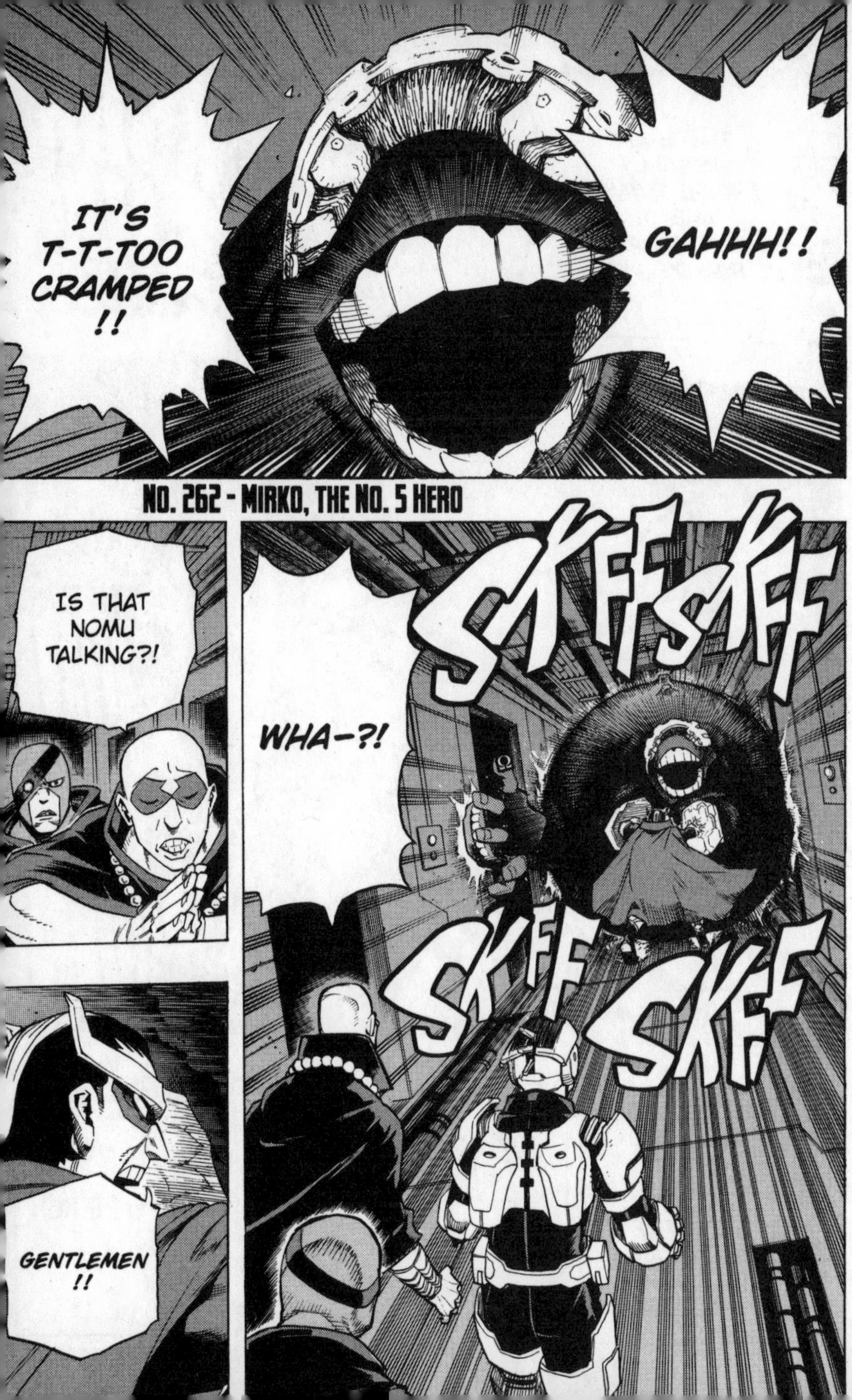
GAHHH!!
IT'S T-T-TOO CRAMPED!!
NO. 262 - MIRKO, THE NO. 5 HERO
SKFF SKFF
WHA-?!
SKFF SKFF
IS THAT NOMU TALKING?!
GENTLEMEN!!

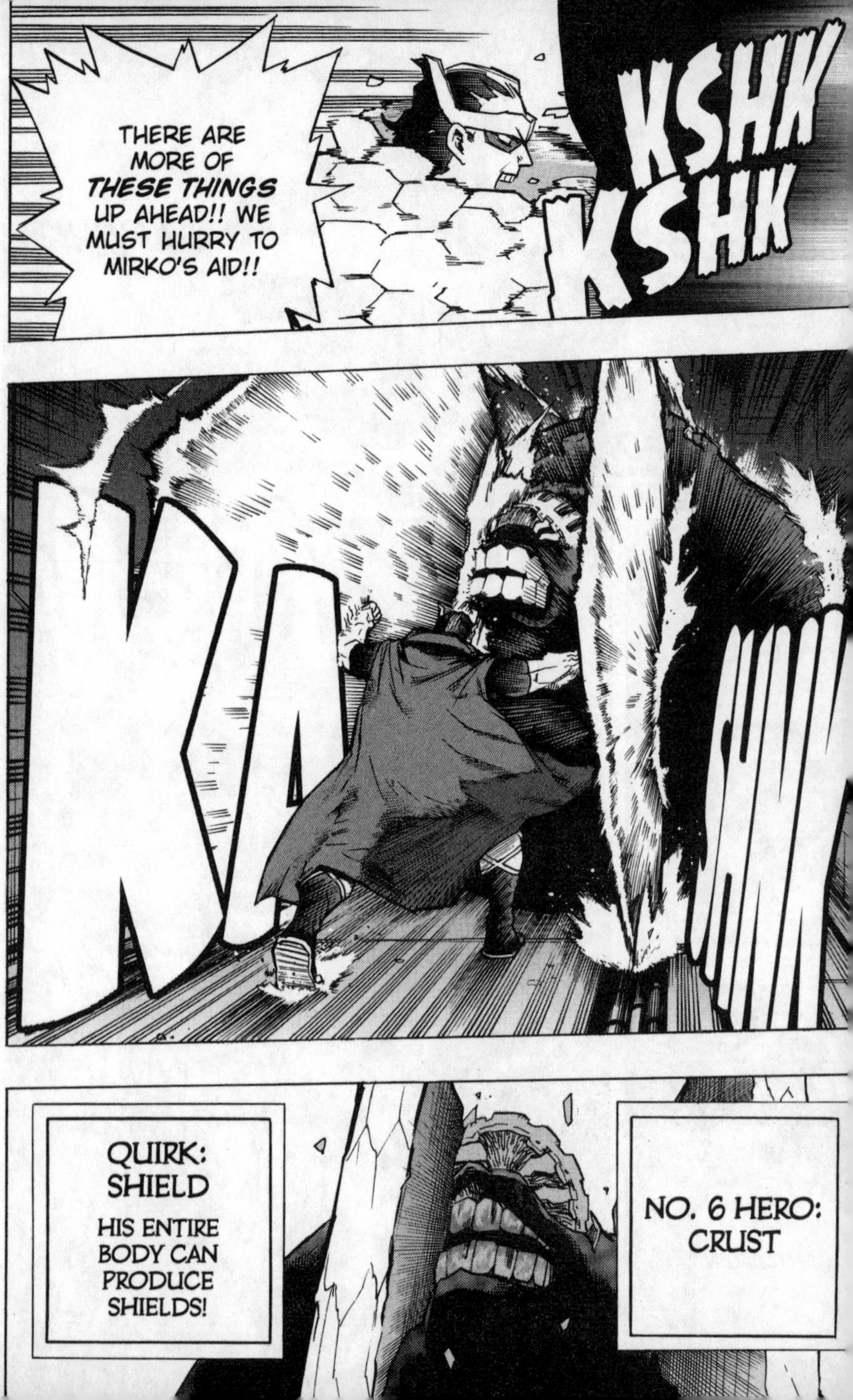
KSHK
KSHK
THERE ARE MORE OF THESE THINGS UP AHEAD!! WE MUST HURRY TO MIRKO'S AID!!
NO. 6 HERO: CRUST
QUIRK: SHIELD
HIS ENTIRE BODY CAN PRODUCE SHIELDS!

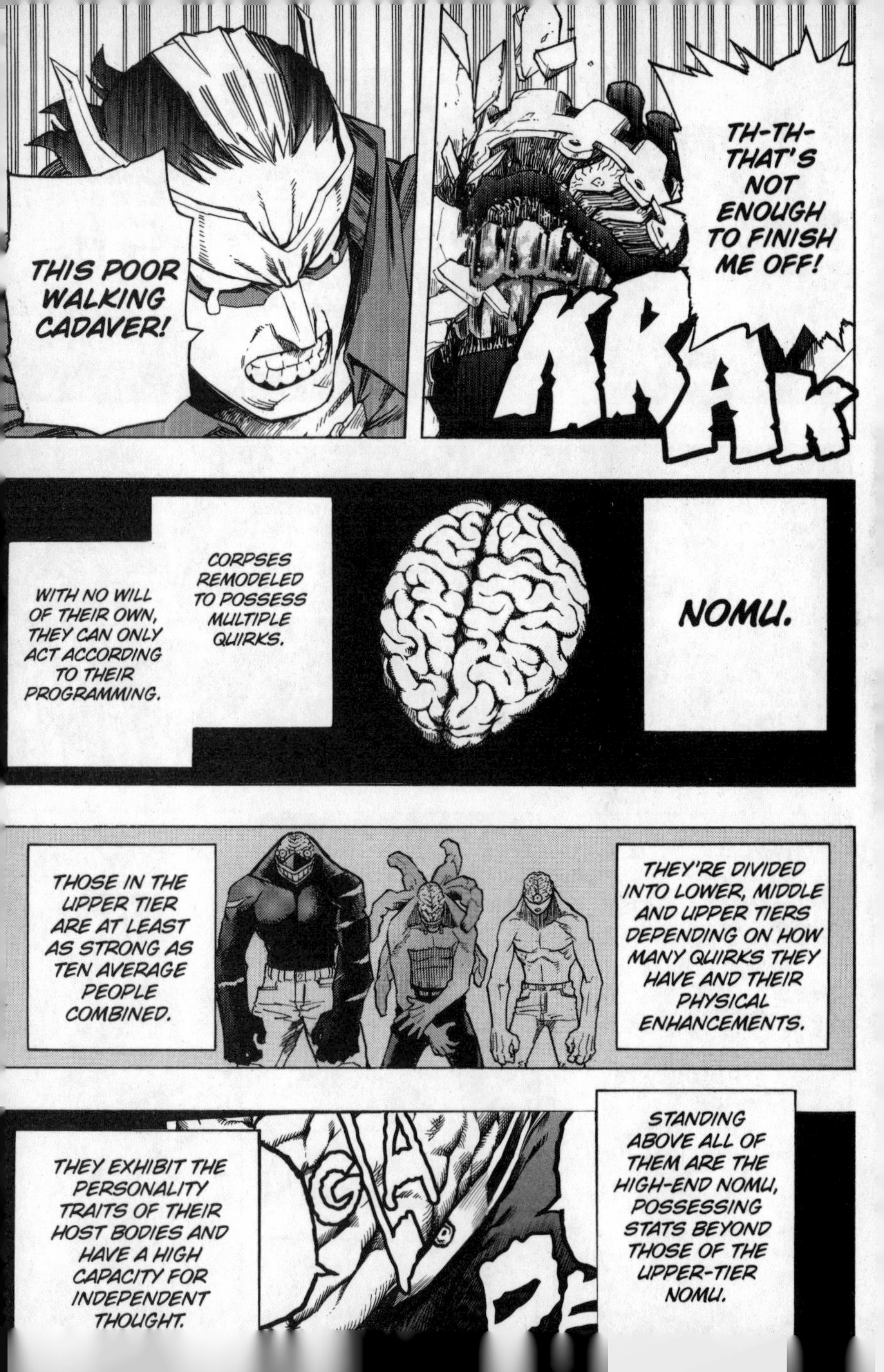
TH-TH-THAT'S NOT ENOUGH TO FINISH ME OFF!
KRAK
THIS POOR WALKING CADAVER!
NOMU.
CORPSES REMODELED TO POSSESS MULTIPLE QUIRKS.
WITH NO WILL OF THEIR OWN, THEY CAN ONLY ACT ACCORDING TO THEIR PROGRAMMING.
THEY'RE DIVIDED INTO LOWER, MIDDLE AND UPPER TIERS DEPENDING ON HOW MANY QUIRKS THEY HAVE AND THEIR PHYSICAL ENHANCEMENTS.
THOSE IN THE UPPER TIER ARE AT LEAST AS STRONG AS TEN AVERAGE PEOPLE COMBINED.
STANDING ABOVE ALL OF THEM ARE THE HIGH-END NOMU, POSSESSING STATS BEYOND THOSE OF THE UPPER-TIER NOMU.
THEY EXHIBIT THE PERSONALITY TRAITS OF THEIR HOST BODIES AND HAVE A HIGH CAPACITY FOR INDEPENDENT THOUGHT.

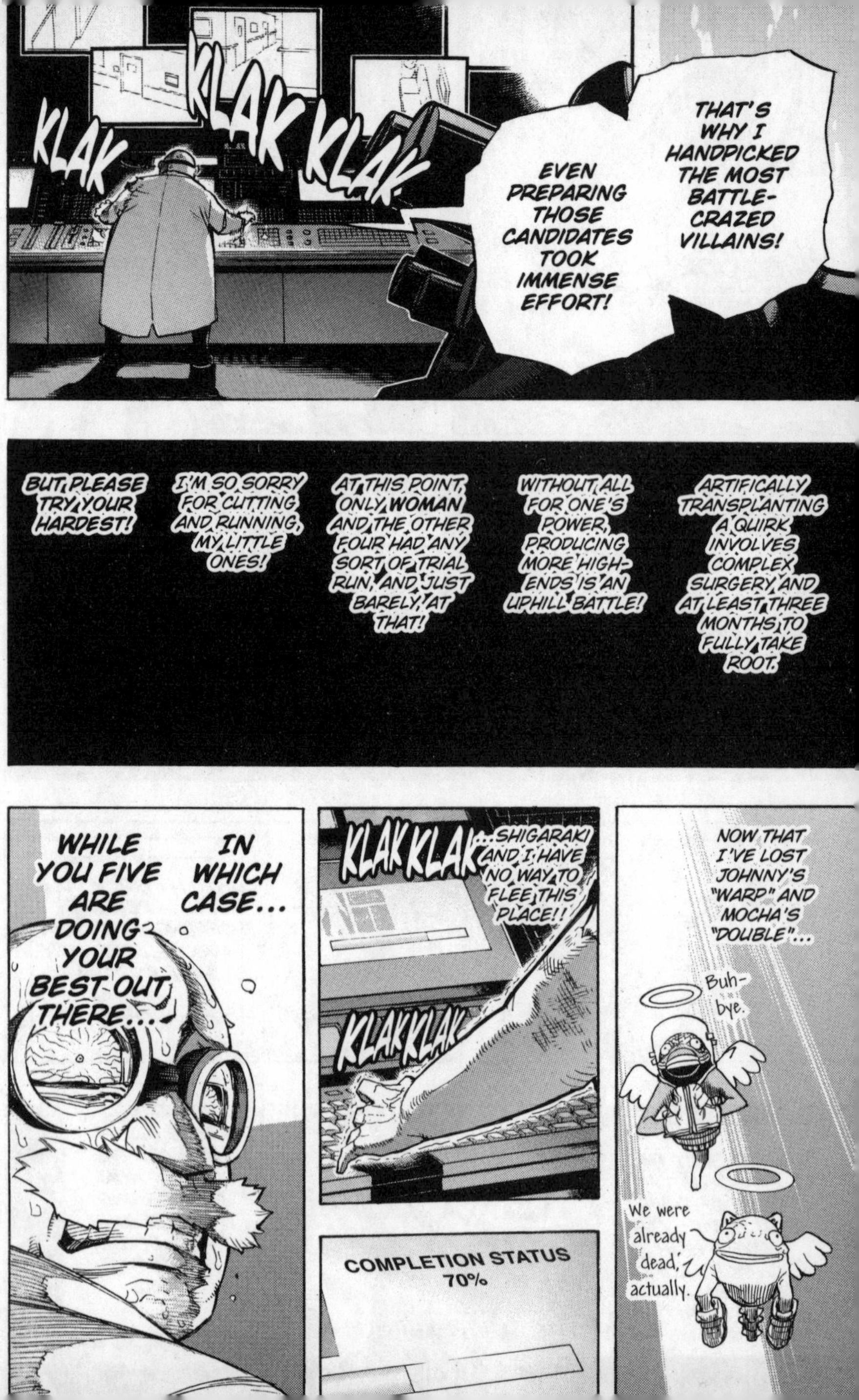
THAT'S WHY I HANDPICKED THE MOST BATTLE-CRAZED VILLAINS!
EVEN PREPARING THOSE CANDIDATES TOOK IMMENSE EFFORT!
KLAK KLAK KLAK
ARTIFICALLY TRANSPLANTING A QUIRK INVOLVES COMPLEX SURGERY AND AT LEAST THREE MONTHS TO FULLY TAKE ROOT.
WITHOUT ALL FOR ONE'S POWER, PRODUCING MORE HIGH-ENDS IS AN UPHILL BATTLE!
AT THIS POINT, ONLY WOMAN AND THE OTHER FOUR HAD ANY SORT OF TRIAL RUN, AND JUST BARELY, AT THAT!
I'M SO SORRY FOR CUTTING AND RUNNING, MY LITTLE ONES!
BUT PLEASE TRY YOUR HARDEST!
NOW THAT I'VE LOST JOHNNY'S "WARP" AND MOCHA'S "DOUBLE"...
Buh-bye.
We were already dead, actually.
KLAK KLAK
...SHIGARAKI AND I HAVE NO WAY TO FLEE THIS PLACE!!
KLAKKLAK
COMPLETION STATUS 70%
IN WHICH CASE...
WHILE YOU FIVE ARE DOING YOUR BEST OUT THERE...

No. 262 - Mirko, the No. 5 Hero

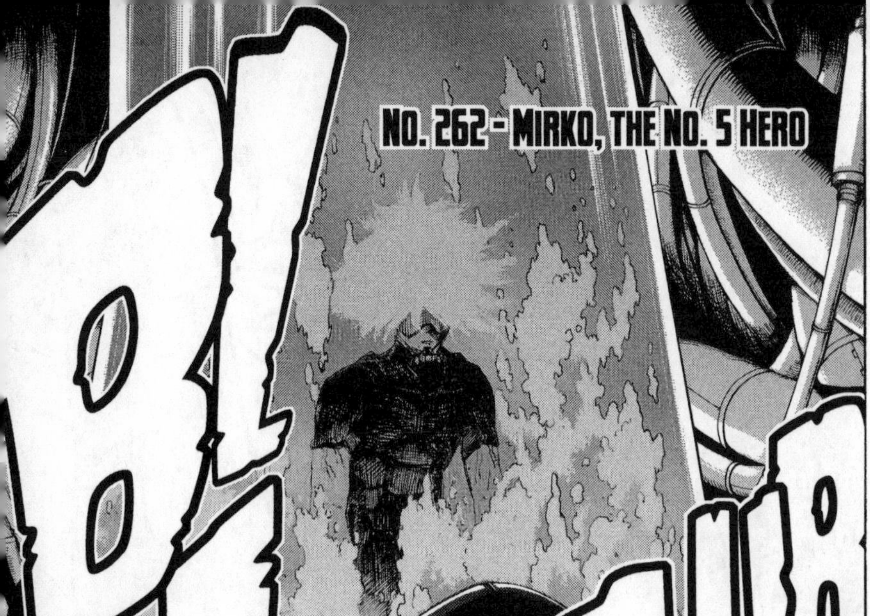
BLUB
BLUB

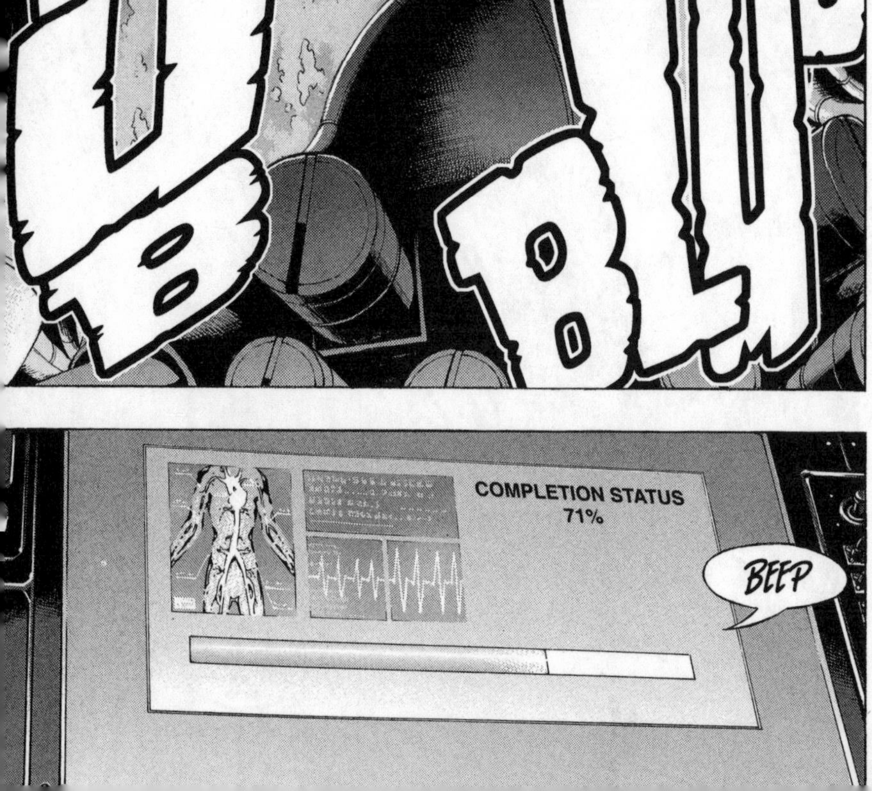
COMPLETION STATUS
71%
BEEP

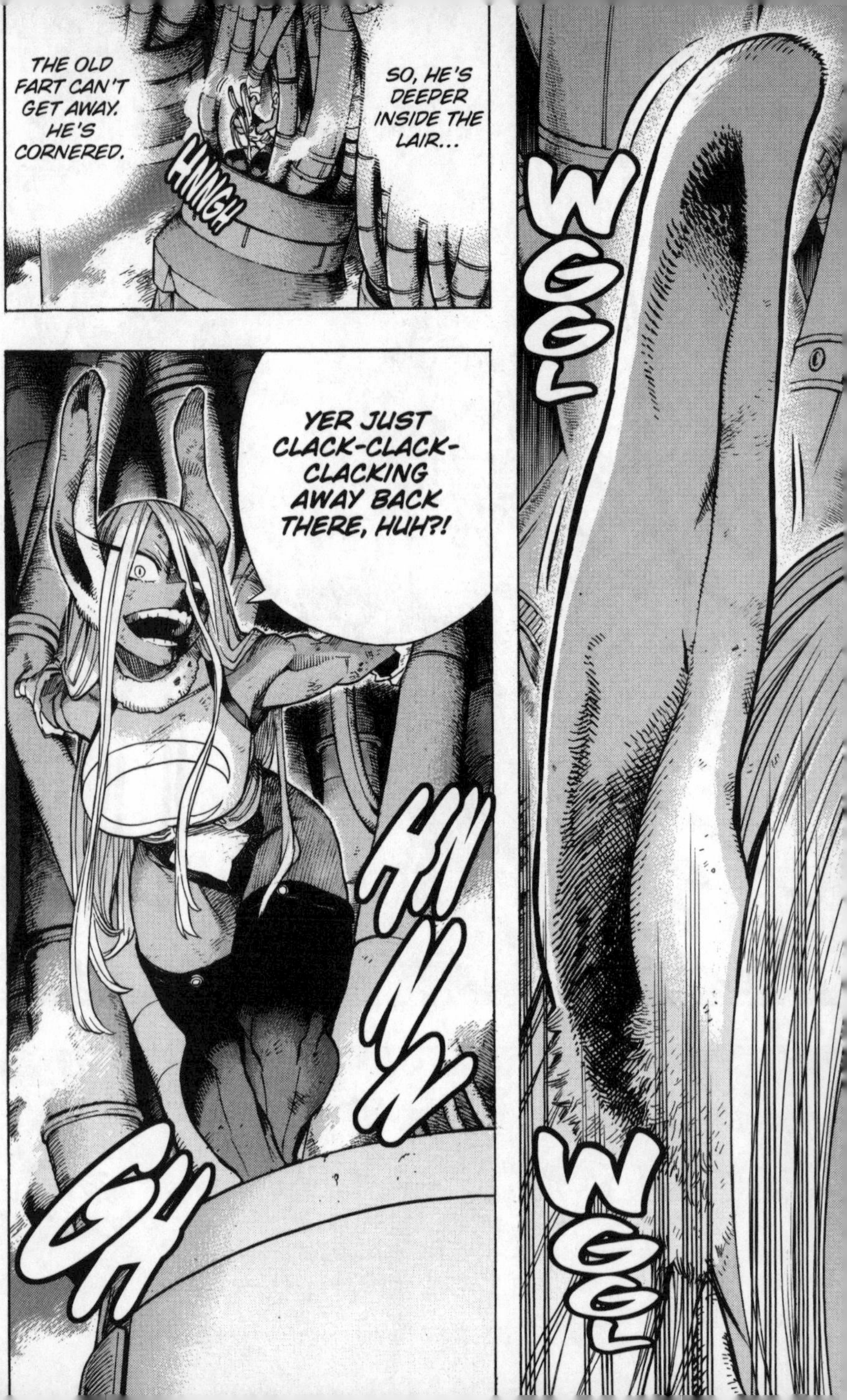
WGGL
WGGL
SO, HE'S DEEPER INSIDE THE LAIR...
THE OLD FART CAN'T GET AWAY. HE'S CORNERED.
HNNGH
YER JUST CLACK-CLACK-CLACKING AWAY BACK THERE, HUH?!

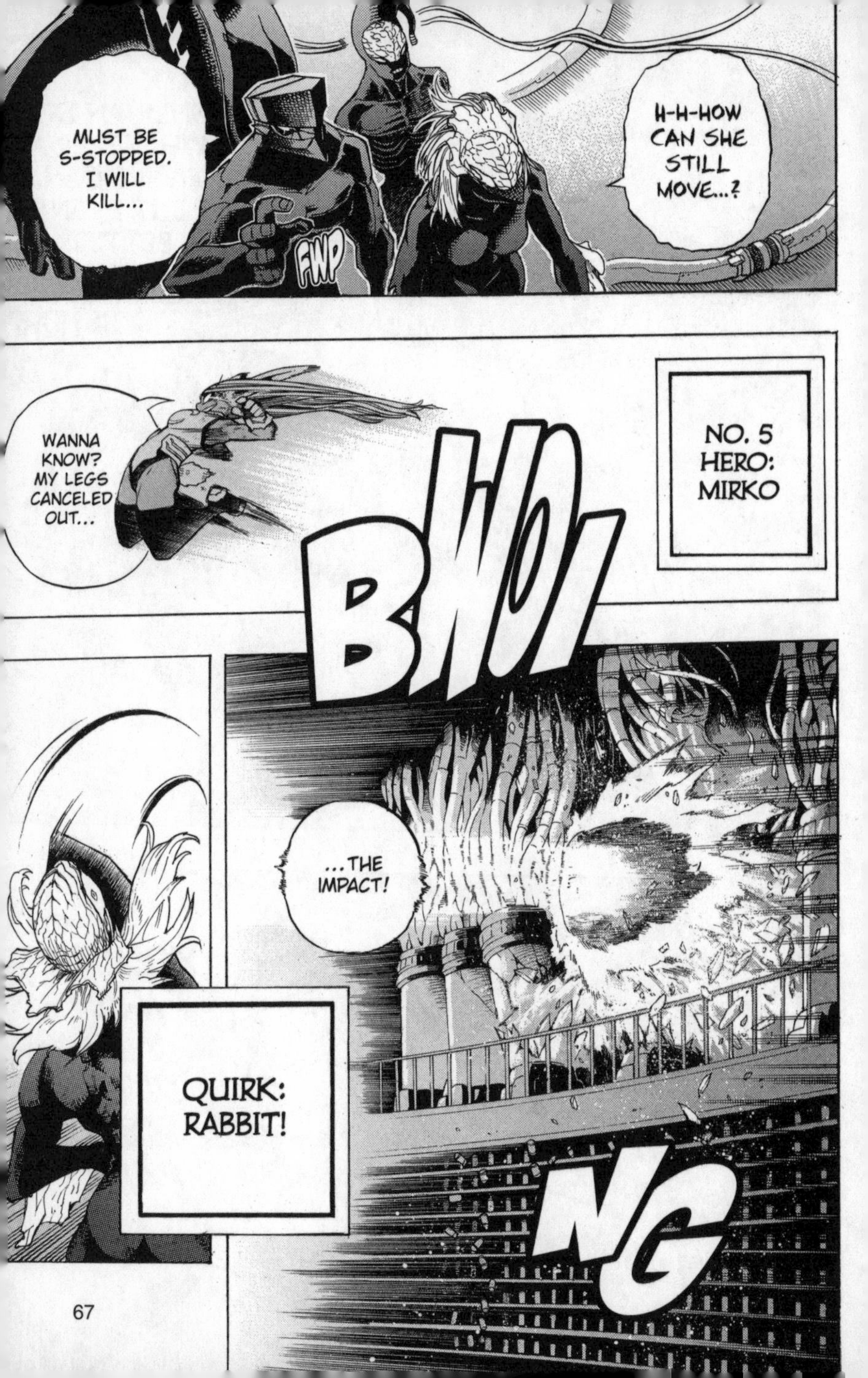
H-H-HOW CAN SHE STILL MOVE...?
MUST BE S-STOPPED. I WILL KILL...
FWP
NO. 5 HERO: MIRKO
WANNA KNOW? MY LEGS CANCELED OUT...
BWOI
...THE IMPACT!
NG
QUIRK: RABBIT!

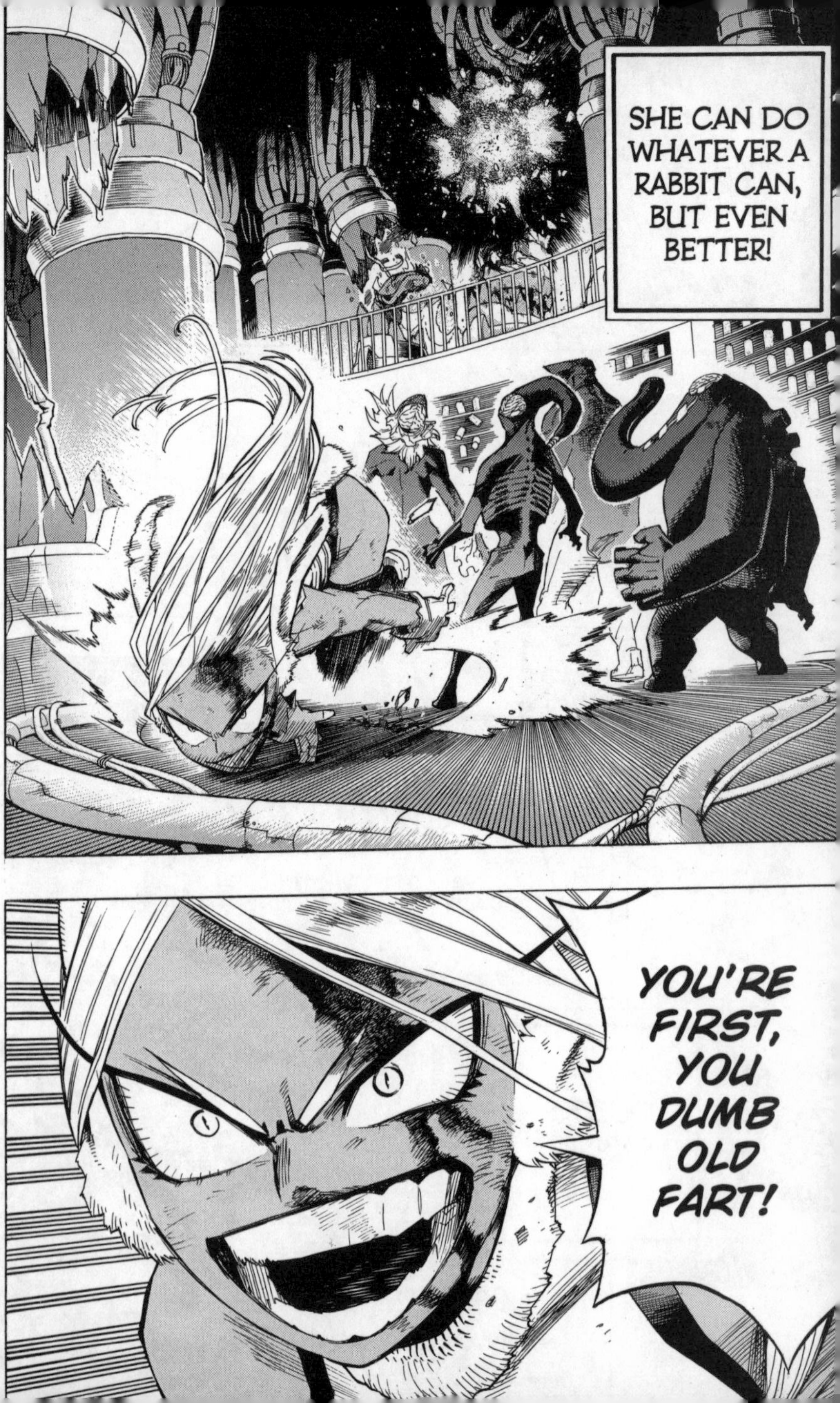
SHE CAN DO WHATEVER A RABBIT CAN, BUT EVEN BETTER!
YOU'RE FIRST, YOU DUMB OLD FART!

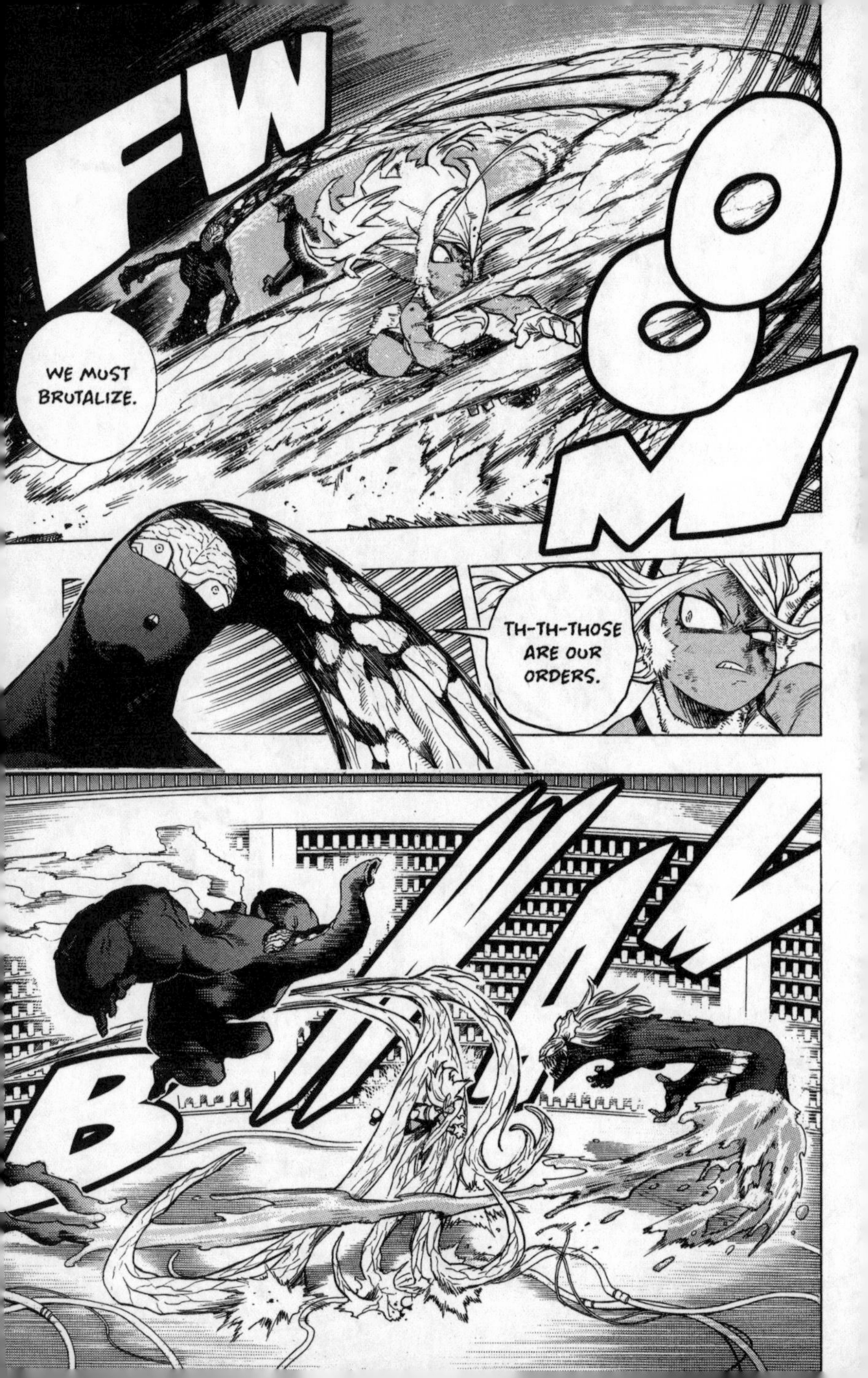
FWOOM
WE MUST BRUTALIZE.
TH-TH-THOSE ARE OUR ORDERS.
BWAM

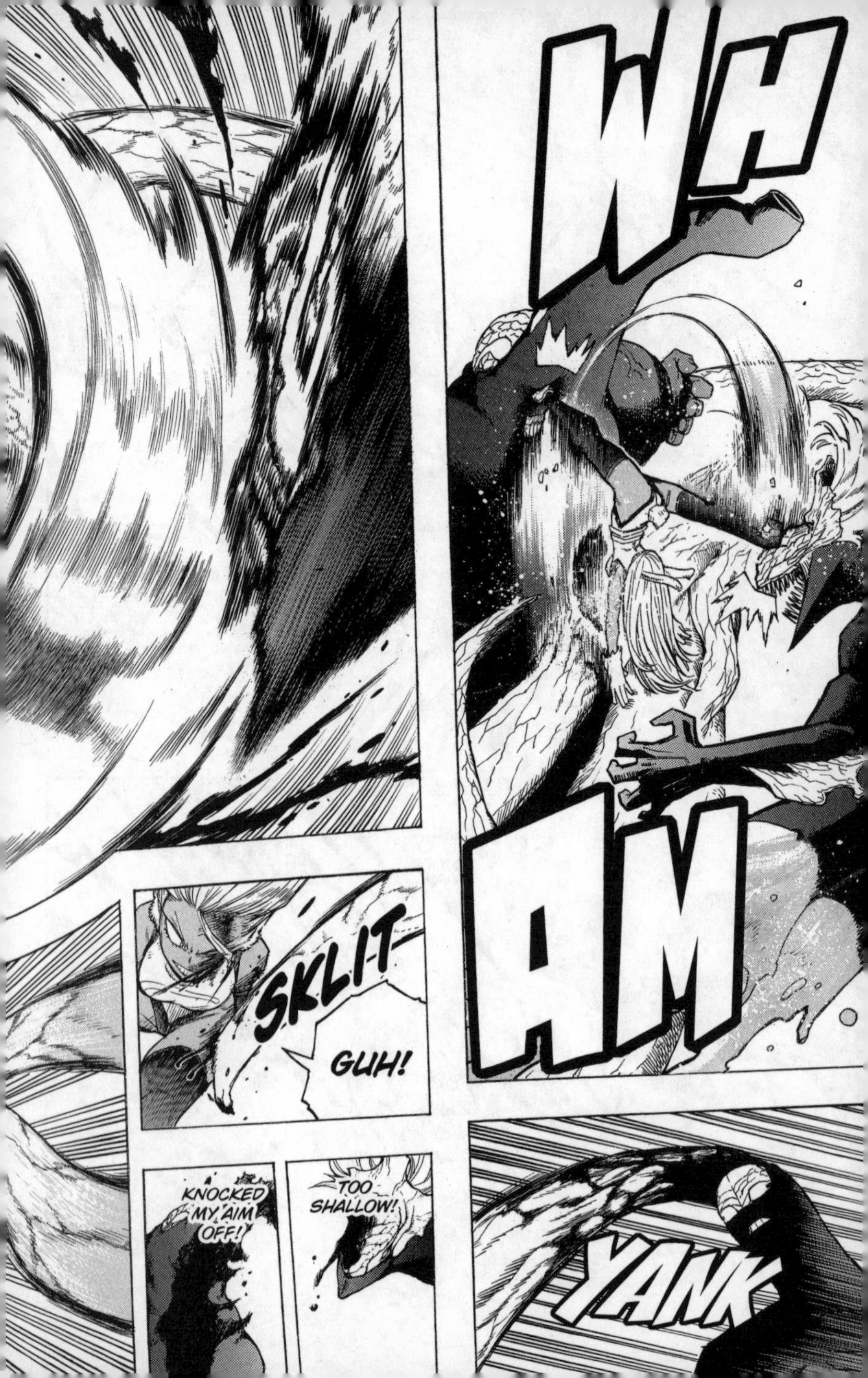
WHAM
SKLIT
GUH!
YANK
TOO SHALLOW!
KNOCKED MY AIM OFF!

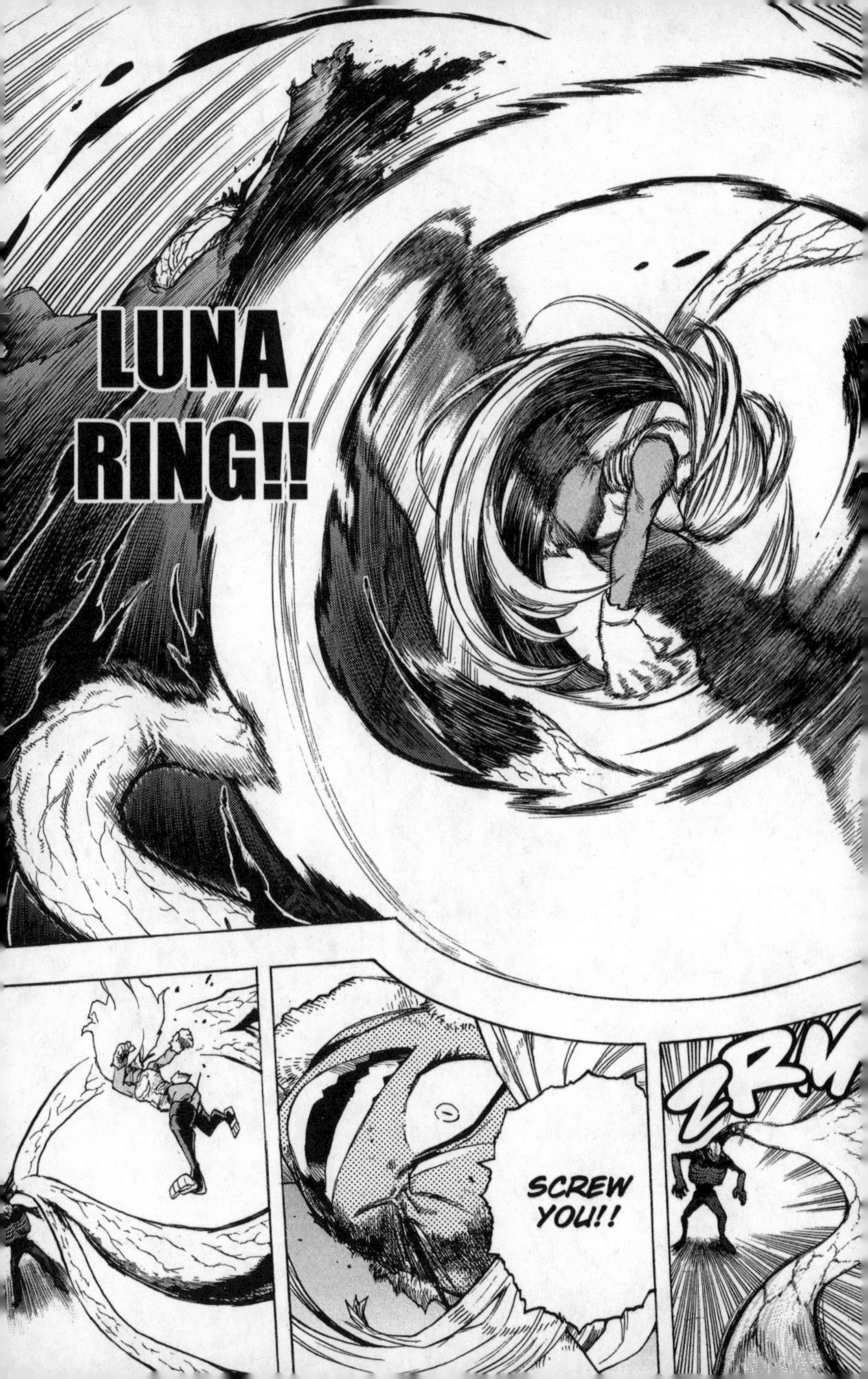
LUNA RING!!
SCREW YOU!!

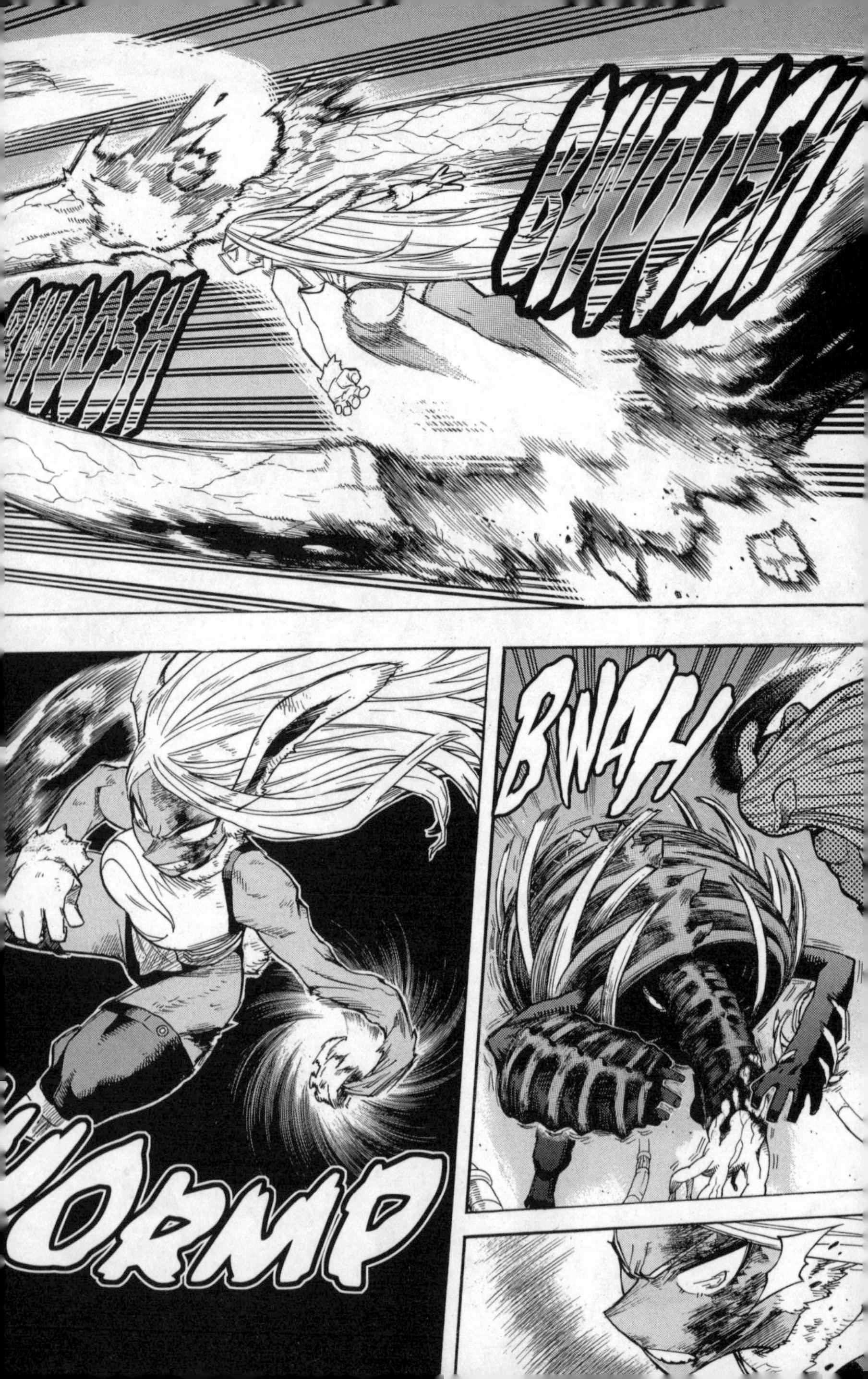
BWAH
ORMP

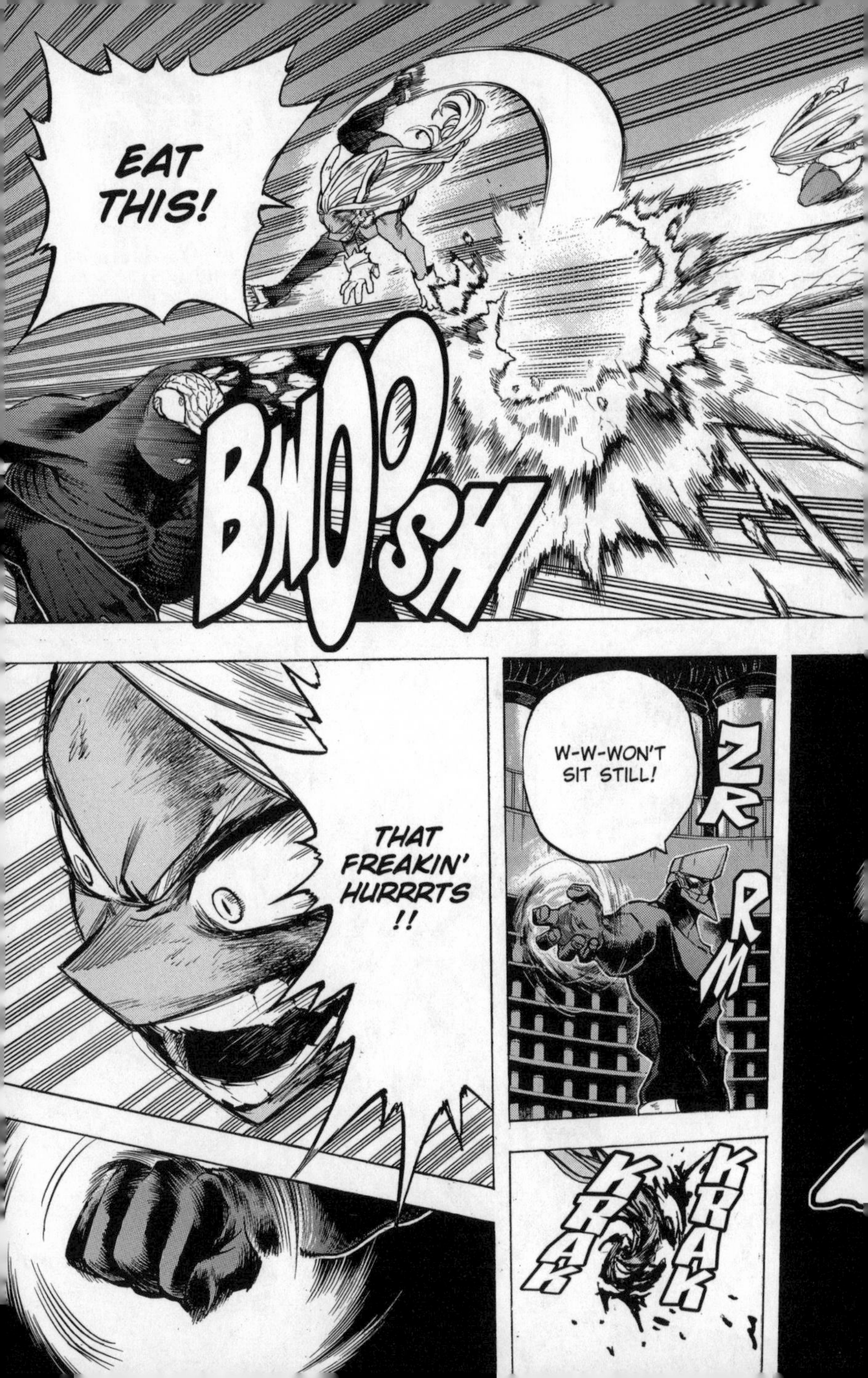
EAT THIS!
BWOOOSH
W-W-WON'T SIT STILL!
ZRRRM
KRAK
KRAK
THAT FREAKIN' HURRRTS!!

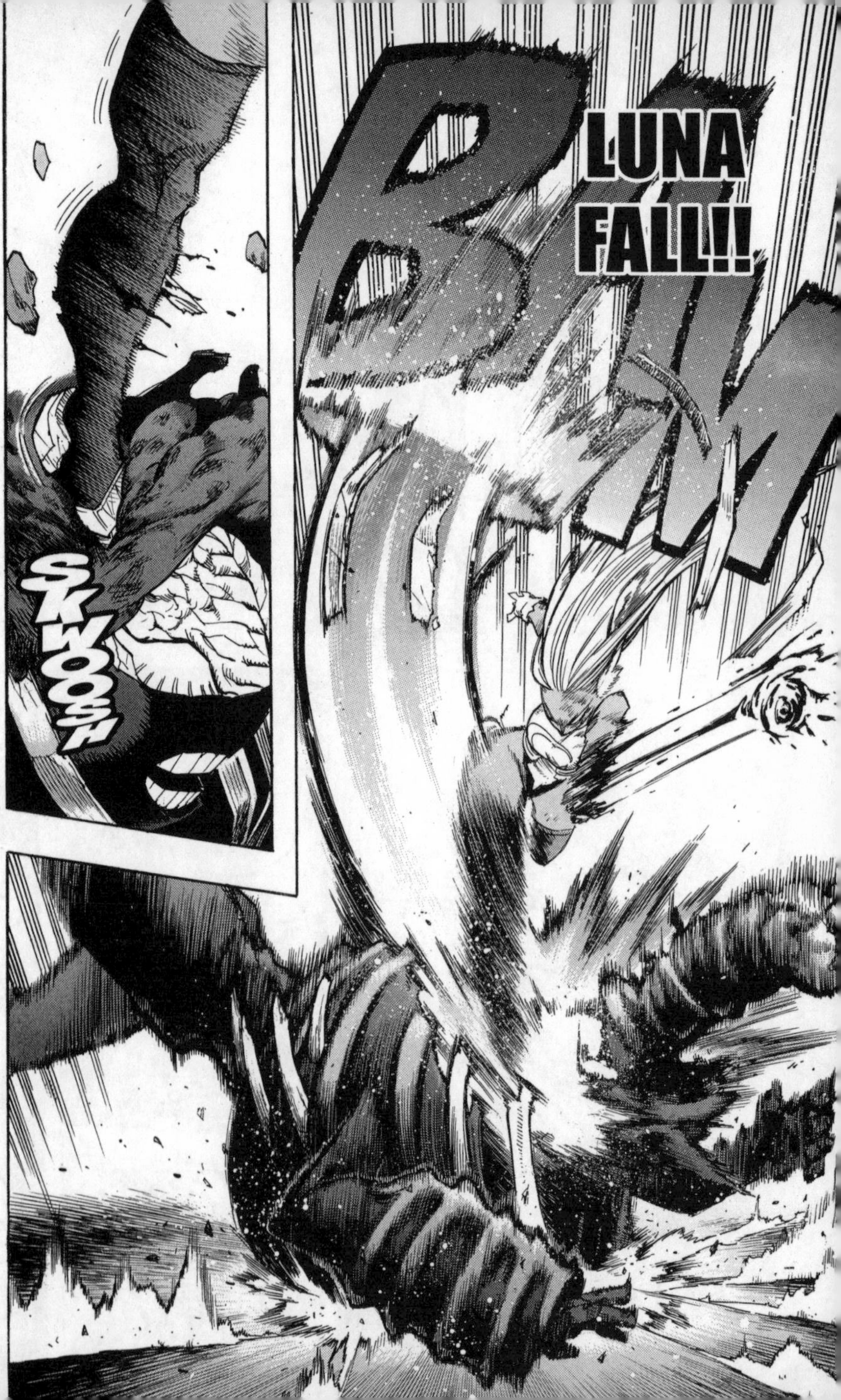
BAM
LUNA FALL!!
SKWOOSH

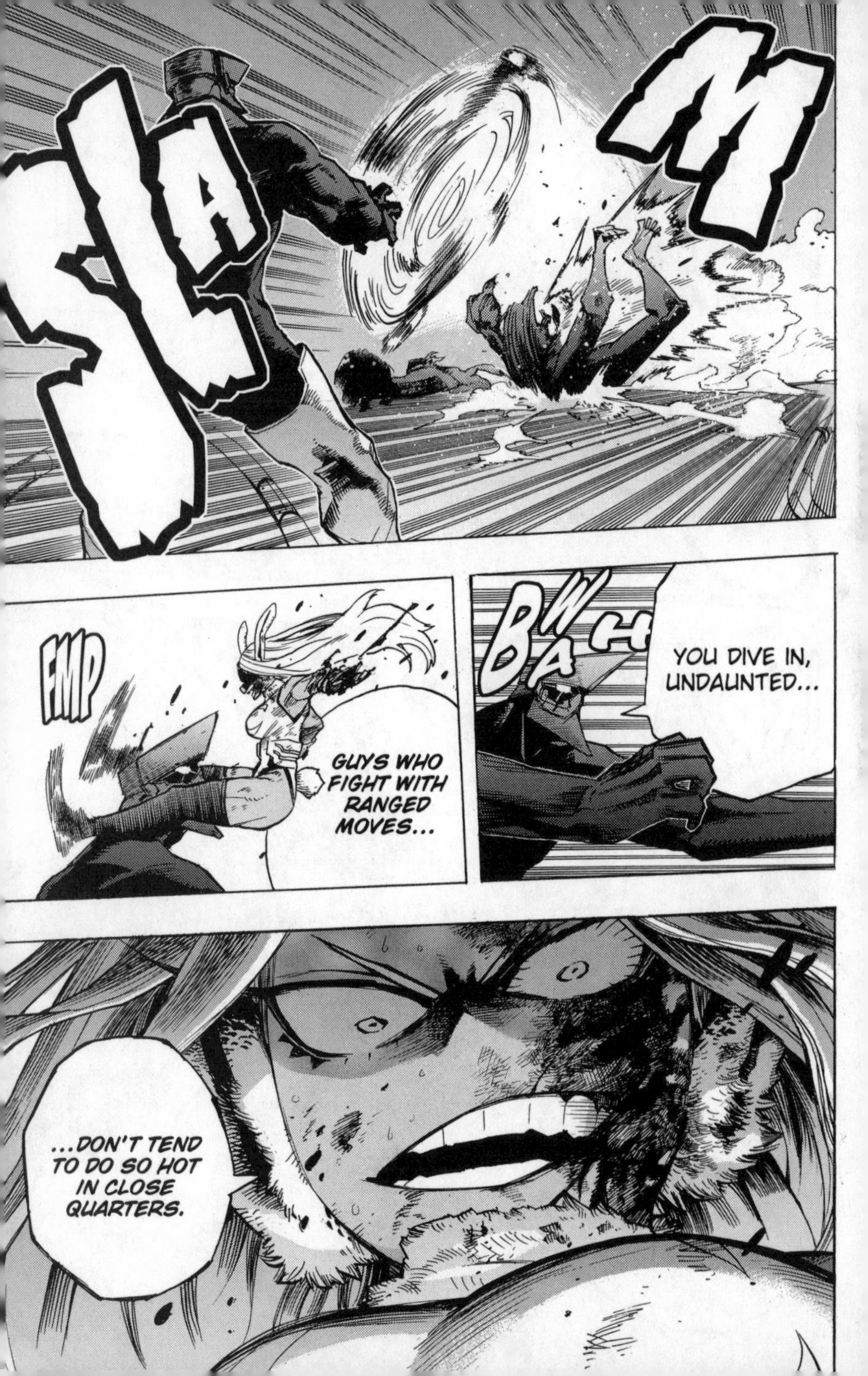
BWAH
YOU DIVE IN, UNDAUNTED...
FMP
GUYS WHO FIGHT WITH RANGED MOVES...
...DON'T TEND TO DO SO HOT IN CLOSE QUARTERS.

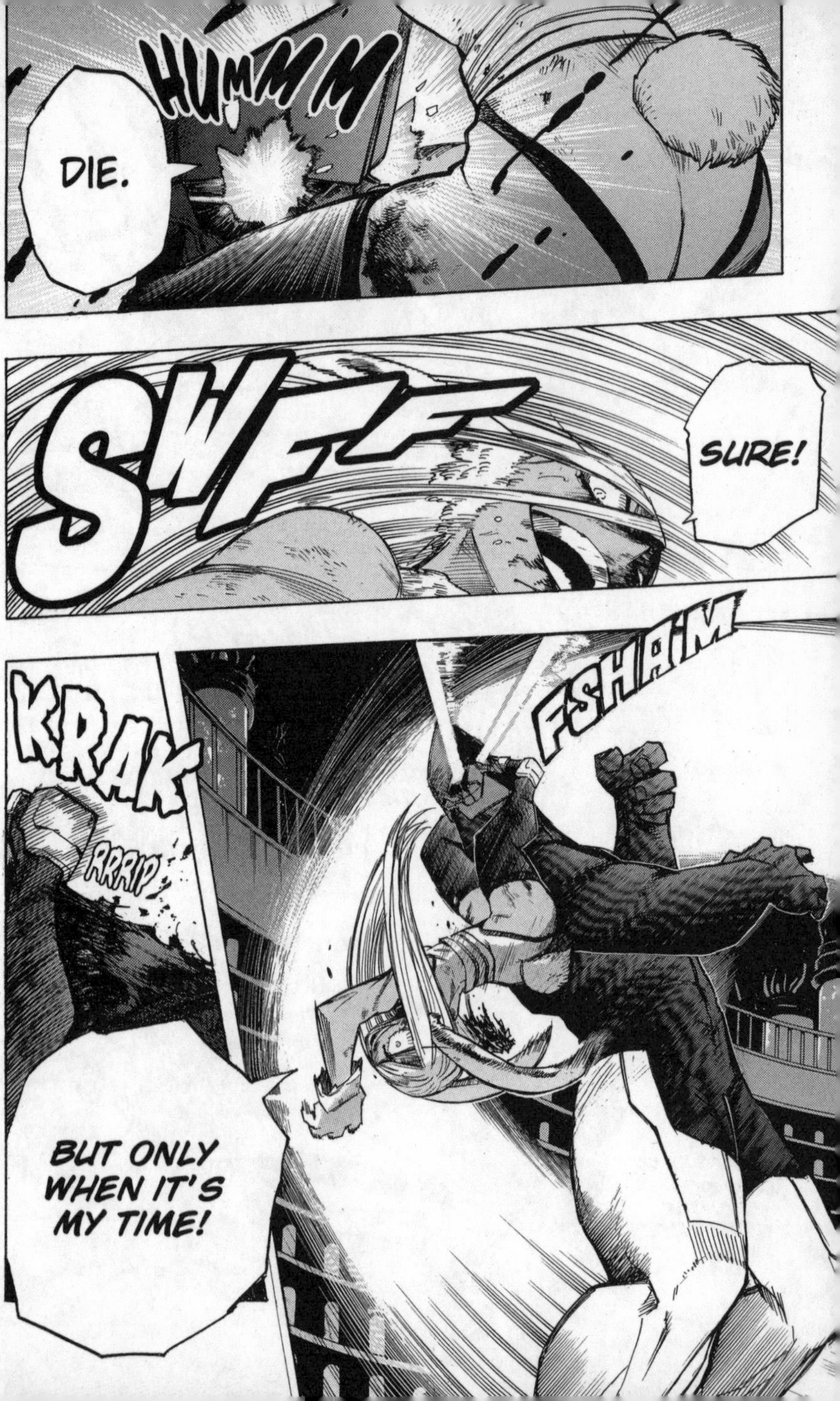
HUMMM
DIE.
SWFF
SURE!
FSHAM
KRAK
RRRIP
BUT ONLY WHEN IT'S MY TIME!

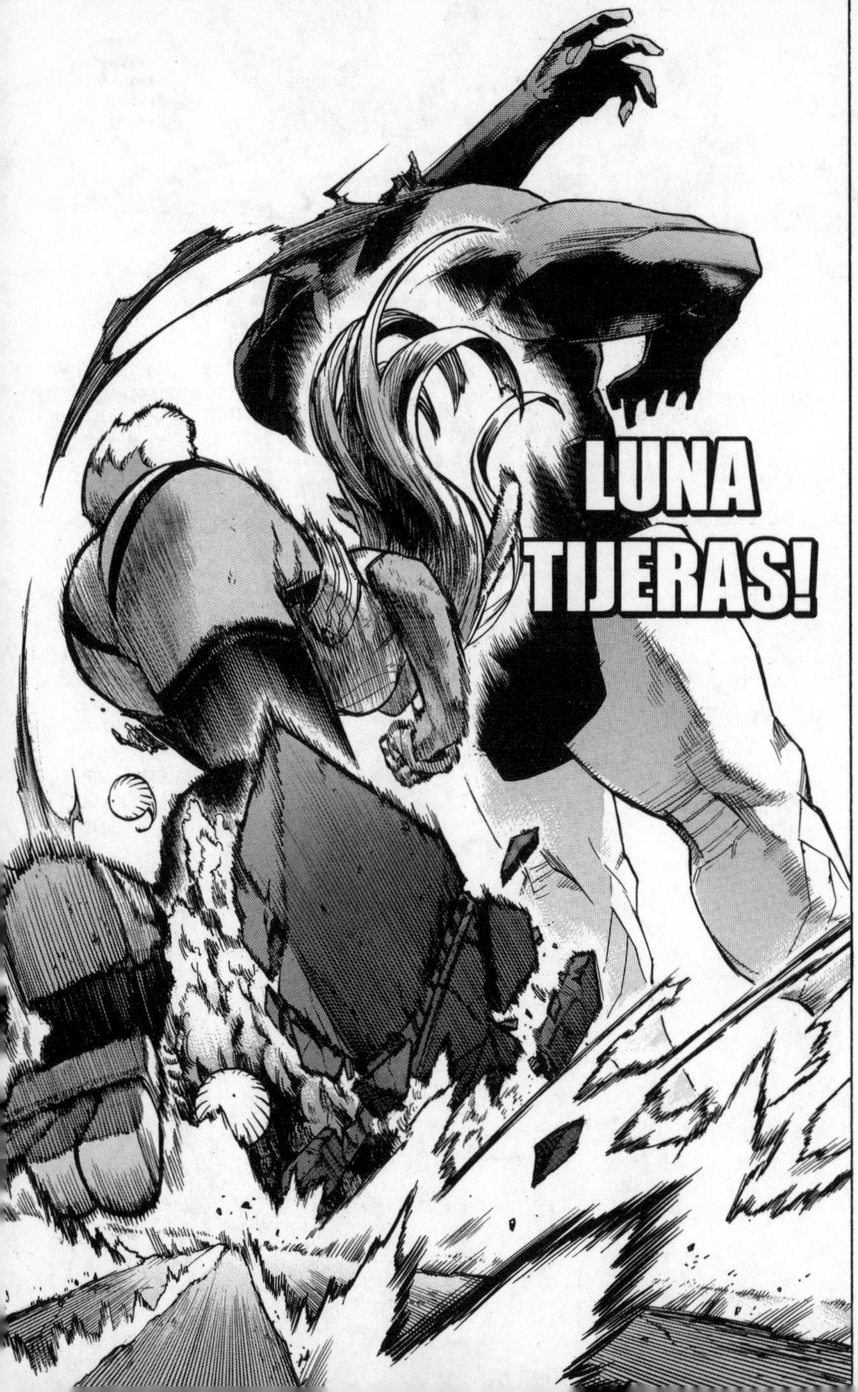
LUNA
TIJERAS!

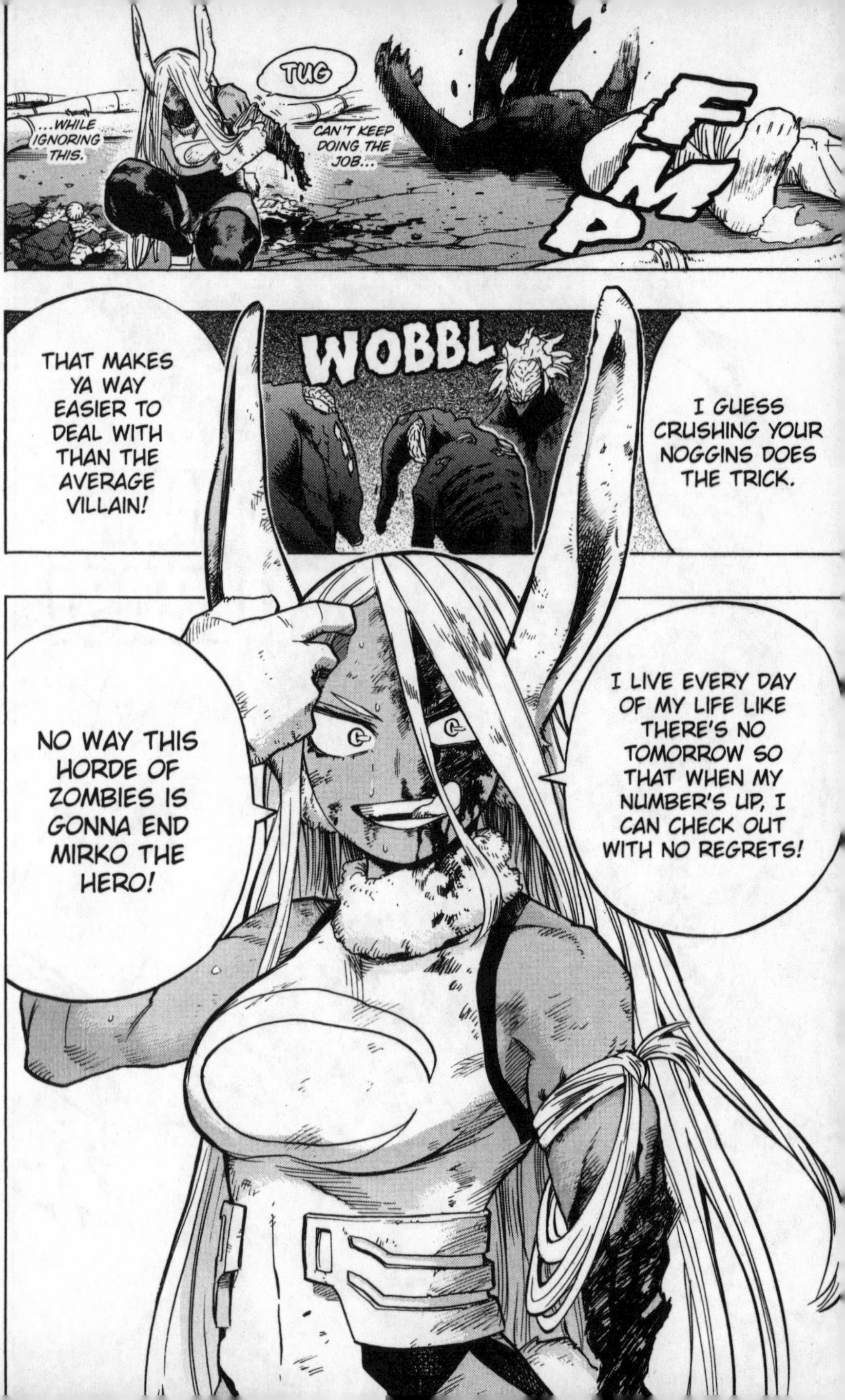
CAN'T KEEP DOING THE JOB...
TUG
...WHILE IGNORING THIS.
I GUESS CRUSHING YOUR NOGGINS DOES THE TRICK.
WOBBL
THAT MAKES YA WAY EASIER TO DEAL WITH THAN THE AVERAGE VILLAIN!
I LIVE EVERY DAY OF MY LIFE LIKE THERE'S NO TOMORROW SO THAT WHEN MY NUMBER'S UP, I CAN CHECK OUT WITH NO REGRETS!
NO WAY THIS HORDE OF ZOMBIES IS GONNA END MIRKO THE HERO!

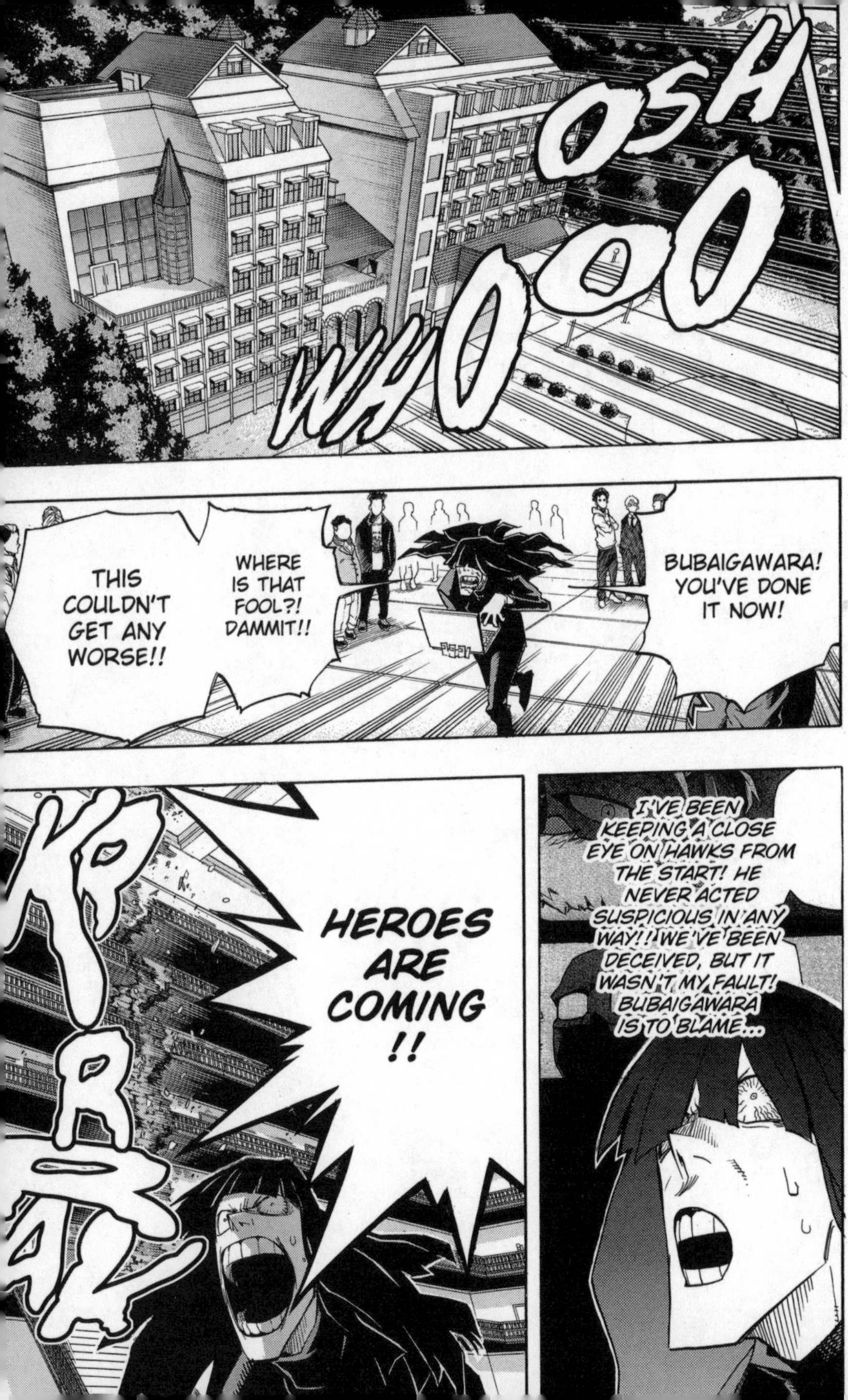
WHOOOOOSH
BUBAIGAWARA! YOU'VE DONE IT NOW!
WHERE IS THAT FOOL?! DAMMIT!!
THIS COULDN'T GET ANY WORSE!!
I'VE BEEN KEEPING A CLOSE EYE ON HAWKS FROM THE START! HE NEVER ACTED SUSPICIOUS IN ANY WAY!! WE'VE BEEN DECEIVED, BUT IT WASN'T MY FAULT! BUBAIGAWARA IS TO BLAME...
HEROES ARE COMING!!

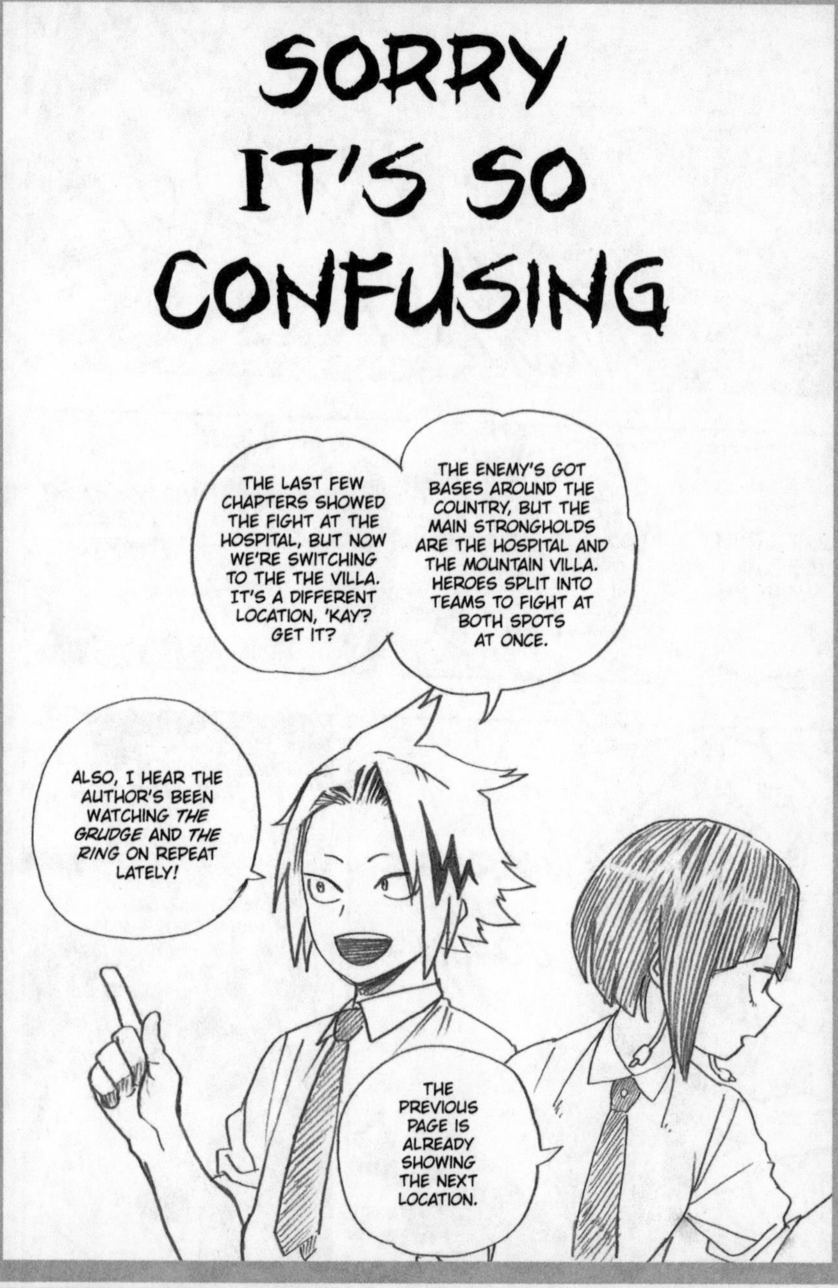
SORRY IT'S SO CONFUSING
THE ENEMY'S GOT BASES AROUND THE COUNTRY, BUT THE MAIN STRONGHOLDS ARE THE HOSPITAL AND THE MOUNTAIN VILLA. HEROES SPLIT INTO TEAMS TO FIGHT AT BOTH SPOTS AT ONCE.
THE LAST FEW CHAPTERS SHOWED THE FIGHT AT THE HOSPITAL, BUT NOW WE'RE SWITCHING TO THE THE VILLA. IT'S A DIFFERENT LOCATION, 'KAY? GET IT?
ALSO, I HEAR THE AUTHOR'S BEEN WATCHING *THE GRUDGE* AND *THE RING* ON REPEAT LATELY!
THE PREVIOUS PAGE IS ALREADY SHOWING THE NEXT LOCATION.

No. 263 - I Wanna Be with You Guys!!

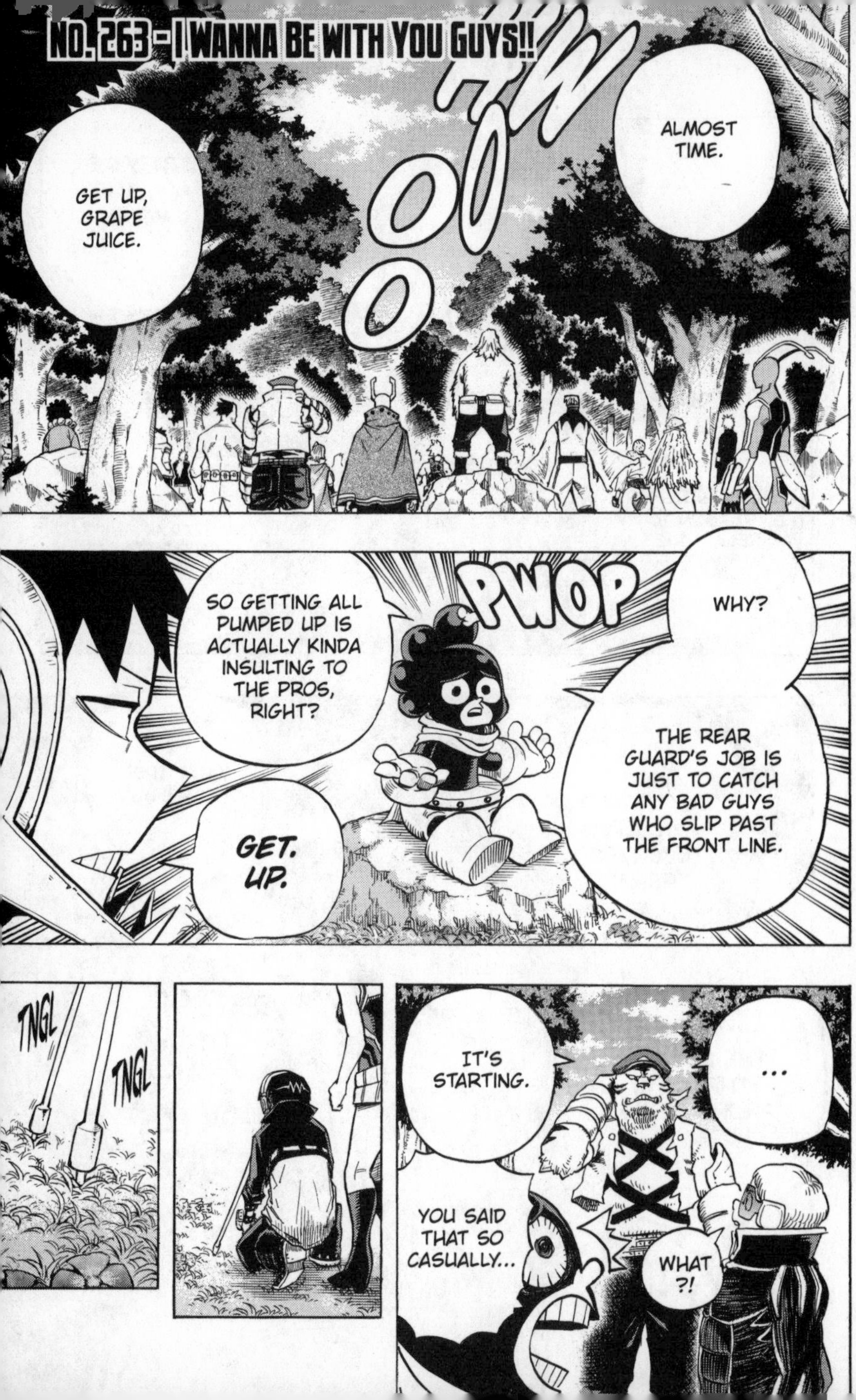
ALMOST TIME.
GET UP, GRAPE JUICE.
WHY?
THE REAR GUARD'S JOB IS JUST TO CATCH ANY BAD GUYS WHO SLIP PAST THE FRONT LINE.
PWOP
SO GETTING ALL PUMPED UP IS ACTUALLY KINDA INSULTING TO THE PROS, RIGHT?
GET. UP.
...
IT'S STARTING.
WHAT?!
YOU SAID THAT SO CASUALLY...
TNGL
TNGL

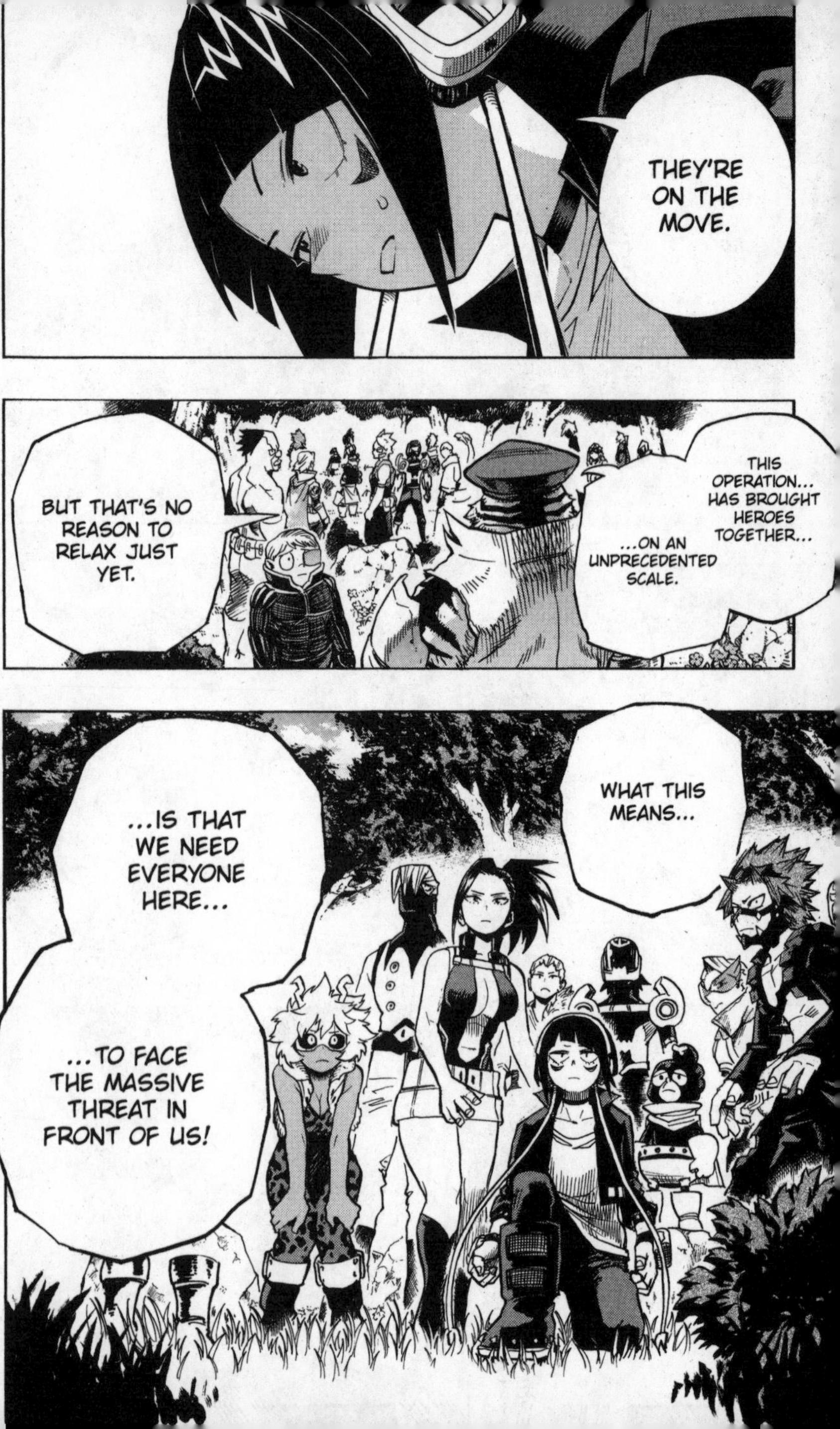
THEY'RE ON THE MOVE.
THIS OPERATION... HAS BROUGHT HEROES TOGETHER...
...ON AN UNPRECEDENTED SCALE.
BUT THAT'S NO REASON TO RELAX JUST YET.
WHAT THIS MEANS...
...IS THAT WE NEED EVERYONE HERE...
...TO FACE THE MASSIVE THREAT IN FRONT OF US!

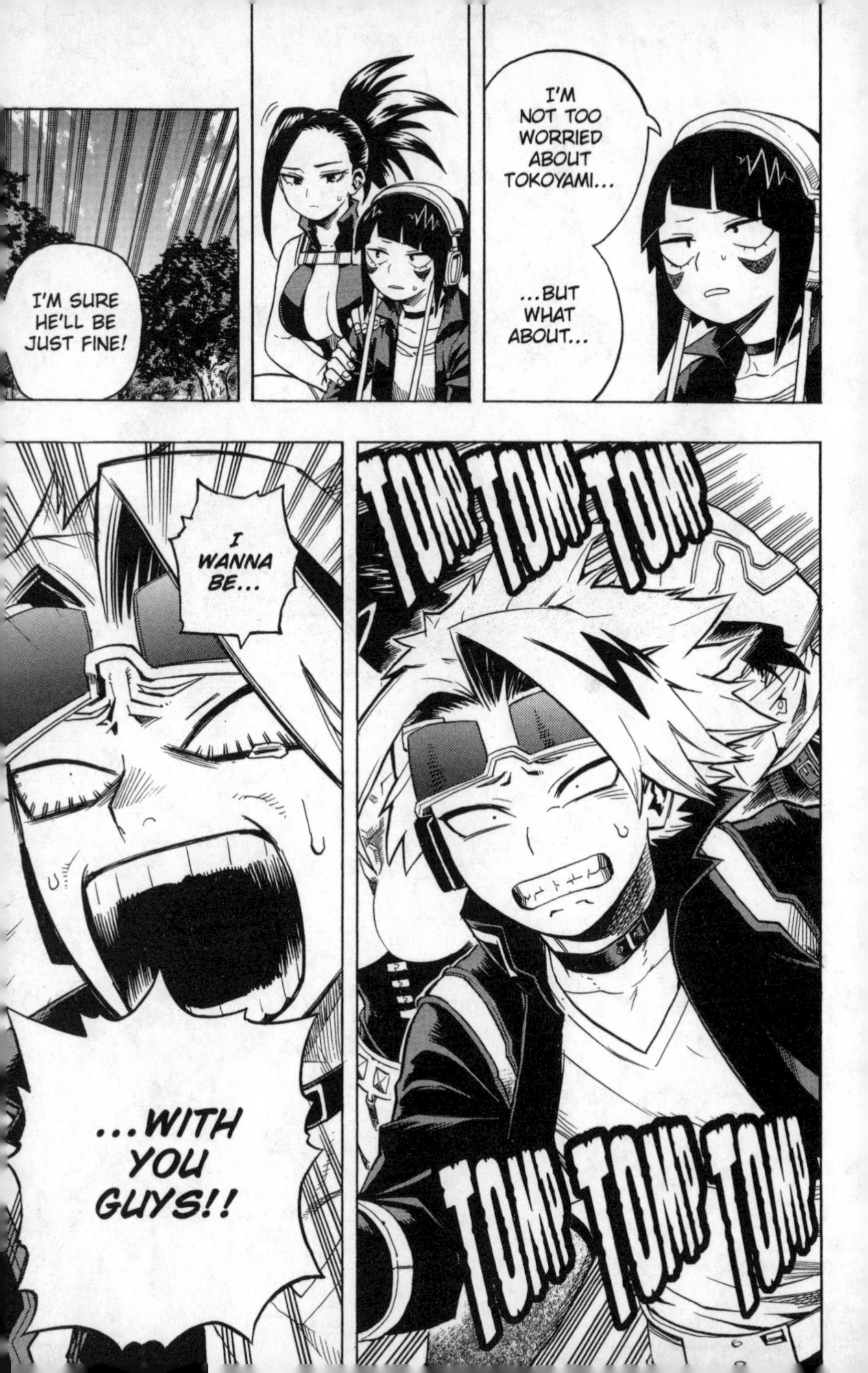
I'M NOT TOO WORRIED ABOUT TOKOYAMI...
...BUT WHAT ABOUT...
I'M SURE HE'LL BE JUST FINE!
TOMP TOMP TOMP
TOMP TOMP TOMP
I WANNA BE...
...WITH YOU GUYS!!

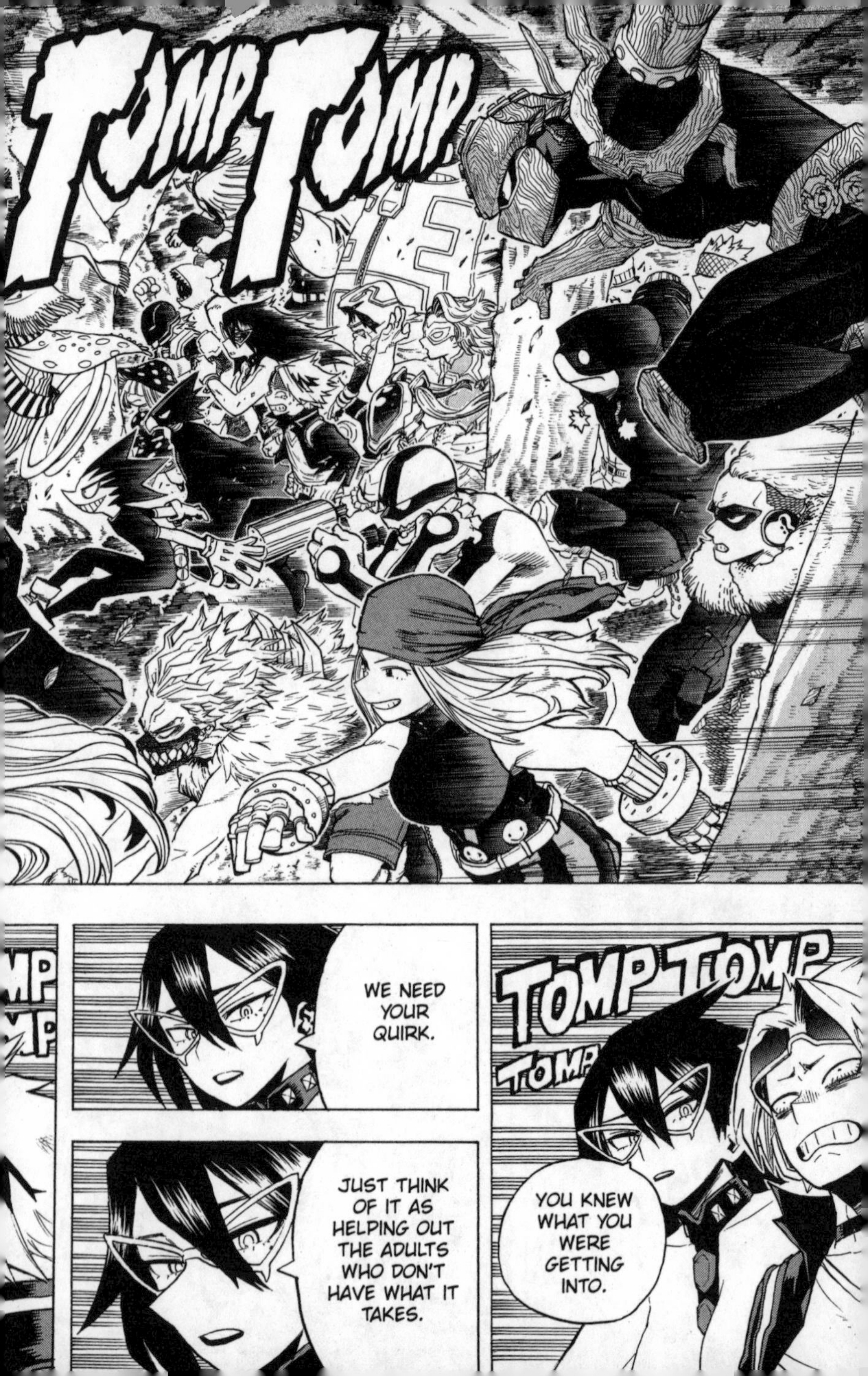
TOMP TOMP
TOMP TOMP
TOMP
YOU KNEW WHAT YOU WERE GETTING INTO.
WE NEED YOUR QUIRK.
JUST THINK OF IT AS HELPING OUT THE ADULTS WHO DON'T HAVE WHAT IT TAKES.

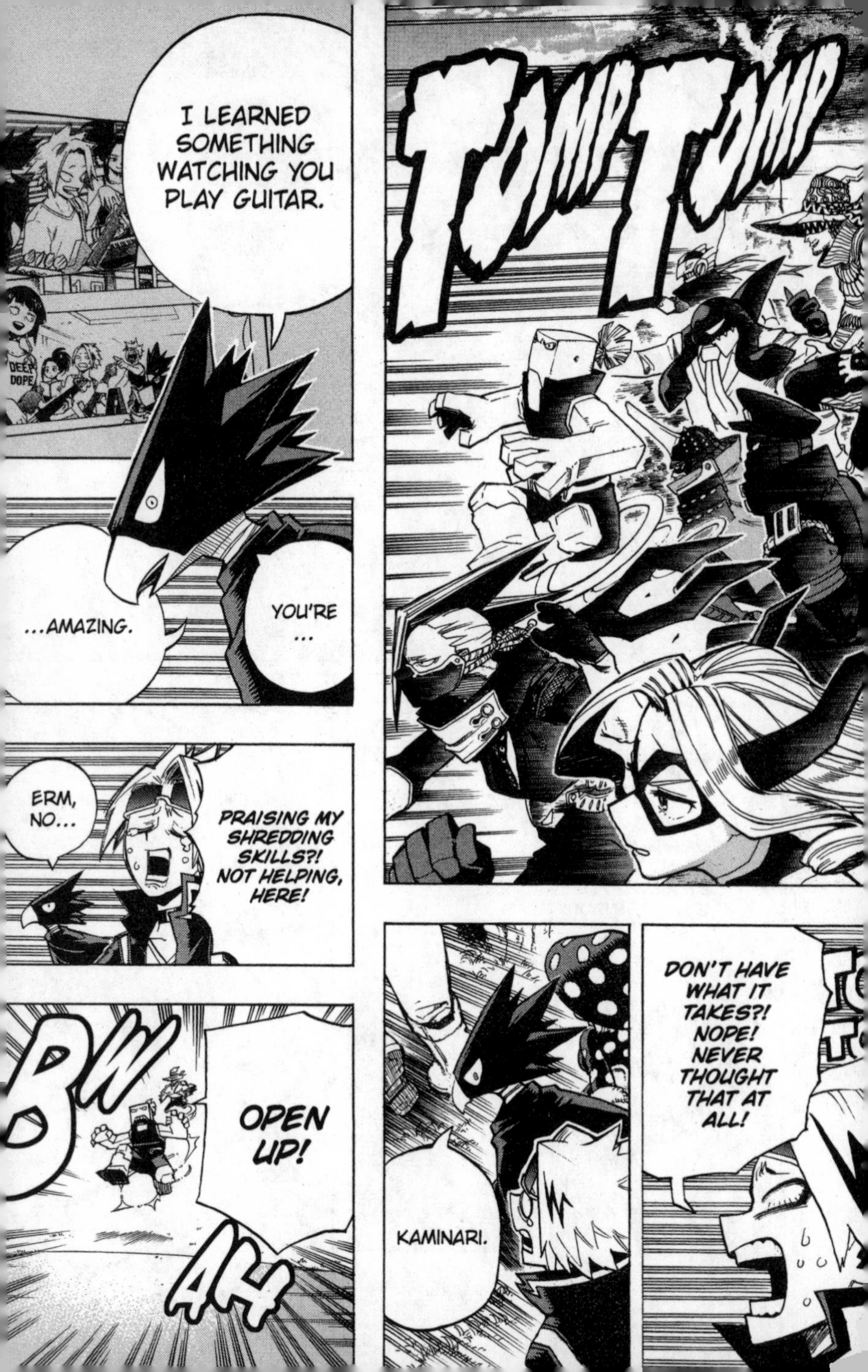
TOMP TOMP
I LEARNED SOMETHING WATCHING YOU PLAY GUITAR.
YOU'RE ...
...AMAZING.
ERM, NO...
PRAISING MY SHREDDING SKILLS?! NOT HELPING, HERE!
DON'T HAVE WHAT IT TAKES?! NOPE! NEVER THOUGHT THAT AT ALL!
KAMINARI.
BN
OPEN UP!
AH
DEEP DOPE

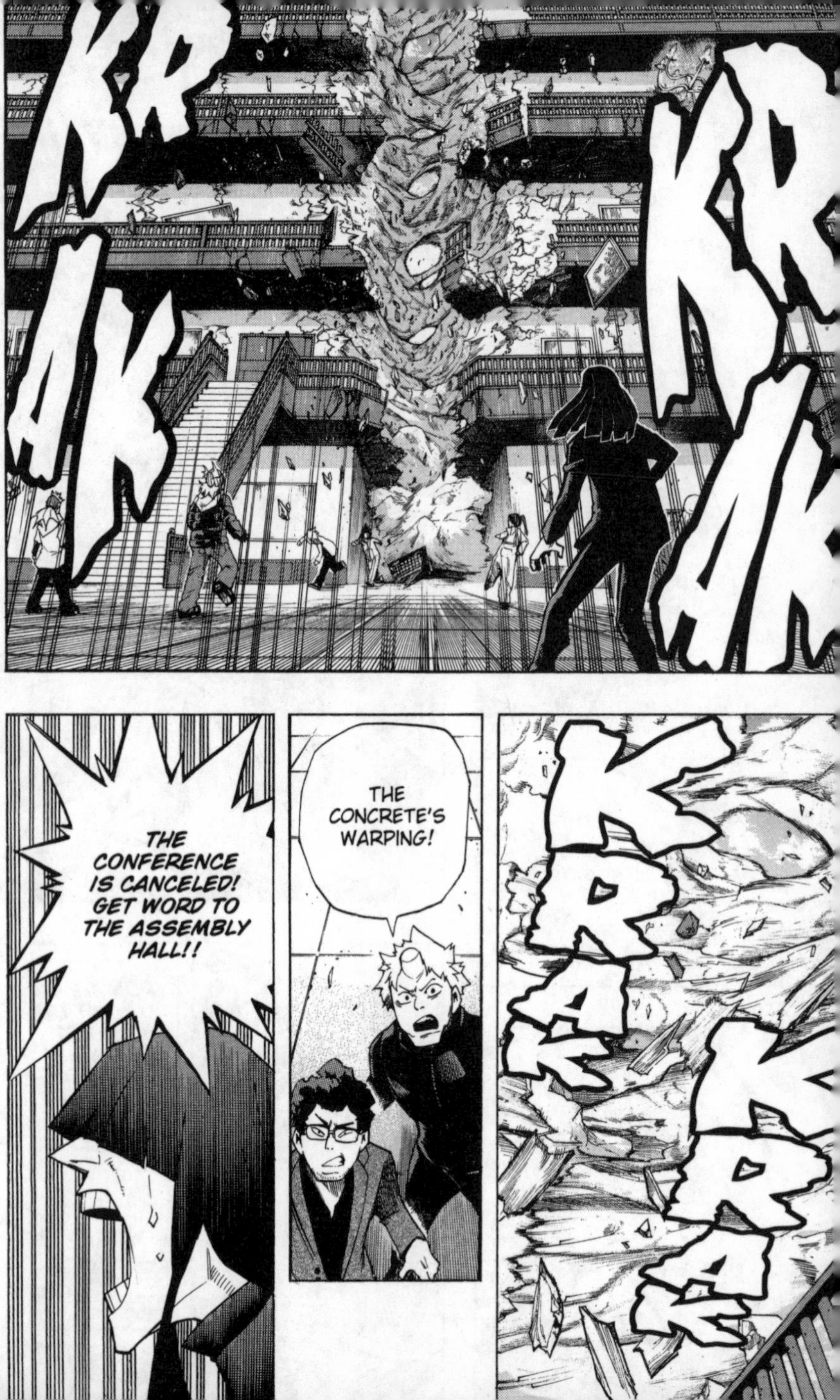
KRAK
KRAK
KRAK
KRAK
THE CONCRETE'S WARPING!
THE CONFERENCE IS CANCELED! GET WORD TO THE ASSEMBLY HALL!!

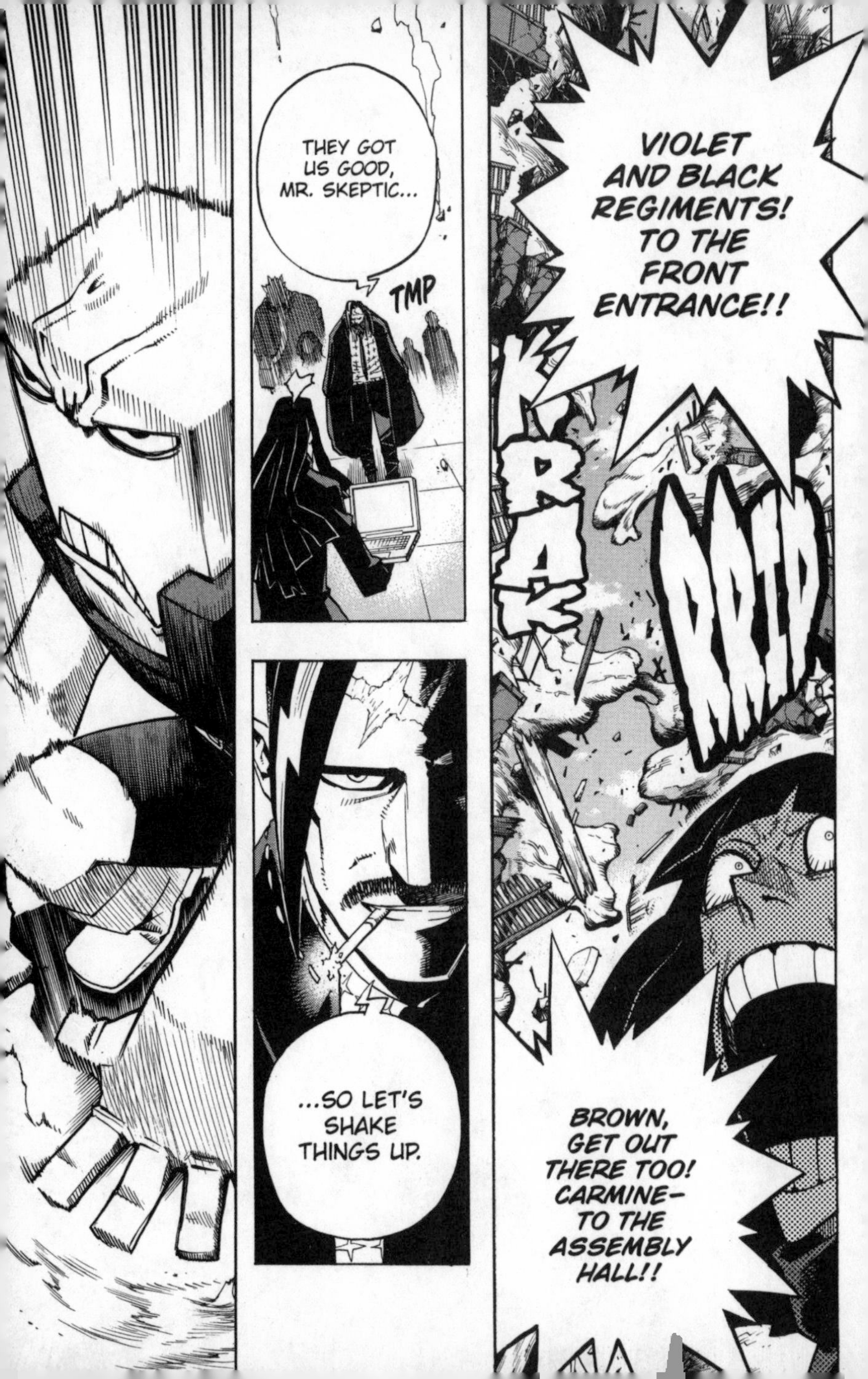
VIOLET AND BLACK REGIMENTS! TO THE FRONT ENTRANCE!!
BROWN, GET OUT THERE TOO! CARMINE- TO THE ASSEMBLY HALL!!
THEY GOT US GOOD, MR. SKEPTIC...
TMP
...SO LET'S SHAKE THINGS UP.

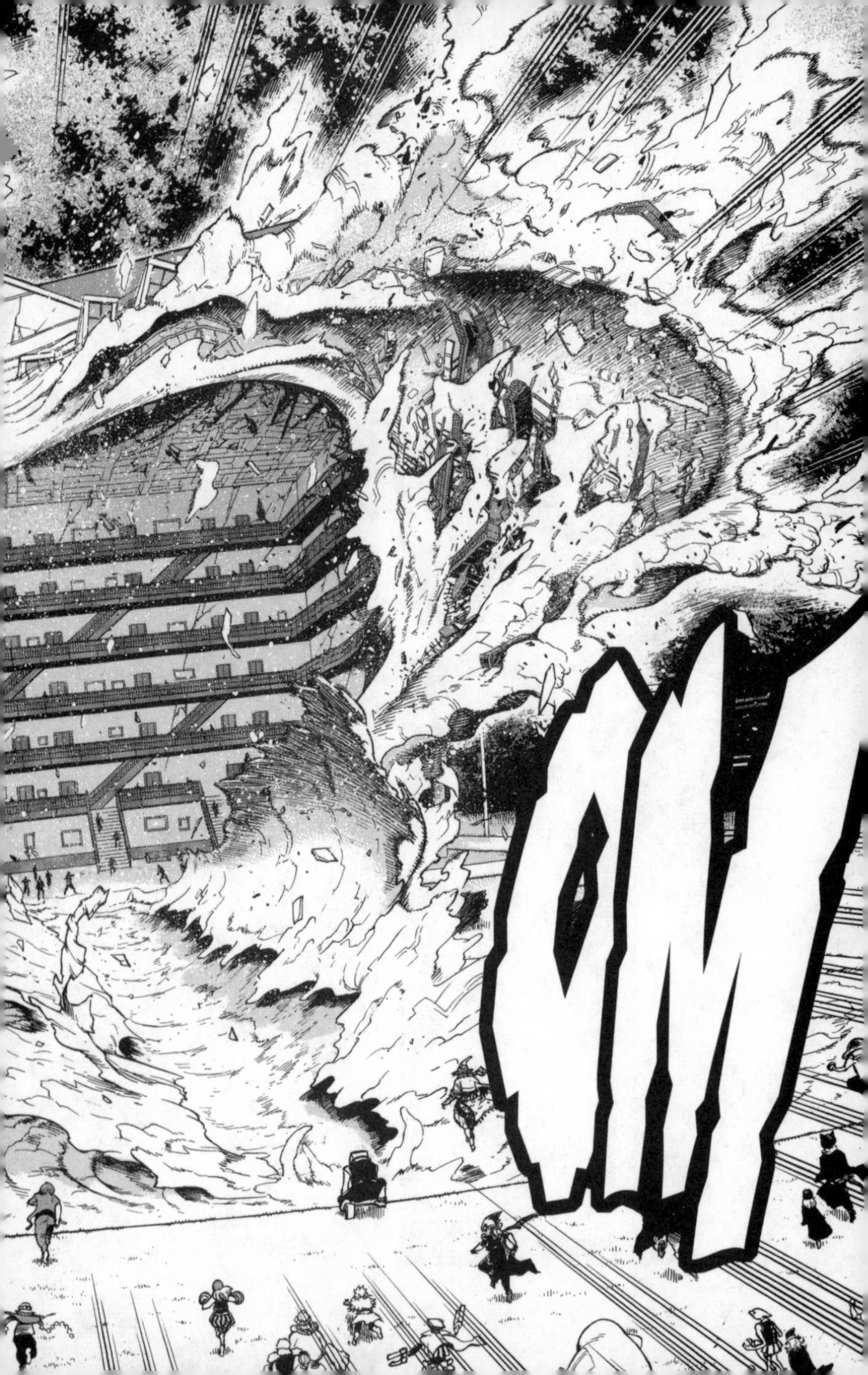
OM

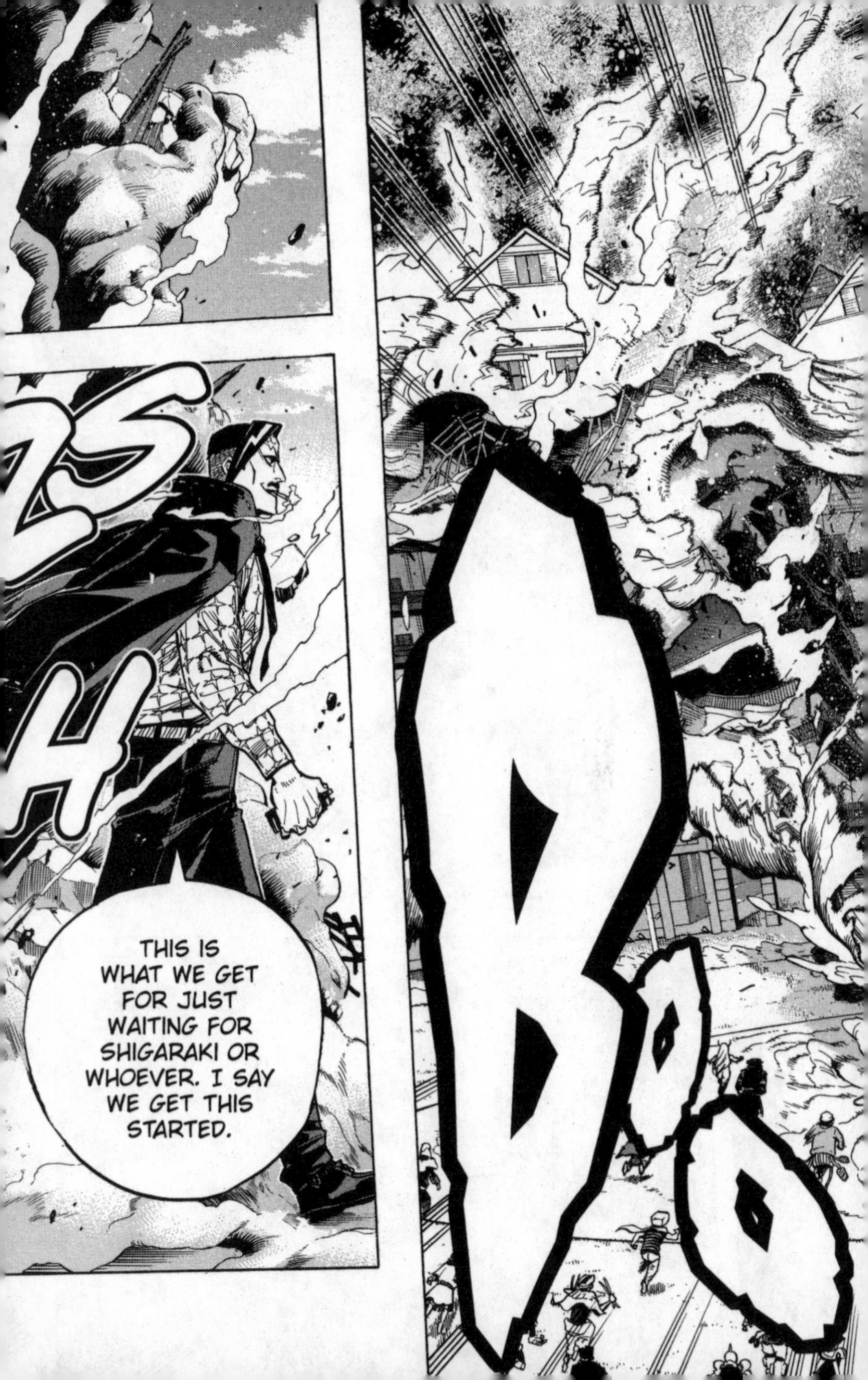
THIS IS WHAT WE GET FOR JUST WAITING FOR SHIGARAKI OR WHOEVER. I SAY WE GET THIS STARTED.

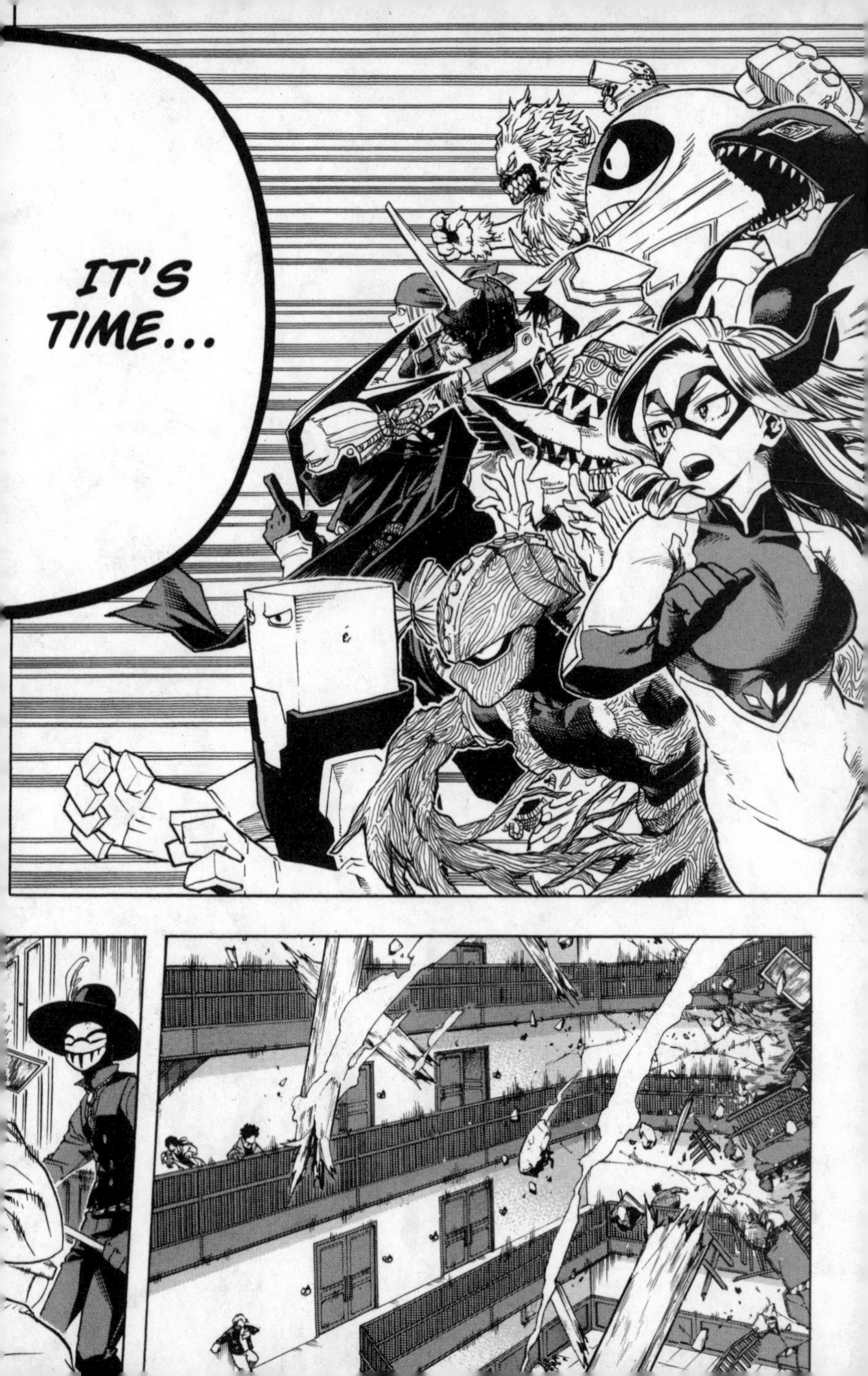
IT'S TIME...

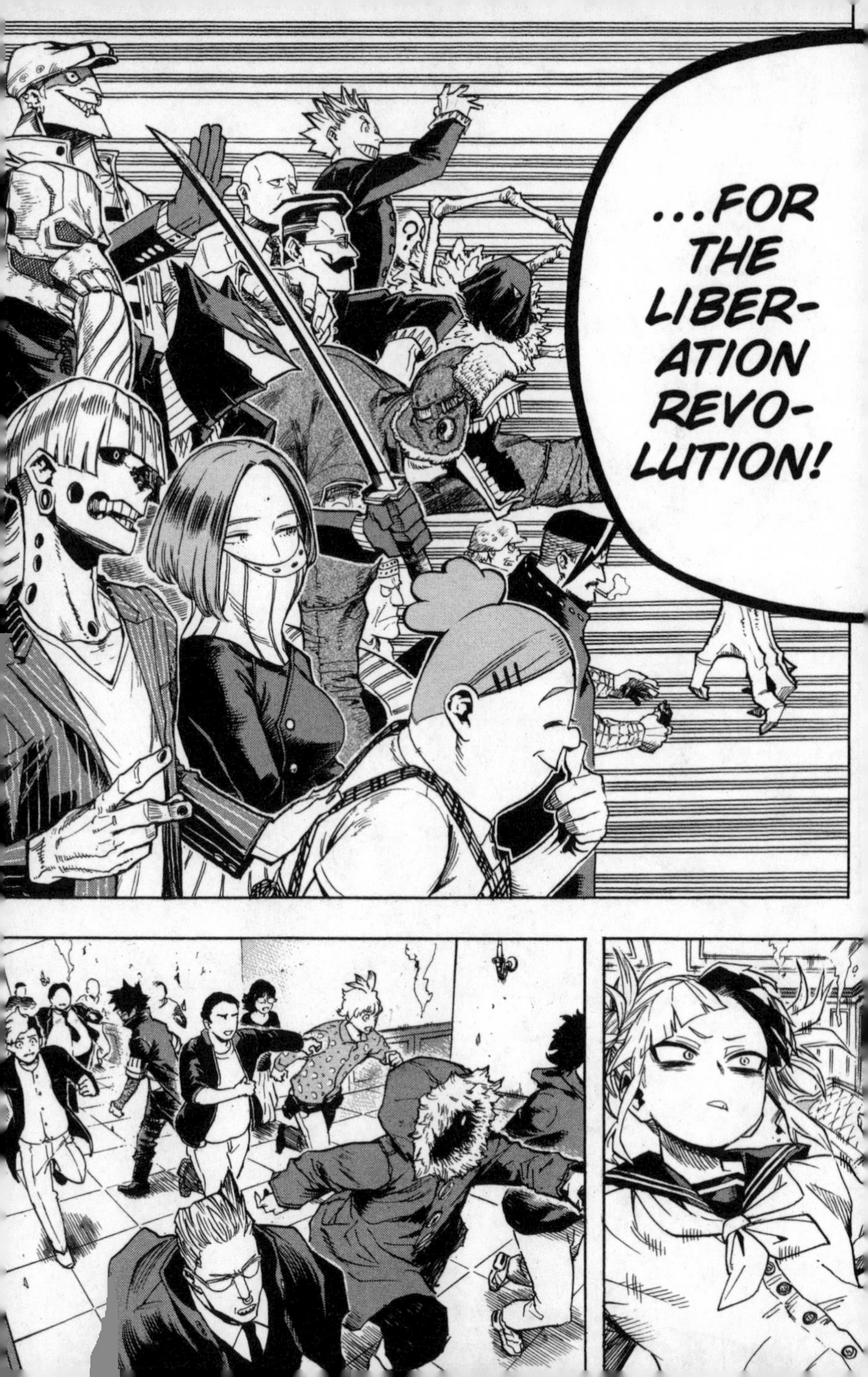
...FOR THE LIBER-ATION REVO-LUTION!

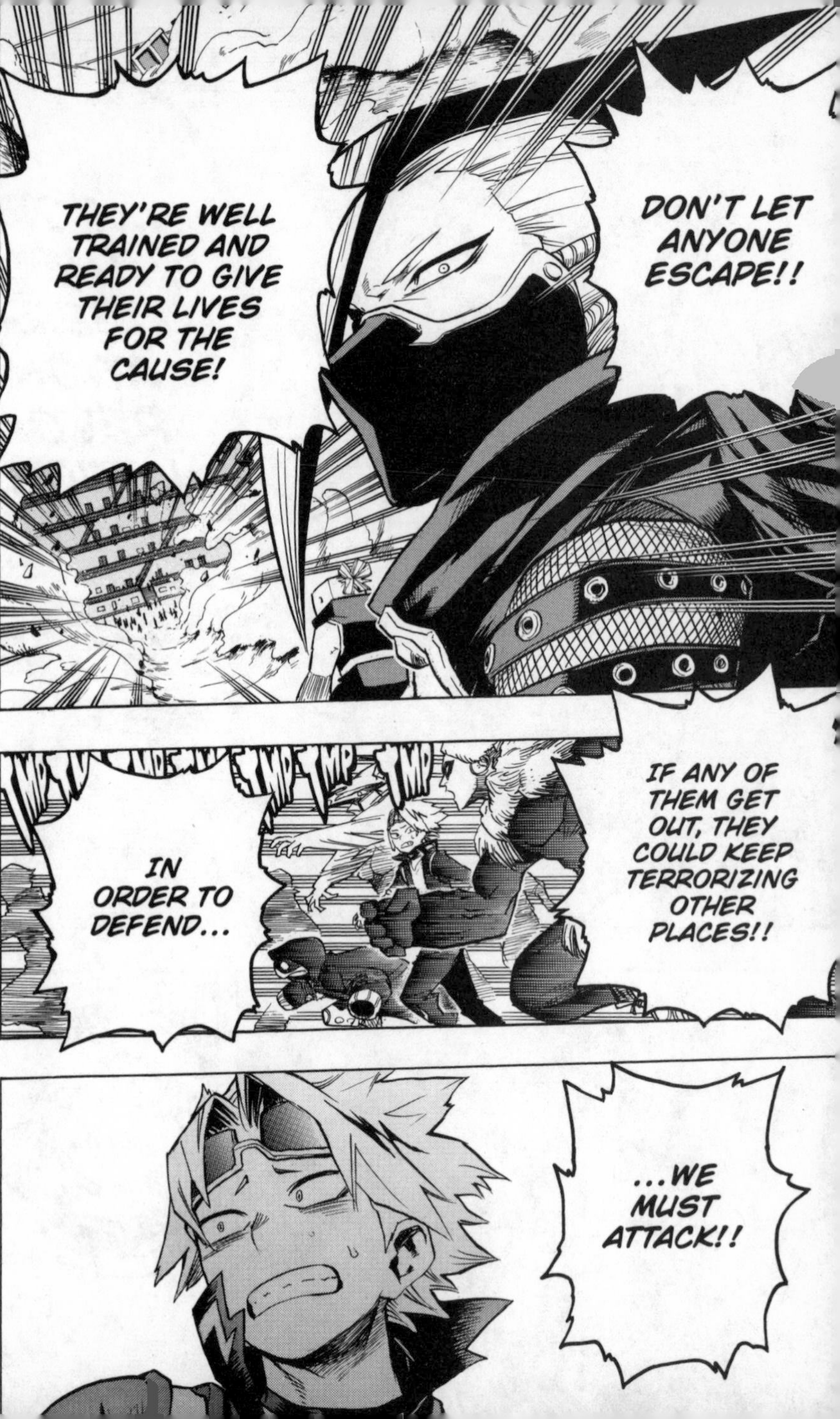
DON'T LET ANYONE ESCAPE!!
THEY'RE WELL TRAINED AND READY TO GIVE THEIR LIVES FOR THE CAUSE!
IF ANY OF THEM GET OUT, THEY COULD KEEP TERRORIZING OTHER PLACES!!
IN ORDER TO DEFEND...
...WE MUST ATTACK!!

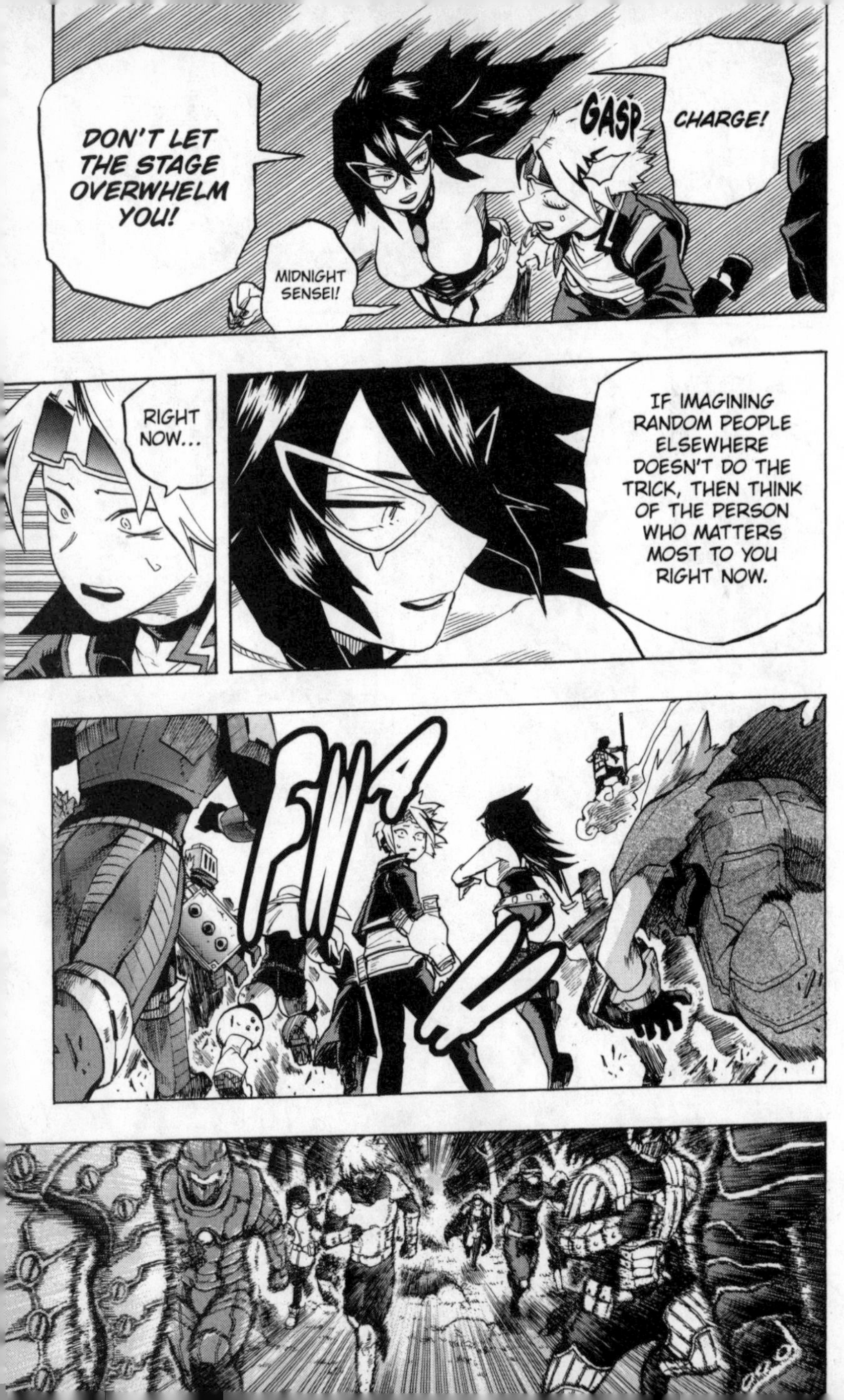
CHARGE!
GASP
DON'T LET THE STAGE OVERWHELM YOU!
MIDNIGHT SENSEI!
IF IMAGINING RANDOM PEOPLE ELSEWHERE DOESN'T DO THE TRICK, THEN THINK OF THE PERSON WHO MATTERS MOST TO YOU RIGHT NOW.
RIGHT NOW...
FWA

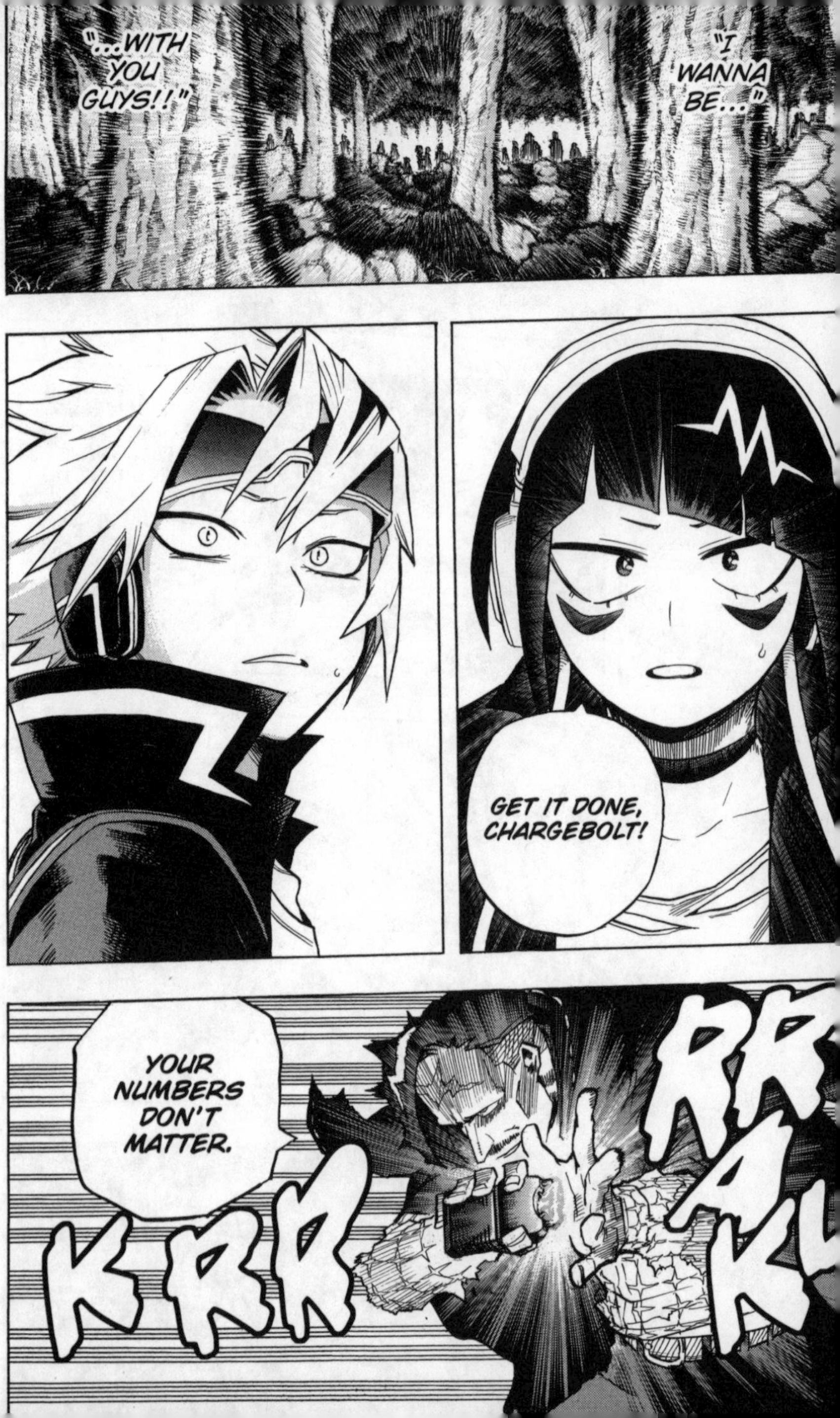
"I WANNA BE..."
"...WITH YOU GUYS!!"
GET IT DONE, CHARGEBOLT!
YOUR NUMBERS DON'T MATTER.
KRR

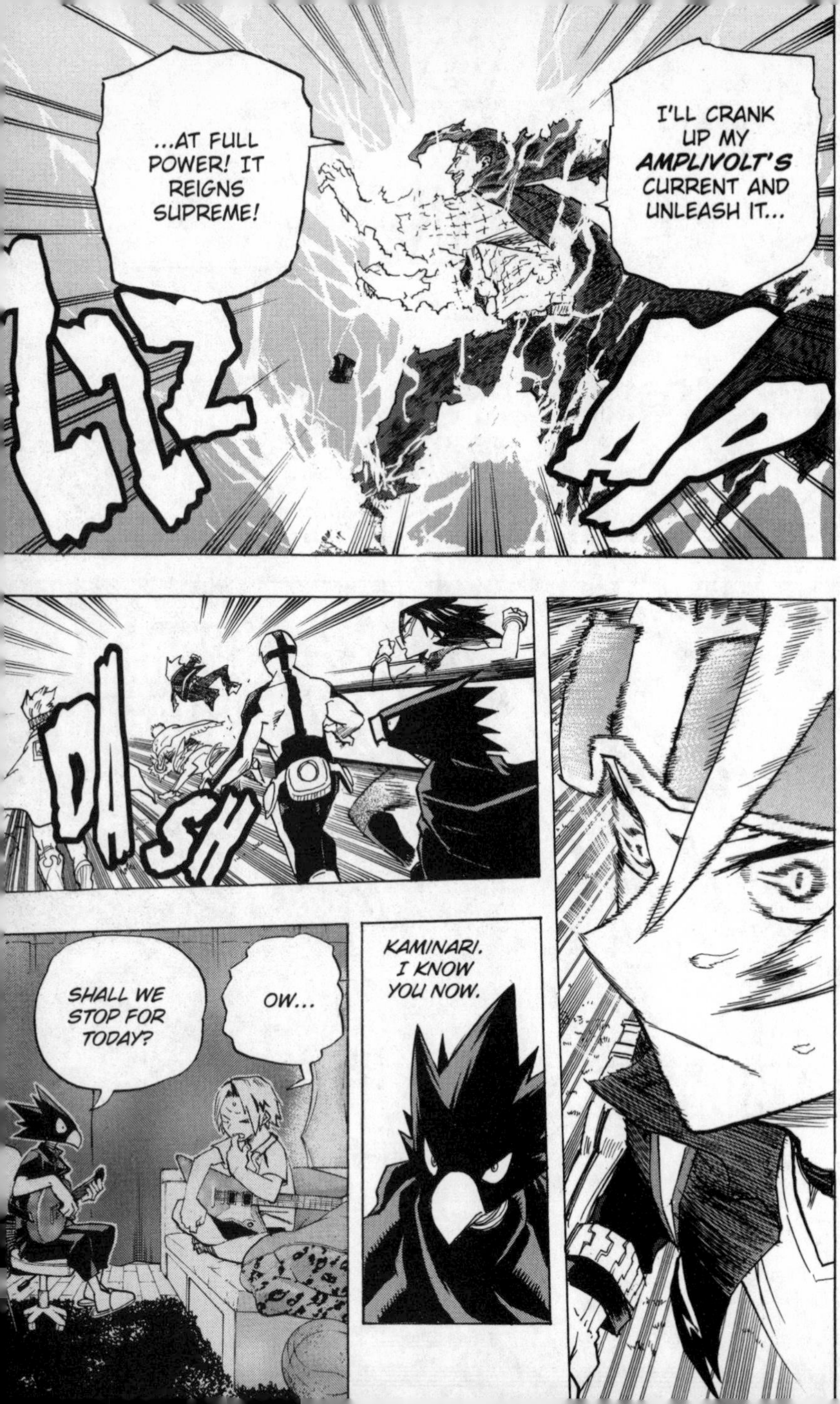
I'LL CRANK UP MY AMPLIVOLT'S CURRENT AND UNLEASH IT...
...AT FULL POWER! IT REIGNS SUPREME!
DASH
KAMINARI. I KNOW YOU NOW.
OW...
SHALL WE STOP FOR TODAY?

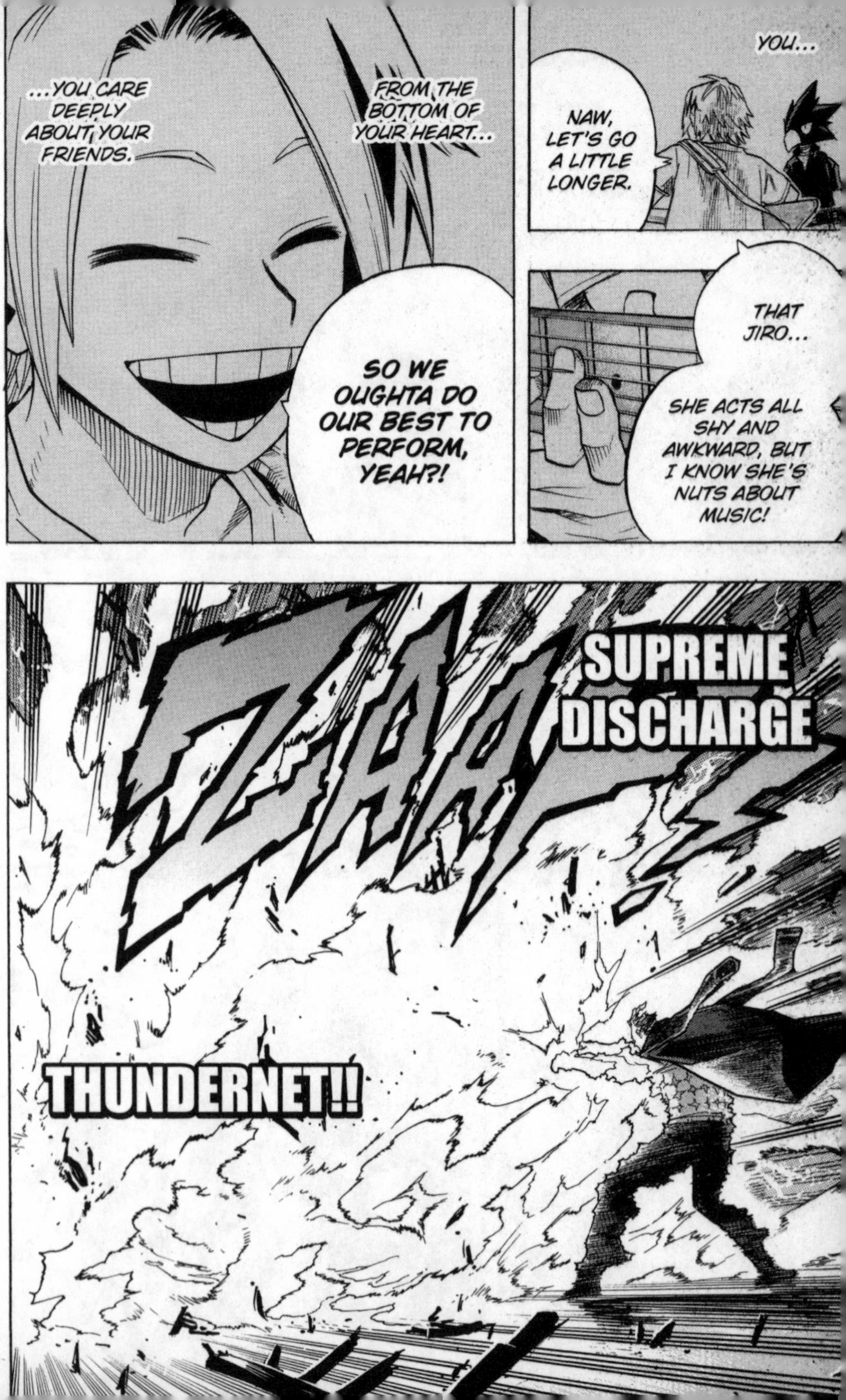
YOU...
NAW, LET'S GO A LITTLE LONGER.
THAT JIRO...
SHE ACTS ALL SHY AND AWKWARD, BUT I KNOW SHE'S NUTS ABOUT MUSIC!
FROM THE BOTTOM OF YOUR HEART...
...YOU CARE DEEPLY ABOUT YOUR FRIENDS.
SO WE OUGHTA DO OUR BEST TO PERFORM, YEAH?!
ZAAA
SUPREME DISCHARGE
THUNDERNET!!

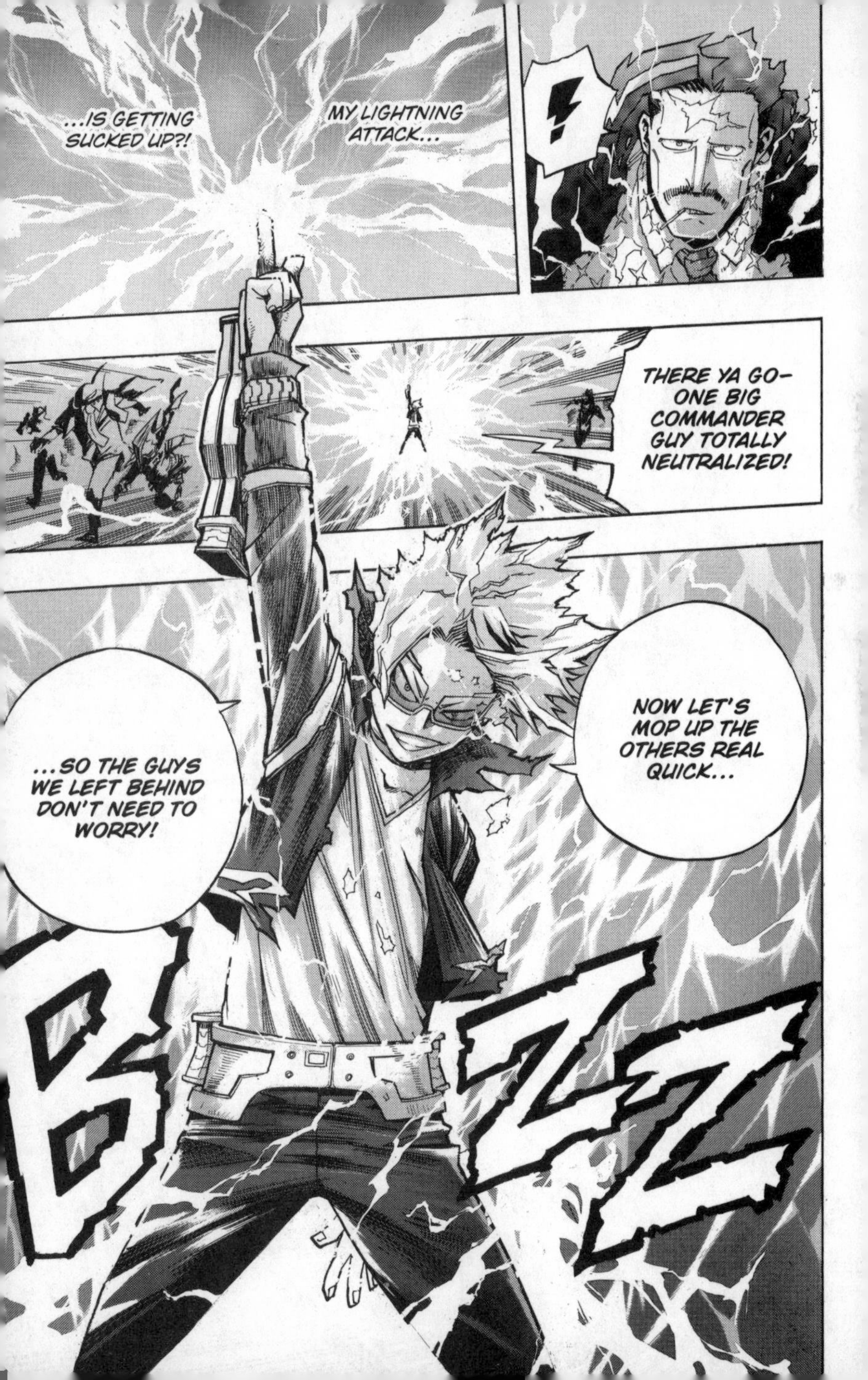
!
MY LIGHTNING ATTACK...
...IS GETTING SUCKED UP?!
THERE YA GO—ONE BIG COMMANDER GUY TOTALLY NEUTRALIZED!
NOW LET'S MOP UP THE OTHERS REAL QUICK...
...SO THE GUYS WE LEFT BEHIND DON'T NEED TO WORRY!
BZZ

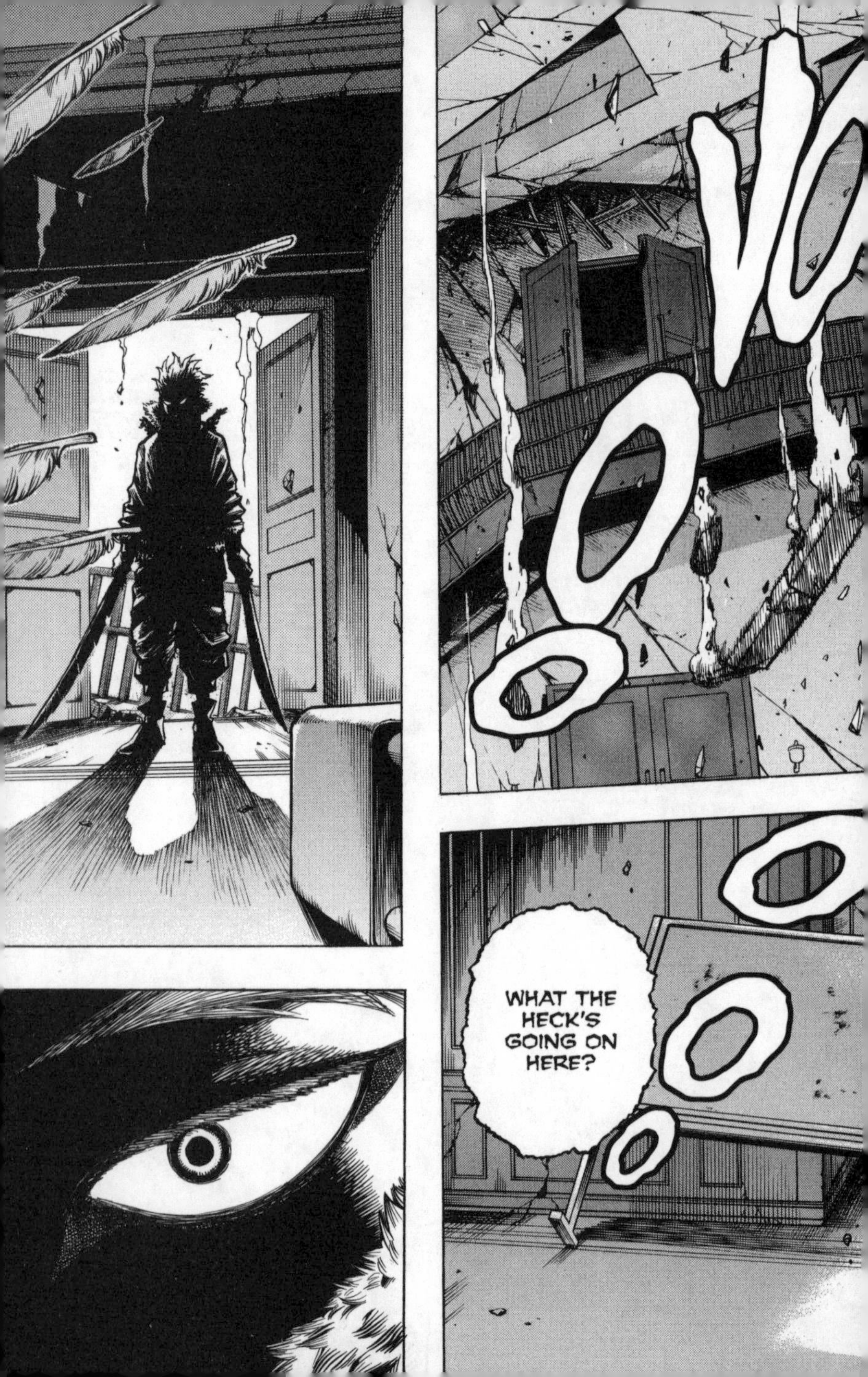
WHAT THE HECK'S GOING ON HERE?

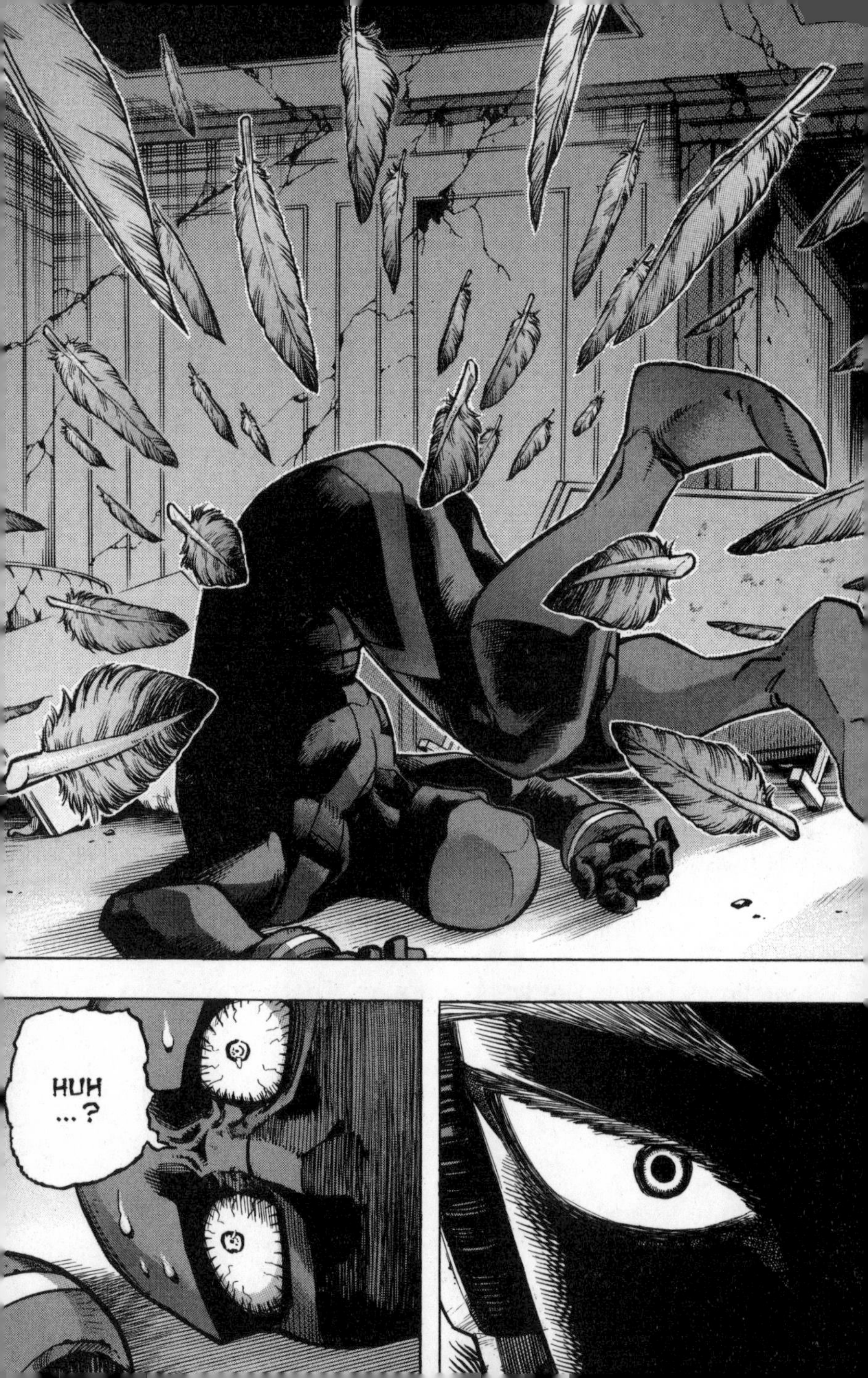
HUH
...?

THE SUBTITLE

One's Justice

This is the title of the *MHA* video game. This volume came out close to the game's release date, so I felt like I had to borrow it for the subtitle of the book. Well, the game is *One's Justice 2*, to be precise.

The game is a ton of fun. I like playing as Twice.

One tends to grow numb to this particular sensation when a series has been running for years, but there's still something wildly shocking about this series—which I draw however the heck I want—being turned into video games, anime, figures, etc. There's a moment when I come to my senses and think, "Huh? Am I actually this happy? Is this reality?"

Sometimes it feels like I'm in a dream. That's how it is to have a long-running series.

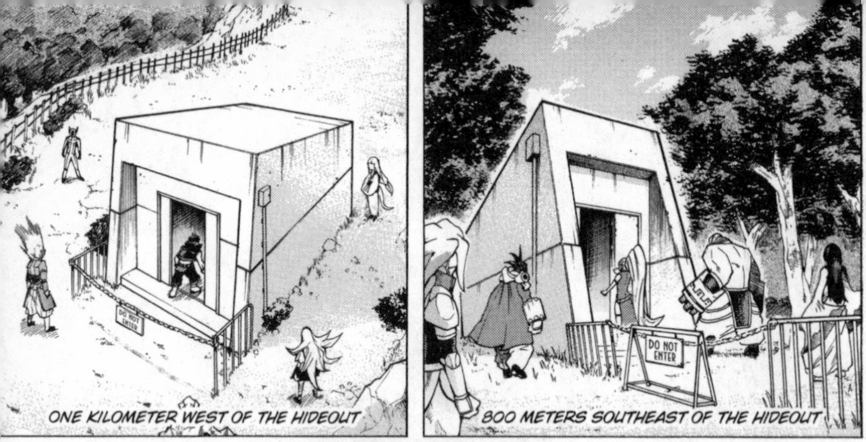
800 METERS SOUTHEAST OF THE HIDEOUT
DO NOT ENTER
ONE KILOMETER WEST OF THE HIDEOUT

No. 264 - One's Justice

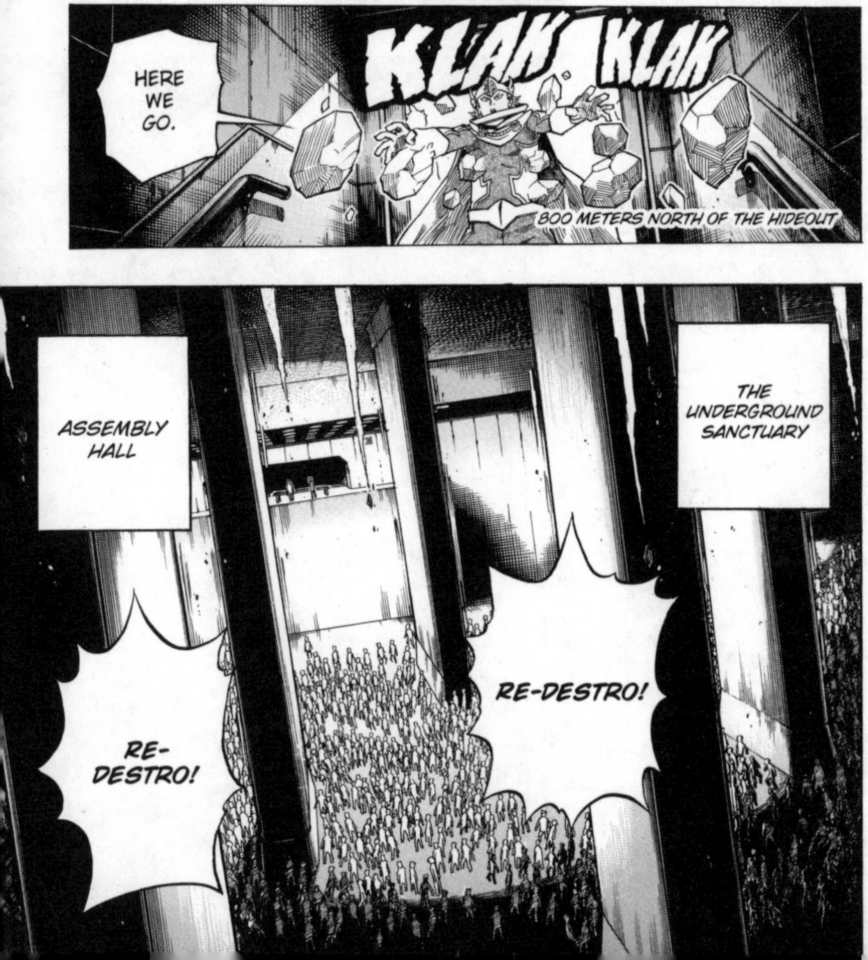
KLAK KLAK
HERE WE GO.
800 METERS NORTH OF THE HIDEOUT
THE UNDERGROUND SANCTUARY
ASSEMBLY HALL
RE-DESTRO!
RE-DESTRO!

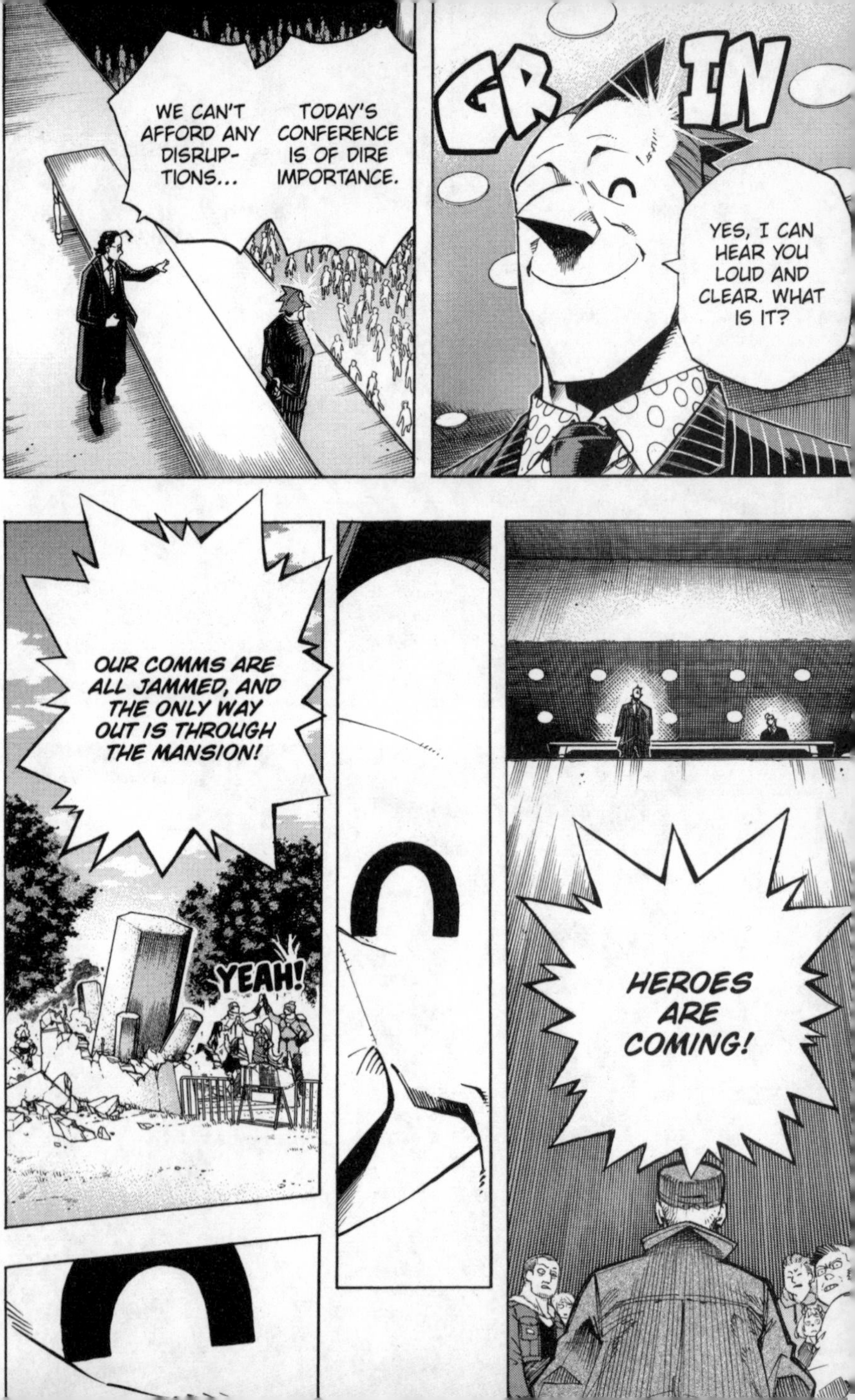
GRIN
YES, I CAN HEAR YOU LOUD AND CLEAR. WHAT IS IT?
TODAY'S CONFERENCE IS OF DIRE IMPORTANCE.
WE CAN'T AFFORD ANY DISRUP-TIONS...
HEROES ARE COMING!
OUR COMMS ARE ALL JAMMED, AND THE ONLY WAY OUT IS THROUGH THE MANSION!
YEAH!

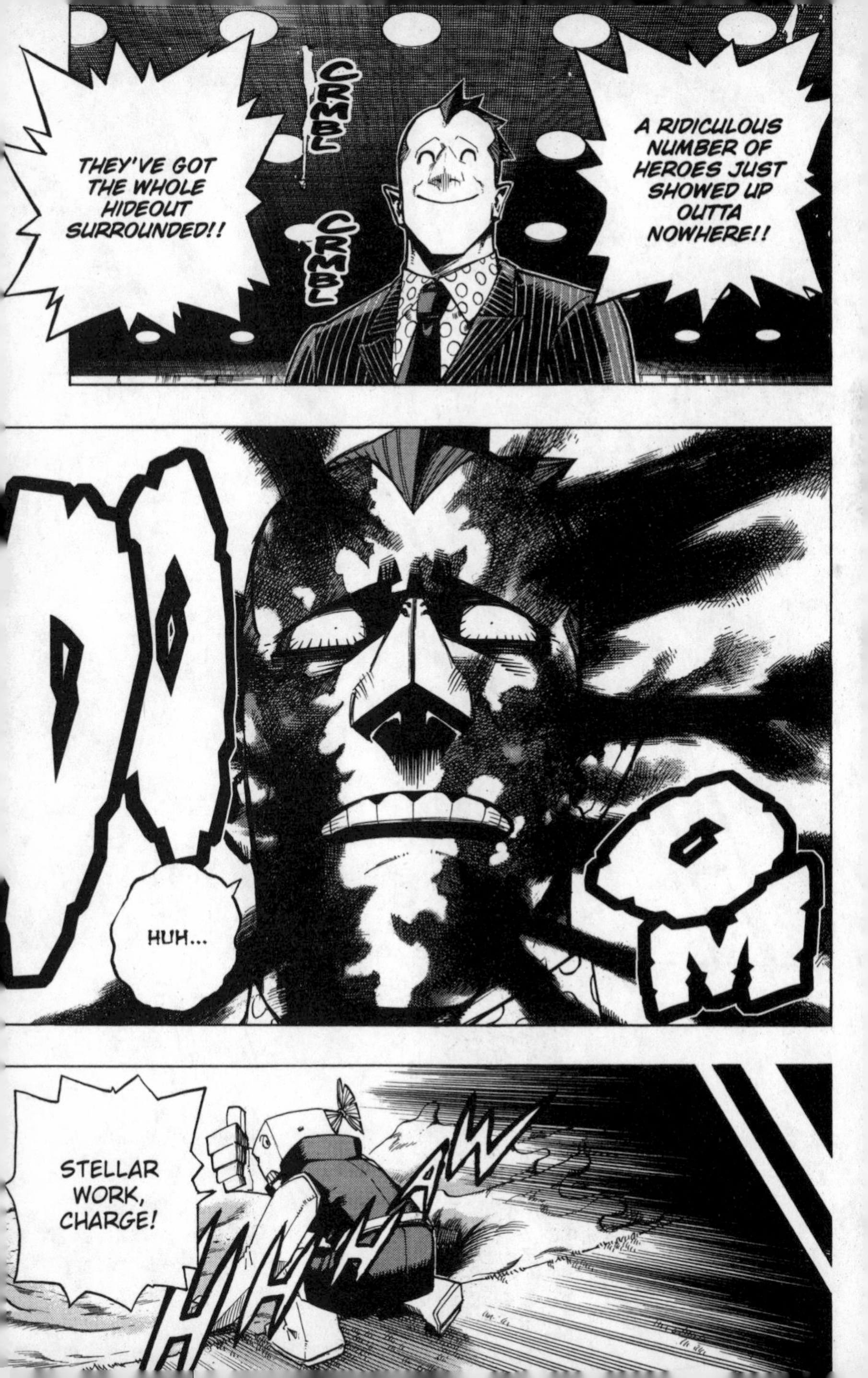
A RIDICULOUS NUMBER OF HEROES JUST SHOWED UP OUTTA NOWHERE!!
CRMBL CRMBL
THEY'VE GOT THE WHOLE HIDEOUT SURROUNDED!!
DOOM
HUH...
STELLAR WORK, CHARGE!

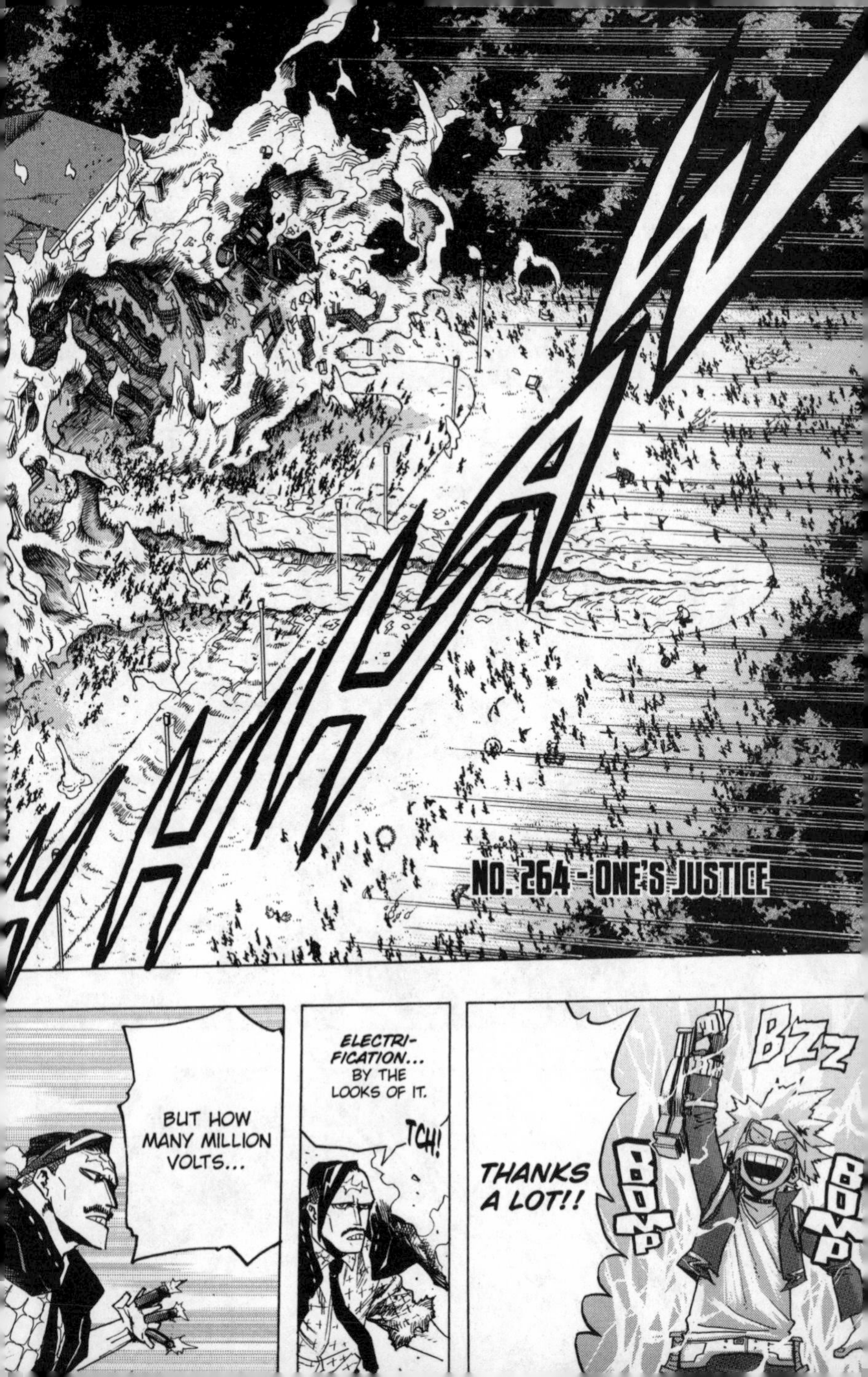
NO. 264 - ONE'S JUSTICE
BZZ
BOMP
BOMP
THANKS A LOT!!
ELECTRI-FICATION... BY THE LOOKS OF IT.
TCH!
BUT HOW MANY MILLION VOLTS...

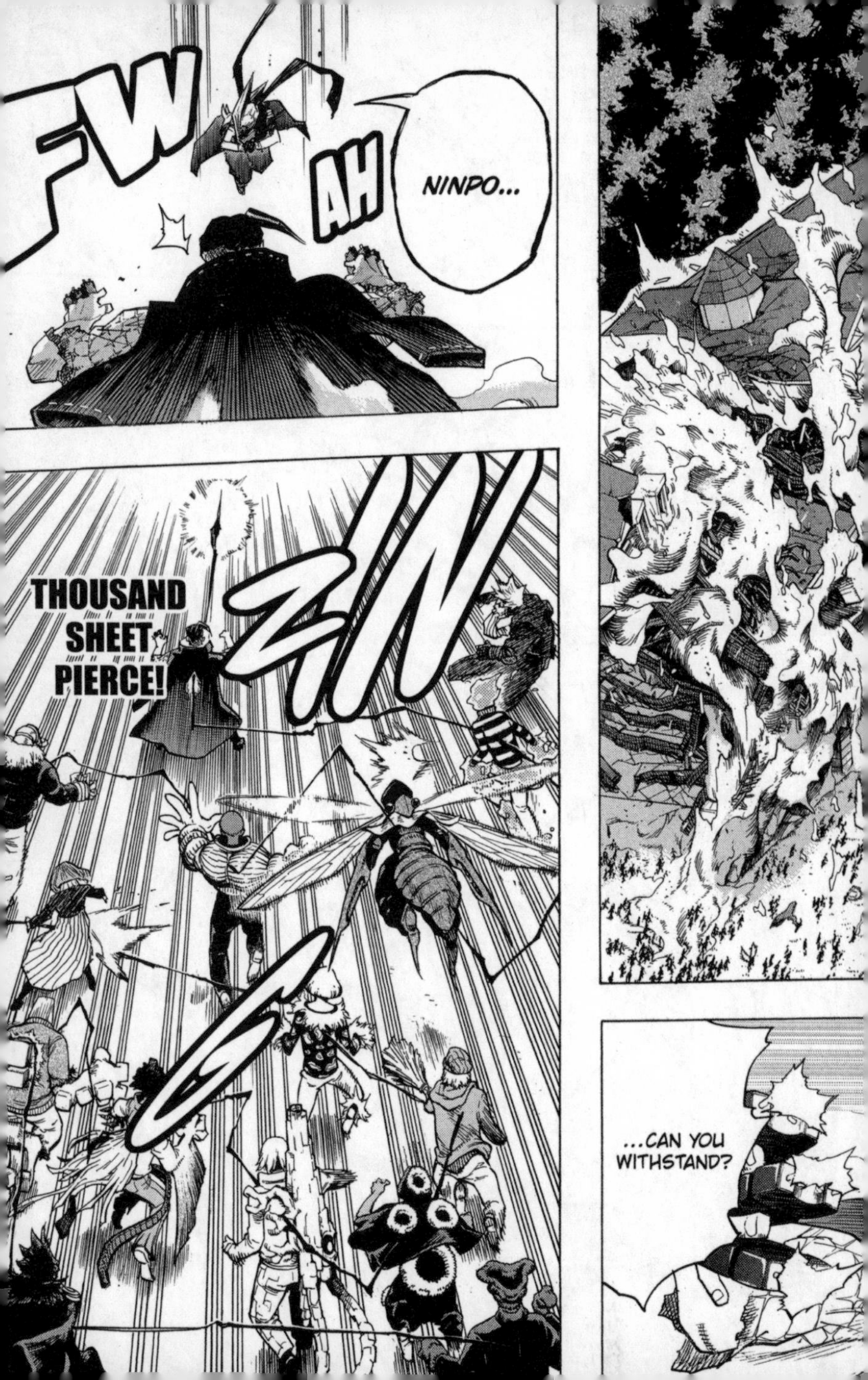
...CAN YOU WITHSTAND?
FWAH
NINPO...
ZIN
THOUSAND SHEET PIERCE!

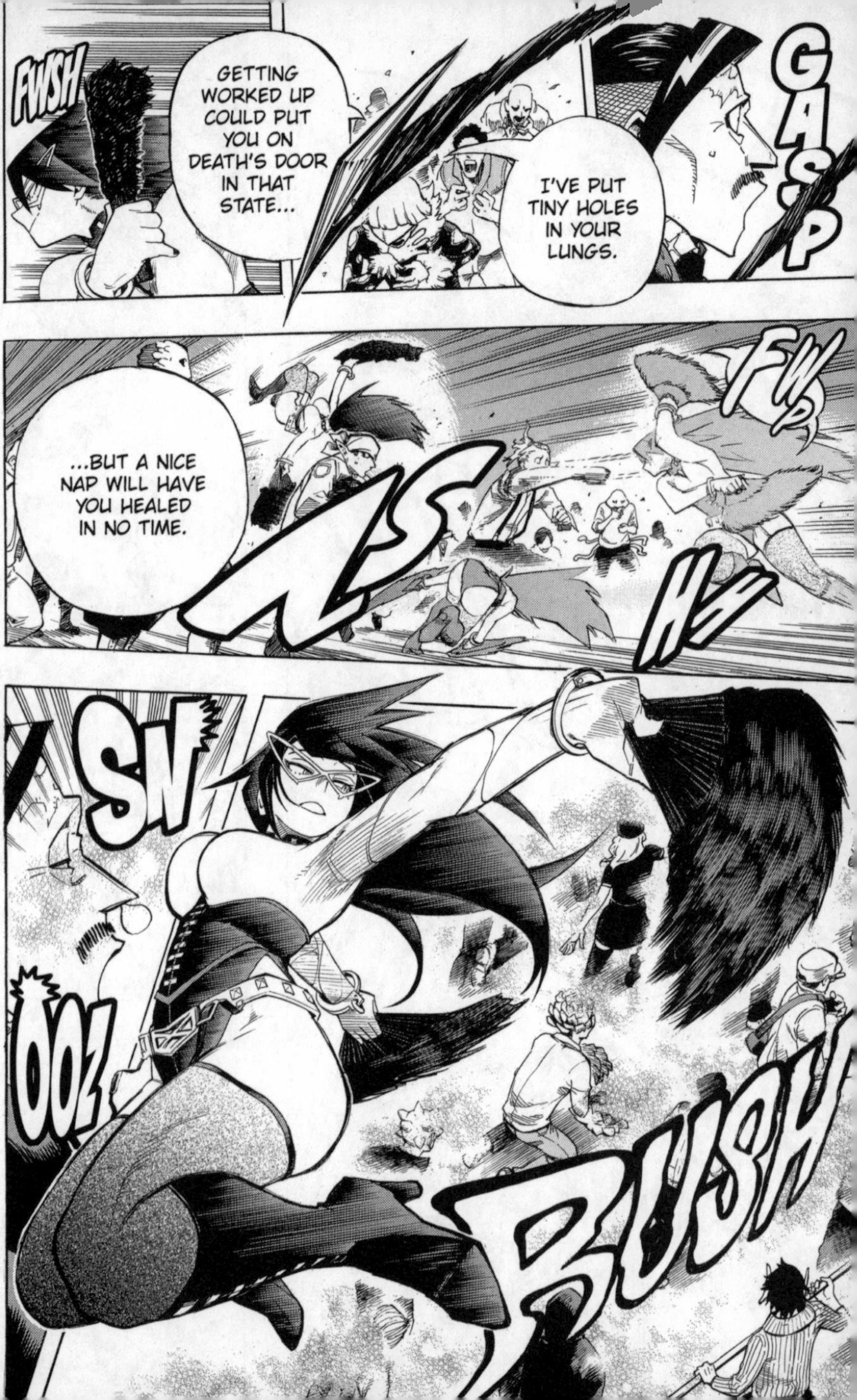
GASP
I'VE PUT TINY HOLES IN YOUR LUNGS.
GETTING WORKED UP COULD PUT YOU ON DEATH'S DOOR IN THAT STATE...
FWSH
FWP
...BUT A NICE NAP WILL HAVE YOU HEALED IN NO TIME.
SN

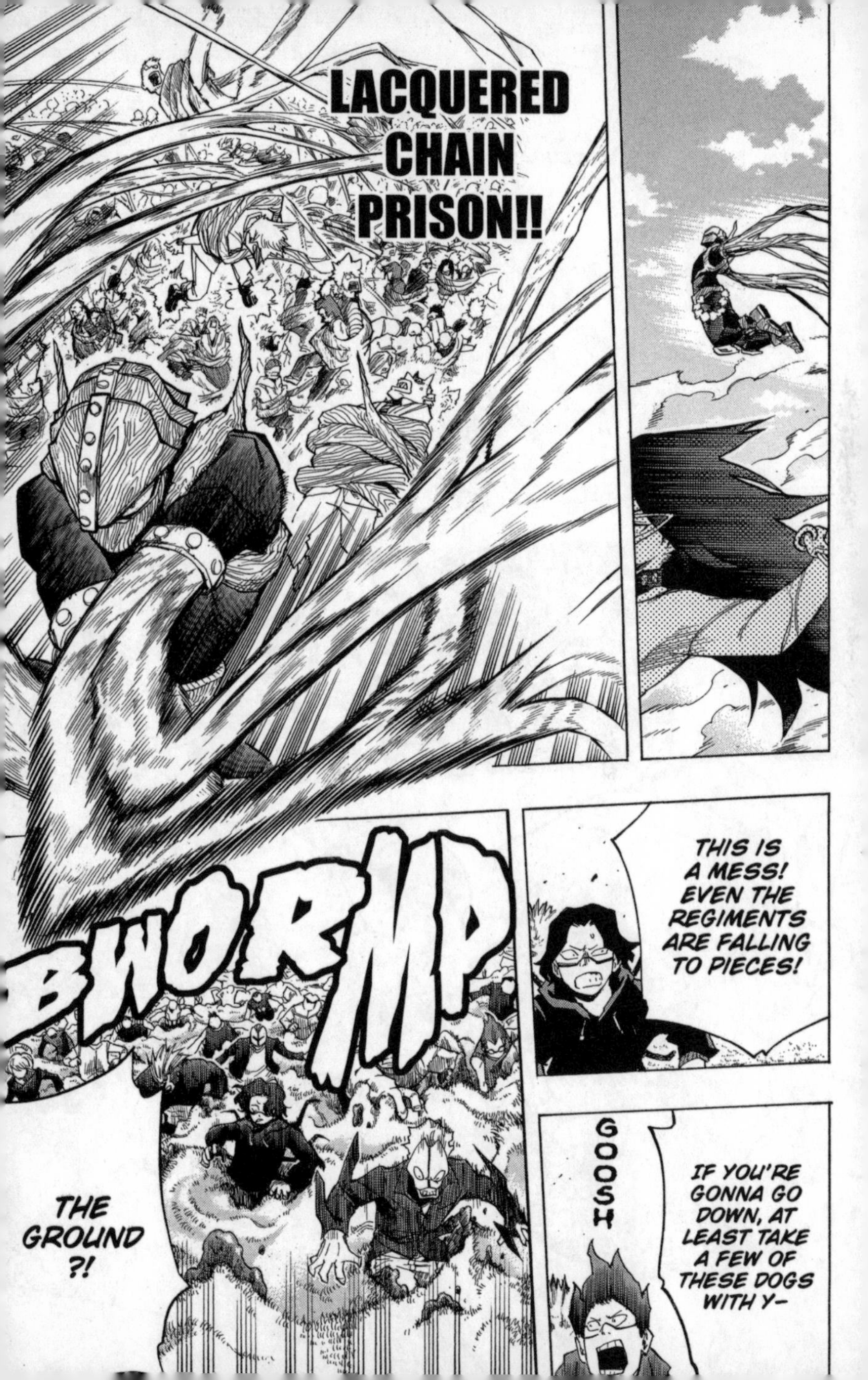
LACQUERED CHAIN PRISON!!
THIS IS A MESS! EVEN THE REGIMENTS ARE FALLING TO PIECES!
GOOSH
IF YOU'RE GONNA GO DOWN, AT LEAST TAKE A FEW OF THESE DOGS WITH Y-
BWORMP
THE GROUND ?!

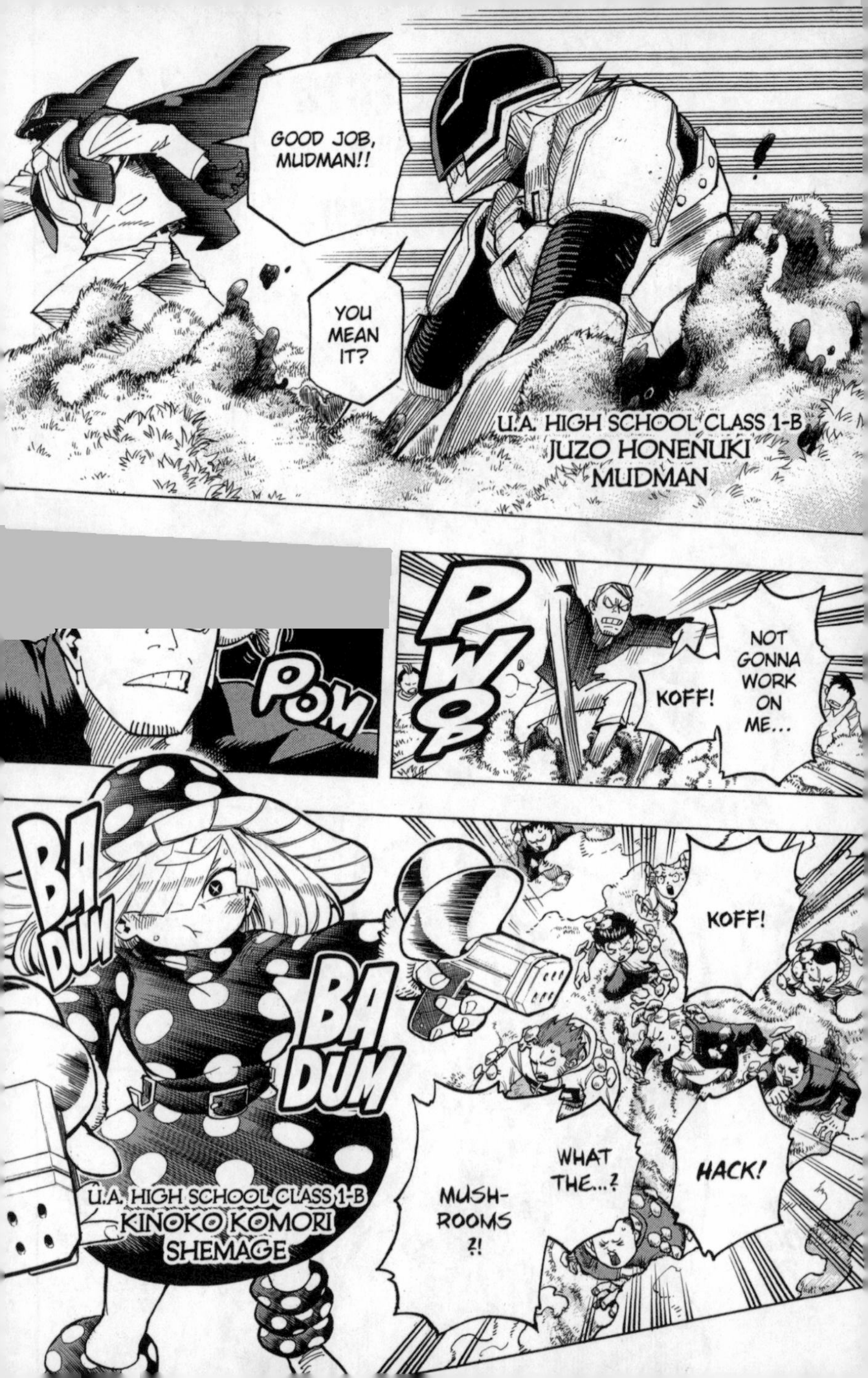
GOOD JOB, MUDMAN!!
YOU MEAN IT?
U.A. HIGH SCHOOL CLASS 1-B
JUZO HONENUKI
MUDMAN
NOT GONNA WORK ON ME...
KOFF!
PWOP
POM
KOFF!
HACK!
WHAT THE...?
MUSH-ROOMS?!
BA DUM
BA DUM
U.A. HIGH SCHOOL CLASS 1-B
KINOKO KOMORI
SHEMAGE

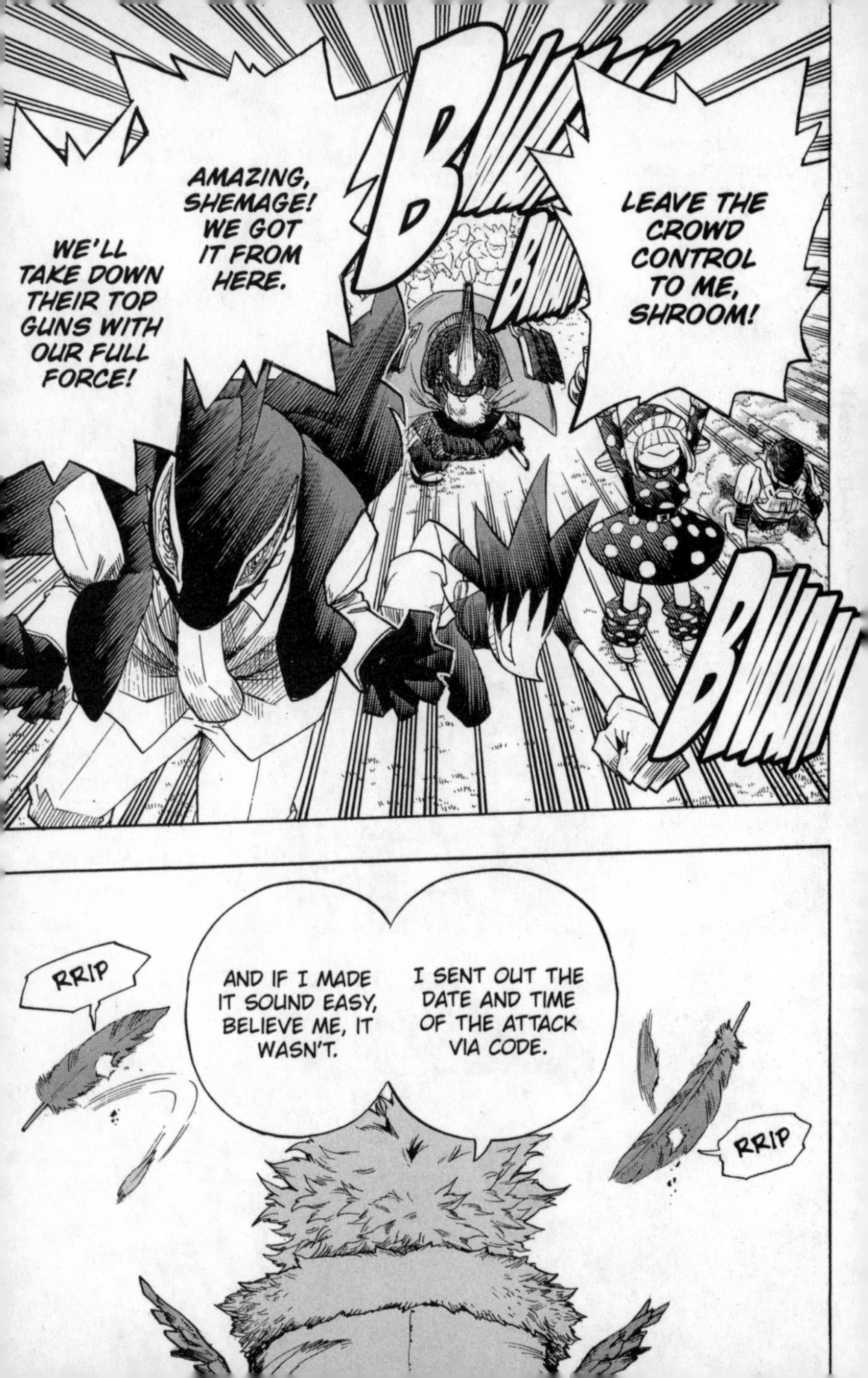
LEAVE THE CROWD CONTROL TO ME, SHROOM!
AMAZING, SHEMAGE! WE GOT IT FROM HERE.
WE'LL TAKE DOWN THEIR TOP GUNS WITH OUR FULL FORCE!
RRIP
I SENT OUT THE DATE AND TIME OF THE ATTACK VIA CODE.
AND IF I MADE IT SOUND EASY, BELIEVE ME, IT WASN'T.
RRIP

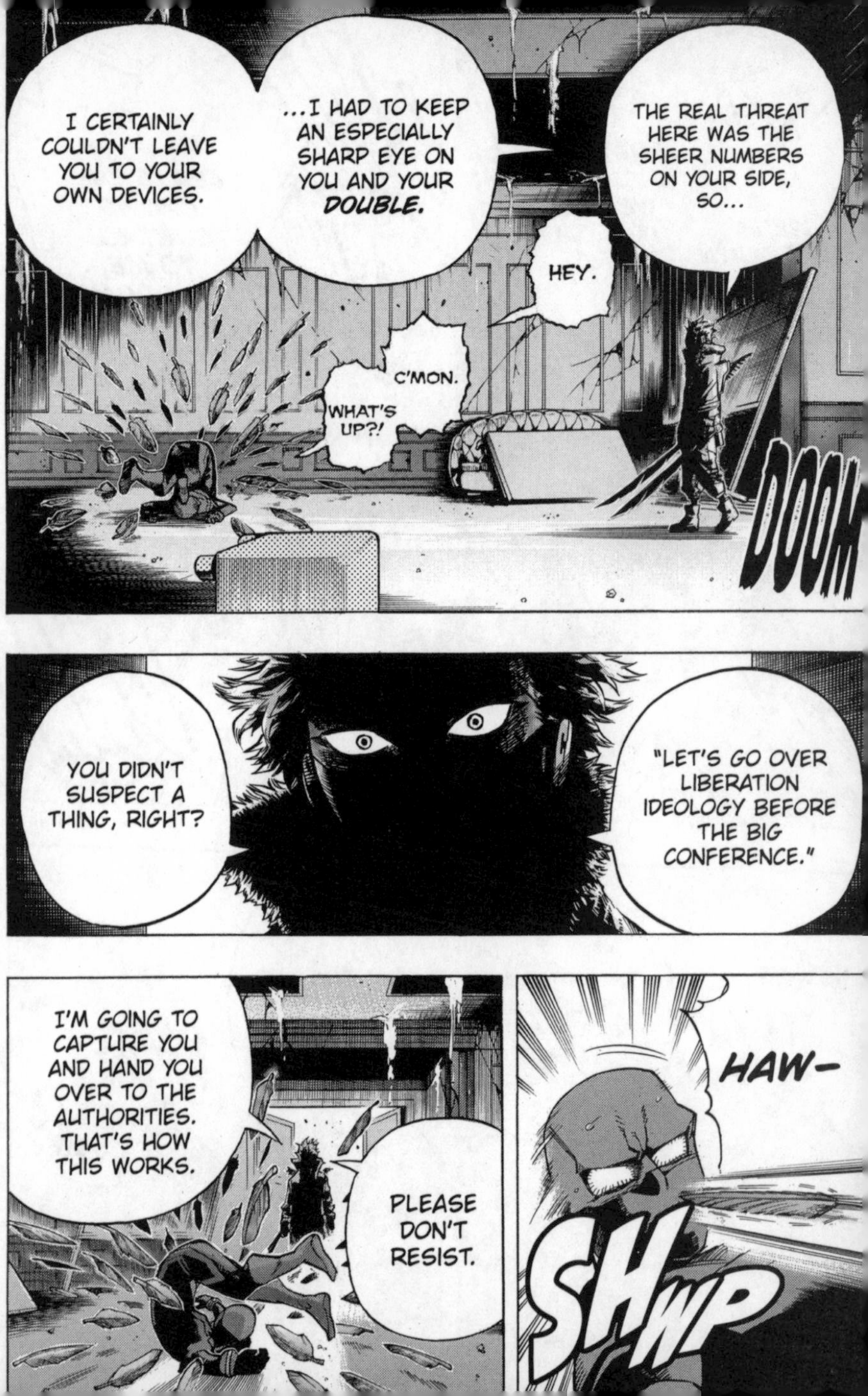
THE REAL THREAT HERE WAS THE SHEER NUMBERS ON YOUR SIDE, SO...
...I HAD TO KEEP AN ESPECIALLY SHARP EYE ON YOU AND YOUR DOUBLE.
I CERTAINLY COULDN'T LEAVE YOU TO YOUR OWN DEVICES.
HEY.
C'MON.
WHAT'S UP?!
DOOM
"LET'S GO OVER LIBERATION IDEOLOGY BEFORE THE BIG CONFERENCE."
YOU DIDN'T SUSPECT A THING, RIGHT?
HAW-
SHWP
I'M GOING TO CAPTURE YOU AND HAND YOU OVER TO THE AUTHORITIES. THAT'S HOW THIS WORKS.
PLEASE DON'T RESIST.

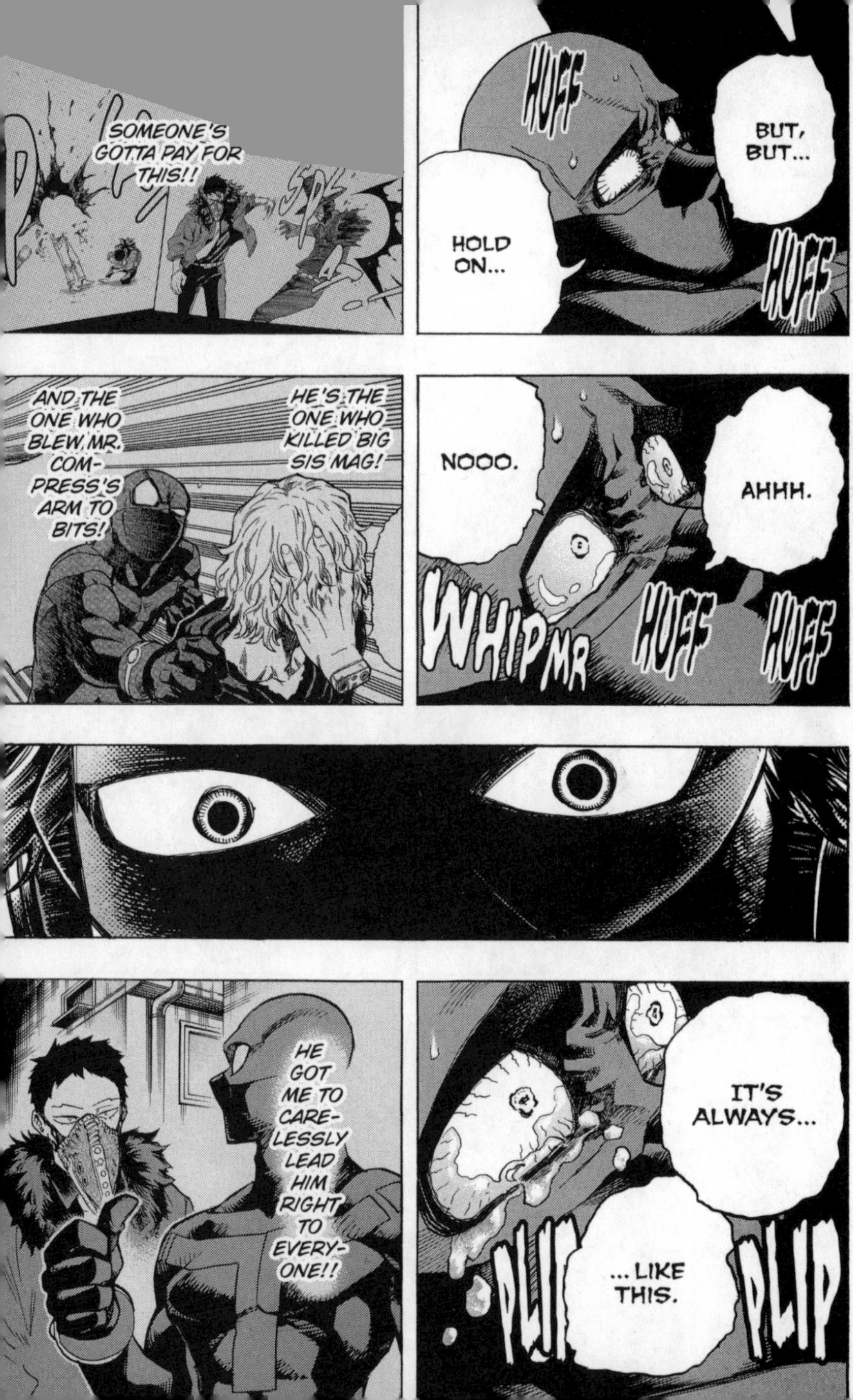
BUT, BUT...
HUFF
HOLD ON...
HUFF
SOMEONE'S GOTTA PAY FOR THIS!!
AHHH.
NOOO.
HUFF
HUFF
WHIP
MR
HE'S THE ONE WHO KILLED BIG SIS MAG!
AND THE ONE WHO BLEW MR. COMPRESS'S ARM TO BITS!
IT'S ALWAYS...
...LIKE THIS.
PLIP
PLIP
HE GOT ME TO CARELESSLY LEAD HIM RIGHT TO EVERYONE!!

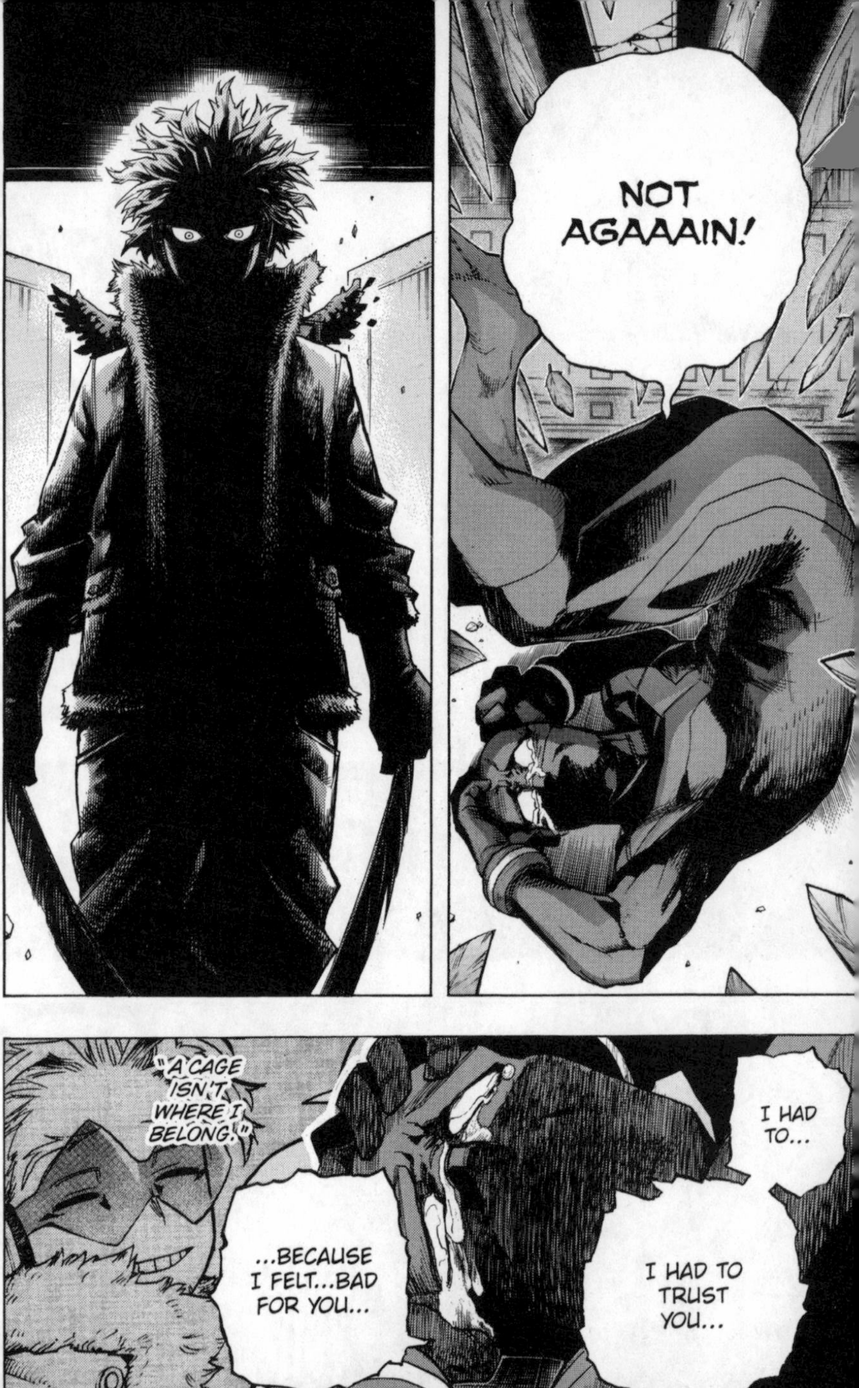
NOT AGAAAIN!
I HAD TO...
I HAD TO TRUST YOU...
...BECAUSE I FELT...BAD FOR YOU...
"A CAGE ISN'T WHERE I BELONG."

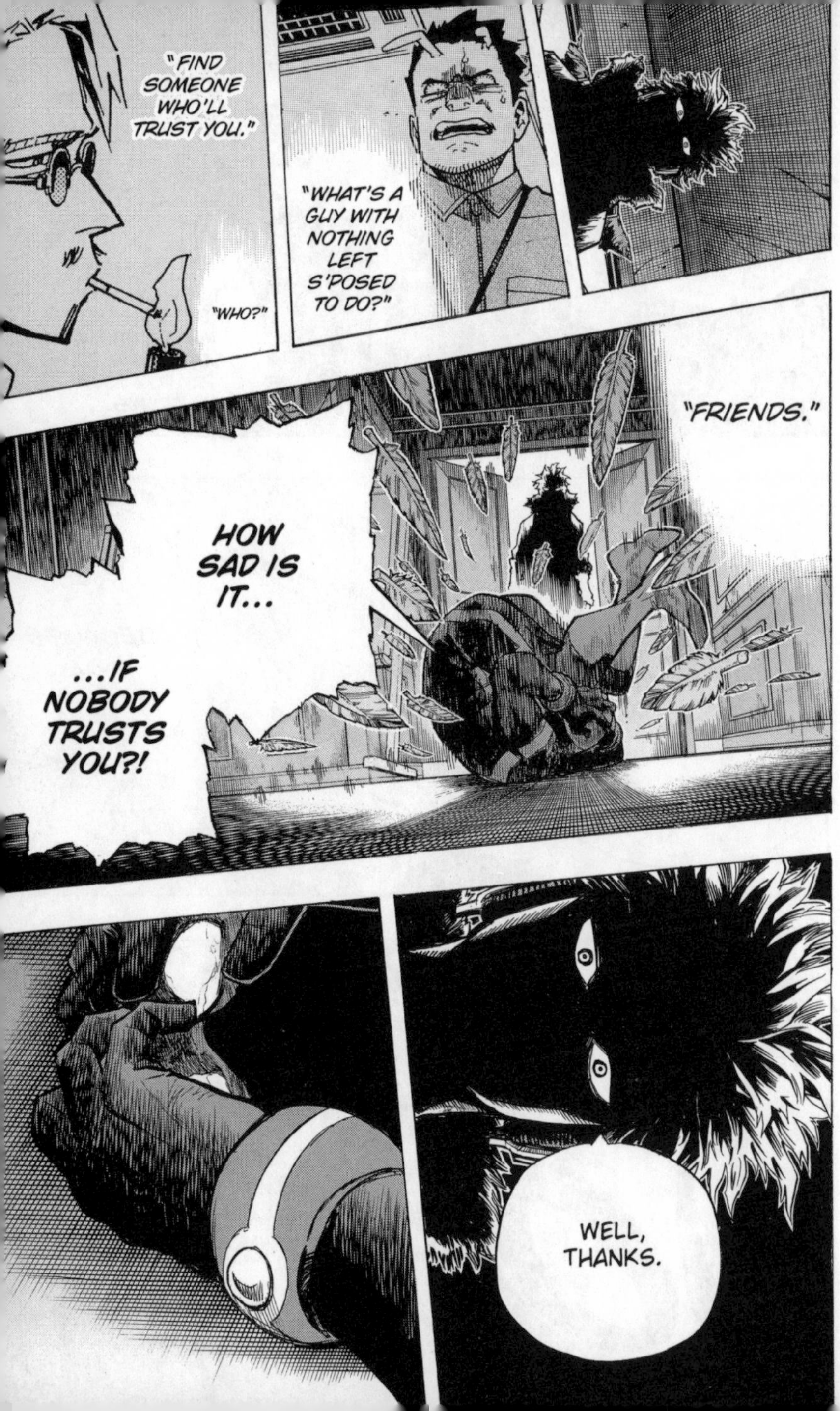
"WHAT'S A GUY WITH NOTHING LEFT S'POSED TO DO?"
"FIND SOMEONE WHO'LL TRUST YOU."
"WHO?"
"FRIENDS."
HOW SAD IS IT...
...IF NOBODY TRUSTS YOU?!
WELL, THANKS.

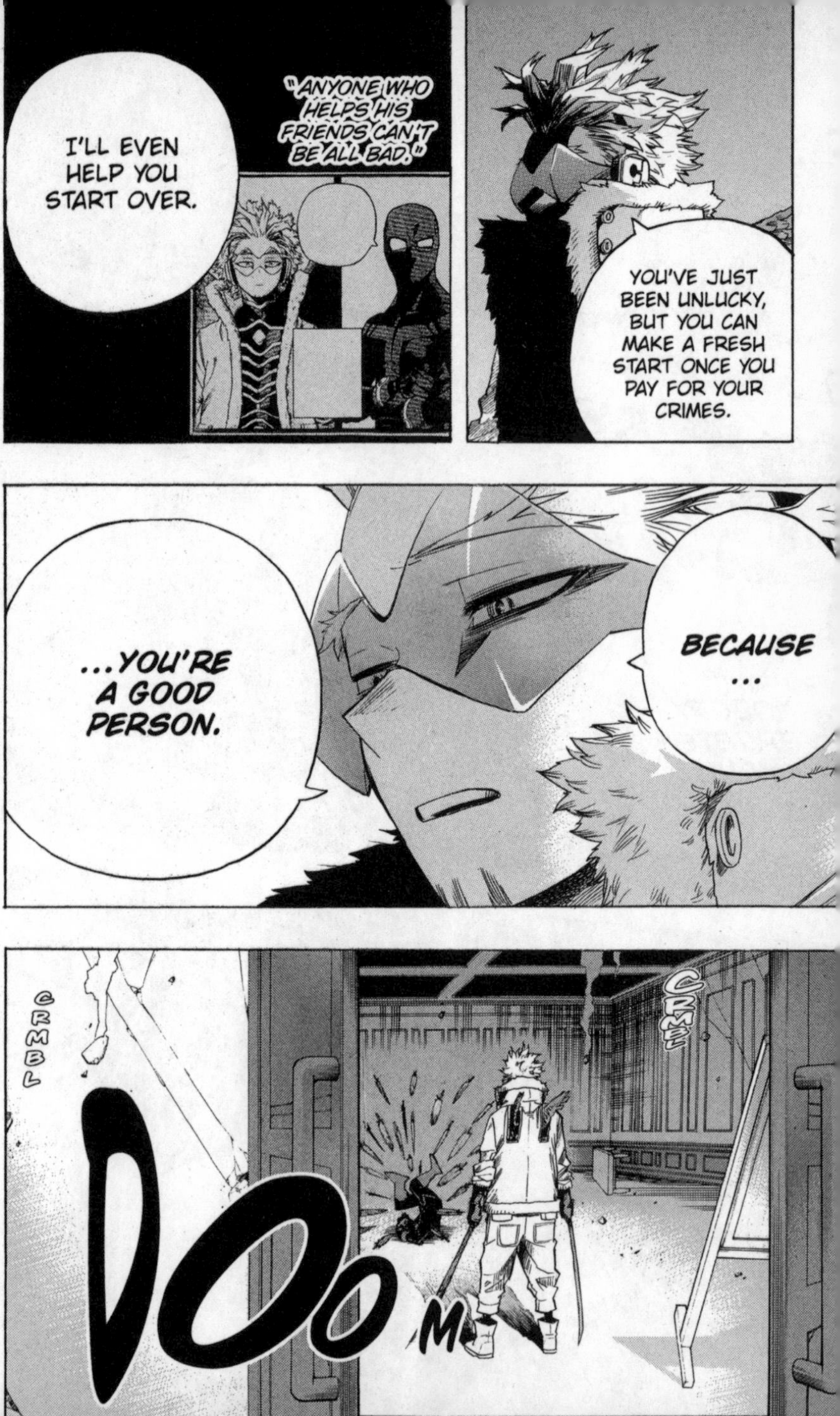
YOU'VE JUST BEEN UNLUCKY, BUT YOU CAN MAKE A FRESH START ONCE YOU PAY FOR YOUR CRIMES.
"ANYONE WHO HELPS HIS FRIENDS CAN'T BE ALL BAD."
I'LL EVEN HELP YOU START OVER.
BECAUSE ...
...YOU'RE A GOOD PERSON.
CRMBL
CRMBL
DOOOM

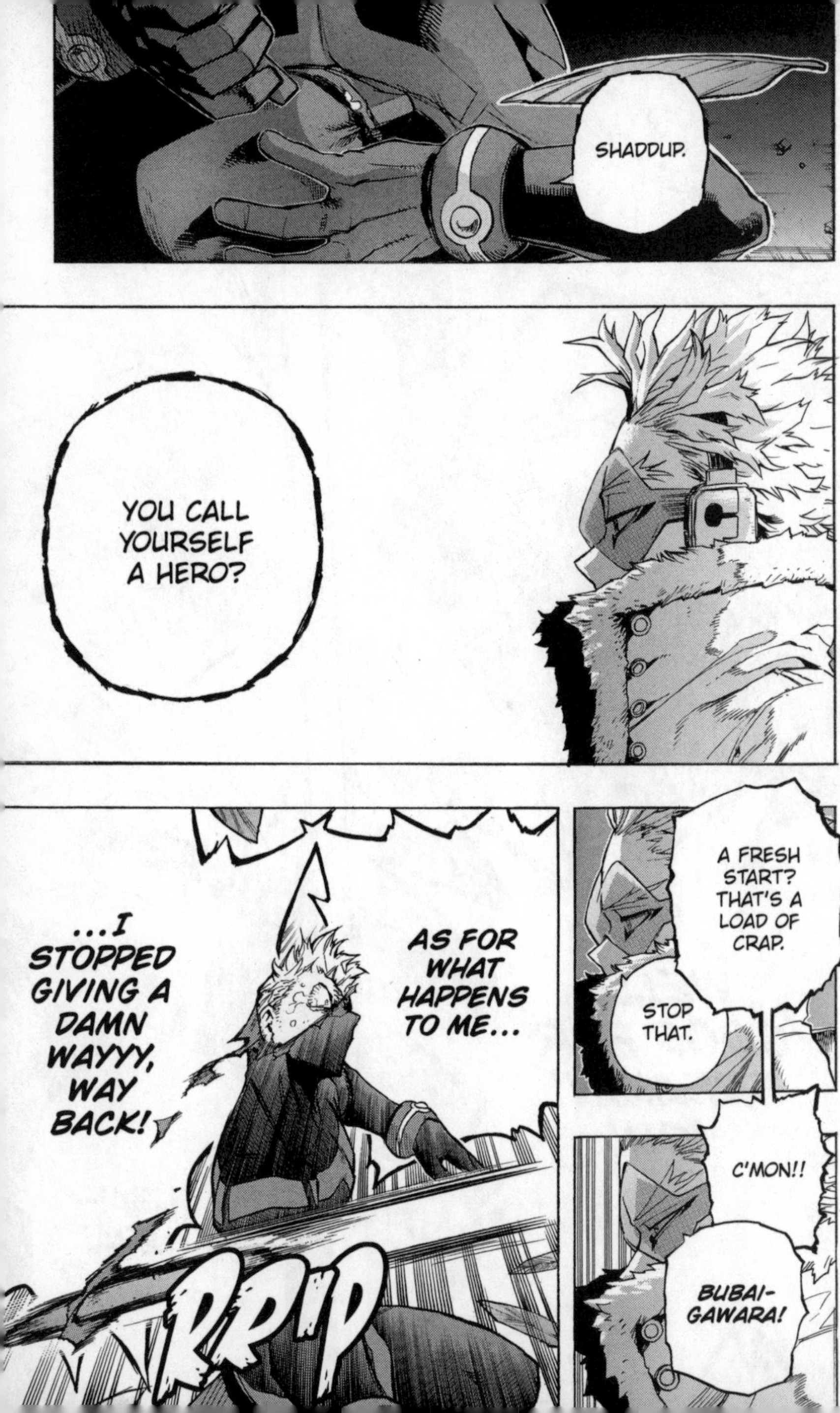
SHADDUP.
YOU CALL YOURSELF A HERO?
A FRESH START? THAT'S A LOAD OF CRAP.
STOP THAT.
C'MON!!
BUBAI-GAWARA!
AS FOR WHAT HAPPENS TO ME...
...I STOPPED GIVING A DAMN WAYYY, WAY BACK!
RRIP

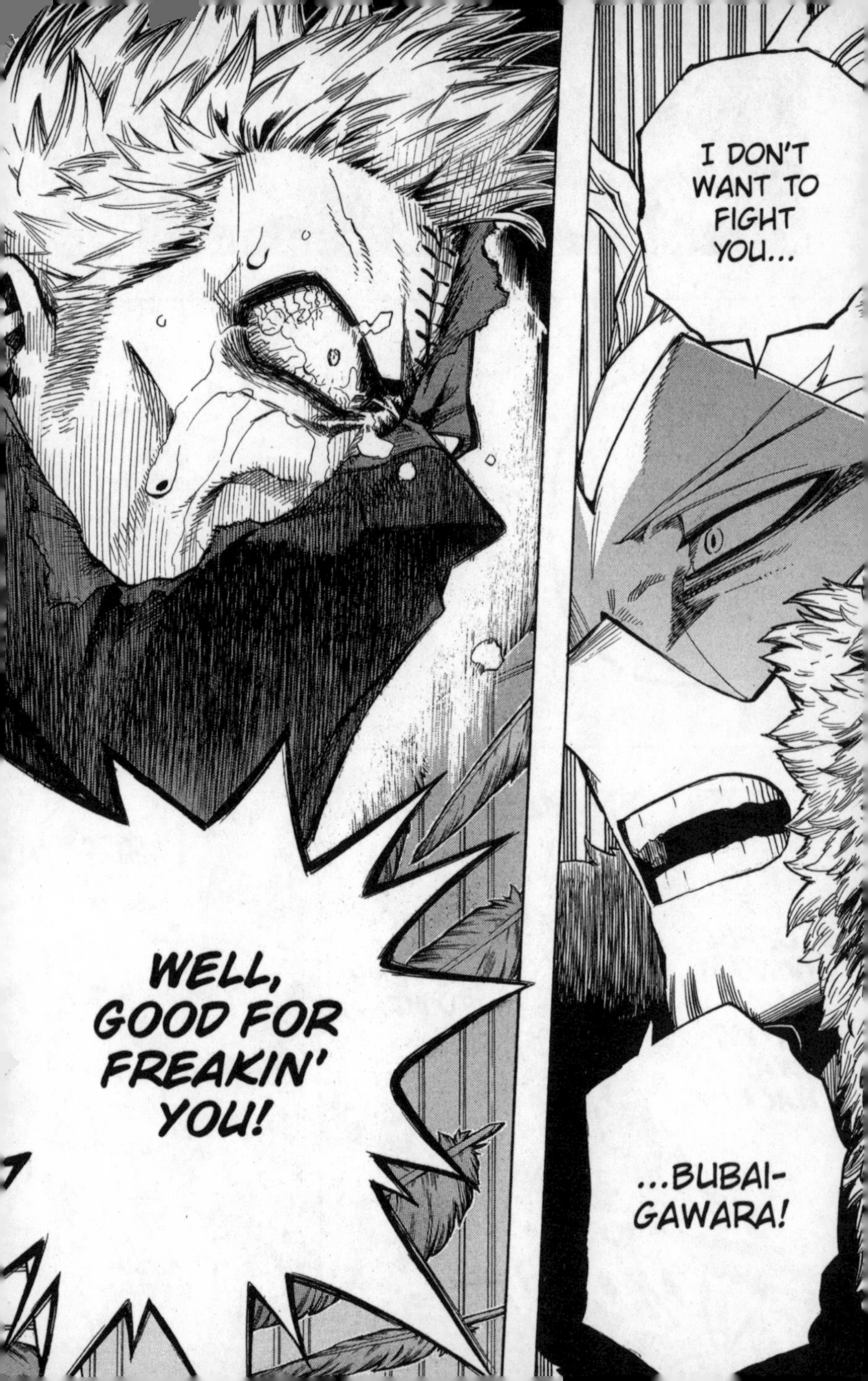
I DON'T WANT TO FIGHT YOU...
...BUBAI-GAWARA!
WELL, GOOD FOR FREAKIN' YOU!

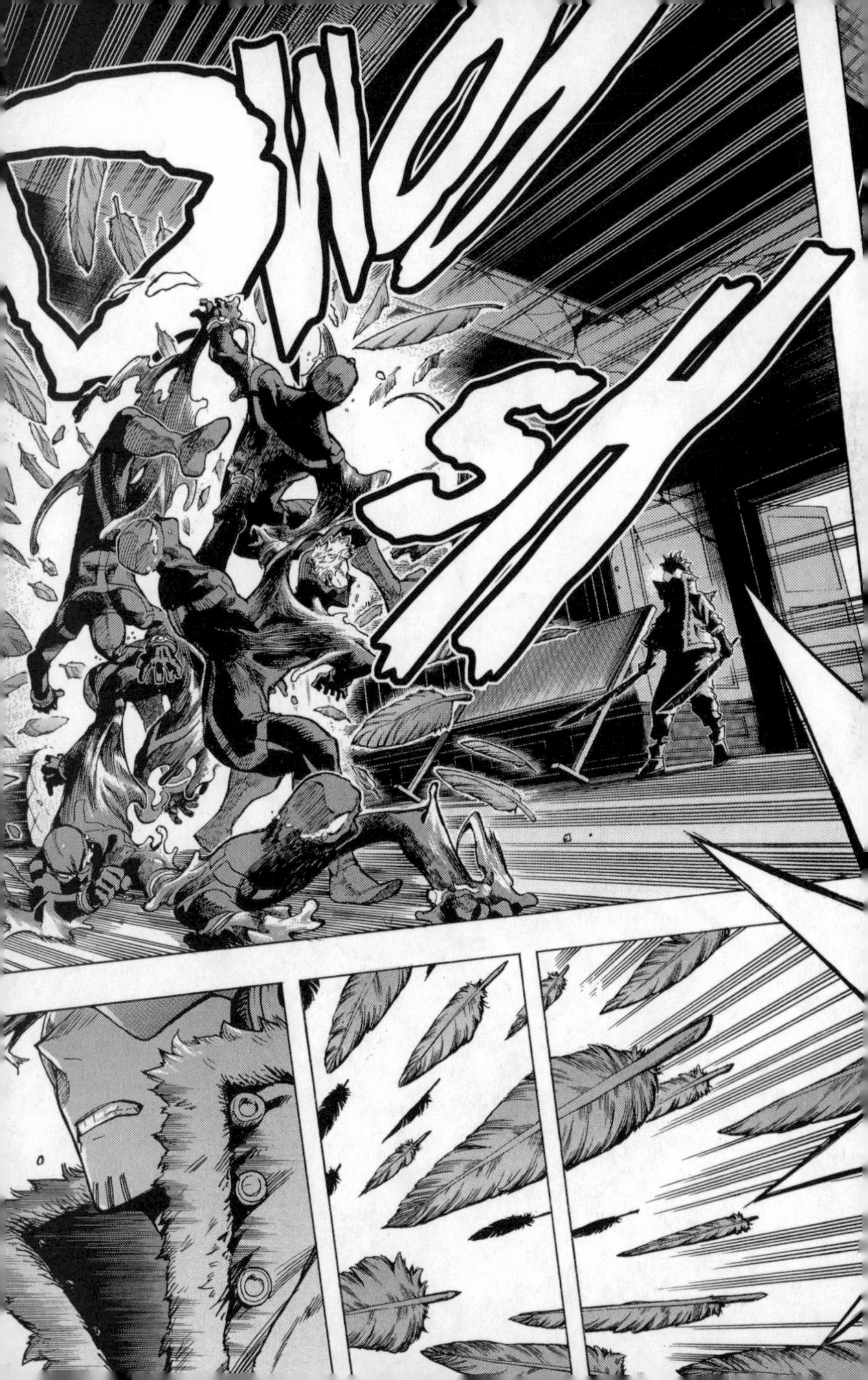
WHOOSH

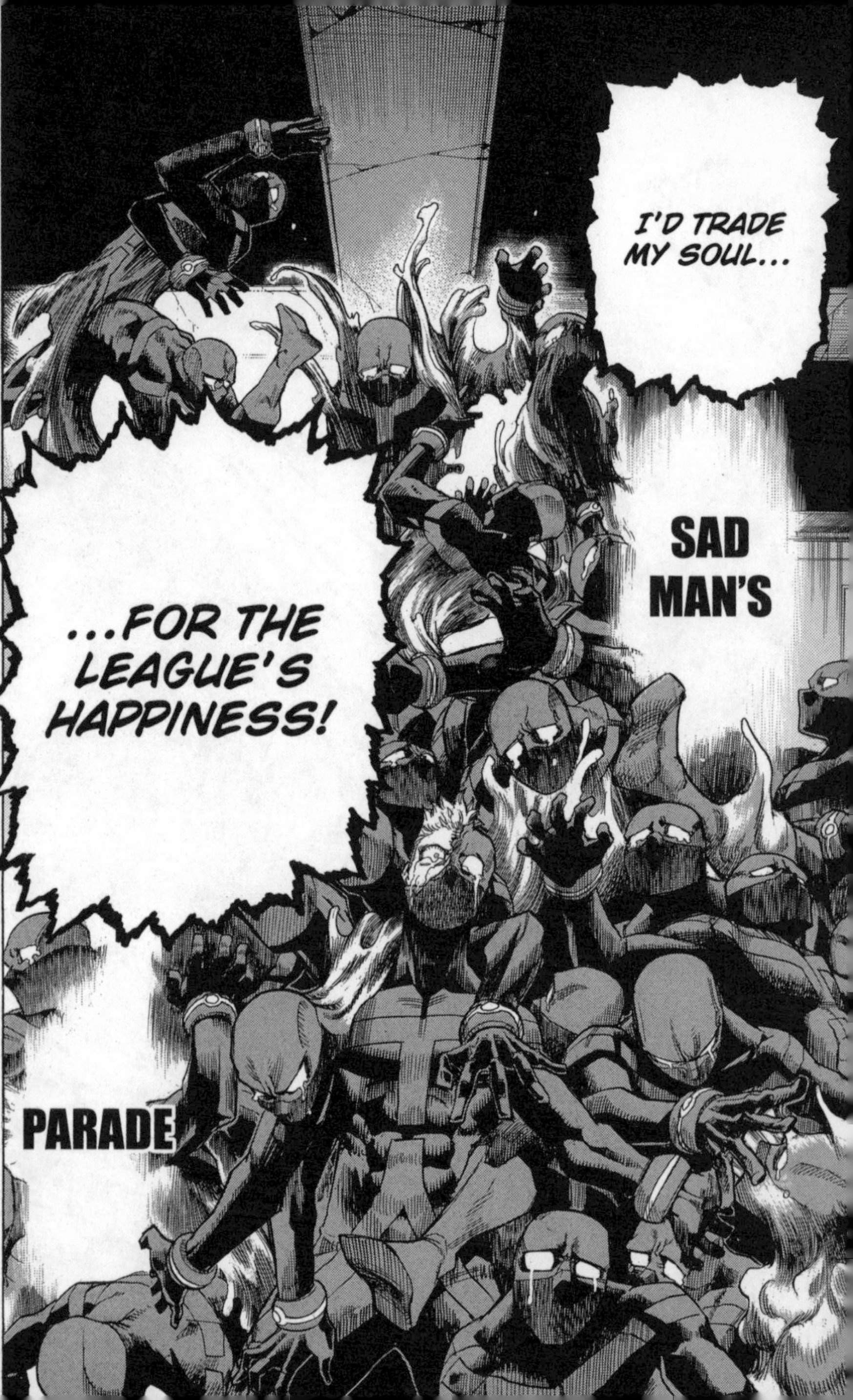
I'D TRADE MY SOUL...
SAD MAN'S
...FOR THE LEAGUE'S HAPPINESS!
PARADE

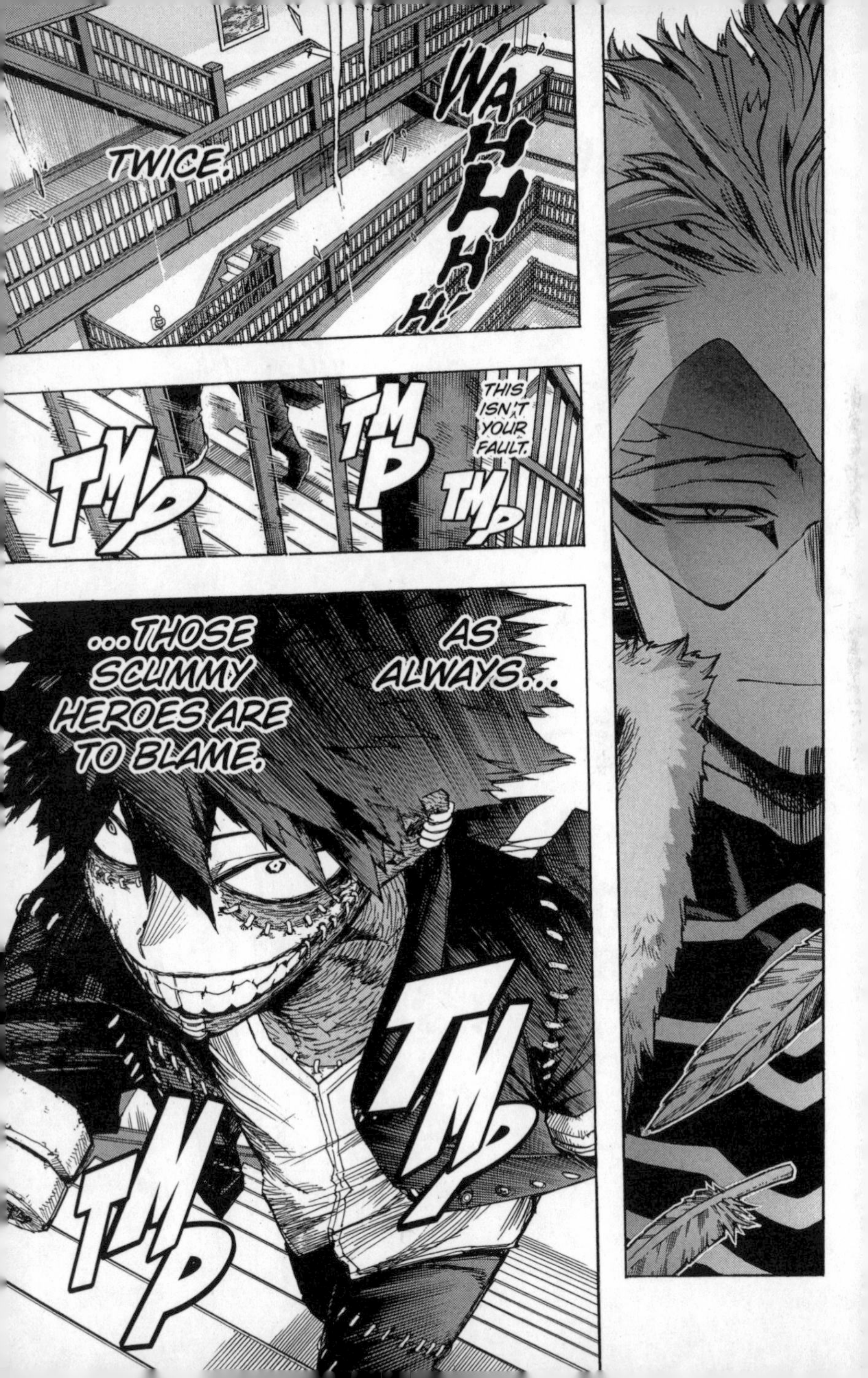
WAHHHHH!
TWICE.
THIS ISN'T YOUR FAULT.
TMP
TMP
TMP
AS ALWAYS...
...THOSE SCUMMY HEROES ARE TO BLAME.
TMP
TMP

MIDNIGHT'S ITEMS

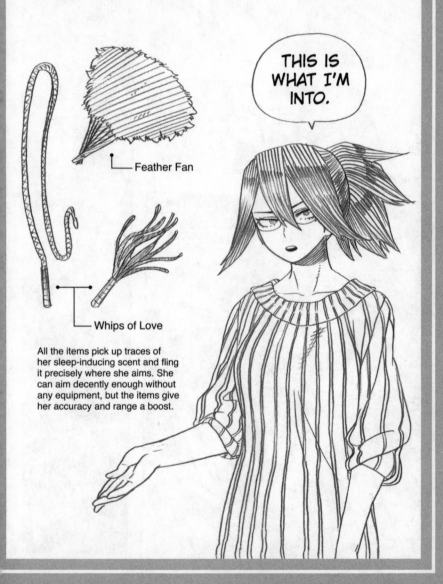

Feather Fan

Whips of Love

THIS IS WHAT I'M INTO.

All the items pick up traces of her sleep-inducing scent and fling it precisely where she aims. She can aim decently enough without any equipment, but the items give her accuracy and range a boost.

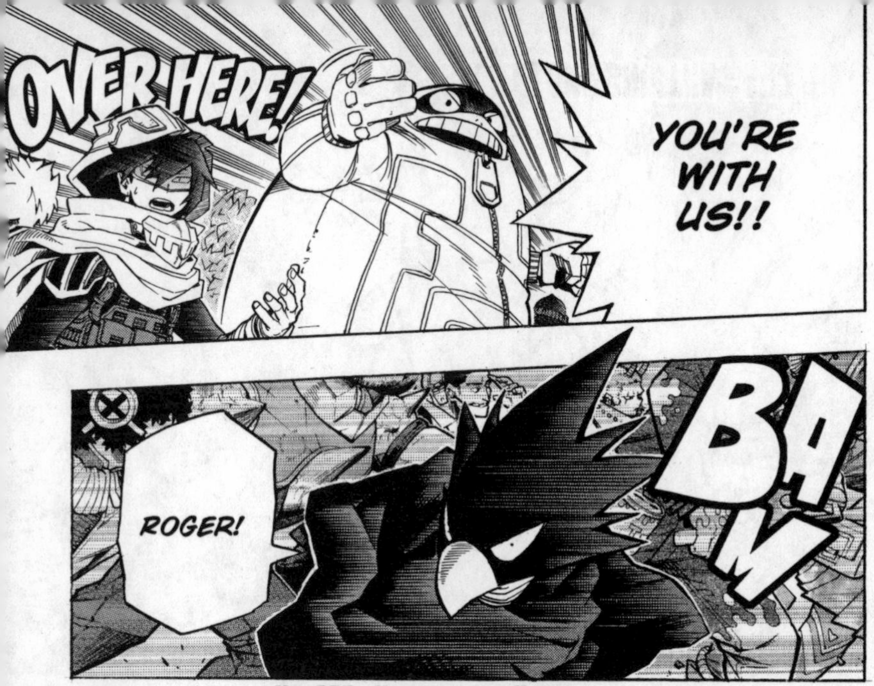
YOU'RE WITH US!!
OVER HERE!
BAM
ROGER!

No. 265 - Villains and Heroes

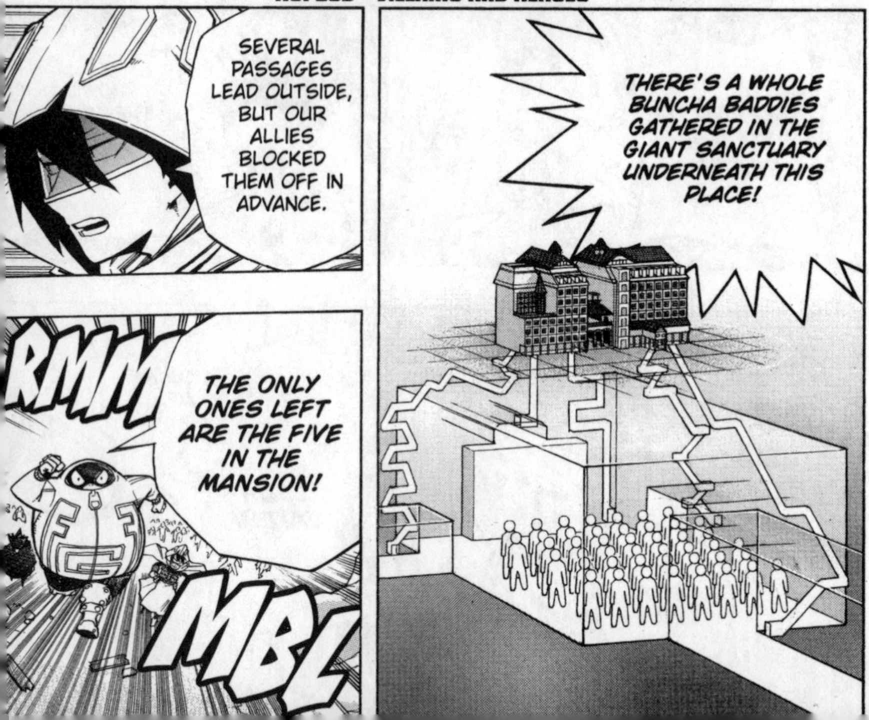
THERE'S A WHOLE BUNCHA BADDIES GATHERED IN THE GIANT SANCTUARY UNDERNEATH THIS PLACE!
SEVERAL PASSAGES LEAD OUTSIDE, BUT OUR ALLIES BLOCKED THEM OFF IN ADVANCE.
RMMMBL
THE ONLY ONES LEFT ARE THE FIVE IN THE MANSION!

No. 265 - Villains and Heroes

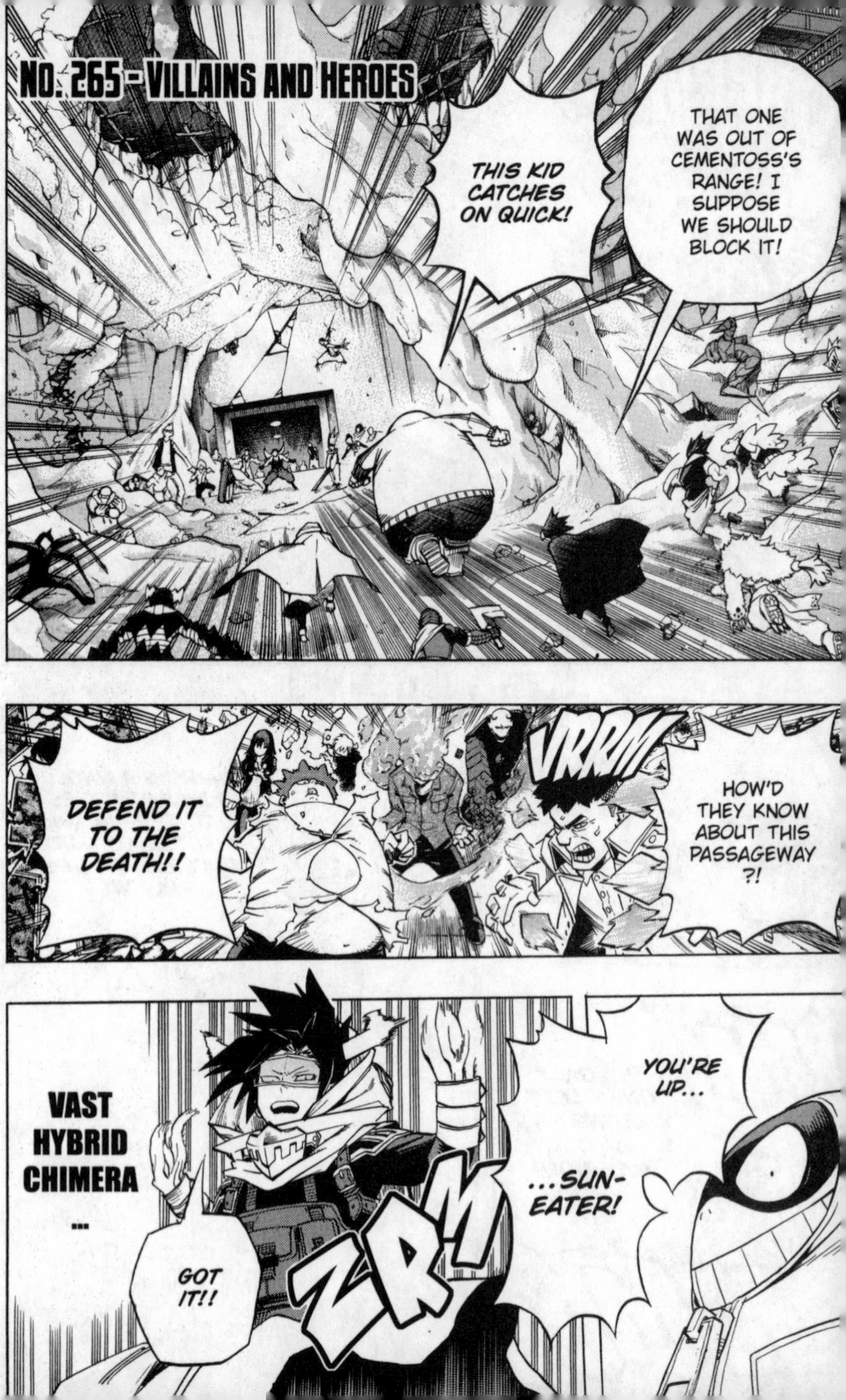
THAT ONE WAS OUT OF CEMENTOSS'S RANGE! I SUPPOSE WE SHOULD BLOCK IT!
THIS KID CATCHES ON QUICK!
HOW'D THEY KNOW ABOUT THIS PASSAGEWAY?!
VRRM
DEFEND IT TO THE DEATH!!
YOU'RE UP...
...SUN-EATER!
ZRM
VAST HYBRID CHIMERA ...
GOT IT!!

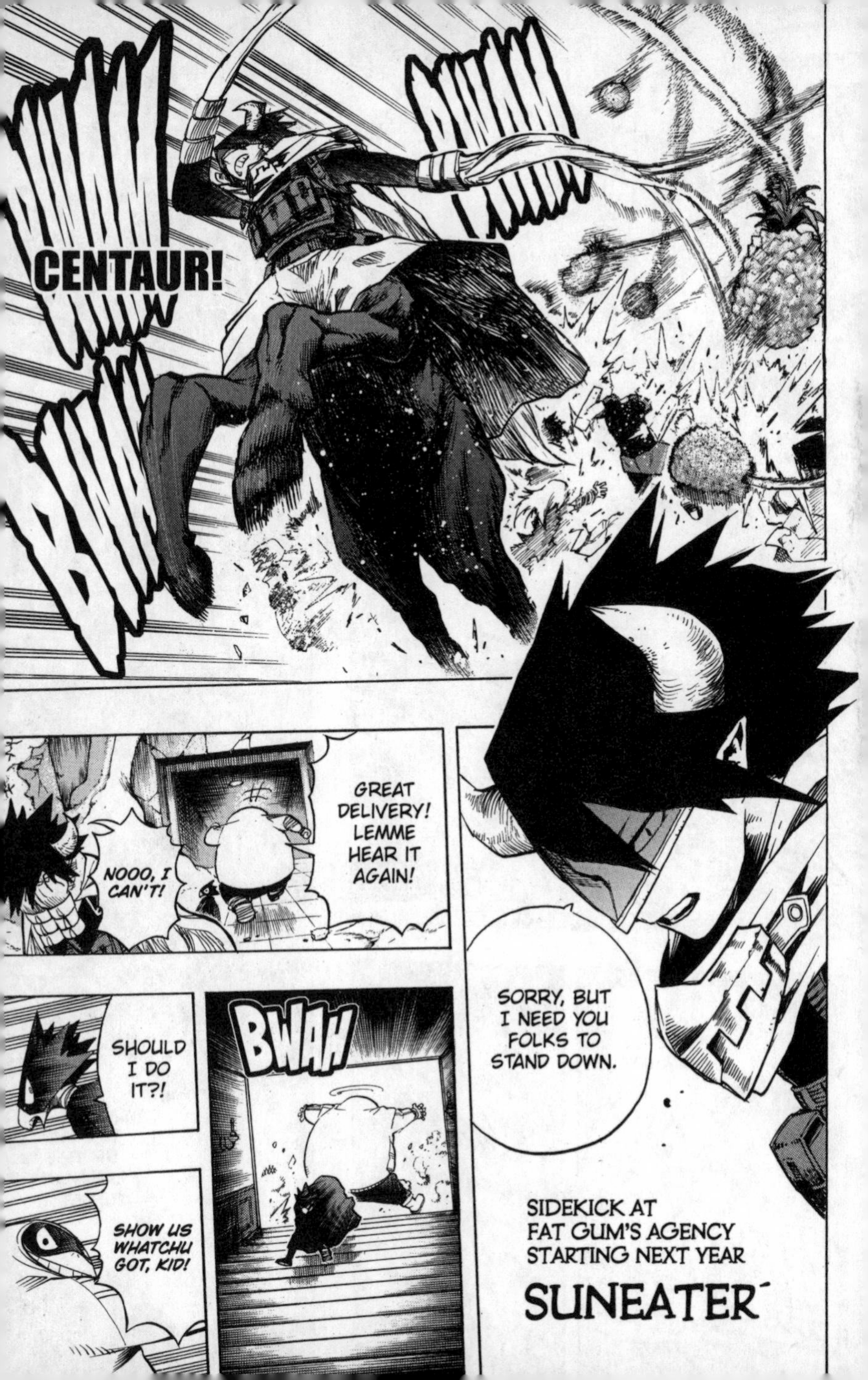
CENTAUR!
SORRY, BUT I NEED YOU FOLKS TO STAND DOWN.
SIDEKICK AT FAT GUM'S AGENCY STARTING NEXT YEAR
SUNEATER
GREAT DELIVERY! LEMME HEAR IT AGAIN!
NOOO, I CAN'T!
BWAH
SHOULD I DO IT?!
SHOW US WHATCHU GOT, KID!

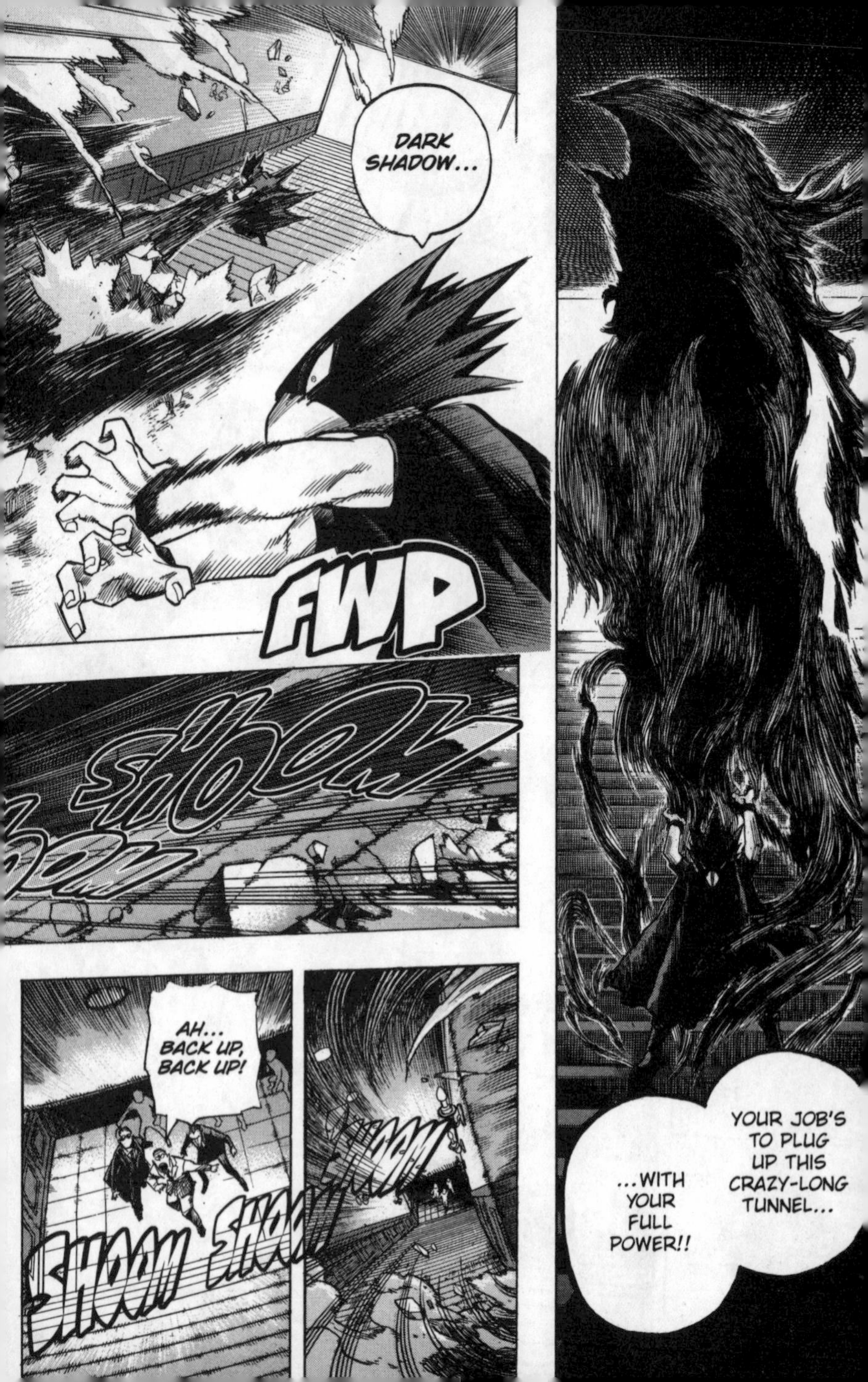
YOUR JOB'S TO PLUG UP THIS CRAZY-LONG TUNNEL...
...WITH YOUR FULL POWER!!
DARK SHADOW...
FWP
AH... BACK UP, BACK UP!
SHOOM SHOOM

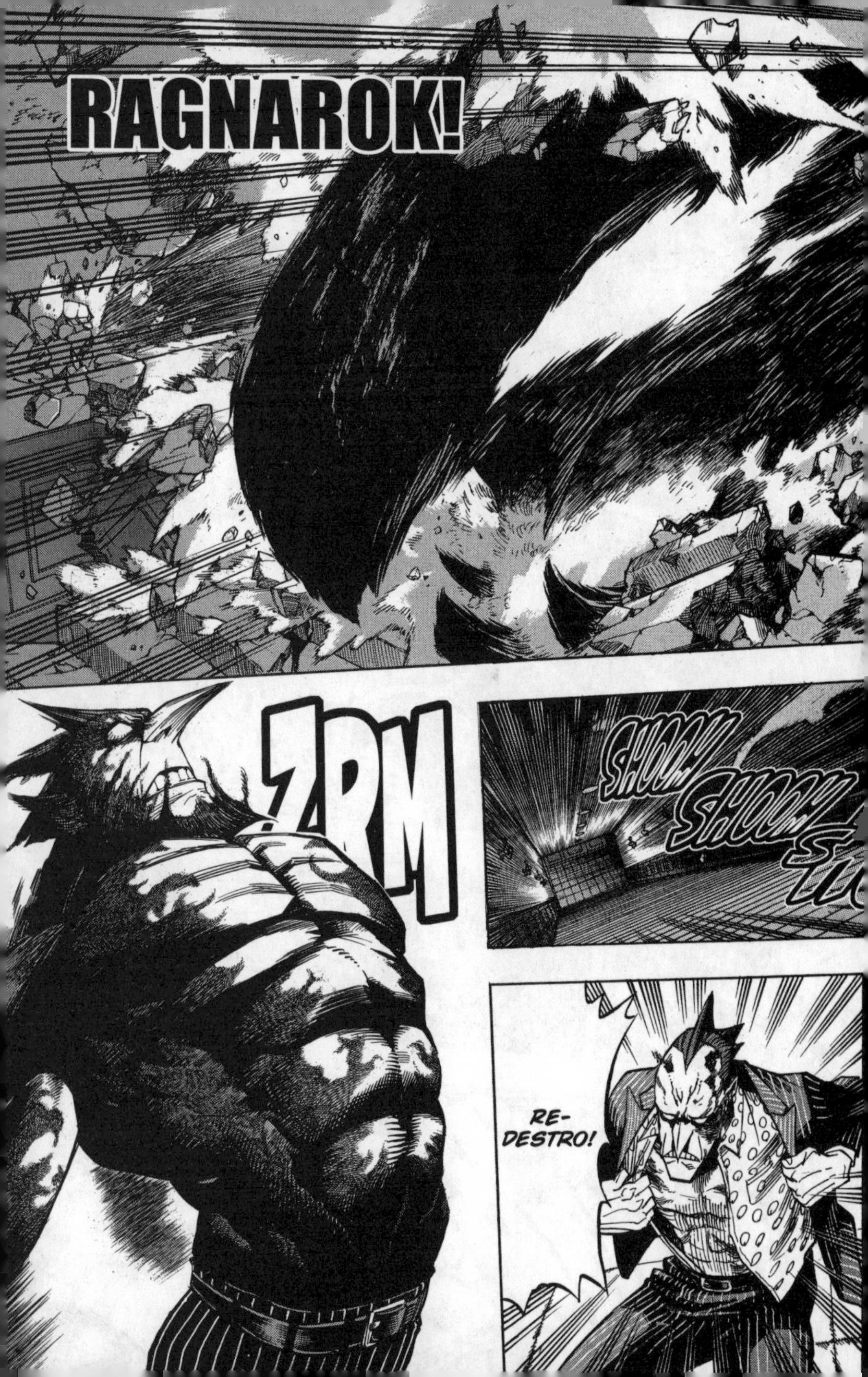
RAGNAROK!
RE-
DESTRO!
ZRM

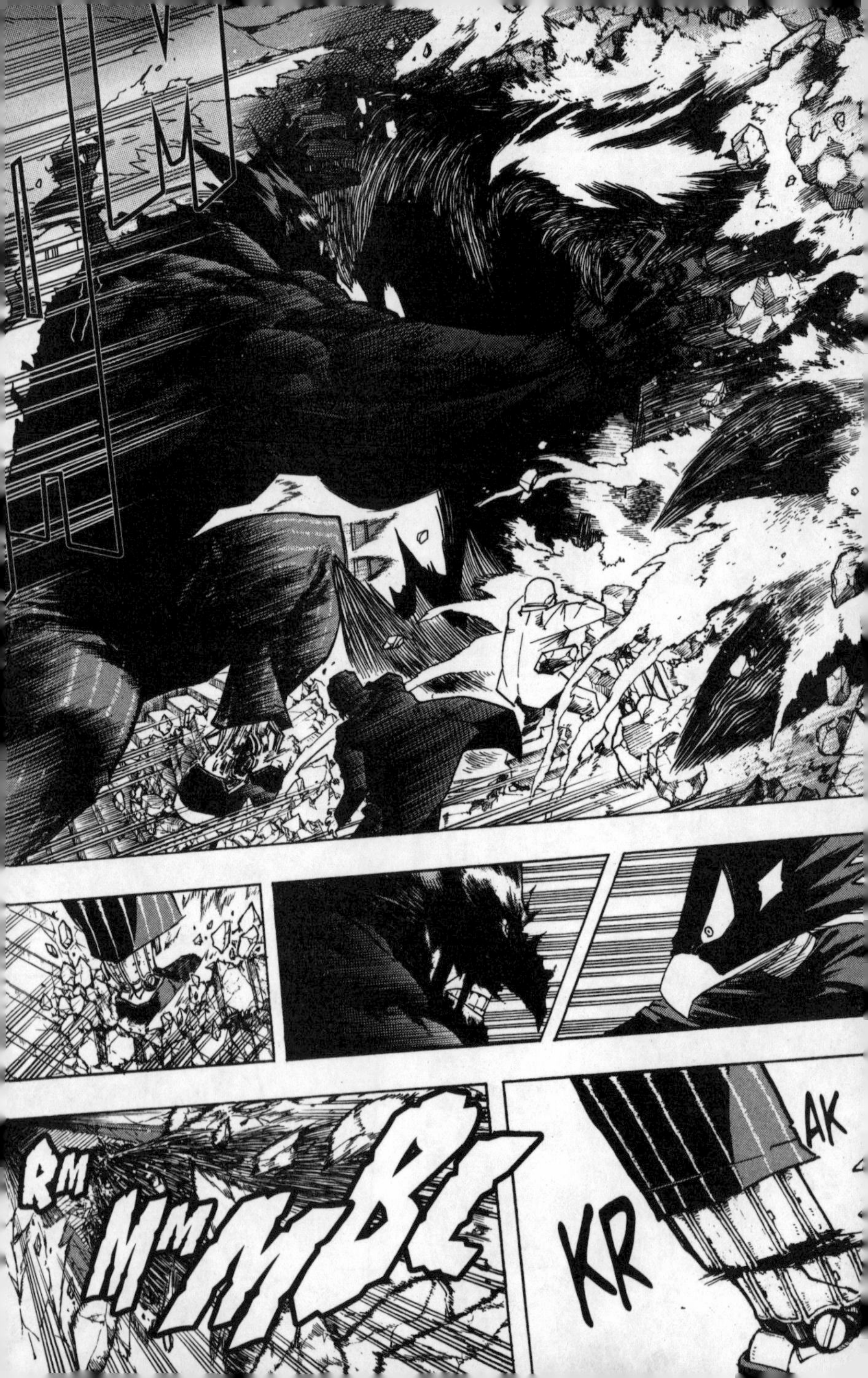
KRAK
RMMMMBL

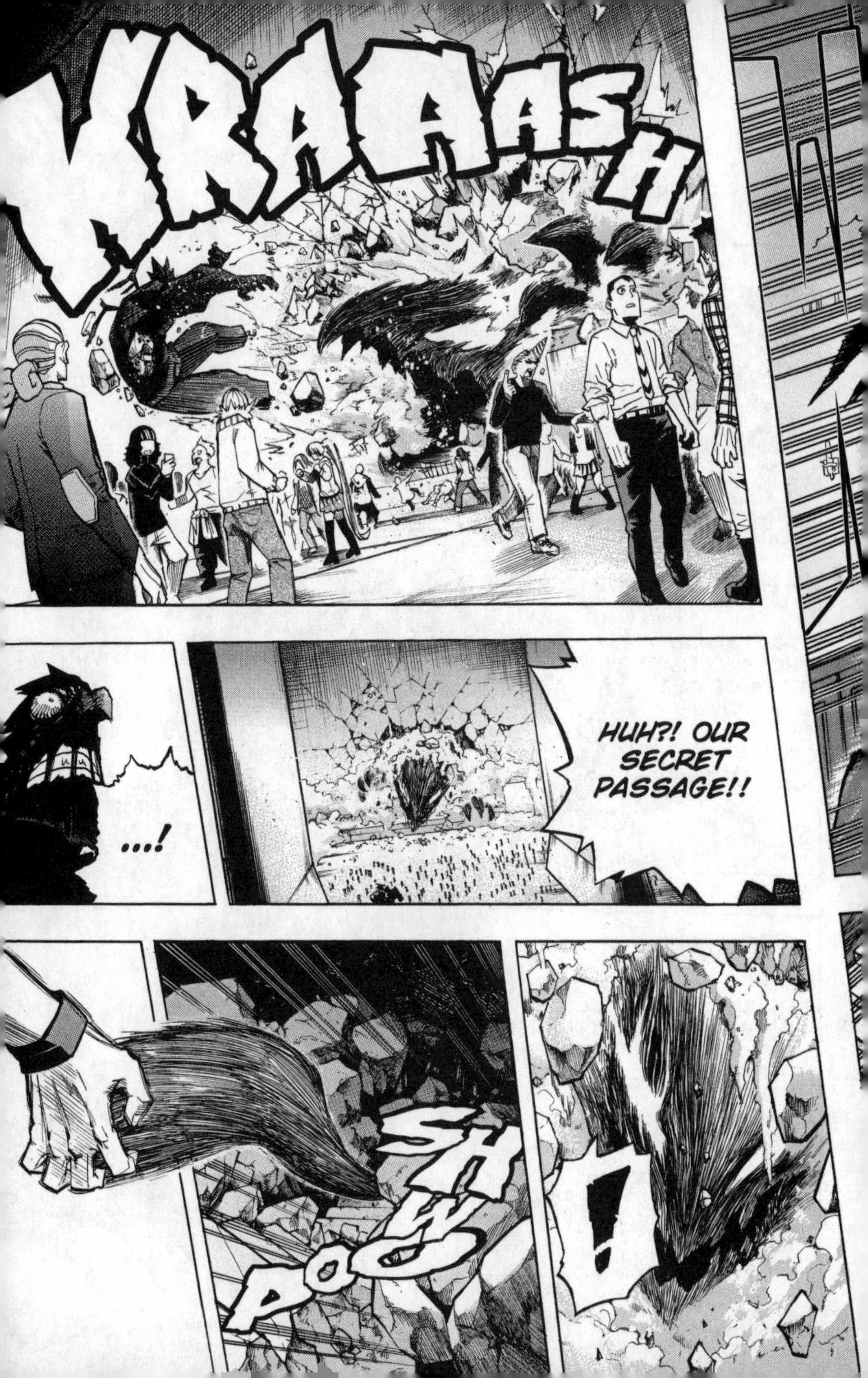
KRAASH
HUH?! OUR SECRET PASSAGE!!
...!
SHWOOP

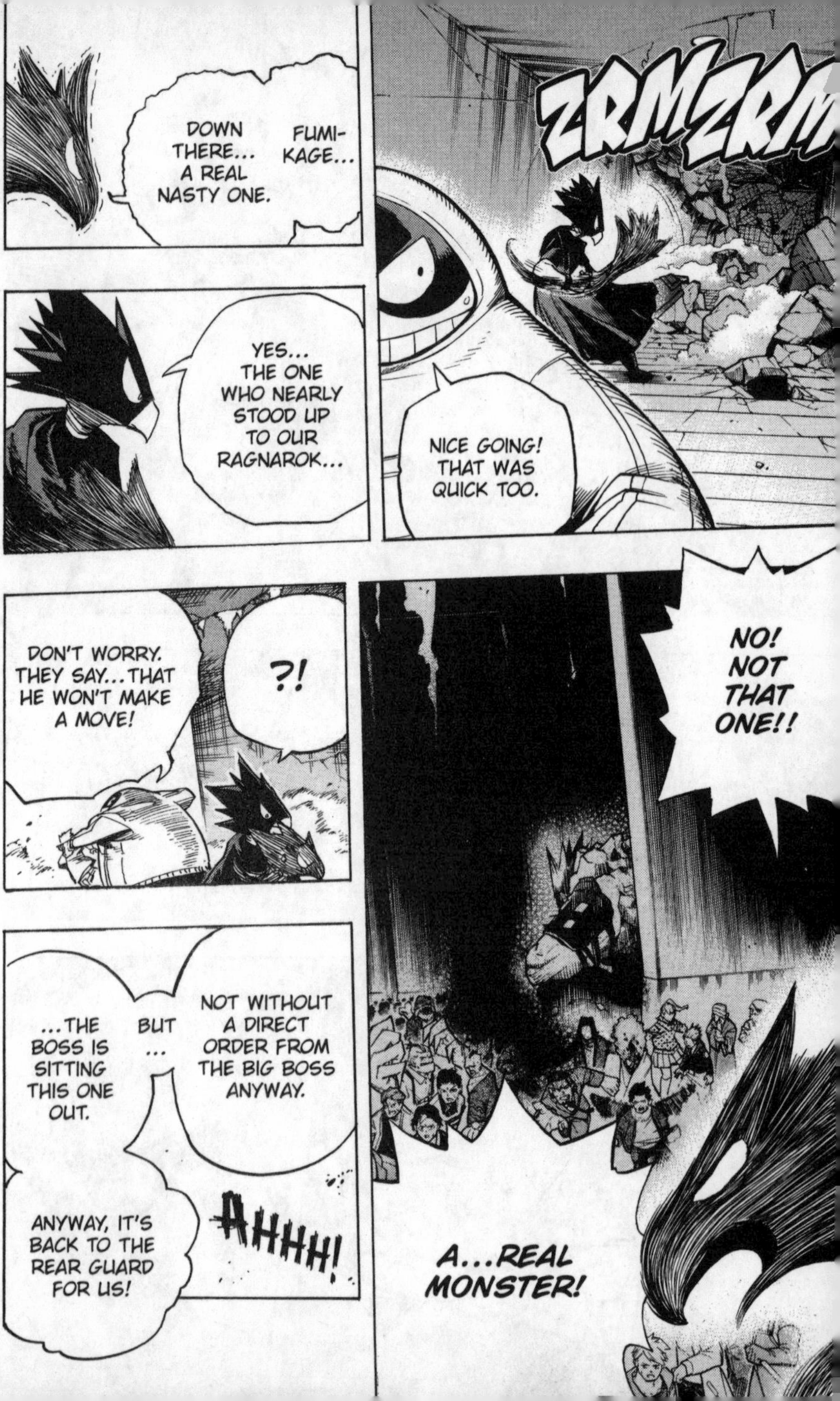
ZRM ZRM
NICE GOING! THAT WAS QUICK TOO.
FUMI-KAGE...
DOWN THERE... A REAL NASTY ONE.
YES... THE ONE WHO NEARLY STOOD UP TO OUR RAGNAROK...
NO! NOT THAT ONE!!
A...REAL MONSTER!
?!
DON'T WORRY. THEY SAY...THAT HE WON'T MAKE A MOVE!
NOT WITHOUT A DIRECT ORDER FROM THE BIG BOSS ANYWAY.
BUT...
...THE BOSS IS SITTING THIS ONE OUT.
AHHH!
ANYWAY, IT'S BACK TO THE REAR GUARD FOR US!

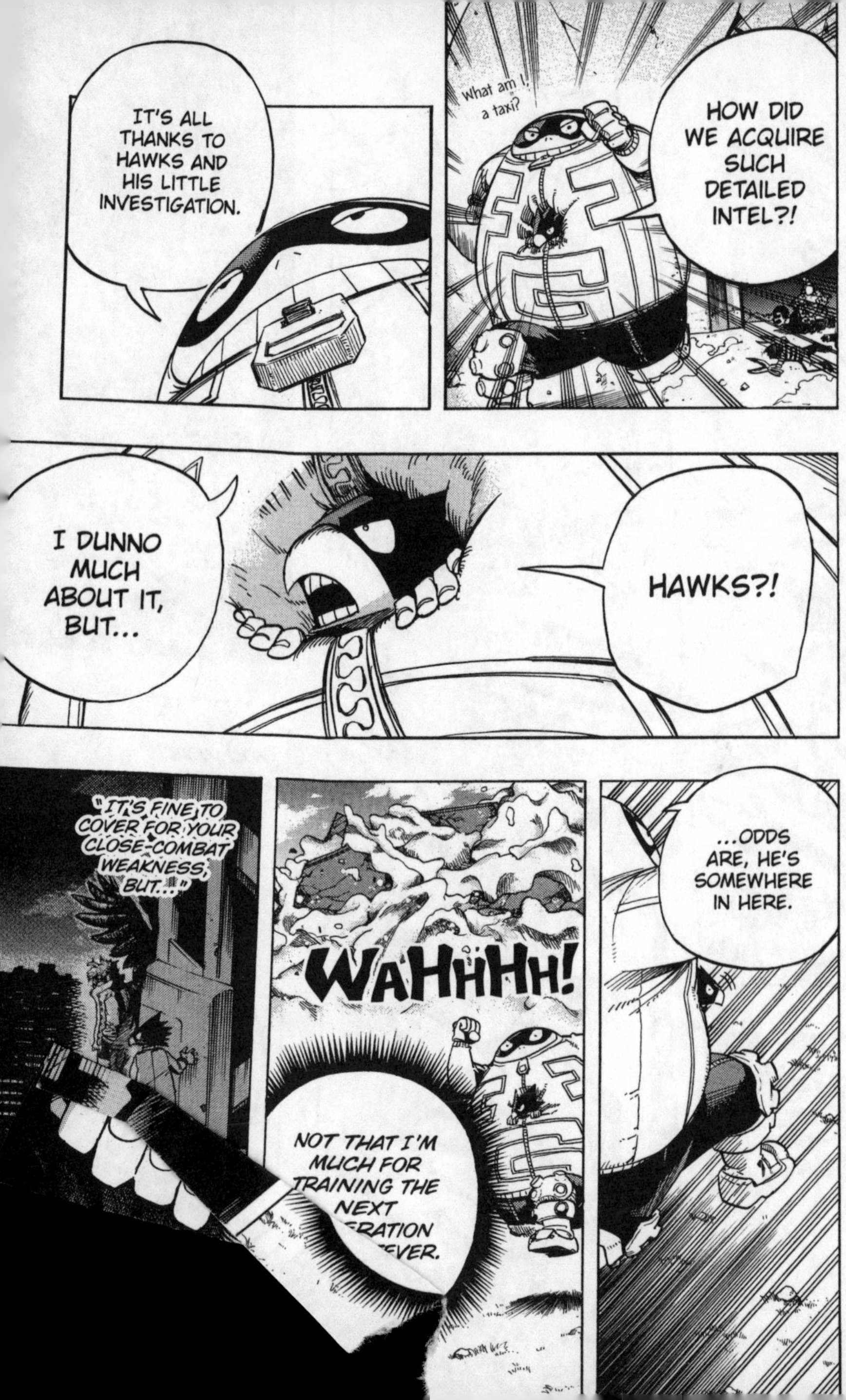

HOW DID WE ACQUIRE SUCH DETAILED INTEL?!
What am I, a taxi?
IT'S ALL THANKS TO HAWKS AND HIS LITTLE INVESTIGATION.
HAWKS?!
I DUNNO MUCH ABOUT IT, BUT...
...ODDS ARE, HE'S SOMEWHERE IN HERE.
WAHHHH!
NOT THAT I'M MUCH FOR TRAINING THE NEXT GRATION EVER.
"IT'S FINE TO COVER FOR YOUR CLOSE-COMBAT WEAKNESS, BUT..."

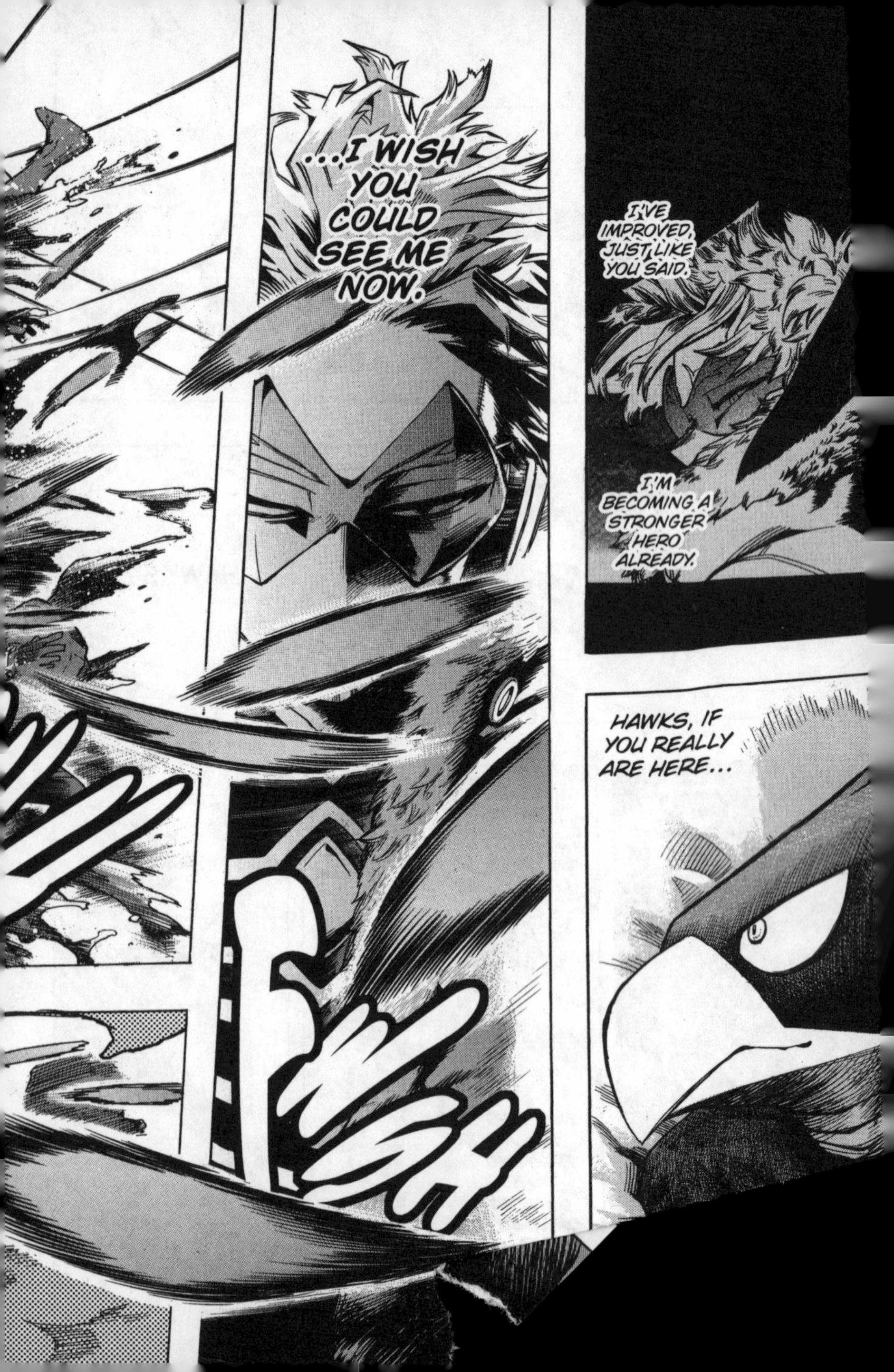
I'VE IMPROVED, JUST LIKE YOU SAID.
I'M BECOMING A STRONGER HERO ALREADY.
HAWKS, IF YOU REALLY ARE HERE...
...I WISH YOU COULD SEE ME NOW.

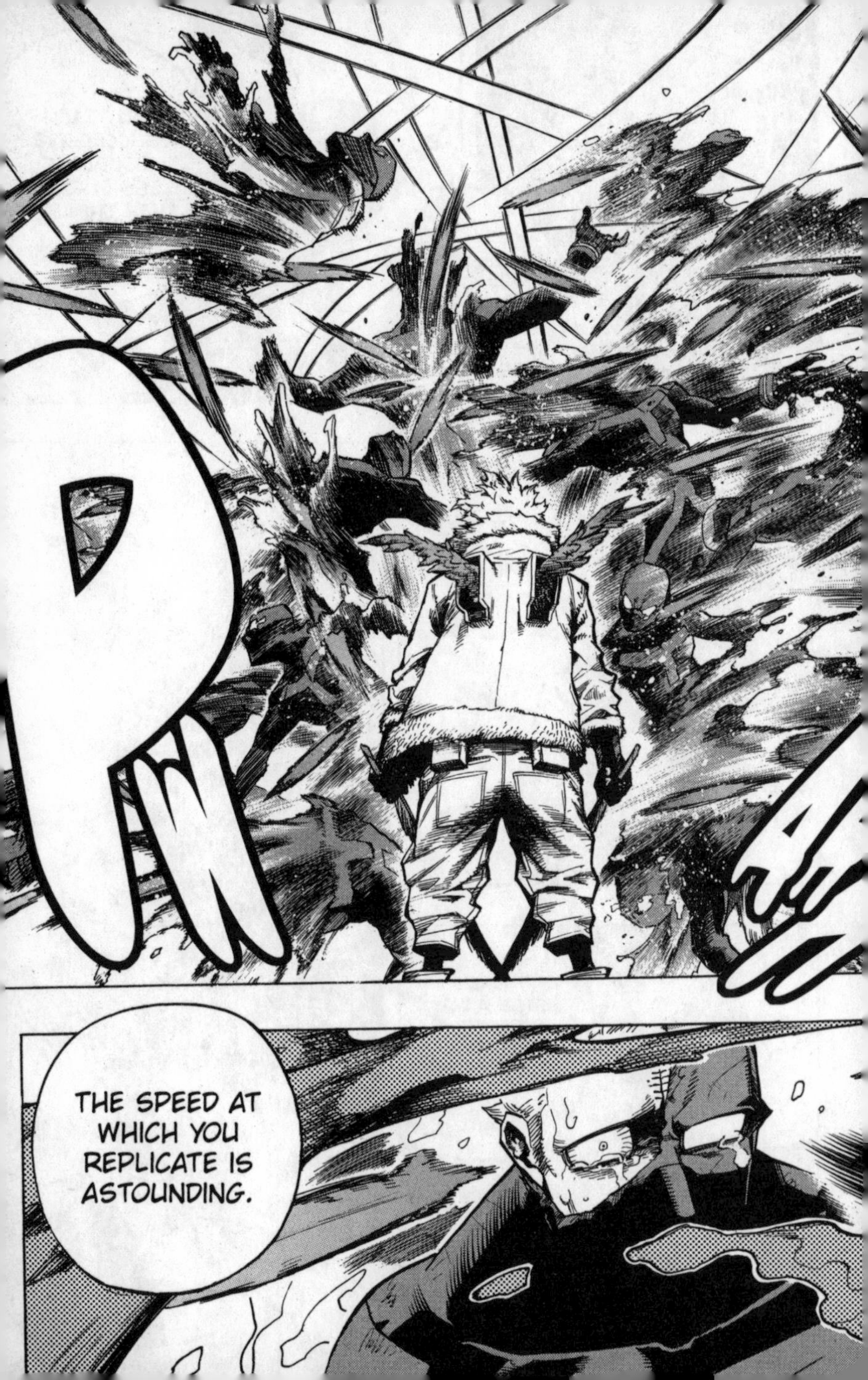
THE SPEED AT WHICH YOU REPLICATE IS ASTOUNDING.

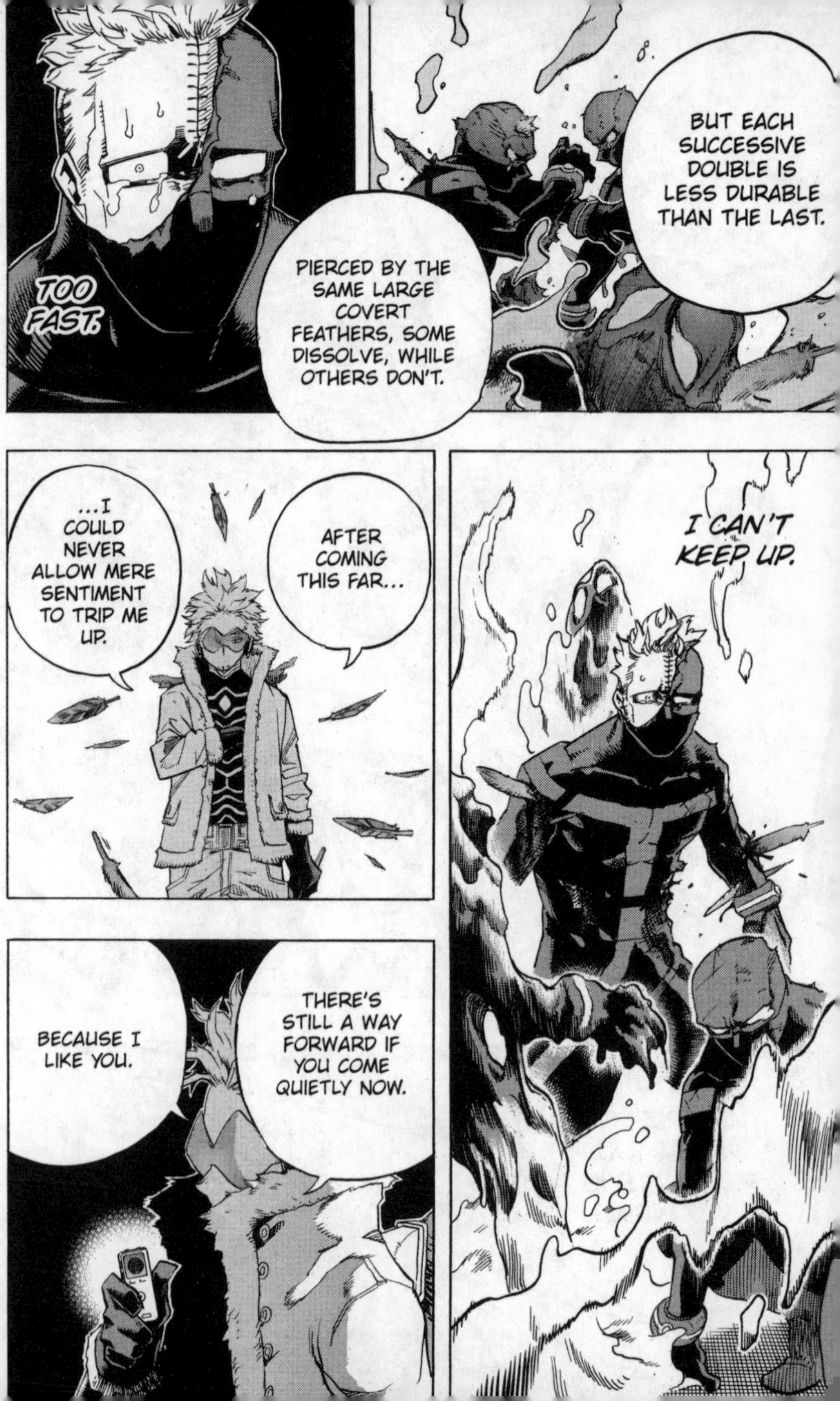
BUT EACH SUCCESSIVE DOUBLE IS LESS DURABLE THAN THE LAST.
PIERCED BY THE SAME LARGE COVERT FEATHERS, SOME DISSOLVE, WHILE OTHERS DON'T.
TOO FAST.
I CAN'T KEEP UP.
AFTER COMING THIS FAR...
...I COULD NEVER ALLOW MERE SENTIMENT TO TRIP ME UP.
THERE'S STILL A WAY FORWARD IF YOU COME QUIETLY NOW.
BECAUSE I LIKE YOU.

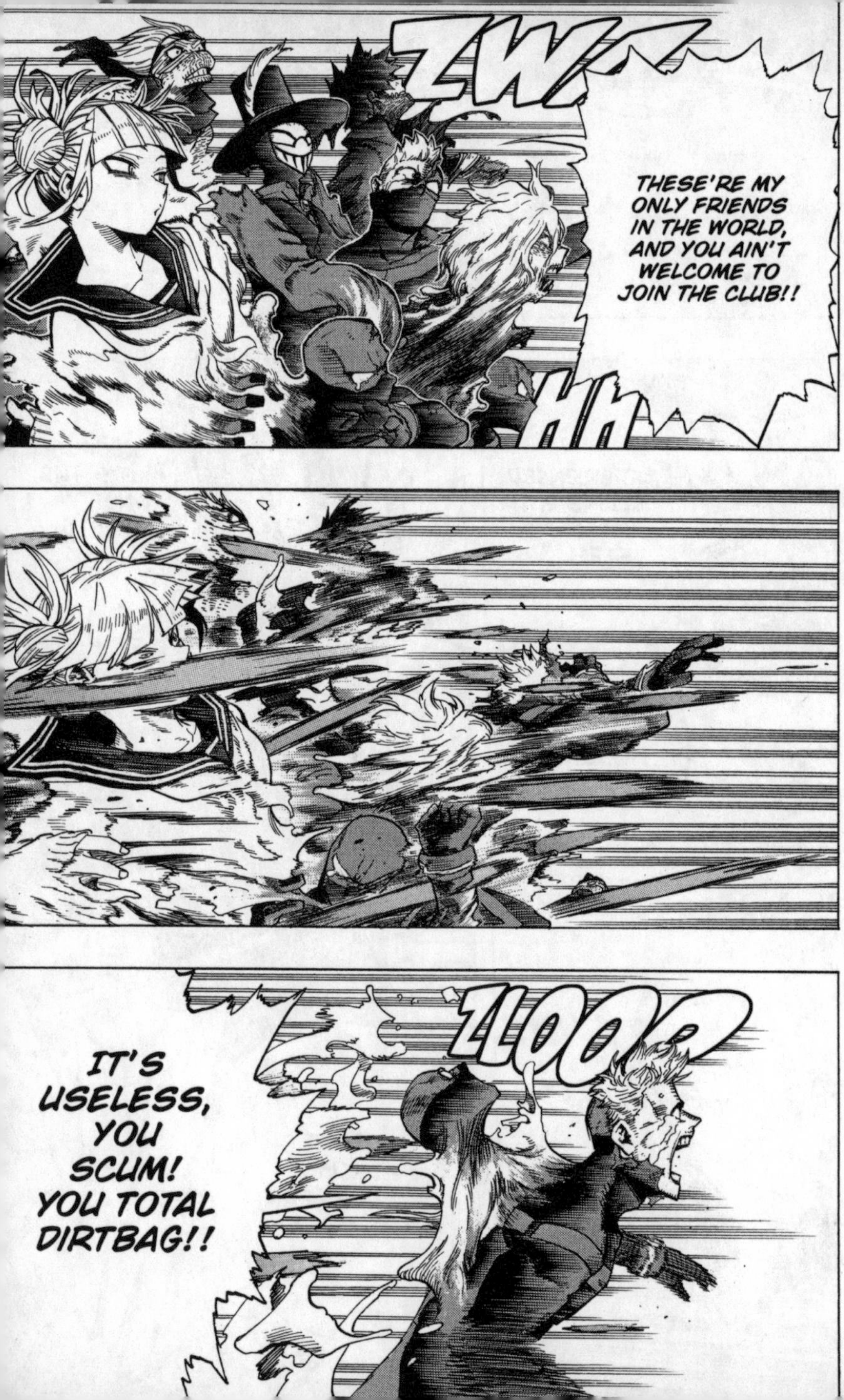
ZW
THESE'RE MY ONLY FRIENDS IN THE WORLD, AND YOU AIN'T WELCOME TO JOIN THE CLUB!!
HH
ZLOO
IT'S USELESS, YOU SCUM! YOU TOTAL DIRTBAG!!

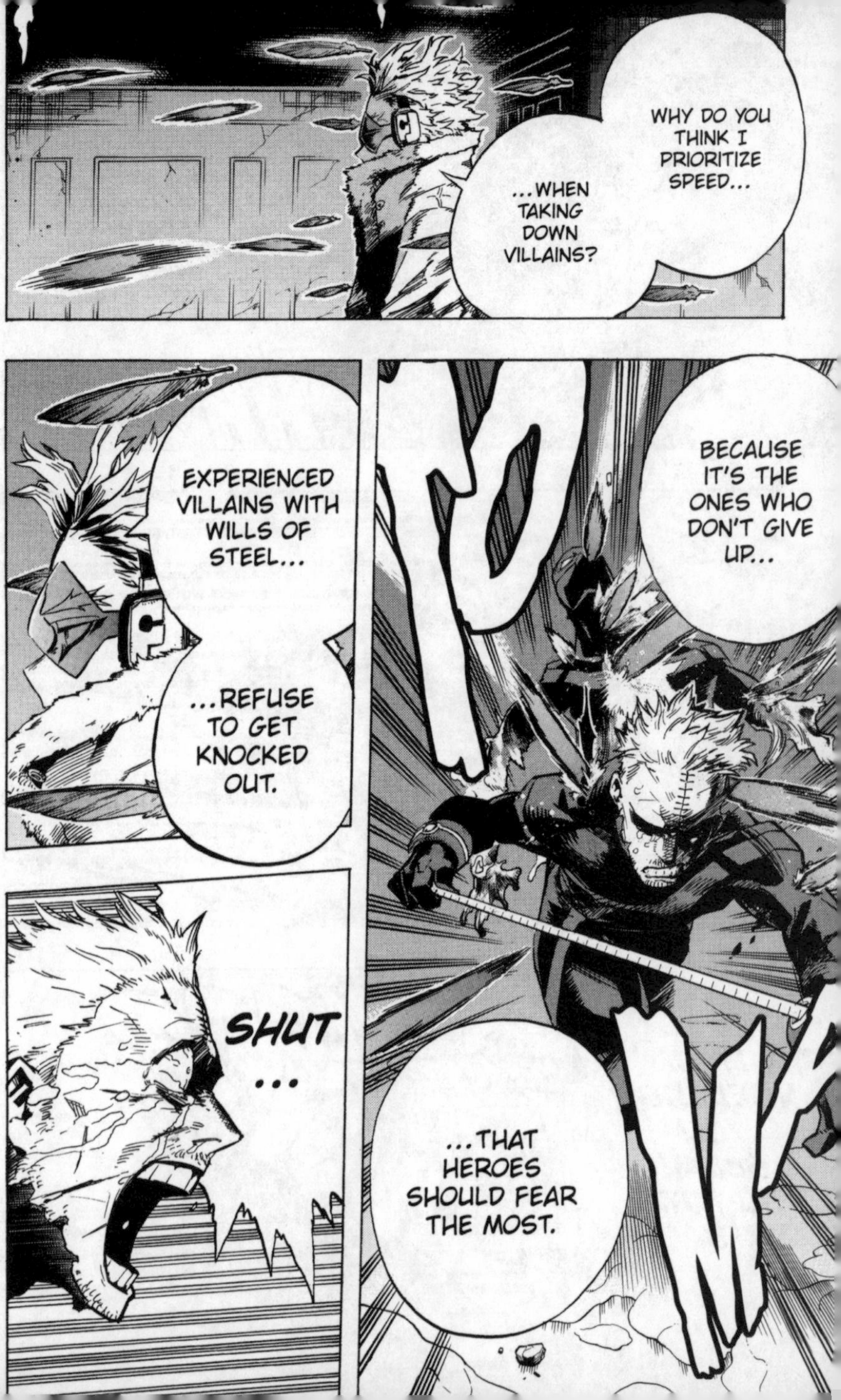
WHY DO YOU THINK I PRIORITIZE SPEED...
...WHEN TAKING DOWN VILLAINS?
BECAUSE IT'S THE ONES WHO DON'T GIVE UP...
...THAT HEROES SHOULD FEAR THE MOST.
EXPERIENCED VILLAINS WITH WILLS OF STEEL...
...REFUSE TO GET KNOCKED OUT.
SHUT ...

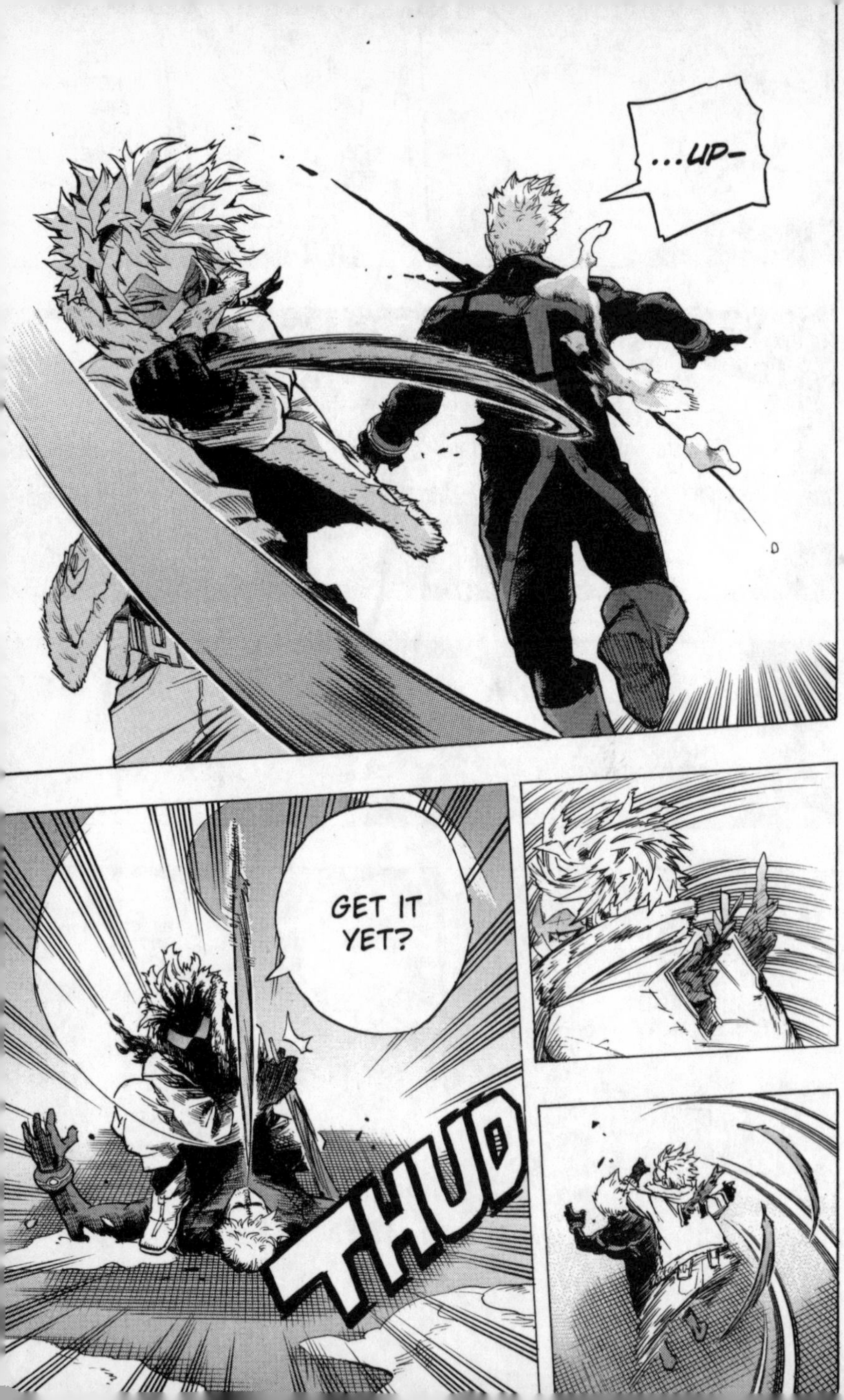
...UP-
GET IT YET?
THUD

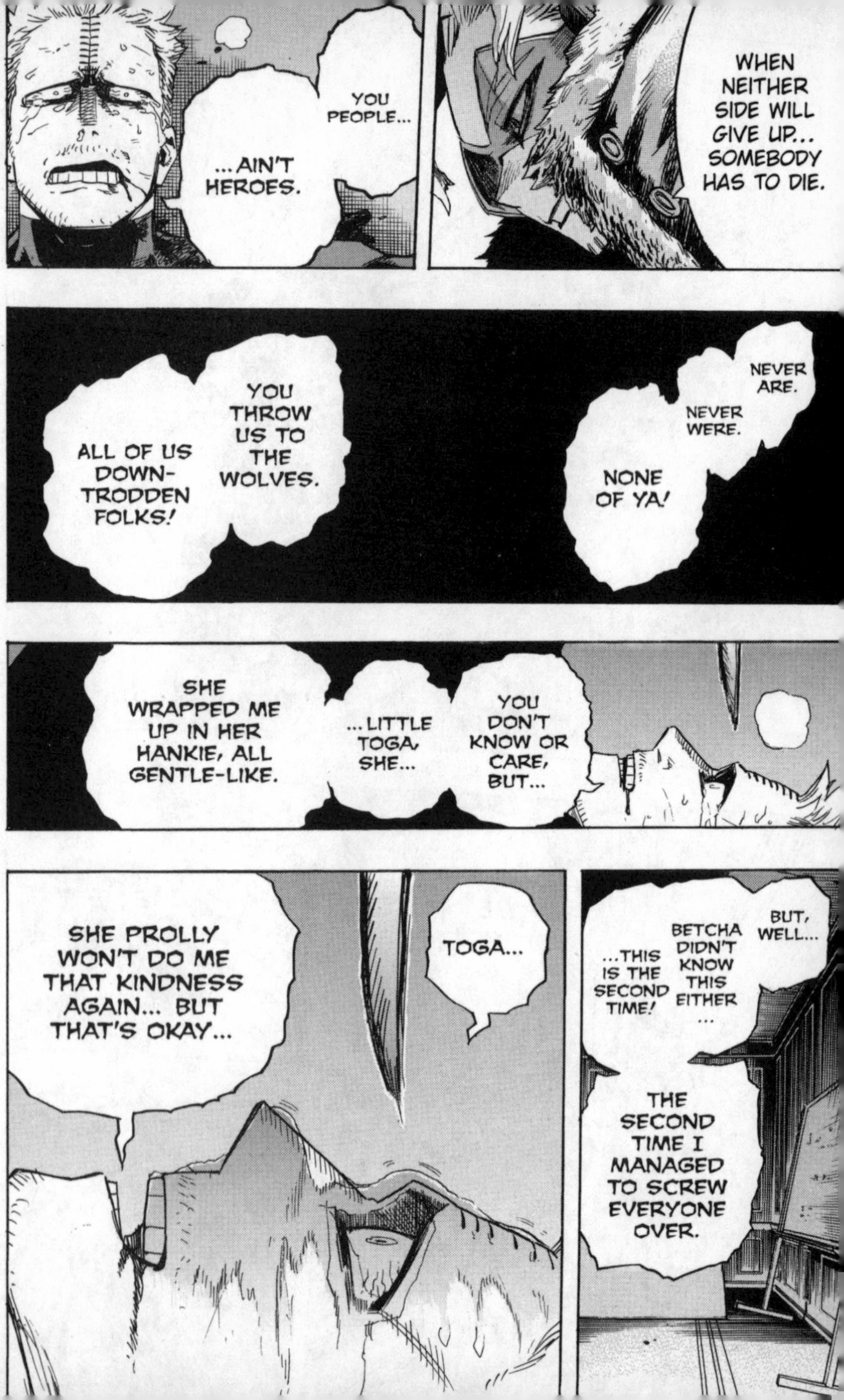
WHEN NEITHER SIDE WILL GIVE UP... SOMEBODY HAS TO DIE.
YOU PEOPLE...
...AIN'T HEROES.
NEVER ARE.
NEVER WERE.
NONE OF YA!
YOU THROW US TO THE WOLVES.
ALL OF US DOWN-TRODDEN FOLKS!
YOU DON'T KNOW OR CARE, BUT...
...LITTLE TOGA, SHE...
SHE WRAPPED ME UP IN HER HANKIE, ALL GENTLE-LIKE.
BUT, WELL...
BETCHA DIDN'T KNOW THIS EITHER...
...THIS IS THE SECOND TIME!
THE SECOND TIME I MANAGED TO SCREW EVERYONE OVER.
TOGA...
SHE PROLLY WON'T DO ME THAT KINDNESS AGAIN... BUT THAT'S OKAY...

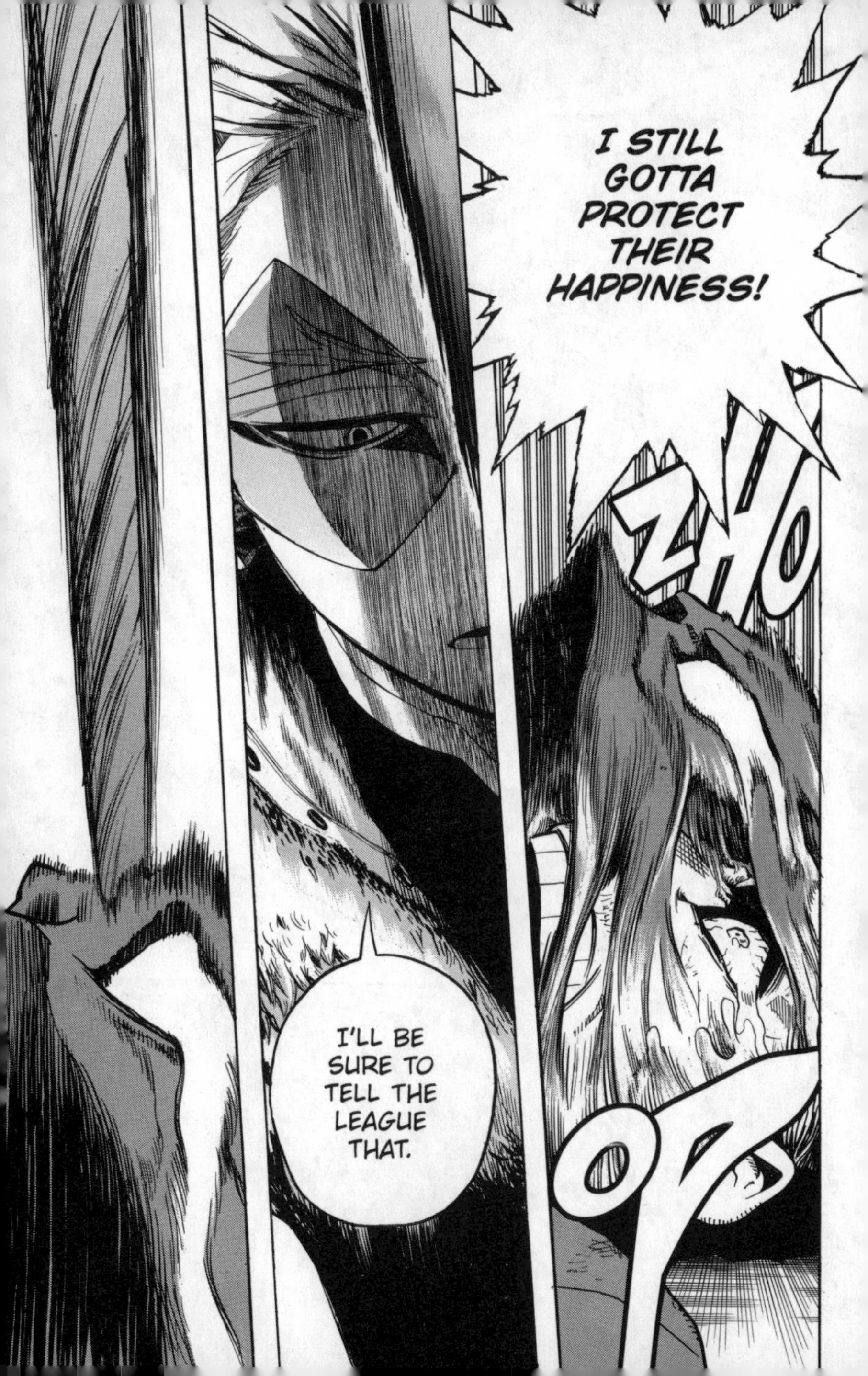
I STILL GOTTA PROTECT THEIR HAPPINESS!
ZHO
I'LL BE SURE TO TELL THE LEAGUE THAT.

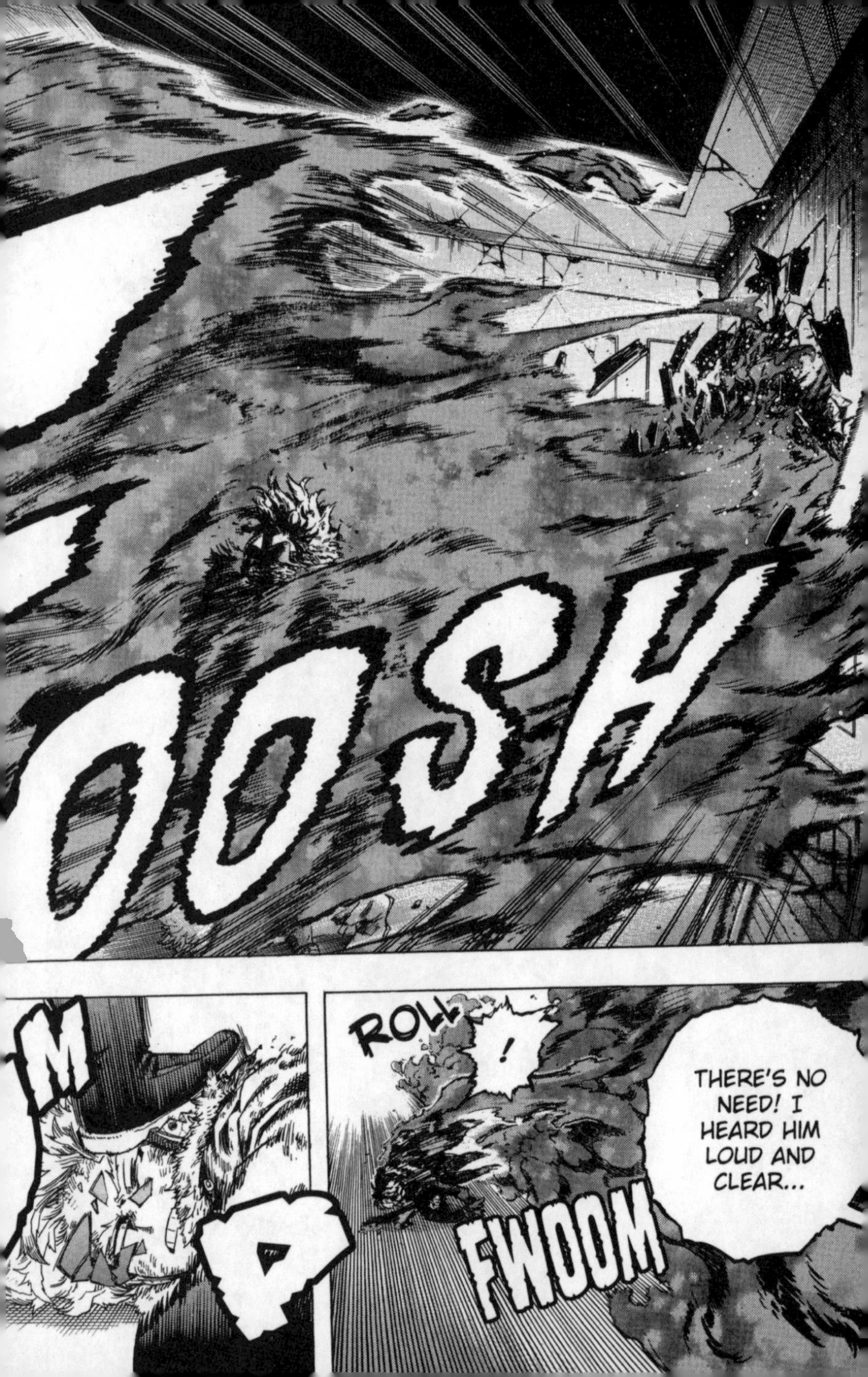
OOSH
THERE'S NO NEED! I HEARD HIM LOUD AND CLEAR...
!
ROLL
FWOOM
M
P

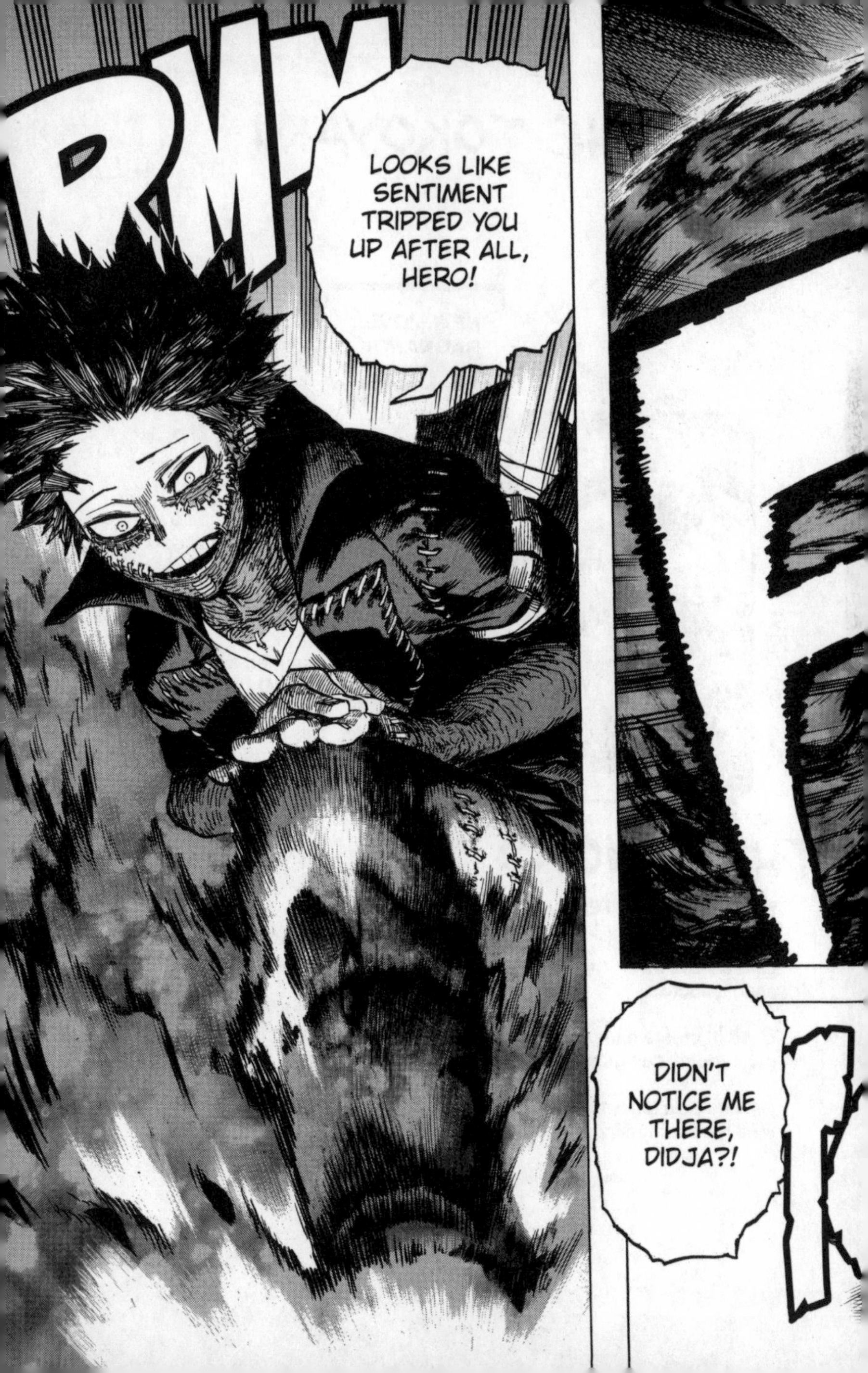
DIDN'T NOTICE ME THERE, DIDJA?!
LOOKS LIKE SENTIMENT TRIPPED YOU UP AFTER ALL, HERO!

THE TOKOYAMI

NEW MOVE: RAGNAROK

[See volume 9 ▼]

Tokoyami has learned to control the rampaging form of Dark Shadow seen in volume 9, and he uses it to great effect. This ultimate move can only be used in the dark, though, and it's nearly responsible for giving the author tendinitis of the wrist.

THE KINOKO

SHROOM-SHOOTER

A pair of spray guns.
One shoots water, and the other shoots spores.

Used to create damp ground where mushrooms can grow easily.

Despite how dinky they look, they have surprising range.

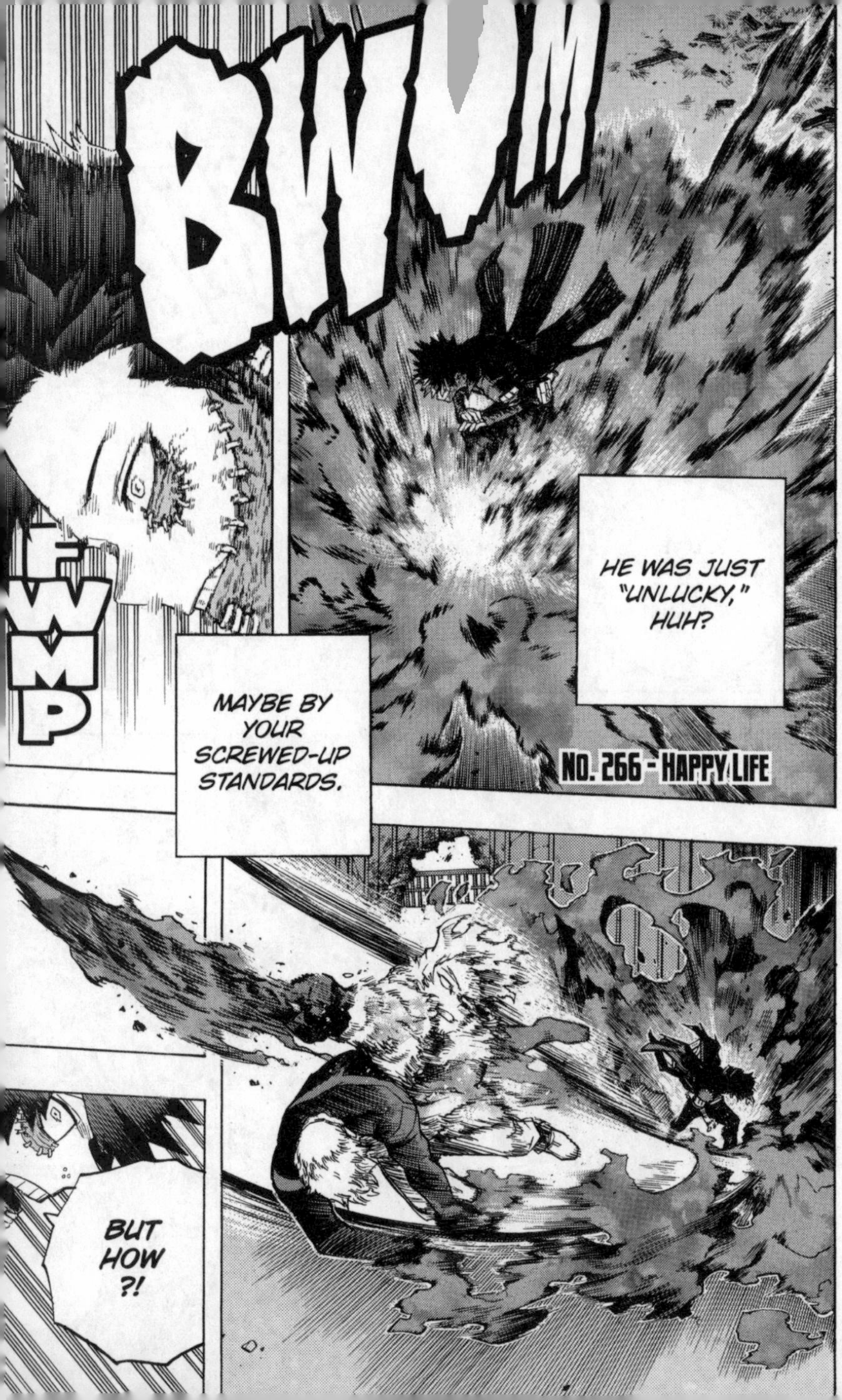
BWOM
HE WAS JUST "UNLUCKY," HUH?
No. 266 - Happy Life
FWMP
MAYBE BY YOUR SCREWED-UP STANDARDS.
BUT HOW ?!

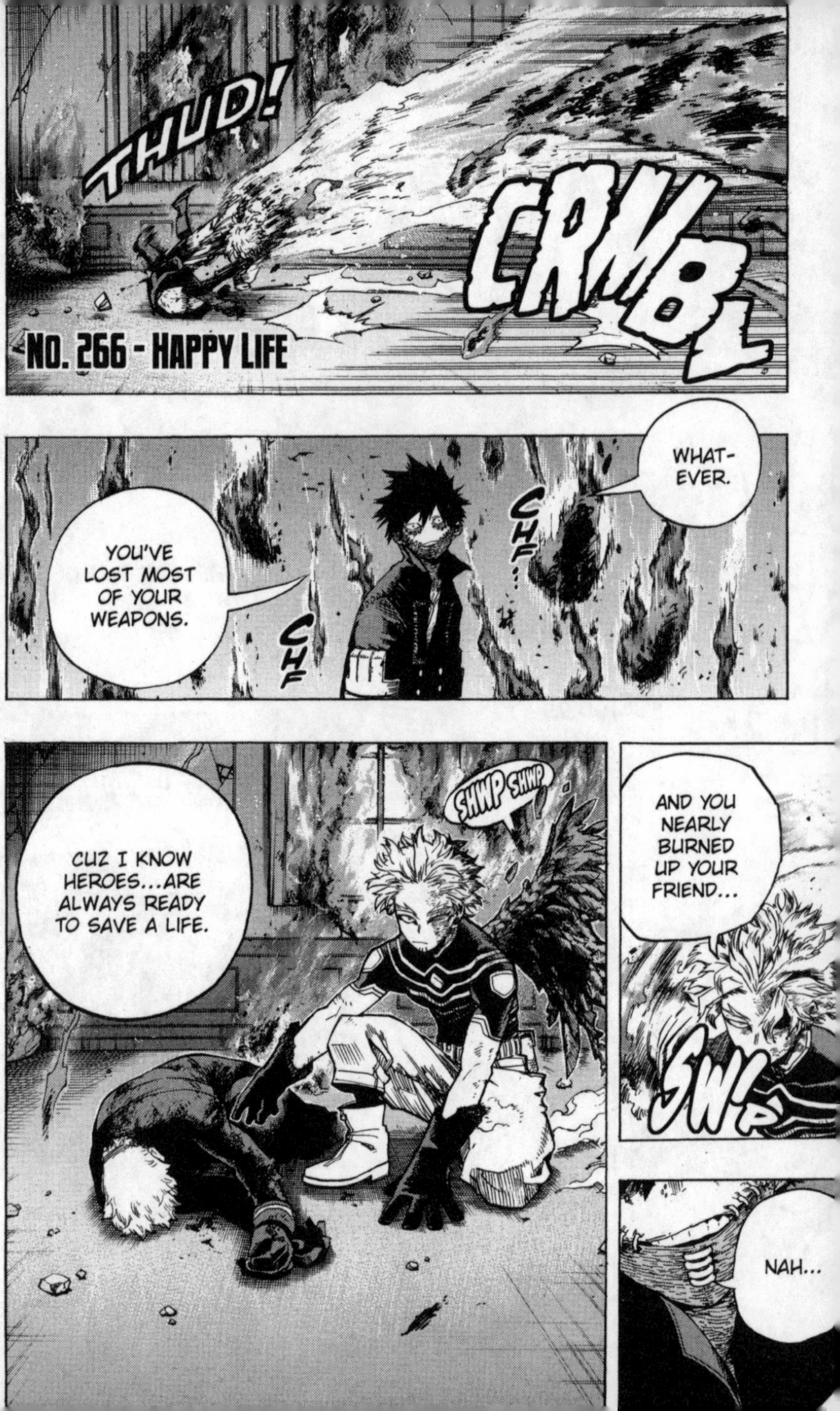

THUD!
CRMBL
No. 266 - Happy Life
WHAT-EVER.
CHF...
YOU'VE LOST MOST OF YOUR WEAPONS.
CHF CHF
AND YOU NEARLY BURNED UP YOUR FRIEND...
SW'P
NAH...
SHWP SHWP
CUZ I KNOW HEROES...ARE ALWAYS READY TO SAVE A LIFE.

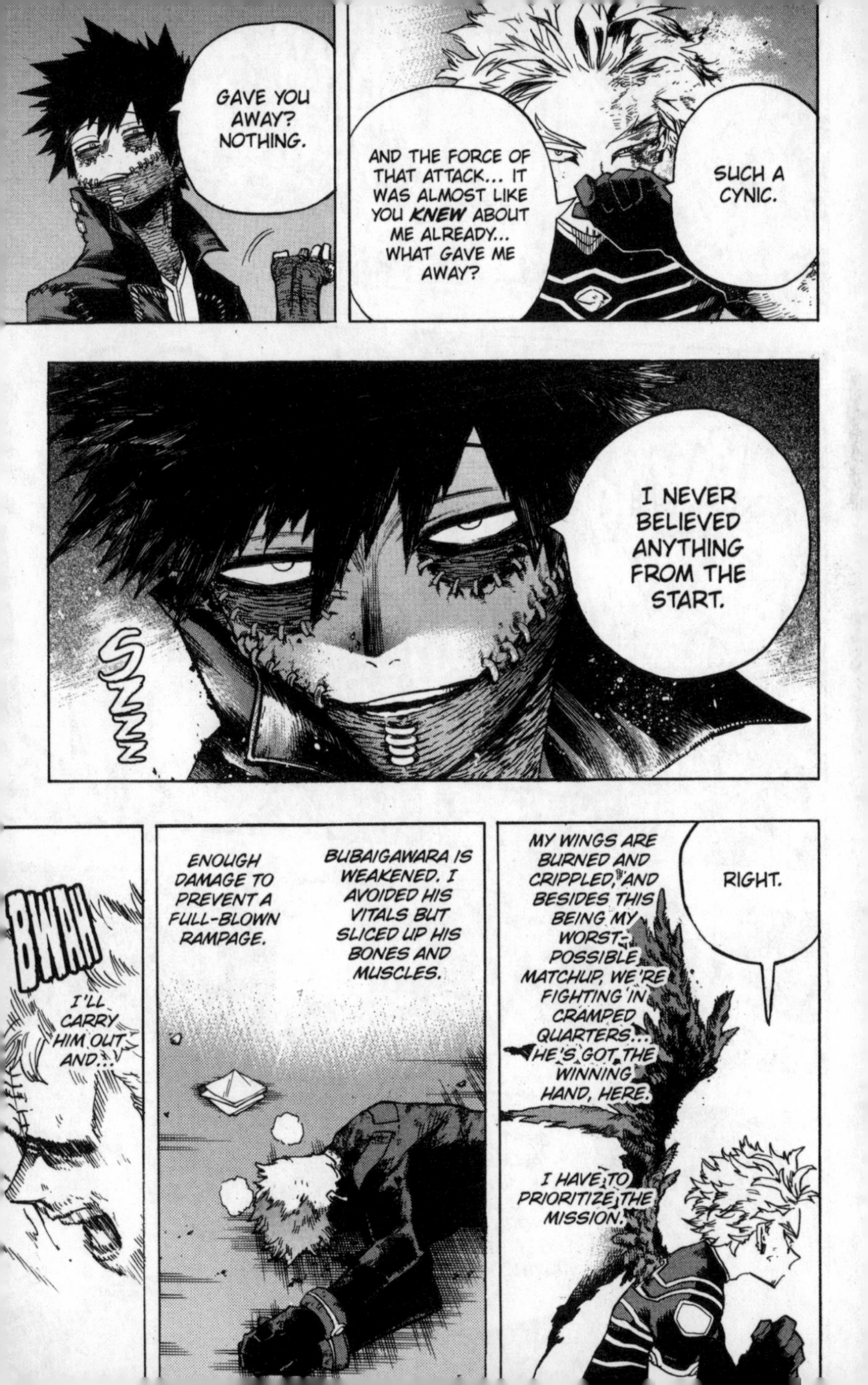
SUCH A CYNIC.
AND THE FORCE OF THAT ATTACK... IT WAS ALMOST LIKE YOU *KNEW* ABOUT ME ALREADY... WHAT GAVE ME AWAY?
GAVE YOU AWAY? NOTHING.
I NEVER BELIEVED ANYTHING FROM THE START.
SZZZ
RIGHT.
MY WINGS ARE BURNED AND CRIPPLED, AND BESIDES THIS BEING MY WORST-POSSIBLE MATCHUP, WE'RE FIGHTING IN CRAMPED QUARTERS... HE'S GOT THE WINNING HAND, HERE.
I HAVE TO PRIORITIZE THE MISSION.
BUBAIGAWARA IS WEAKENED. I AVOIDED HIS VITALS BUT SLICED UP HIS BONES AND MUSCLES.
ENOUGH DAMAGE TO PREVENT A FULL-BLOWN RAMPAGE.
BWAH
I'LL CARRY HIM OUT AND...

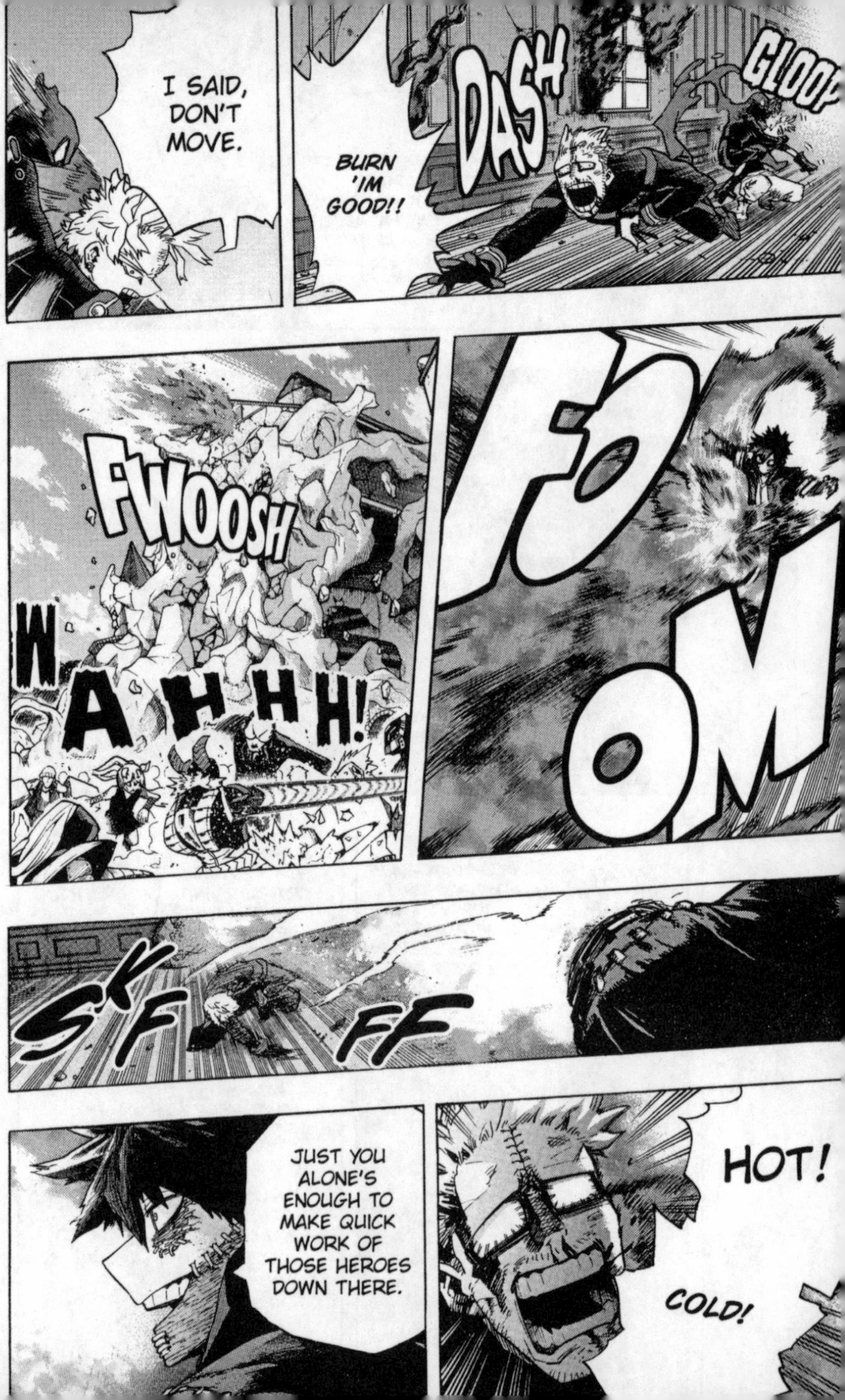
GLOOP
DASH
BURN 'IM GOOD!!
I SAID, DON'T MOVE.
FOOM
FWOOSH
WAHHH!
SKFFF
HOT!
COLD!
JUST YOU ALONE'S ENOUGH TO MAKE QUICK WORK OF THOSE HEROES DOWN THERE.

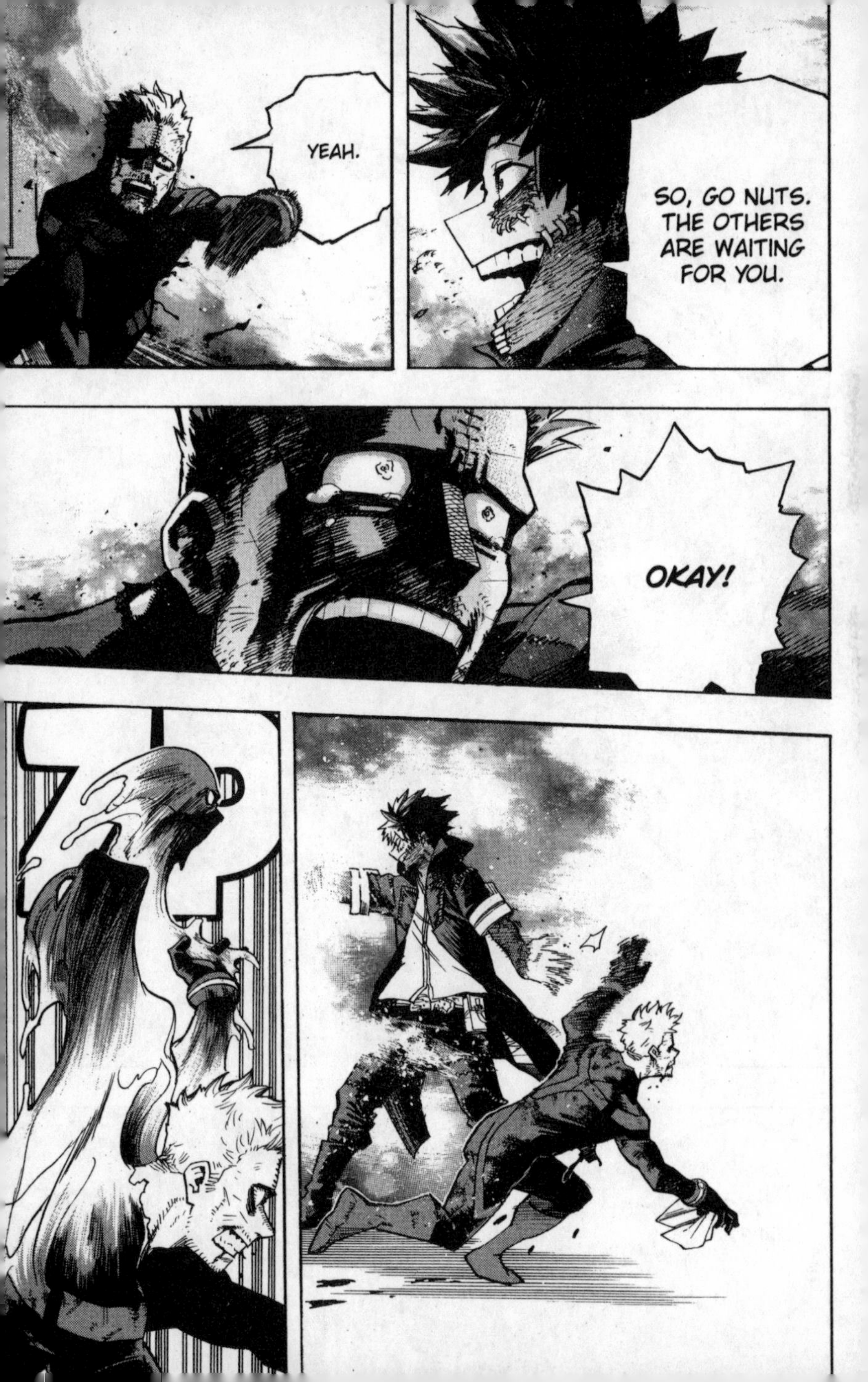
SO, GO NUTS. THE OTHERS ARE WAITING FOR YOU.
YEAH.
OKAY!

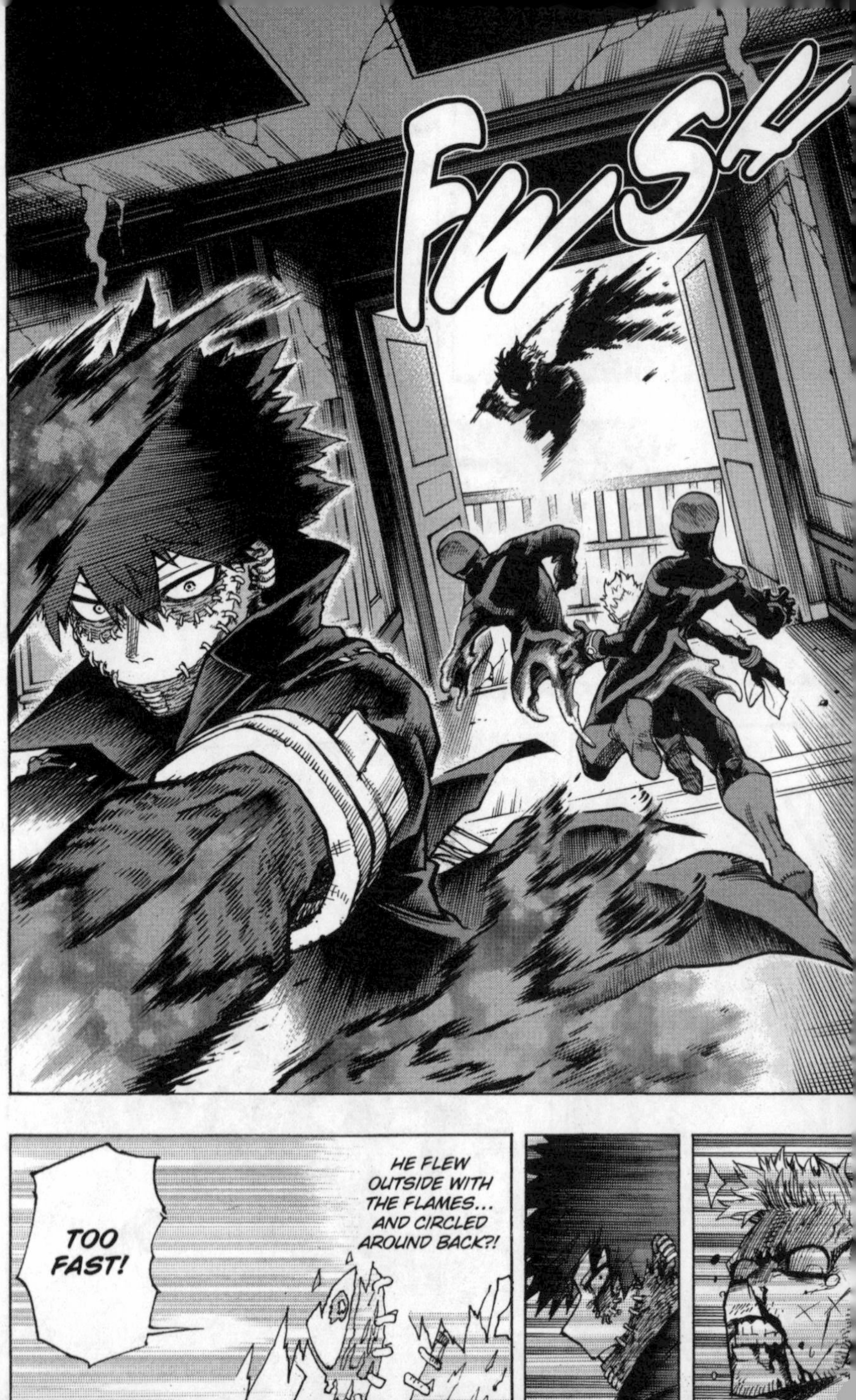
FWSH
HE FLEW OUTSIDE WITH THE FLAMES... AND CIRCLED AROUND BACK?!
TOO FAST!

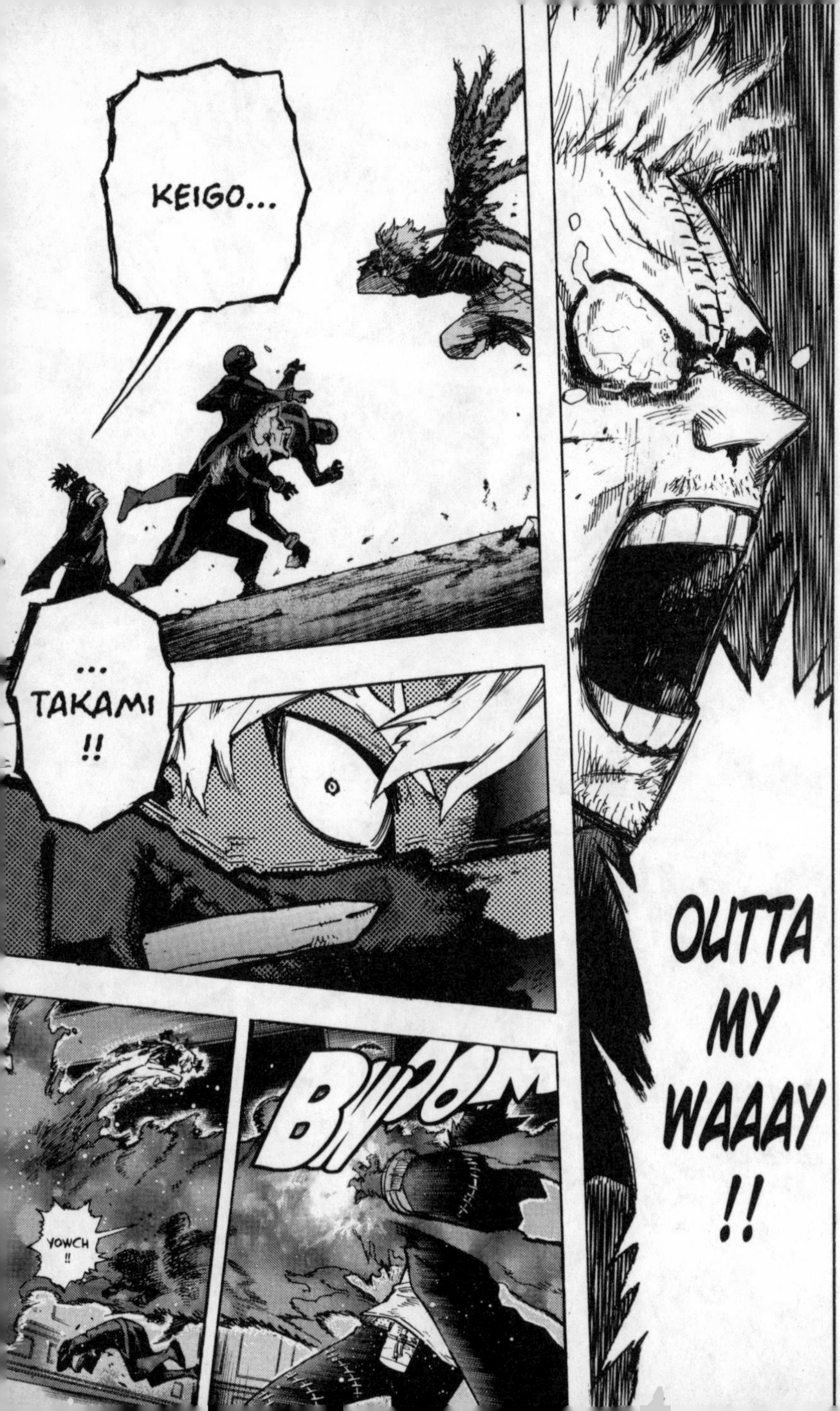
OUTTA MY WAAAY!!
KEIGO...
...TAKAMI!!
BWOOM
YOWCH!!

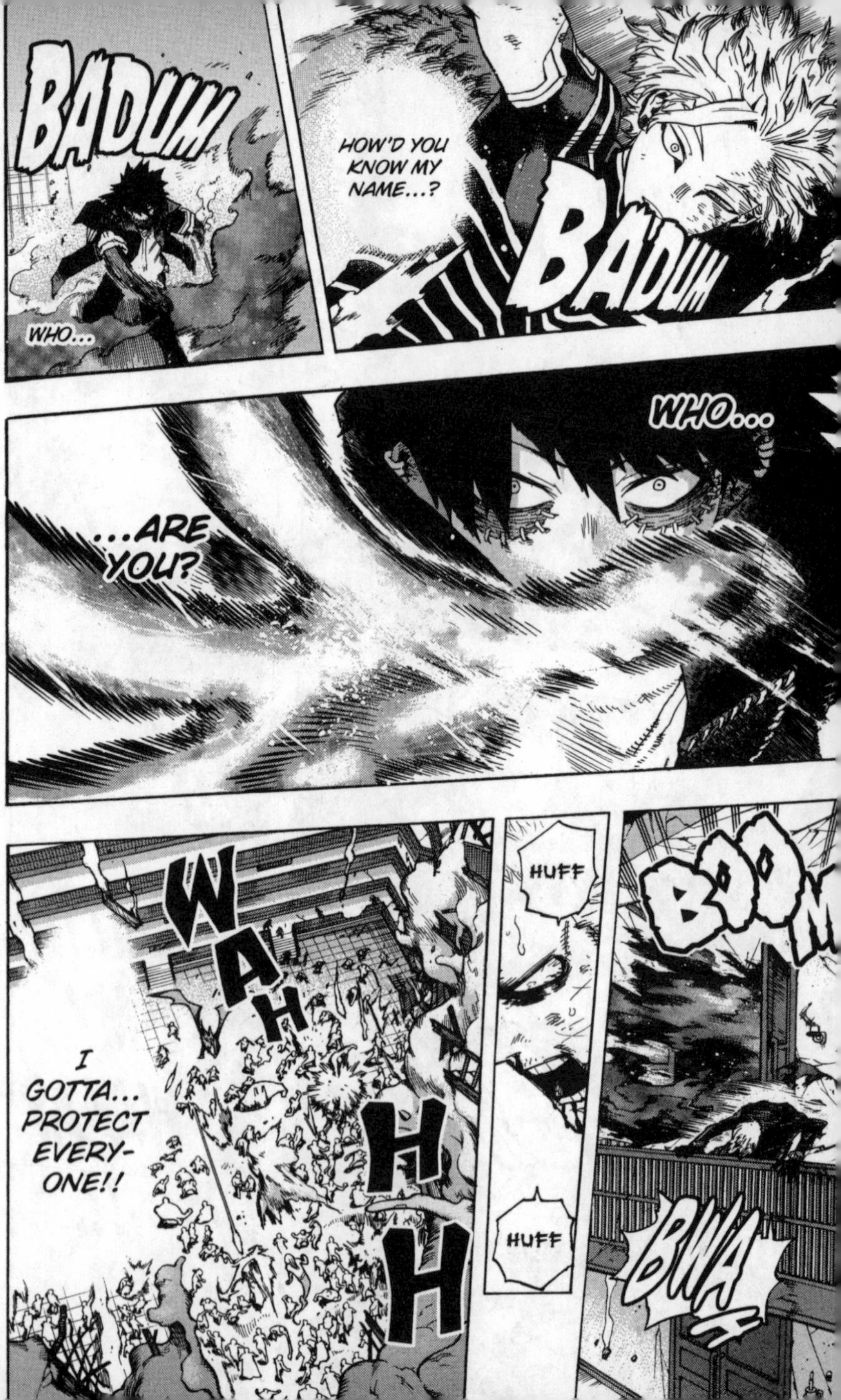
HOW'D YOU KNOW MY NAME...?
BADUM
BADUM
WHO...
WHO...
...ARE YOU?
BOOM
BWAH
HUFF
HUFF
WAHHH
I GOTTA... PROTECT EVERY-ONE!!

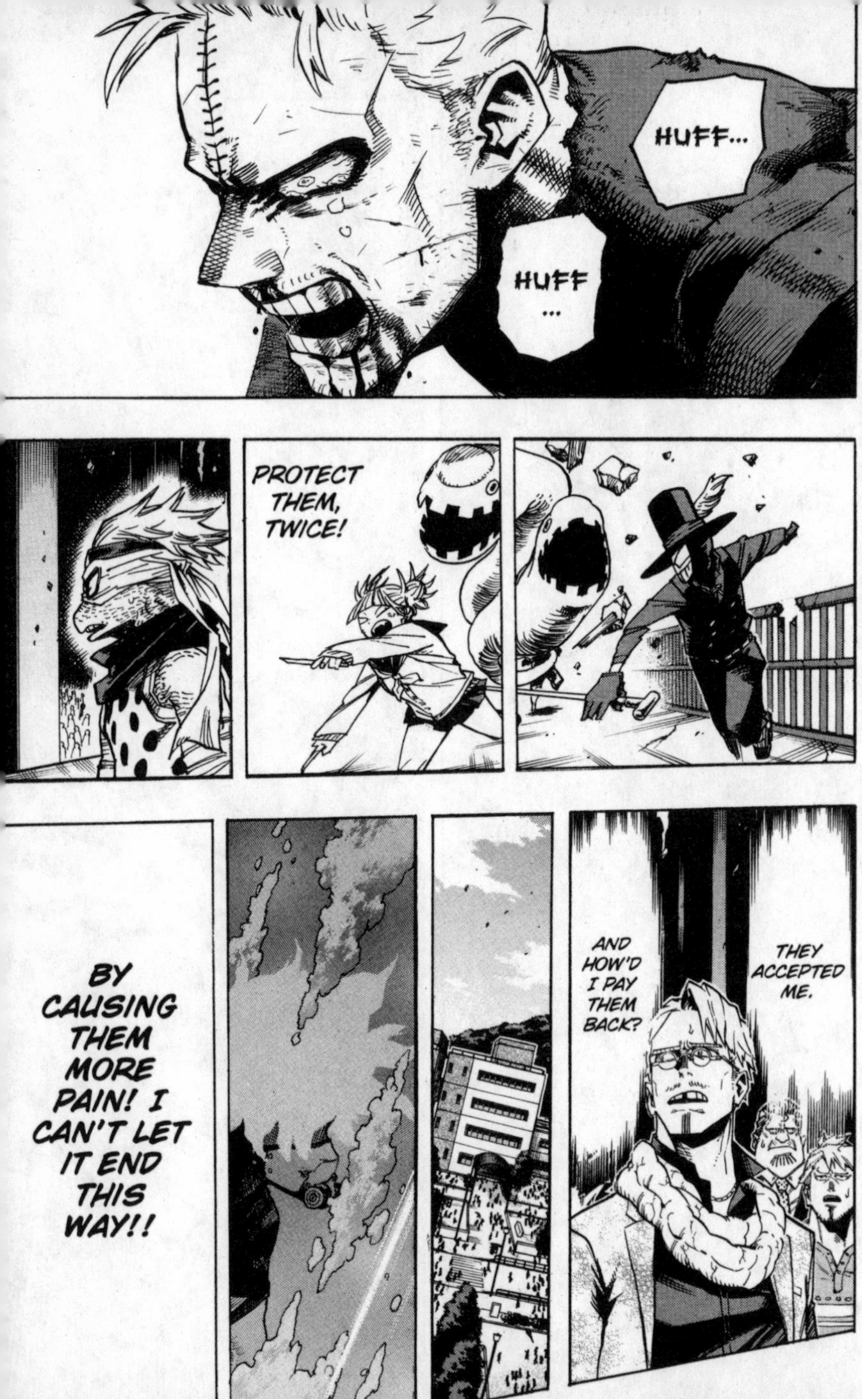
HUFF...
HUFF ...
PROTECT THEM, TWICE!
THEY ACCEPTED ME.
AND HOW'D I PAY THEM BACK?
BY CAUSING THEM MORE PAIN! I CAN'T LET IT END THIS WAY!!

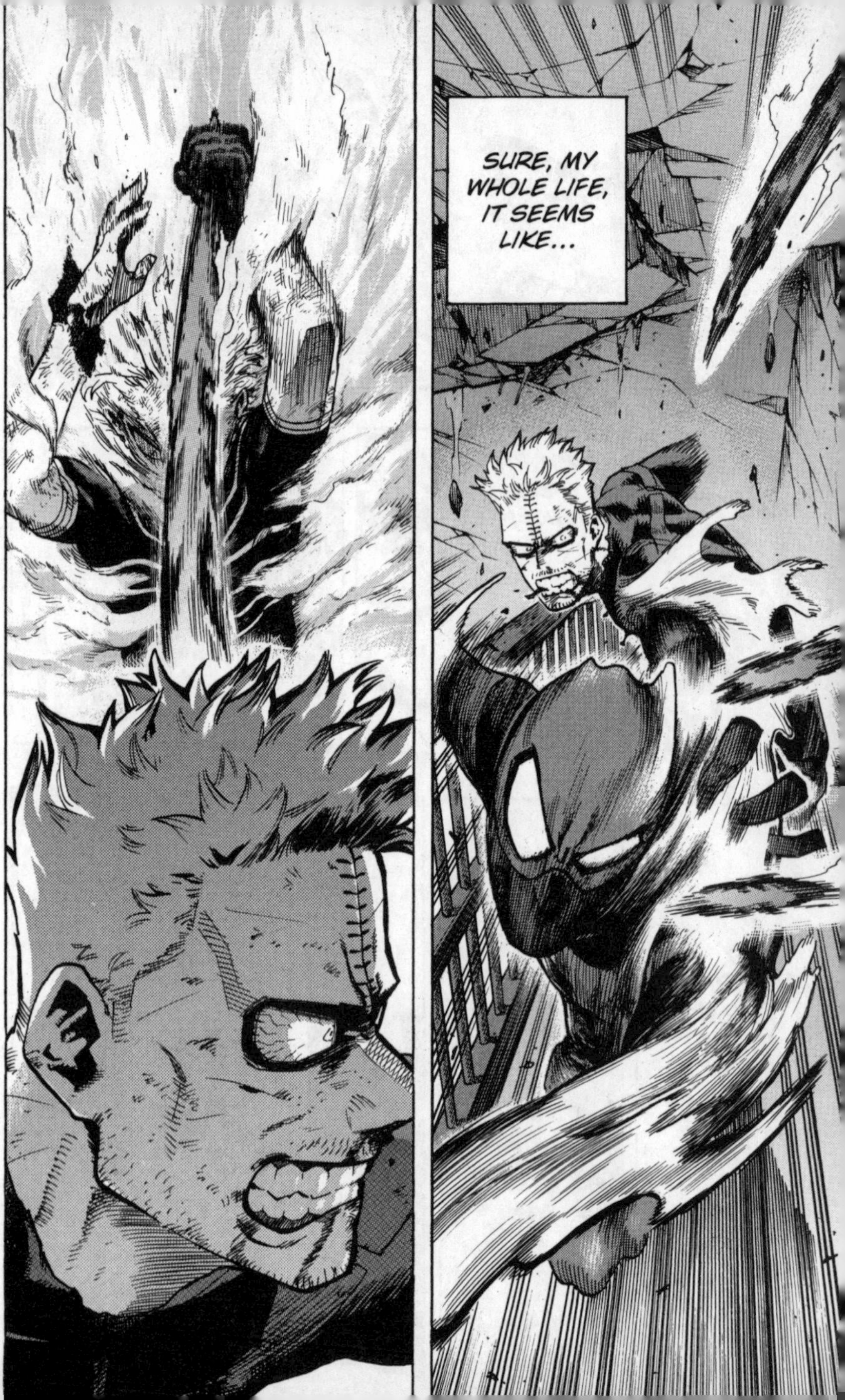
SURE, MY WHOLE LIFE, IT SEEMS LIKE...

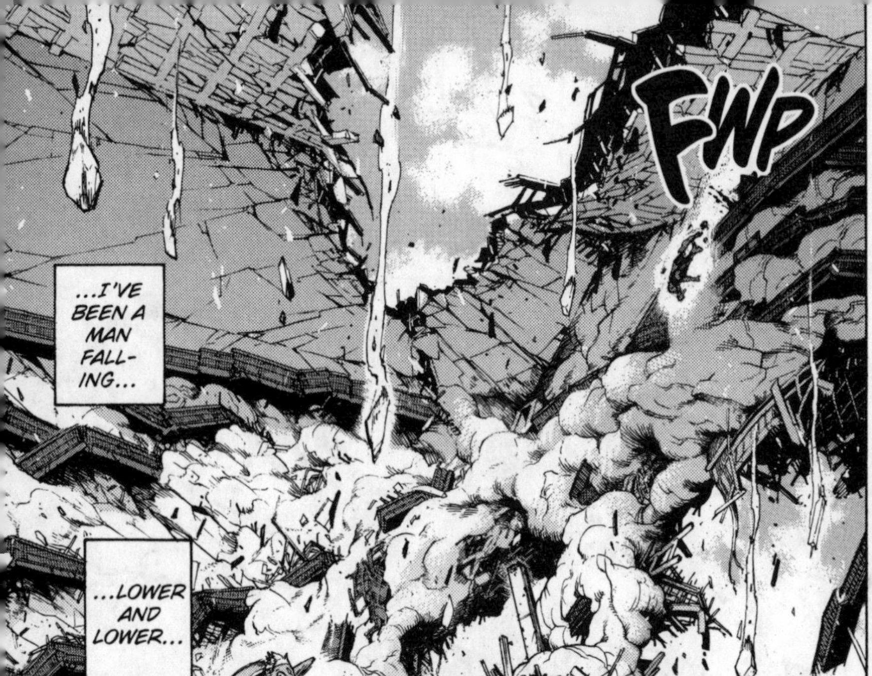
FWP
...I'VE BEEN A MAN FALLING...
...LOWER AND LOWER...
GETTING DUPED.
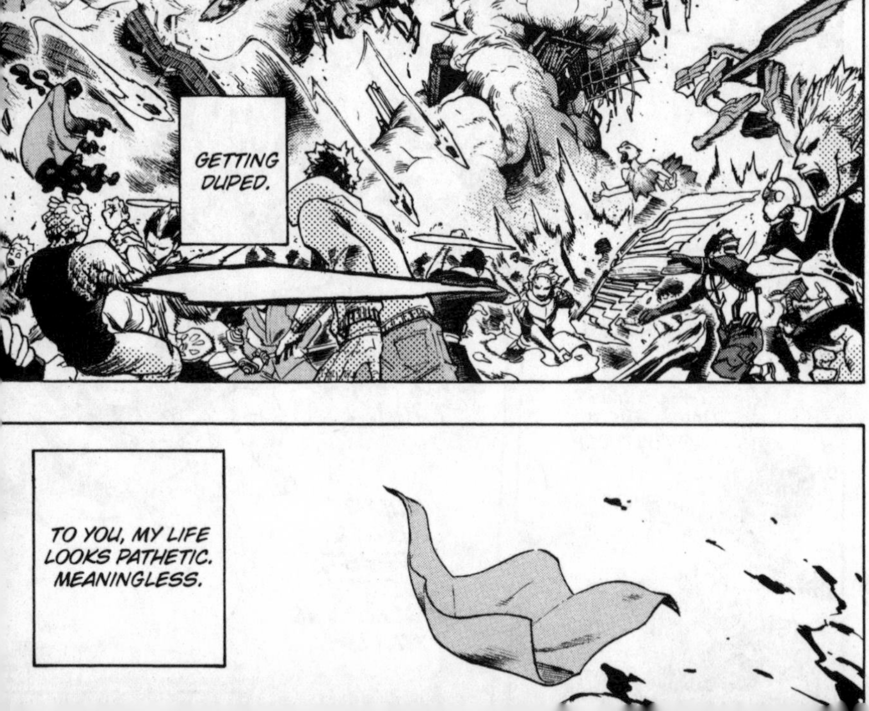
TO YOU, MY LIFE LOOKS PATHETIC. MEANINGLESS.

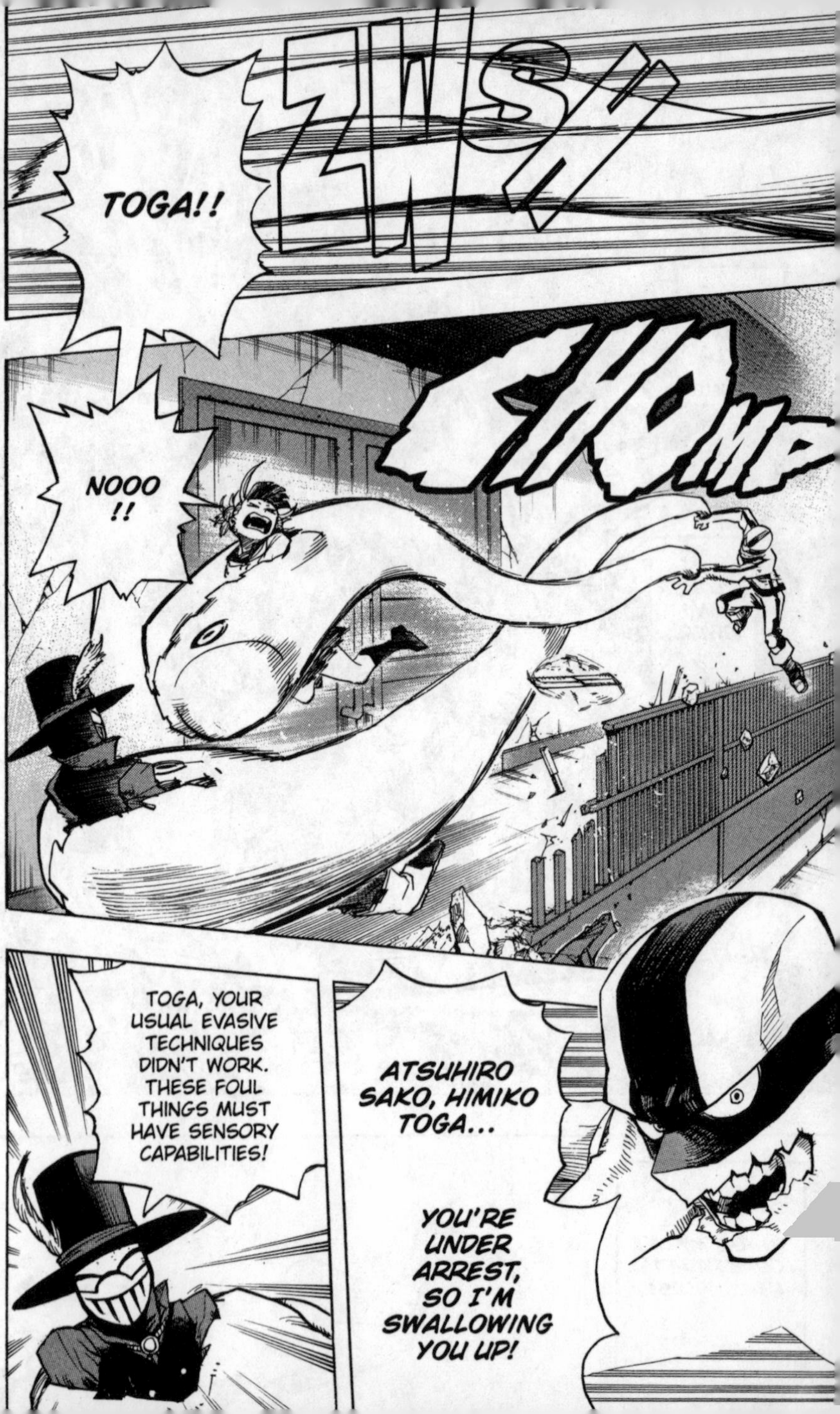
ZWSH
TOGA!!
THOMP
NOOO!!
ATSUHIRO SAKO, HIMIKO TOGA...
YOU'RE UNDER ARREST, SO I'M SWALLOWING YOU UP!
TOGA, YOUR USUAL EVASIVE TECHNIQUES DIDN'T WORK. THESE FOUL THINGS MUST HAVE SENSORY CAPABILITIES!

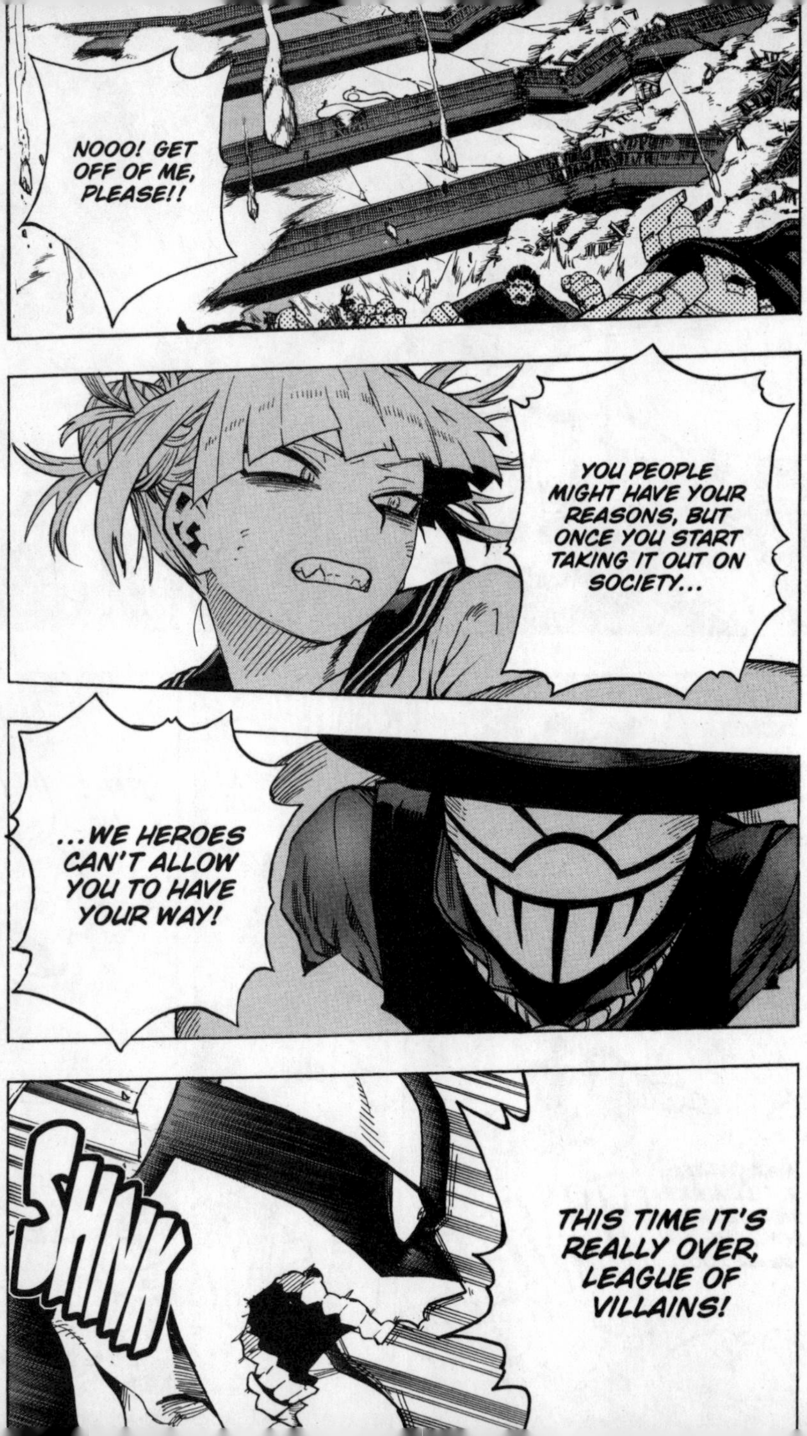
NOOO! GET OFF OF ME, PLEASE!!
YOU PEOPLE MIGHT HAVE YOUR REASONS, BUT ONCE YOU START TAKING IT OUT ON SOCIETY...
...WE HEROES CAN'T ALLOW YOU TO HAVE YOUR WAY!
THIS TIME IT'S REALLY OVER, LEAGUE OF VILLAINS!
SHINK

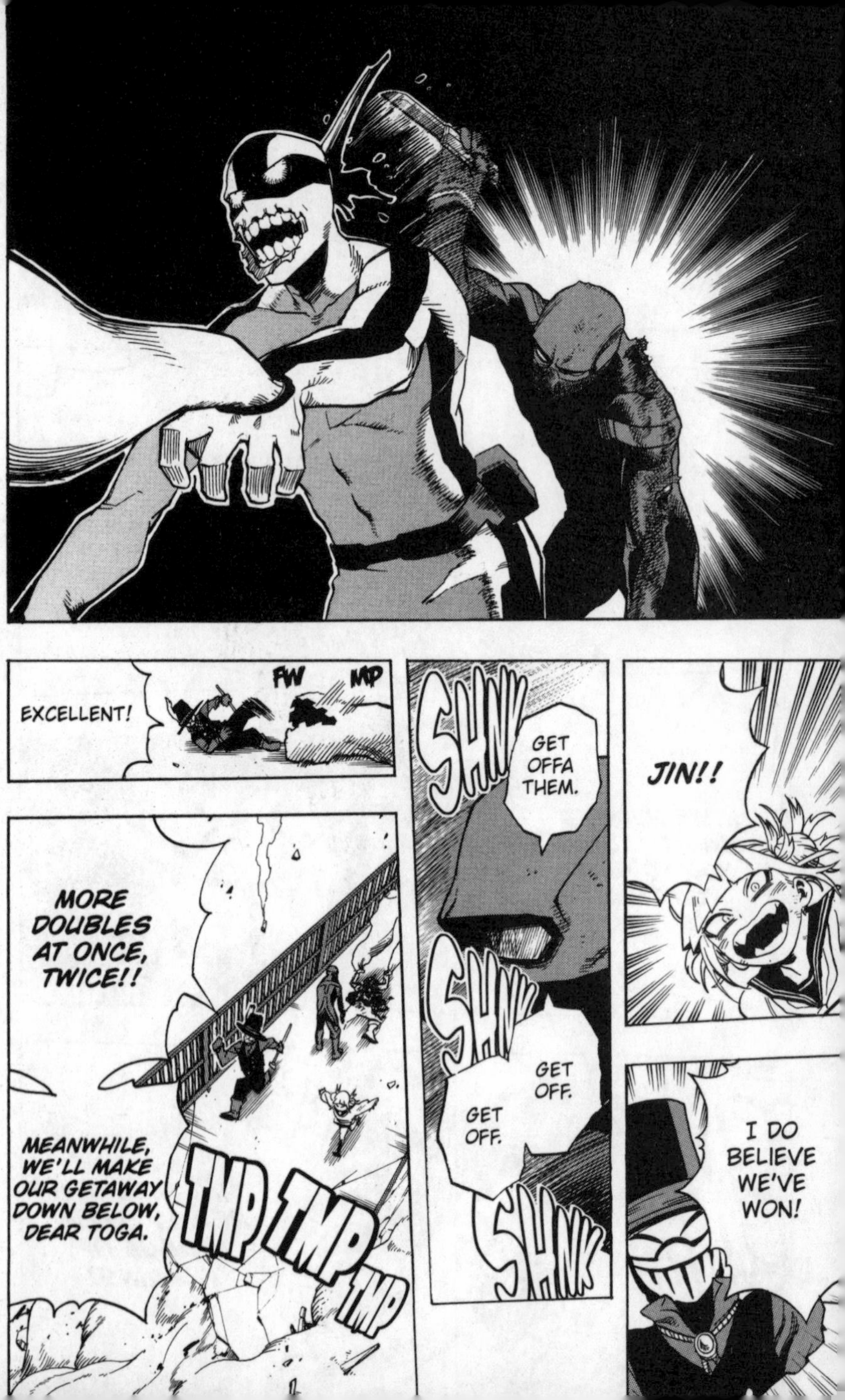
JIN!!
I DO BELIEVE WE'VE WON!
SHNK
GET OFFA THEM.
SHNK
GET OFF.
GET OFF.
SHNK
EXCELLENT!
FWMP
MORE DOUBLES AT ONCE, TWICE!!
MEANWHILE, WE'LL MAKE OUR GETAWAY DOWN BELOW, DEAR TOGA.
TMP TMP TMP

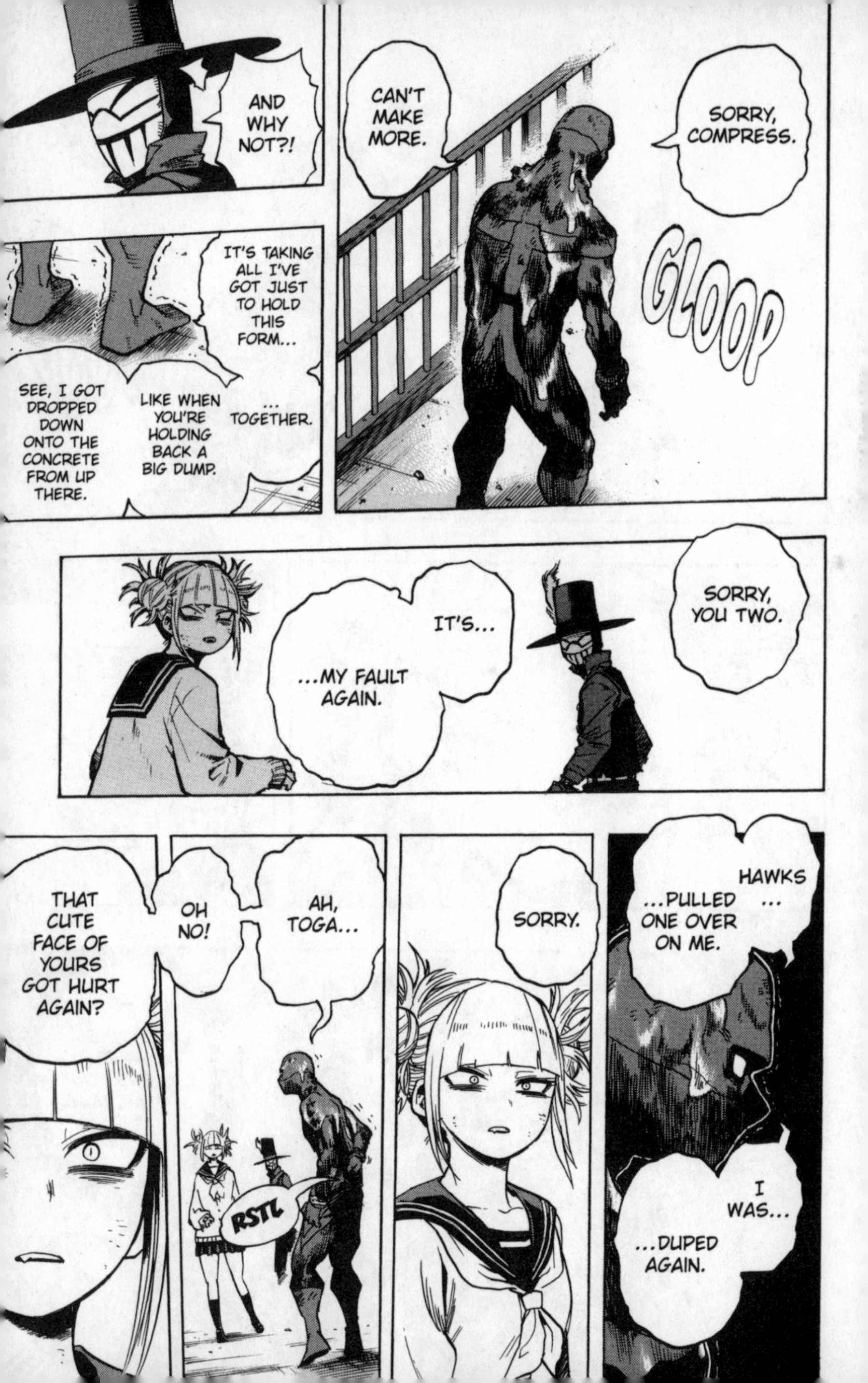
SORRY, COMPRESS.
GLOOP
CAN'T MAKE MORE.
AND WHY NOT?!
IT'S TAKING ALL I'VE GOT JUST TO HOLD THIS FORM...
...TOGETHER.
LIKE WHEN YOU'RE HOLDING BACK A BIG DUMP.
SEE, I GOT DROPPED DOWN ONTO THE CONCRETE FROM UP THERE.
SORRY, YOU TWO.
IT'S...
...MY FAULT AGAIN.
HAWKS...
...PULLED ONE OVER ON ME.
I WAS...
...DUPED AGAIN.
SORRY.
AH, TOGA...
RSTL
OH NO!
THAT CUTE FACE OF YOURS GOT HURT AGAIN?

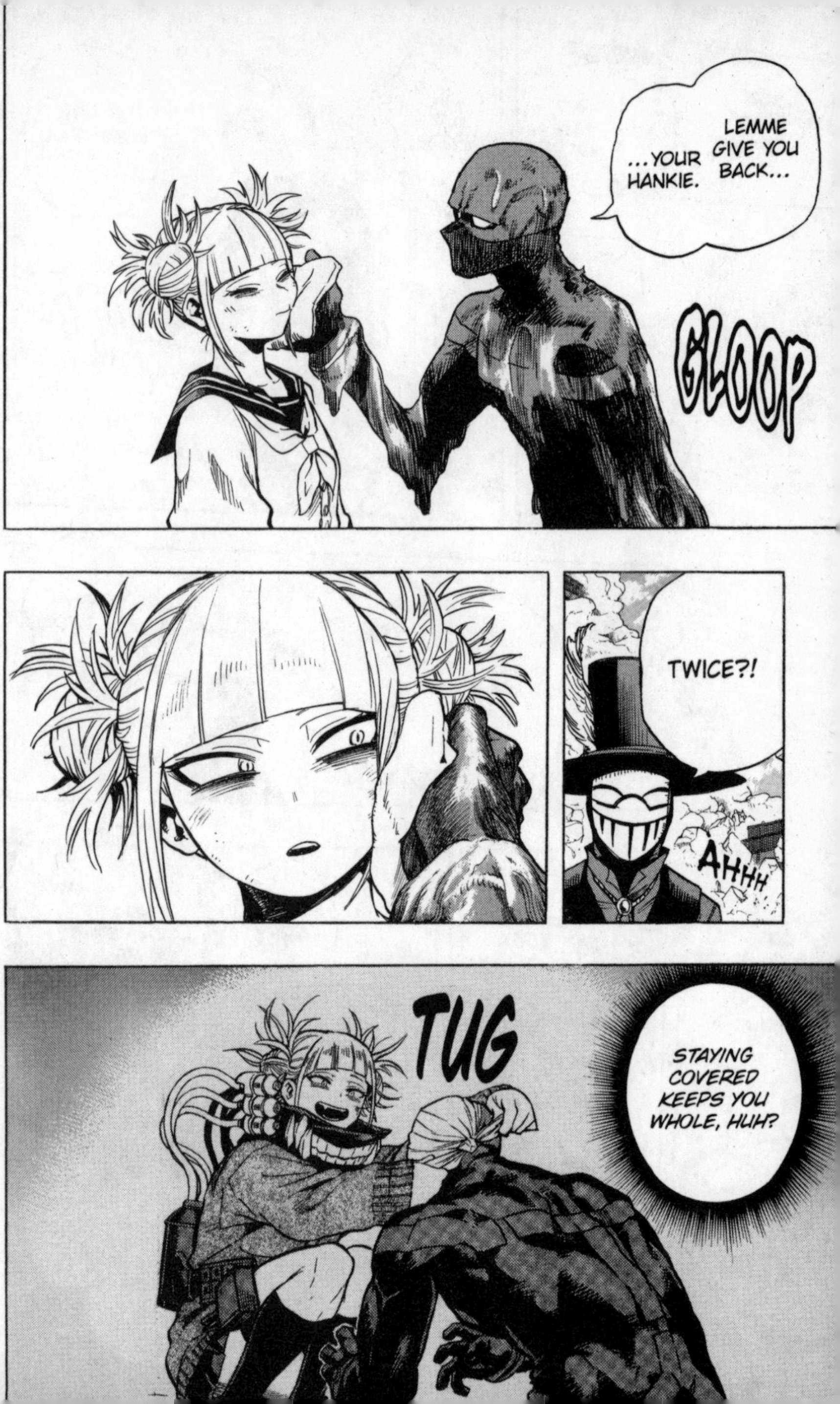
LEMME GIVE YOU BACK... ...YOUR HANKIE.
GLOOP
TWICE?!
AHHH
TUG
STAYING COVERED KEEPS YOU WHOLE, HUH?

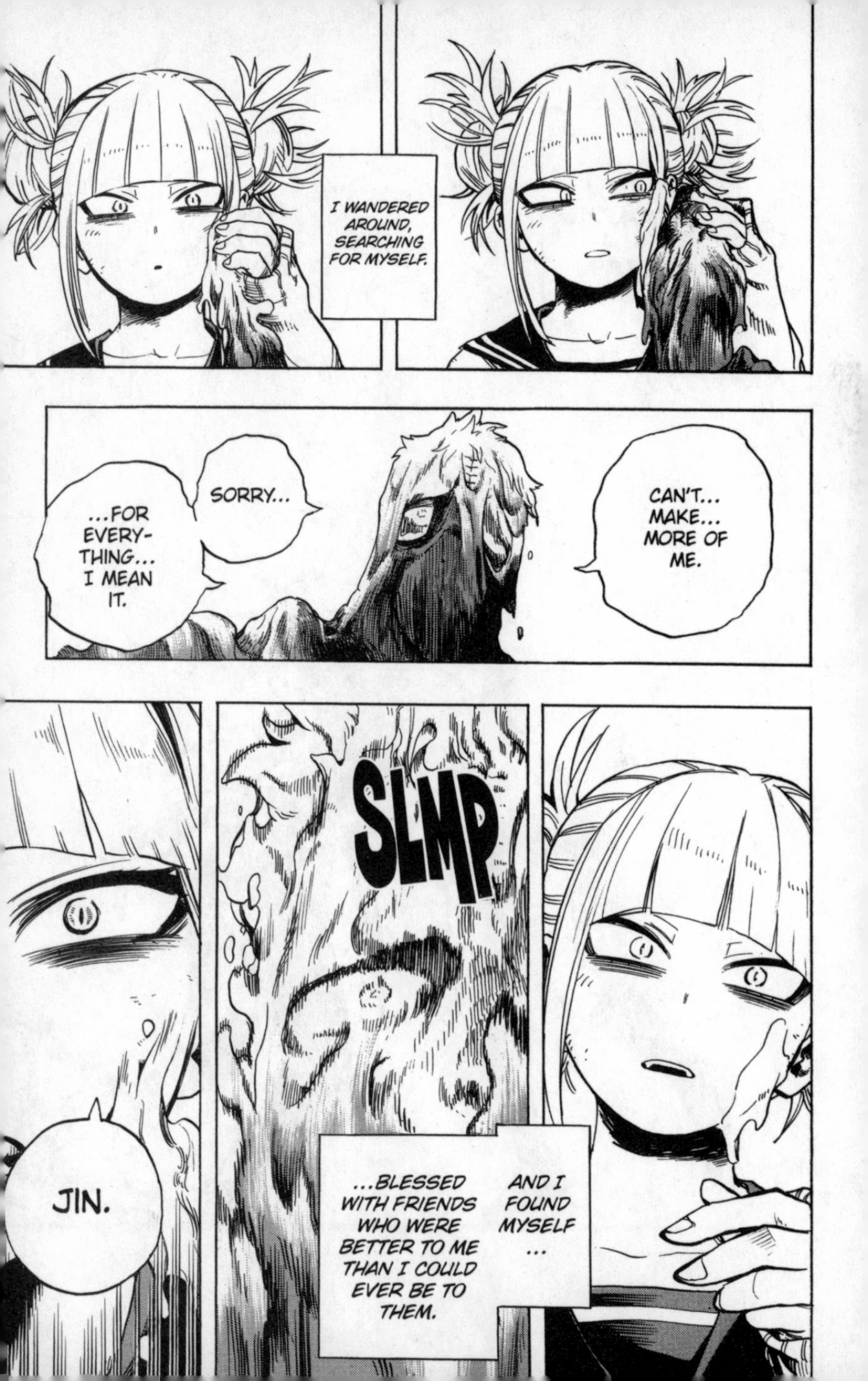
I WANDERED AROUND, SEARCHING FOR MYSELF.
CAN'T... MAKE... MORE OF ME.
SORRY...
...FOR EVERY-THING... I MEAN IT.
AND I FOUND MYSELF ...
...BLESSED WITH FRIENDS WHO WERE BETTER TO ME THAN I COULD EVER BE TO THEM.
SLMP
JIN.

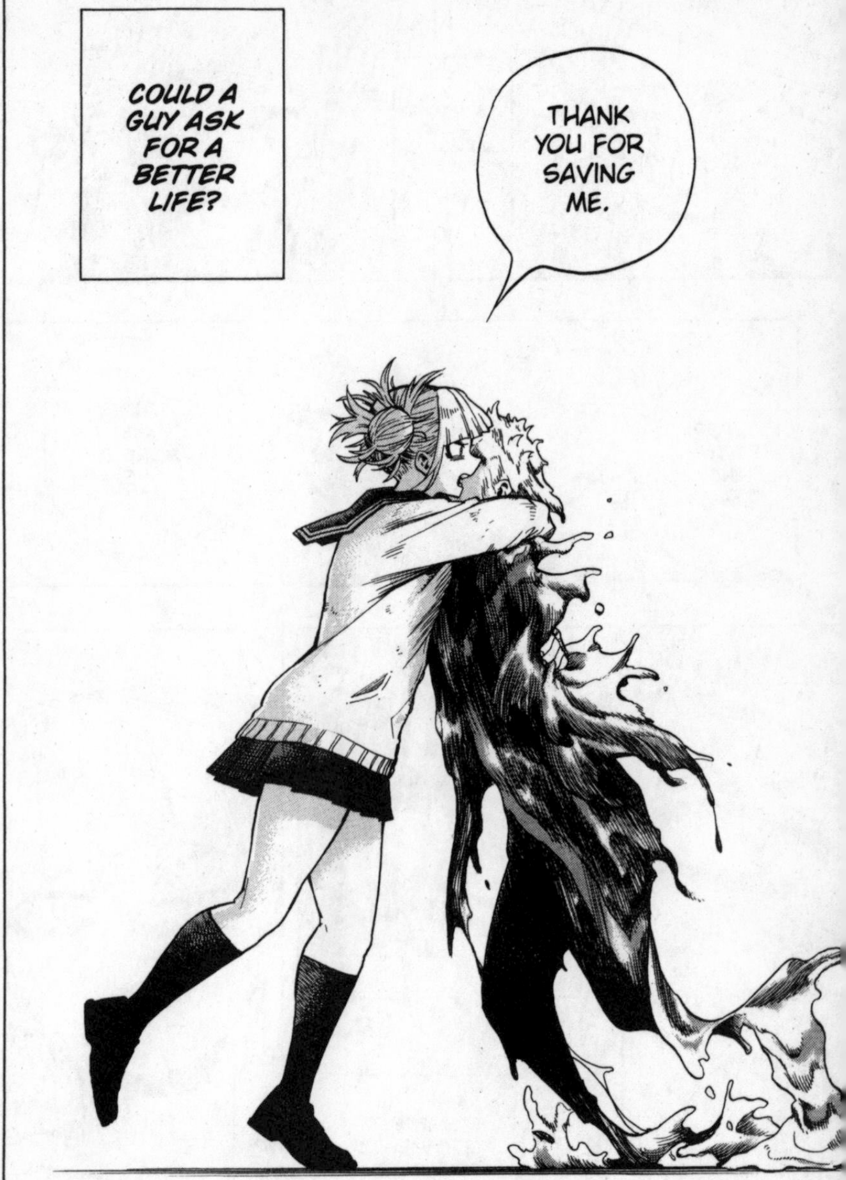
THANK YOU FOR SAVING ME.
COULD A GUY ASK FOR A BETTER LIFE?

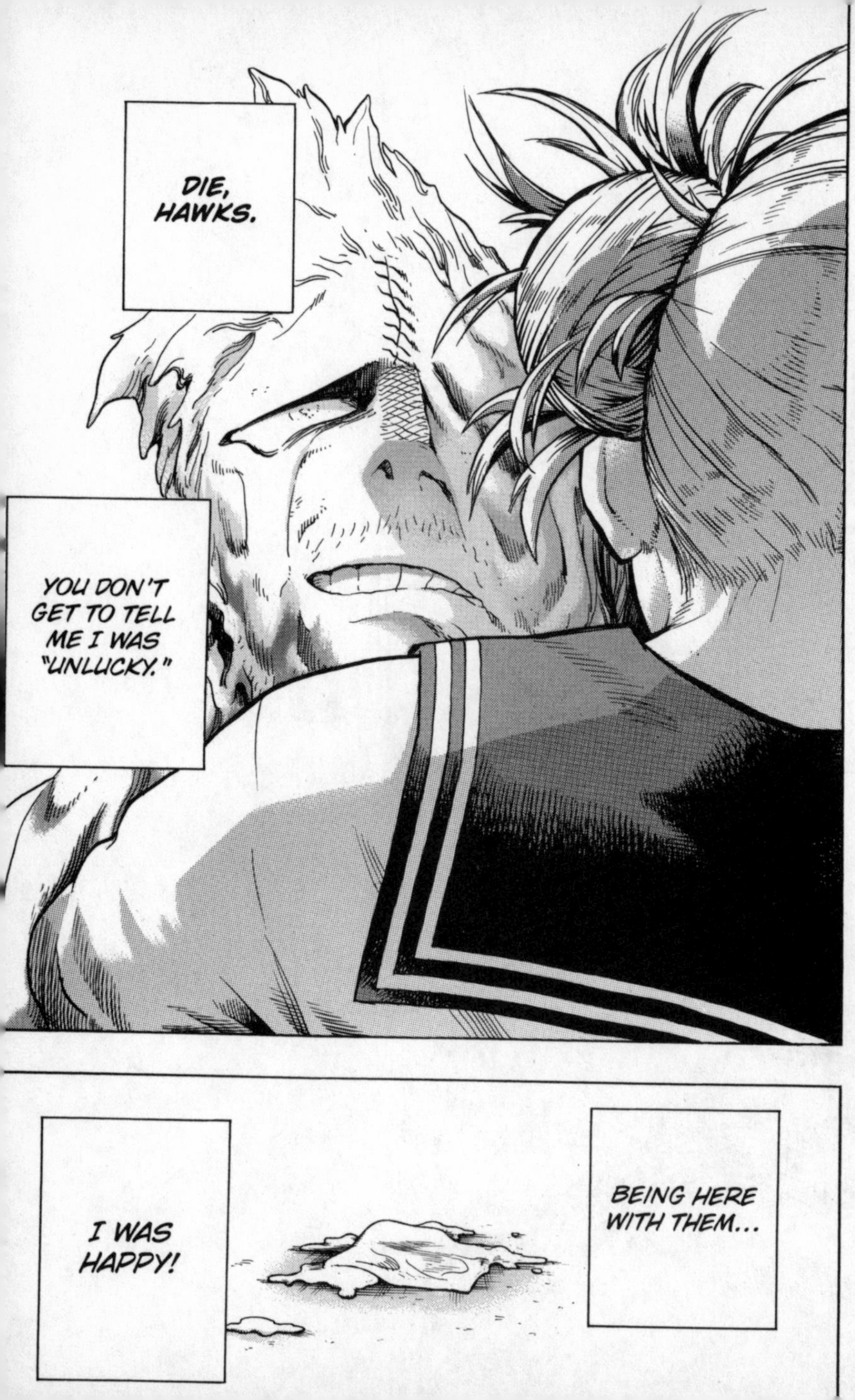
DIE, HAWKS.
YOU DON'T GET TO TELL ME I WAS "UNLUCKY."
BEING HERE WITH THEM...
I WAS HAPPY!

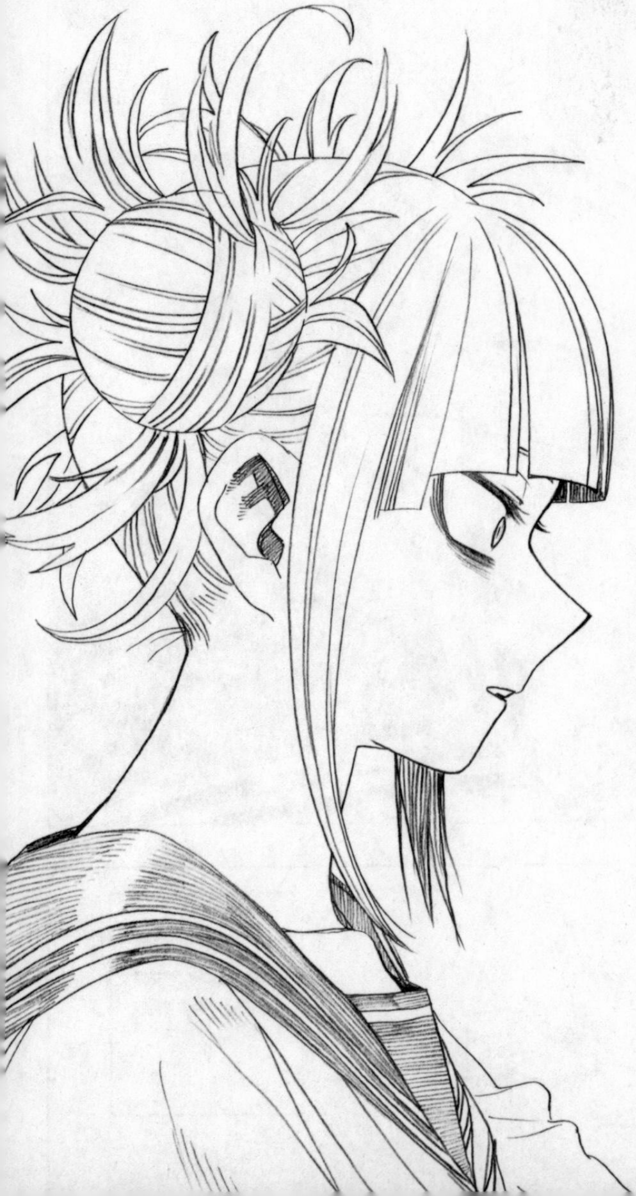

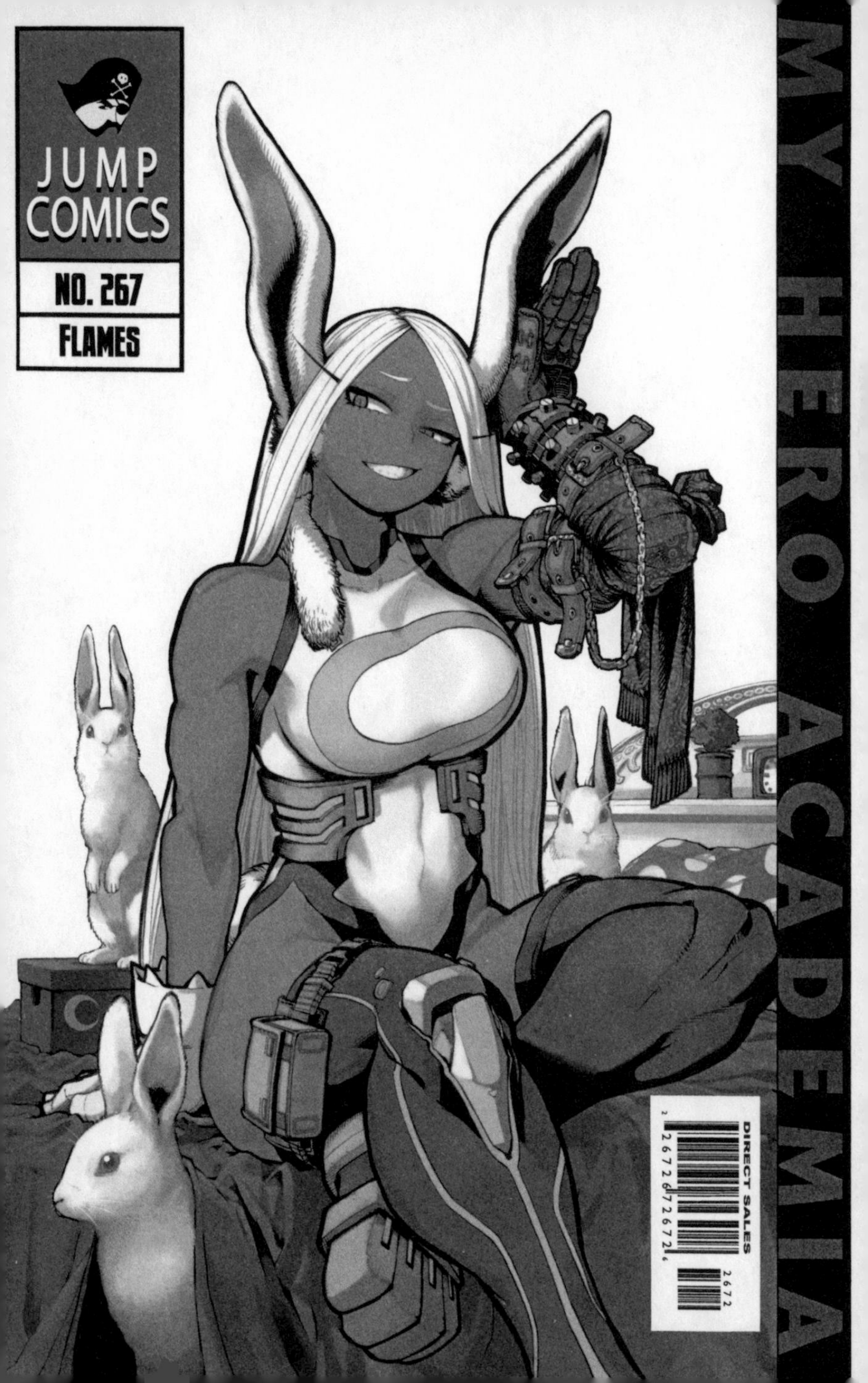
JUMP COMICS
NO. 267
FLAMES
MY HERO ACADEMIA
DIRECT SALES

MY HERO ACADEMIA

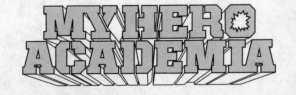

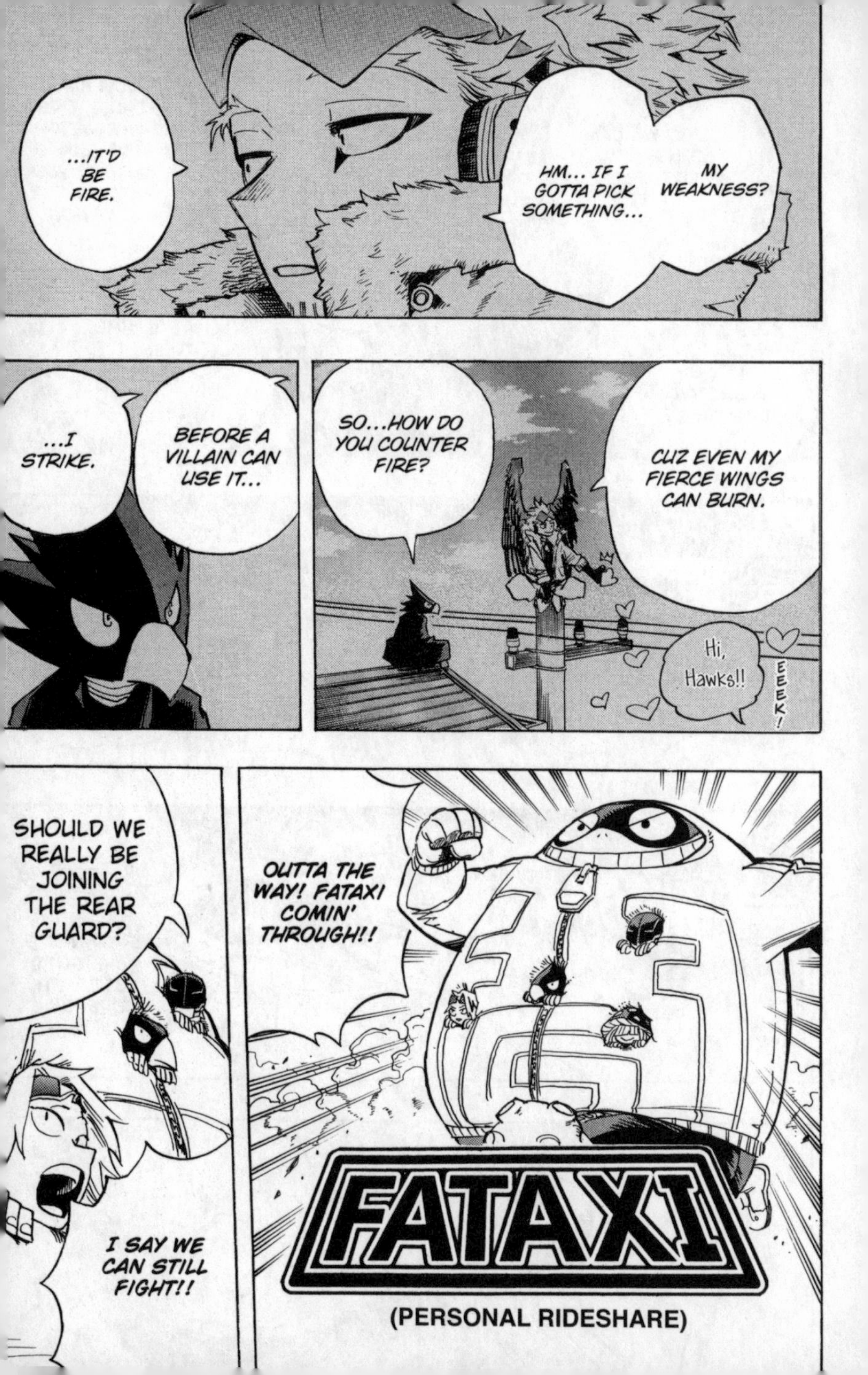
MY WEAKNESS?
HM... IF I GOTTA PICK SOMETHING...
...IT'D BE FIRE.
CUZ EVEN MY FIERCE WINGS CAN BURN.
Hi, Hawks!!
EEEK!
SO...HOW DO YOU COUNTER FIRE?
BEFORE A VILLAIN CAN USE IT...
...I STRIKE.
OUTTA THE WAY! FATAXI COMIN' THROUGH!!
FATAXI
(PERSONAL RIDESHARE)
SHOULD WE REALLY BE JOINING THE REAR GUARD?
I SAY WE CAN STILL FIGHT!!

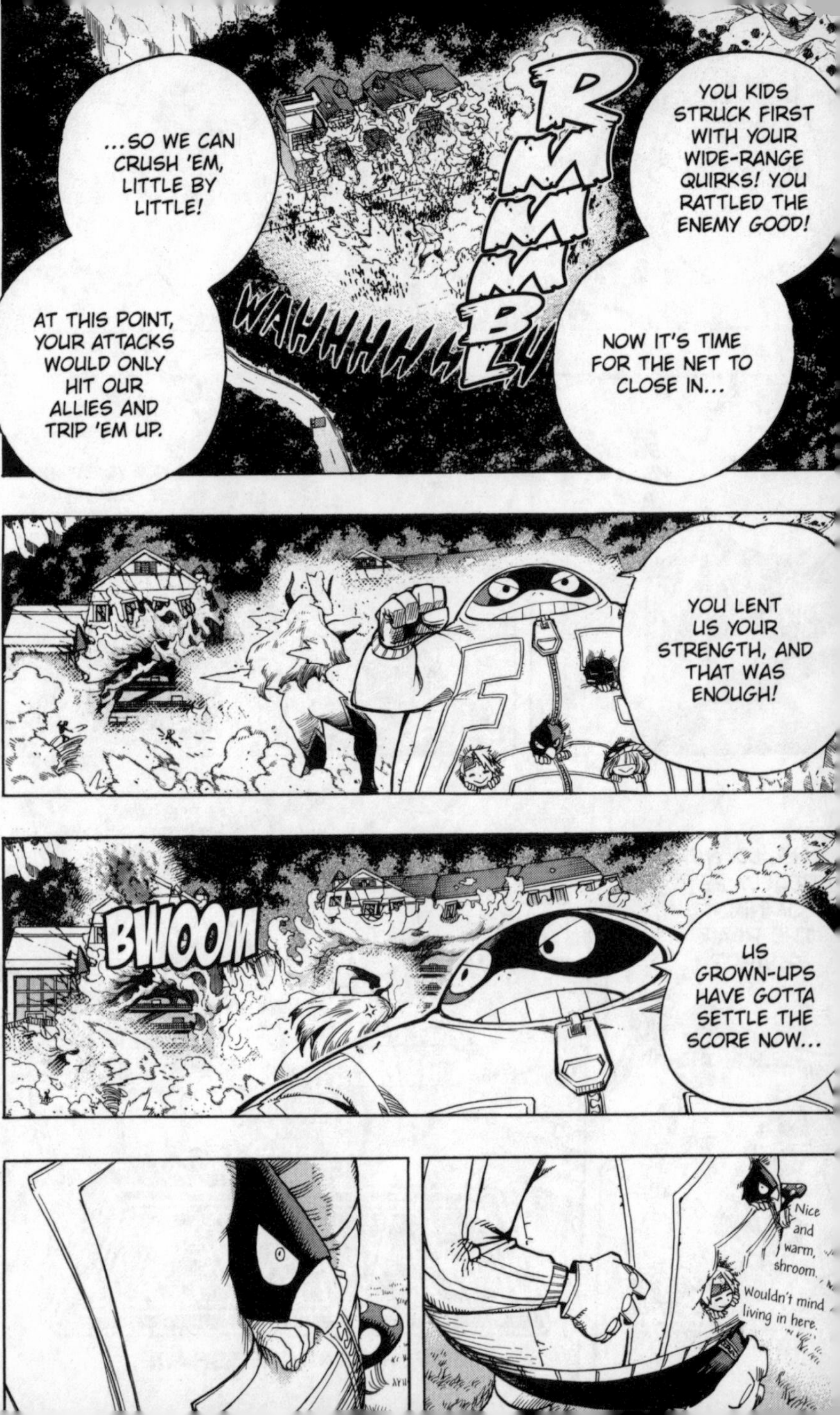
YOU KIDS STRUCK FIRST WITH YOUR WIDE-RANGE QUIRKS! YOU RATTLED THE ENEMY GOOD!
NOW IT'S TIME FOR THE NET TO CLOSE IN...
...SO WE CAN CRUSH 'EM, LITTLE BY LITTLE!
AT THIS POINT, YOUR ATTACKS WOULD ONLY HIT OUR ALLIES AND TRIP 'EM UP.
YOU LENT US YOUR STRENGTH, AND THAT WAS ENOUGH!
US GROWN-UPS HAVE GOTTA SETTLE THE SCORE NOW...
BWOOM
Nice and warm, shroom.
Wouldn't mind living in here.

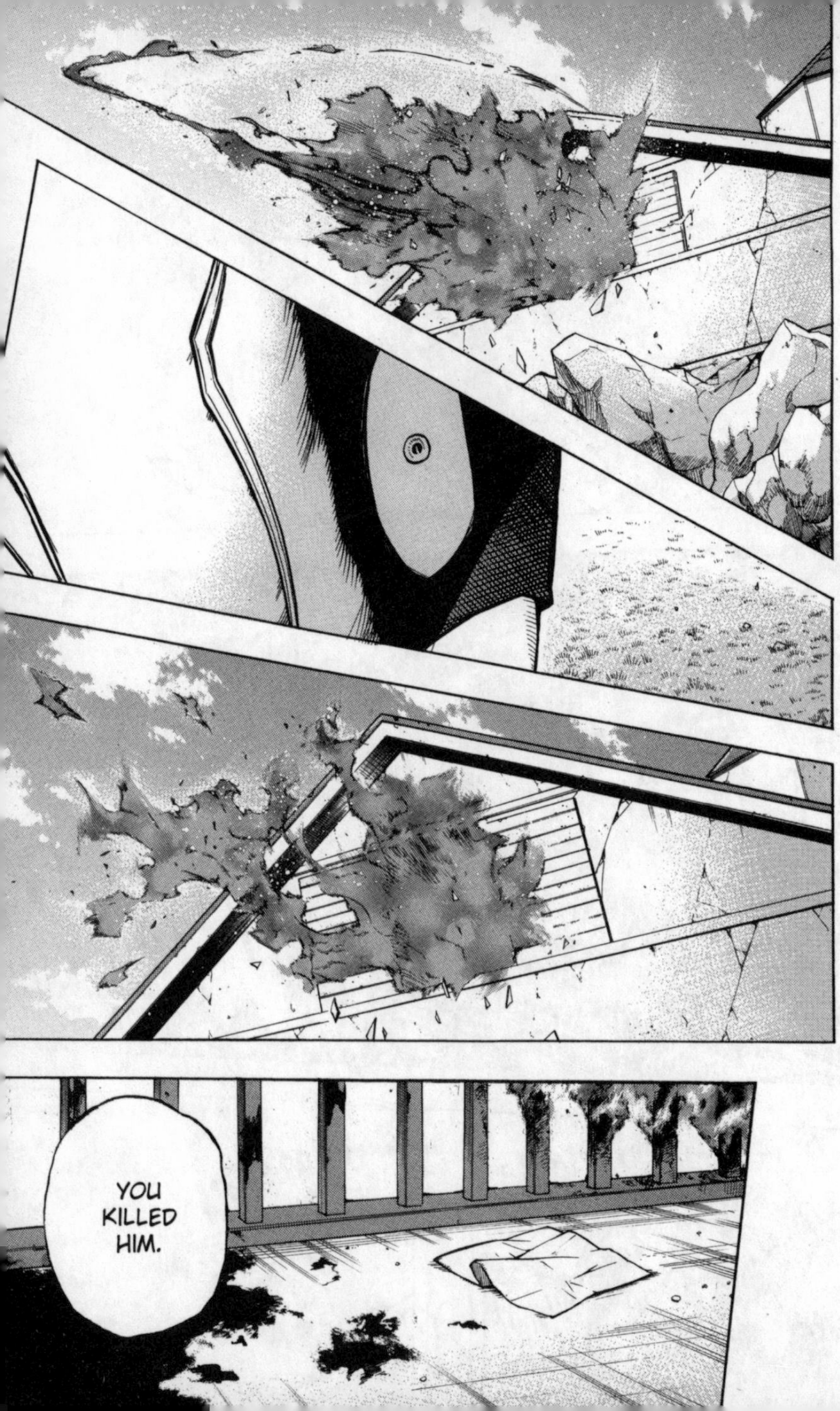
YOU KILLED HIM.

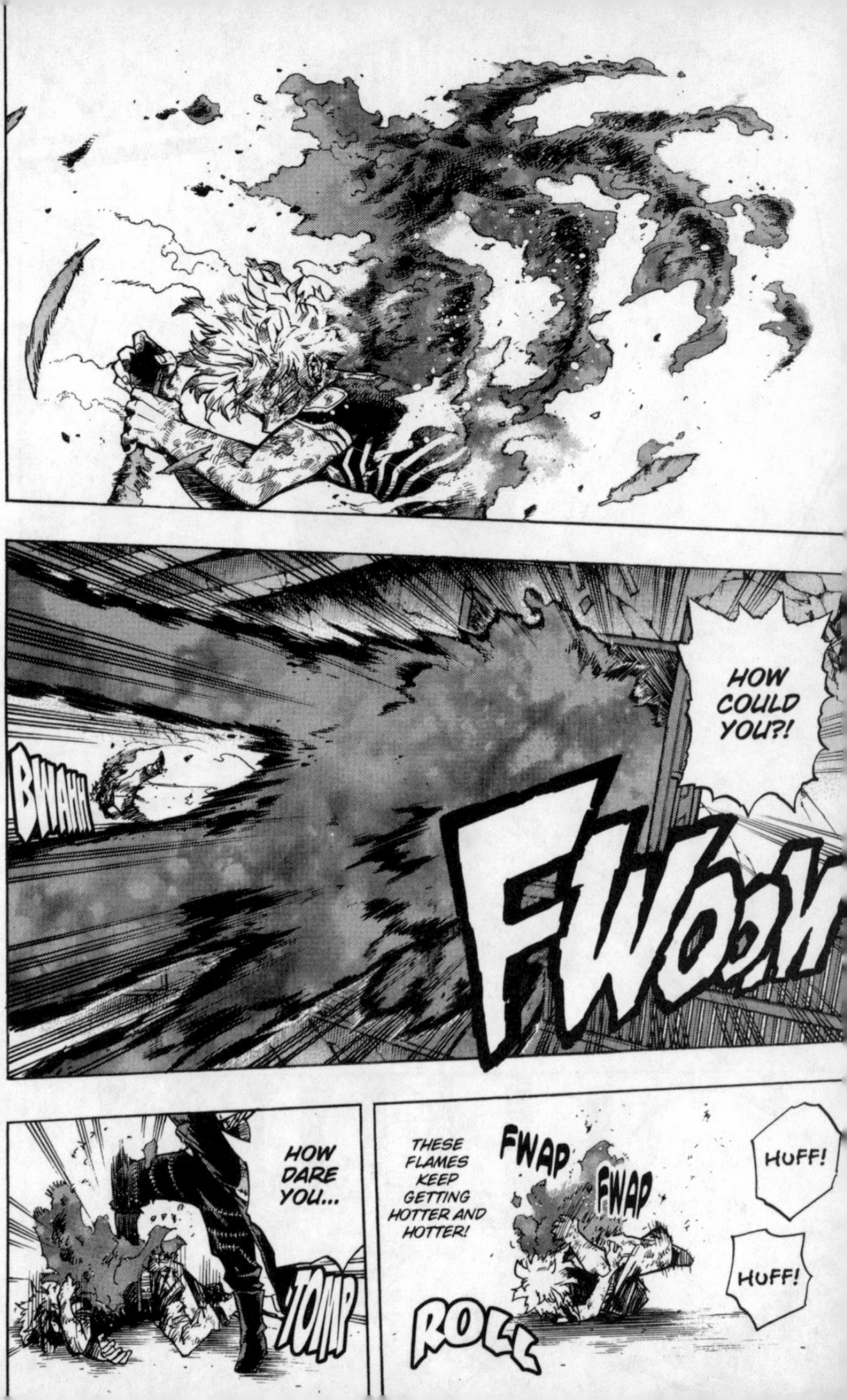
HOW COULD YOU?!
FWOOM
BWAHH
HUFF!
HUFF!
FWAP
FWAP
THESE FLAMES KEEP GETTING HOTTER AND HOTTER!
ROLL
HOW DARE YOU...
TOMP

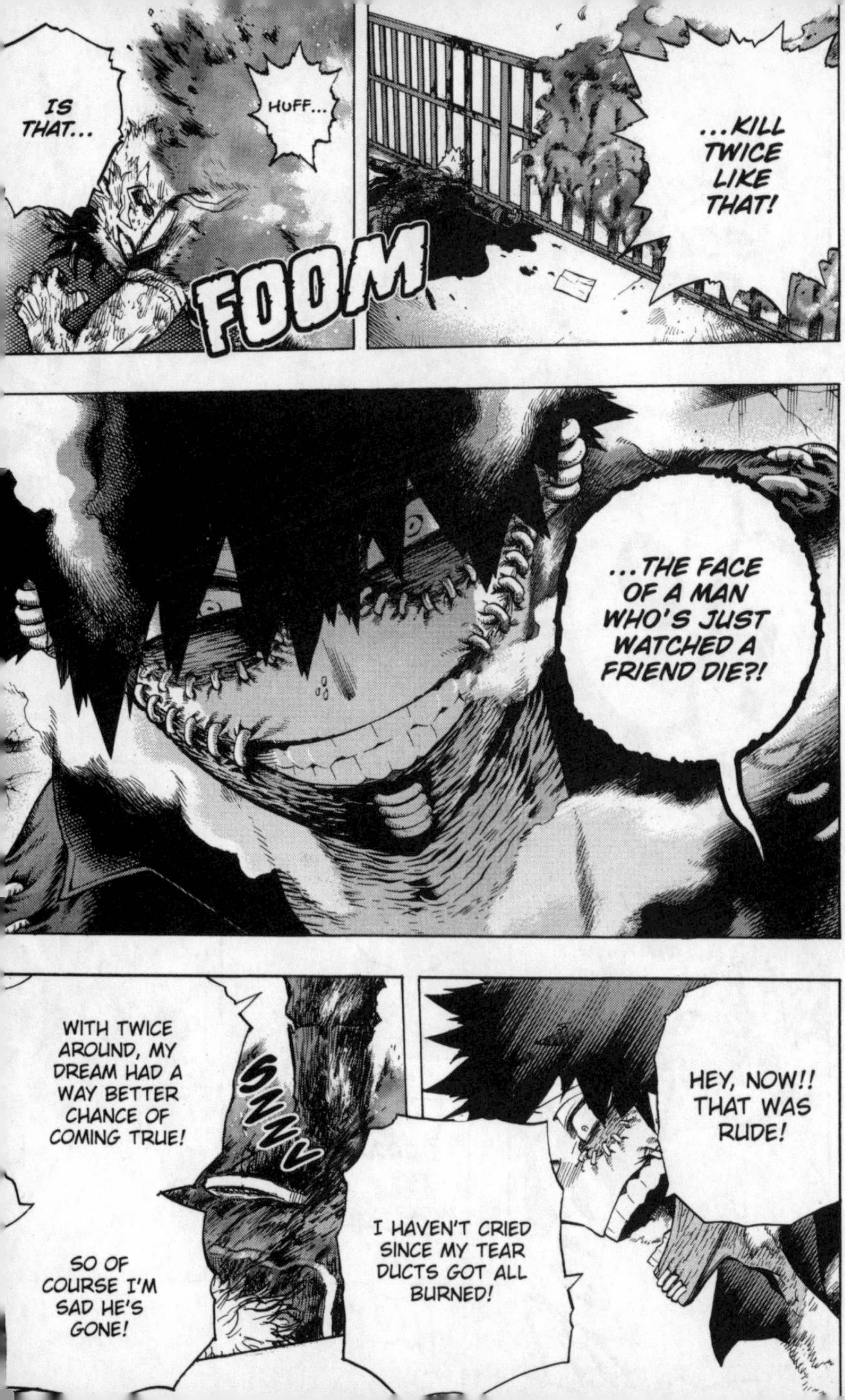
...KILL TWICE LIKE THAT!
IS THAT...
HUFF...
FOOM
...THE FACE OF A MAN WHO'S JUST WATCHED A FRIEND DIE?!
HEY, NOW!! THAT WAS RUDE!
I HAVEN'T CRIED SINCE MY TEAR DUCTS GOT ALL BURNED!
WITH TWICE AROUND, MY DREAM HAD A WAY BETTER CHANCE OF COMING TRUE!
SO OF COURSE I'M SAD HE'S GONE!

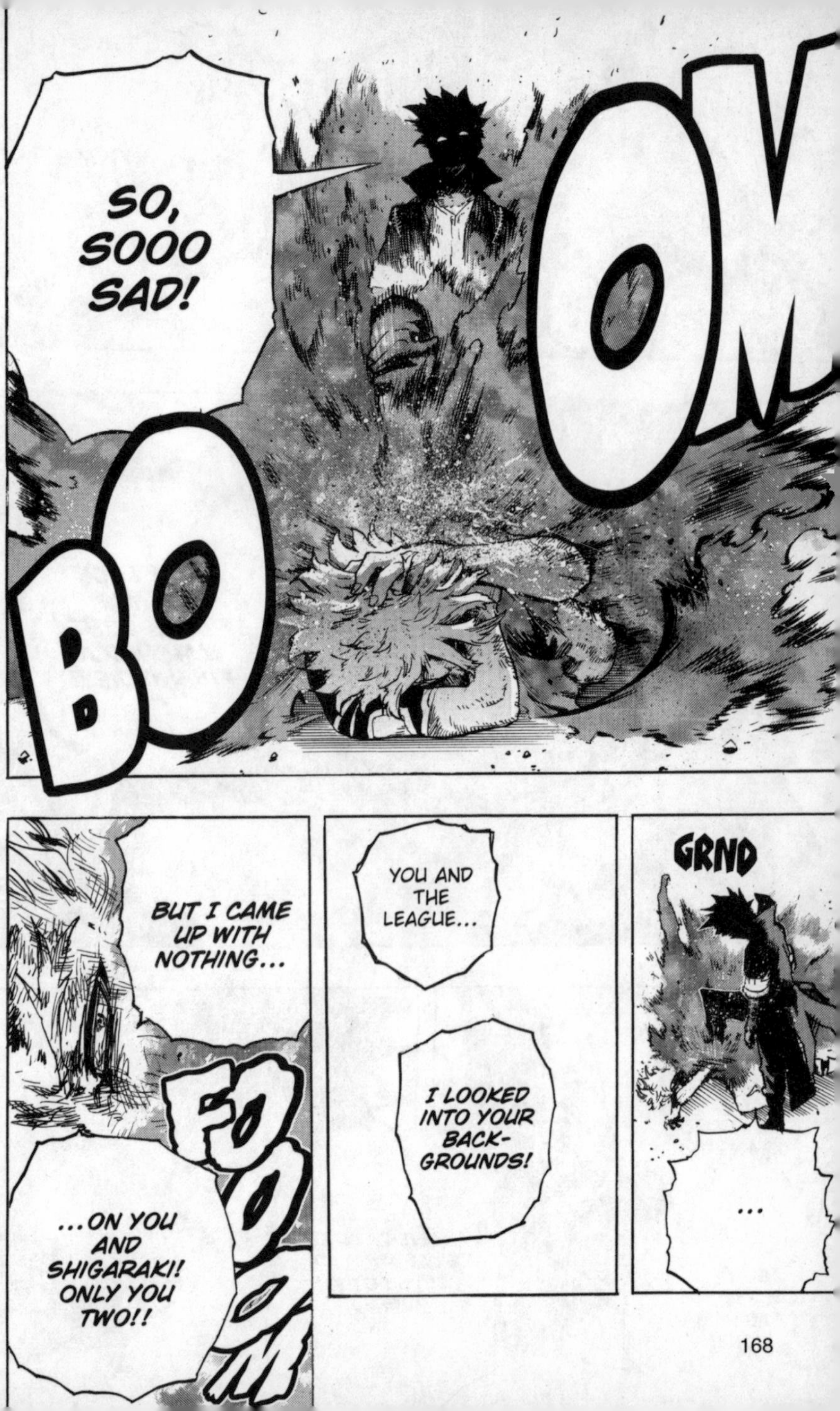
SO, SOOO SAD!
BOOOM
GRND
...
YOU AND THE LEAGUE...
I LOOKED INTO YOUR BACK-GROUNDS!
BUT I CAME UP WITH NOTHING...
FOOOM
...ON YOU AND SHIGARAKI! ONLY YOU TWO!!

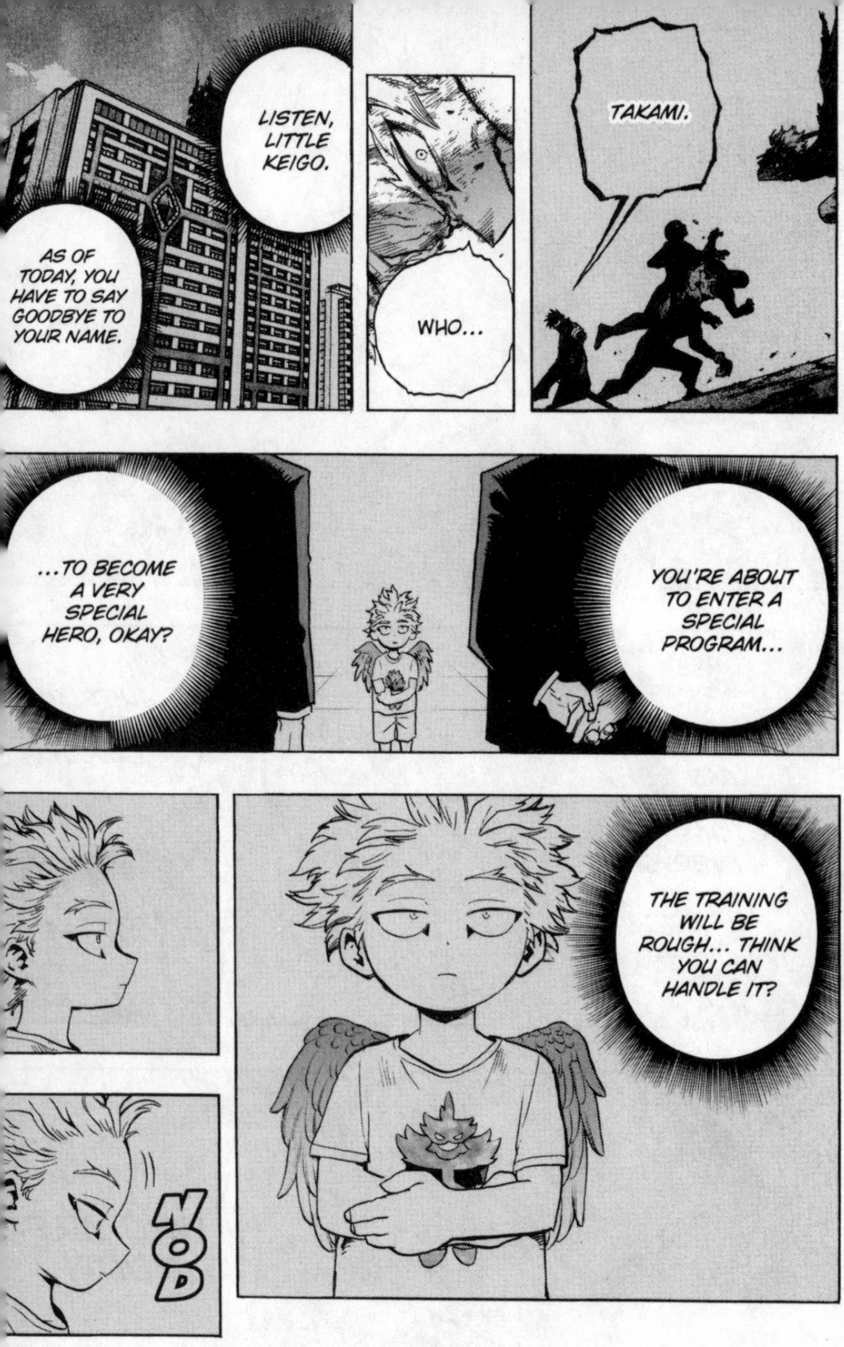
TAKAMI.
WHO...
LISTEN, LITTLE KEIGO.
AS OF TODAY, YOU HAVE TO SAY GOODBYE TO YOUR NAME.
YOU'RE ABOUT TO ENTER A SPECIAL PROGRAM...
...TO BECOME A VERY SPECIAL HERO, OKAY?
THE TRAINING WILL BE ROUGH... THINK YOU CAN HANDLE IT?
NOD

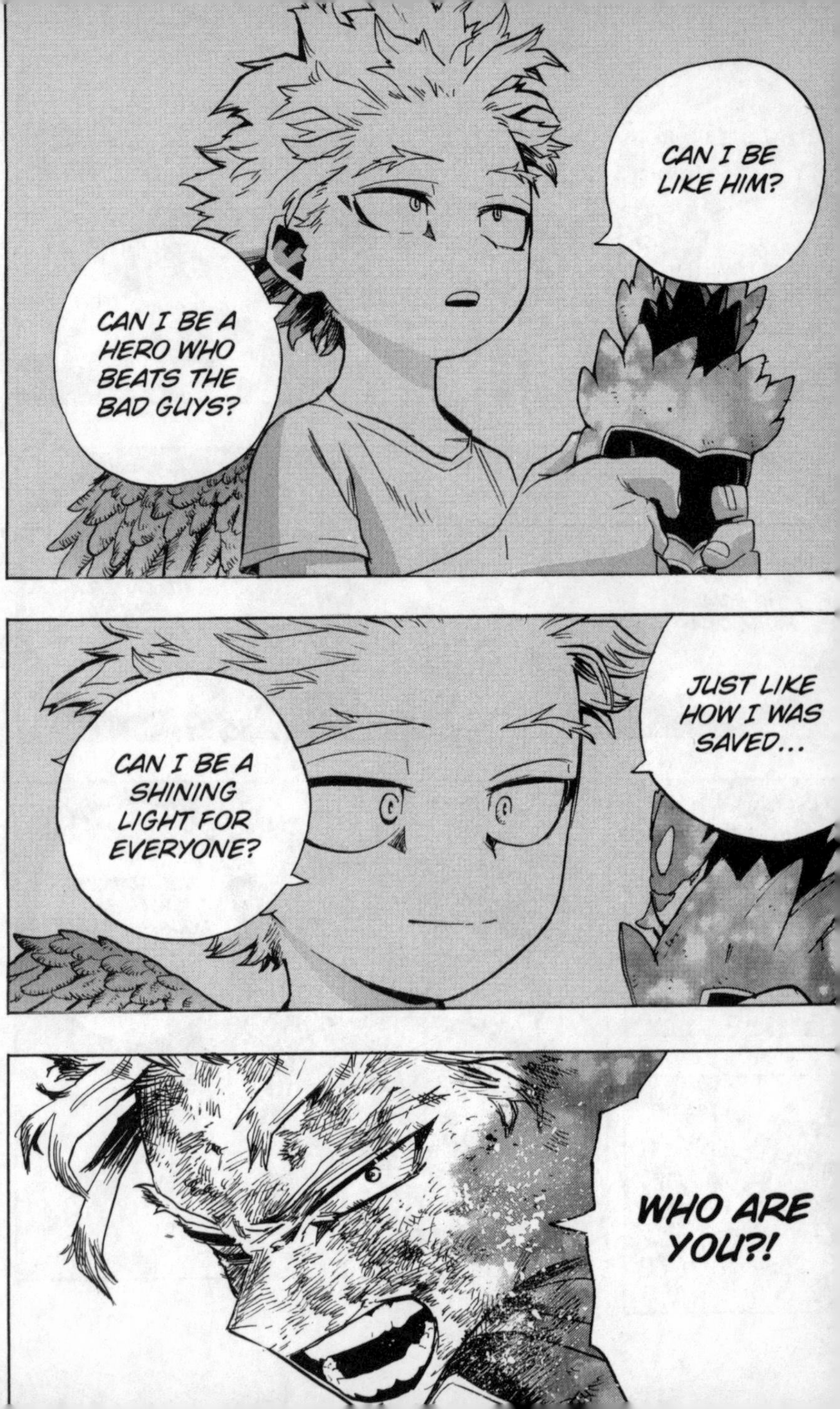
CAN I BE LIKE HIM?
CAN I BE A HERO WHO BEATS THE BAD GUYS?
JUST LIKE HOW I WAS SAVED...
CAN I BE A SHINING LIGHT FOR EVERYONE?
WHO ARE YOU?!

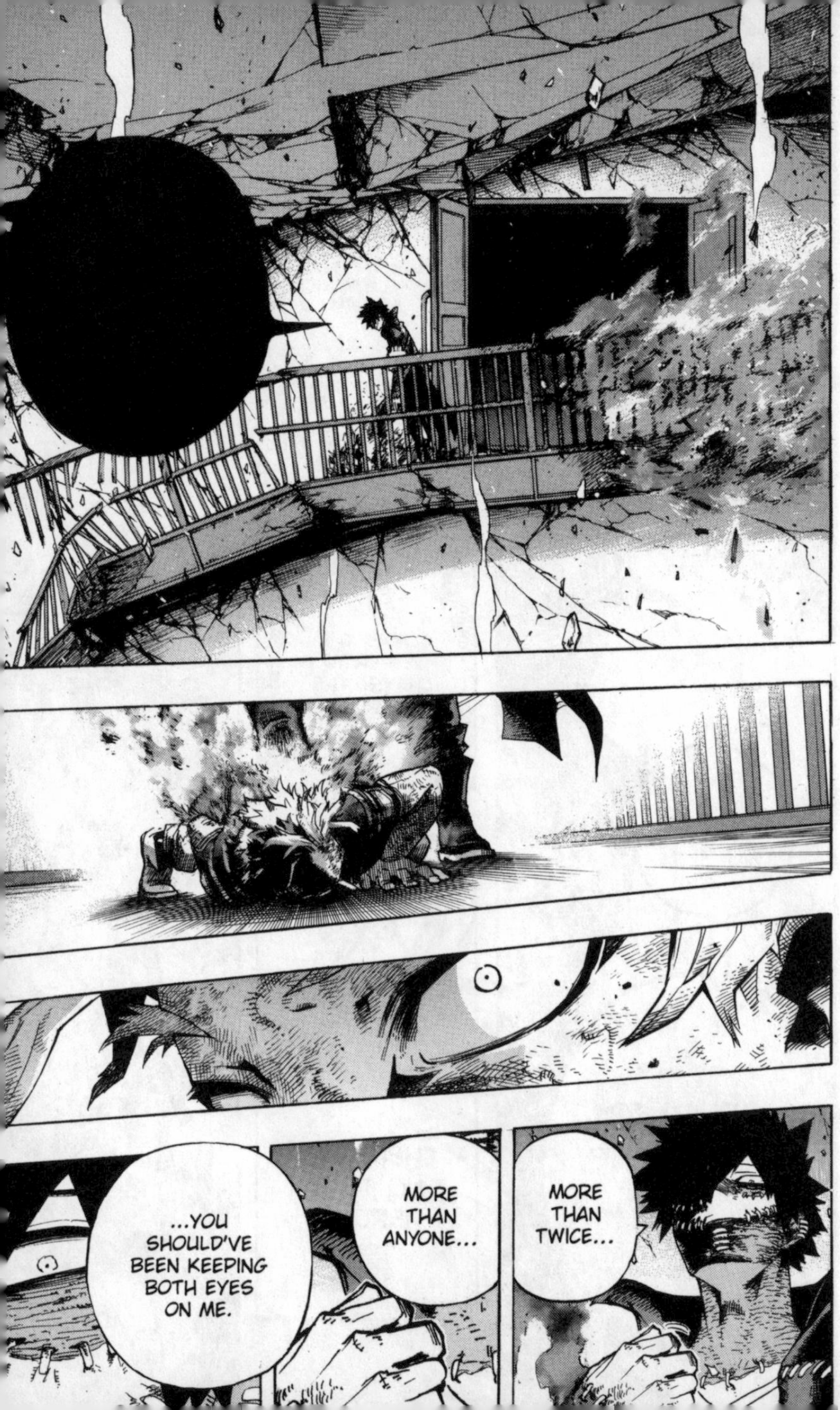
MORE THAN TWICE...
MORE THAN ANYONE...
...YOU SHOULD'VE BEEN KEEPING BOTH EYES ON ME.

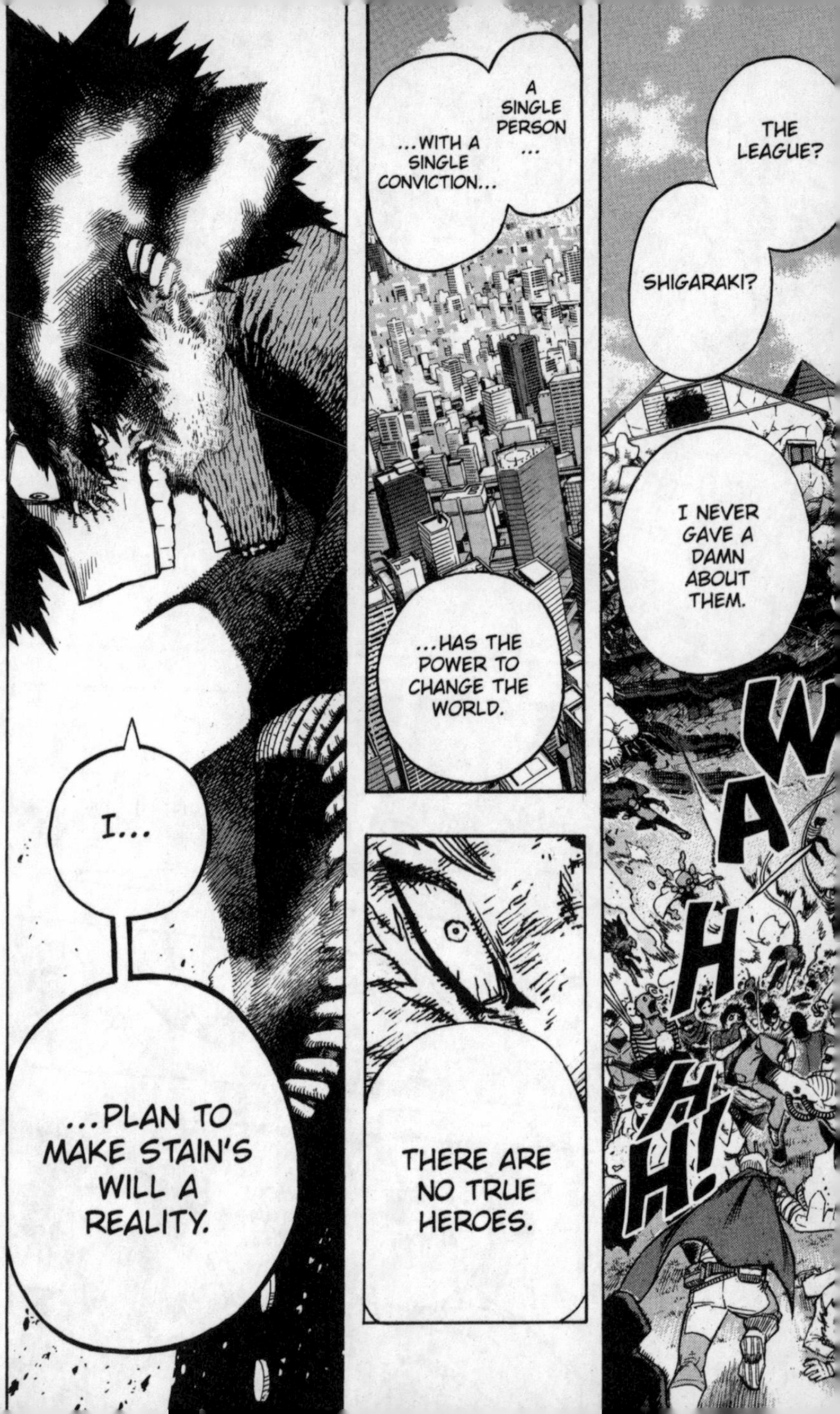
THE LEAGUE?
SHIGARAKI?
I NEVER GAVE A DAMN ABOUT THEM.
WAHHH!
A SINGLE PERSON...
...WITH A SINGLE CONVICTION...
...HAS THE POWER TO CHANGE THE WORLD.
THERE ARE NO TRUE HEROES.
I...
...PLAN TO MAKE STAIN'S WILL A REALITY.

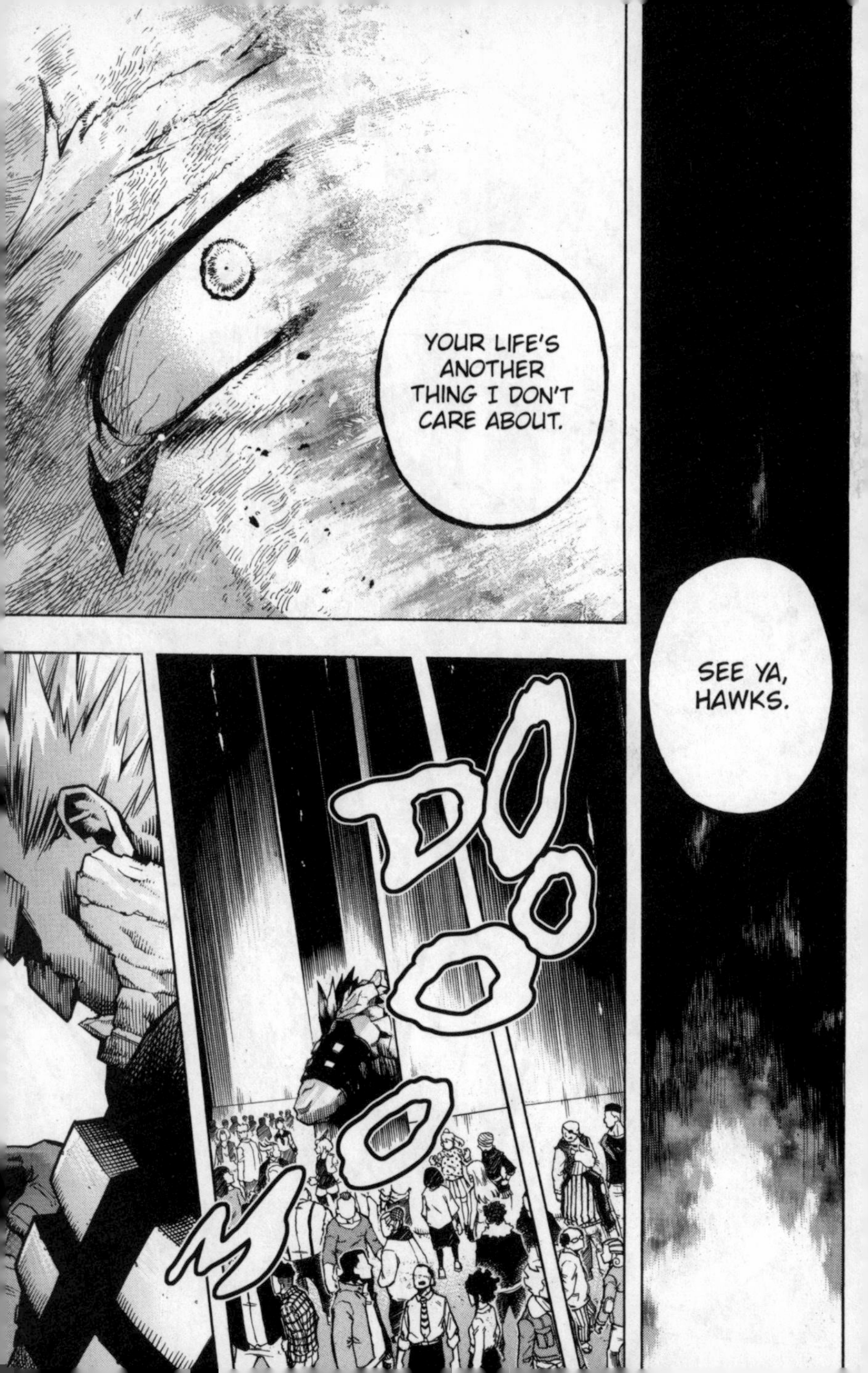
SEE YA, HAWKS.
YOUR LIFE'S ANOTHER THING I DON'T CARE ABOUT.
DOOOOM

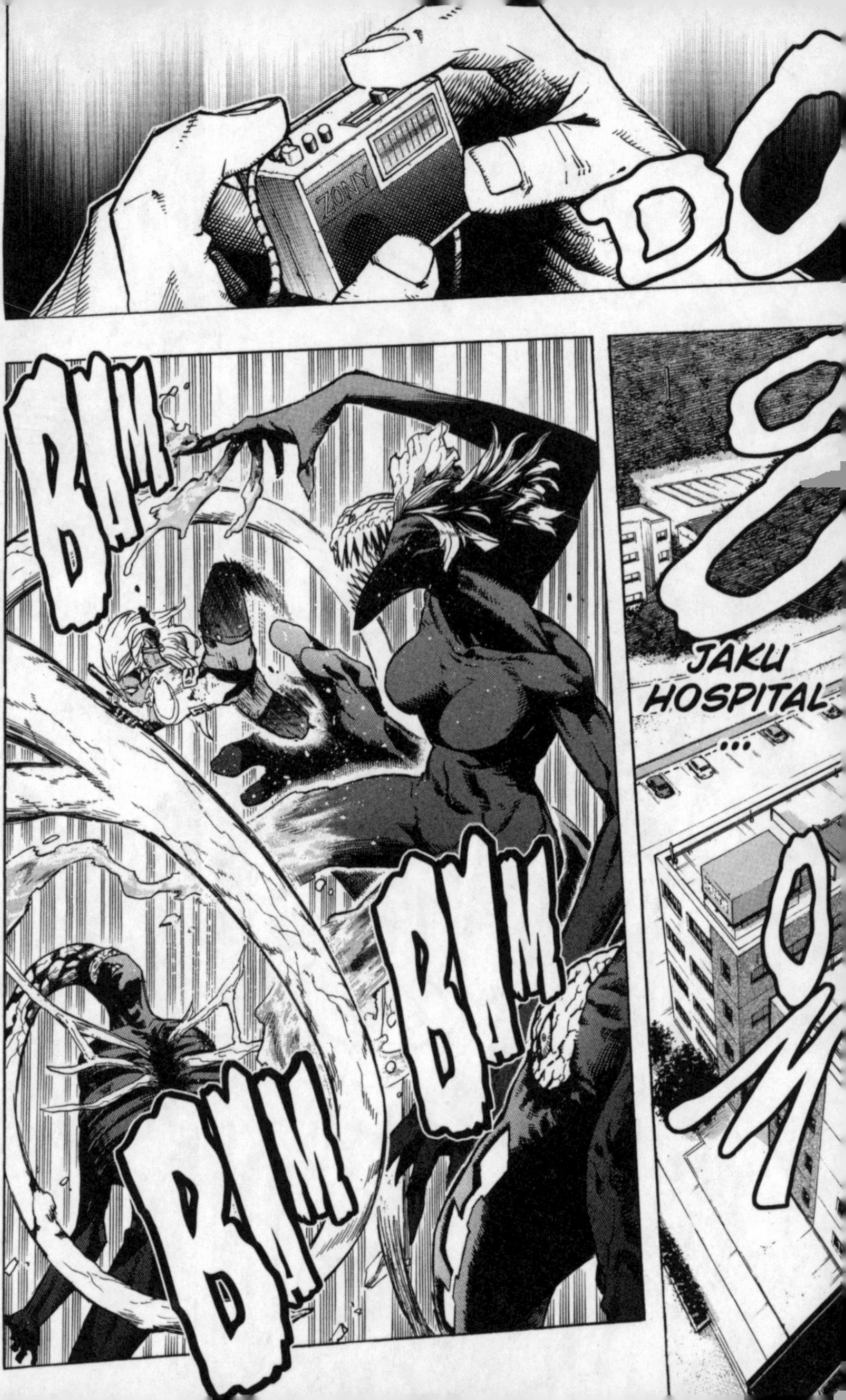
DOOOM
JAKU HOSPITAL...
BAM
BAM
BAM

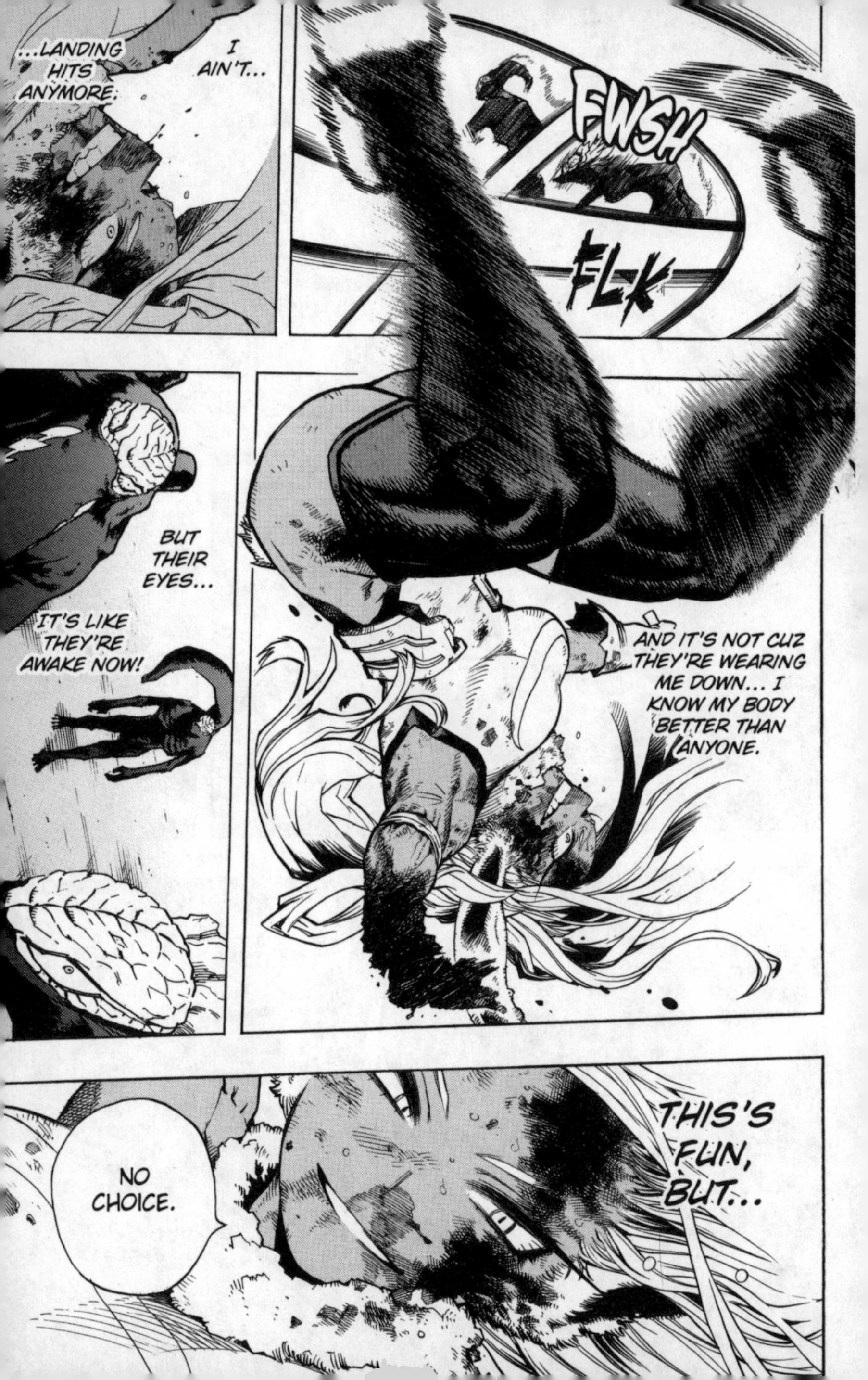
FWSH
FLK
I AIN'T...
...LANDING HITS ANYMORE.
AND IT'S NOT CUZ THEY'RE WEARING ME DOWN... I KNOW MY BODY BETTER THAN ANYONE.
BUT THEIR EYES...
IT'S LIKE THEY'RE AWAKE NOW!
THIS'S FUN, BUT...
NO CHOICE.

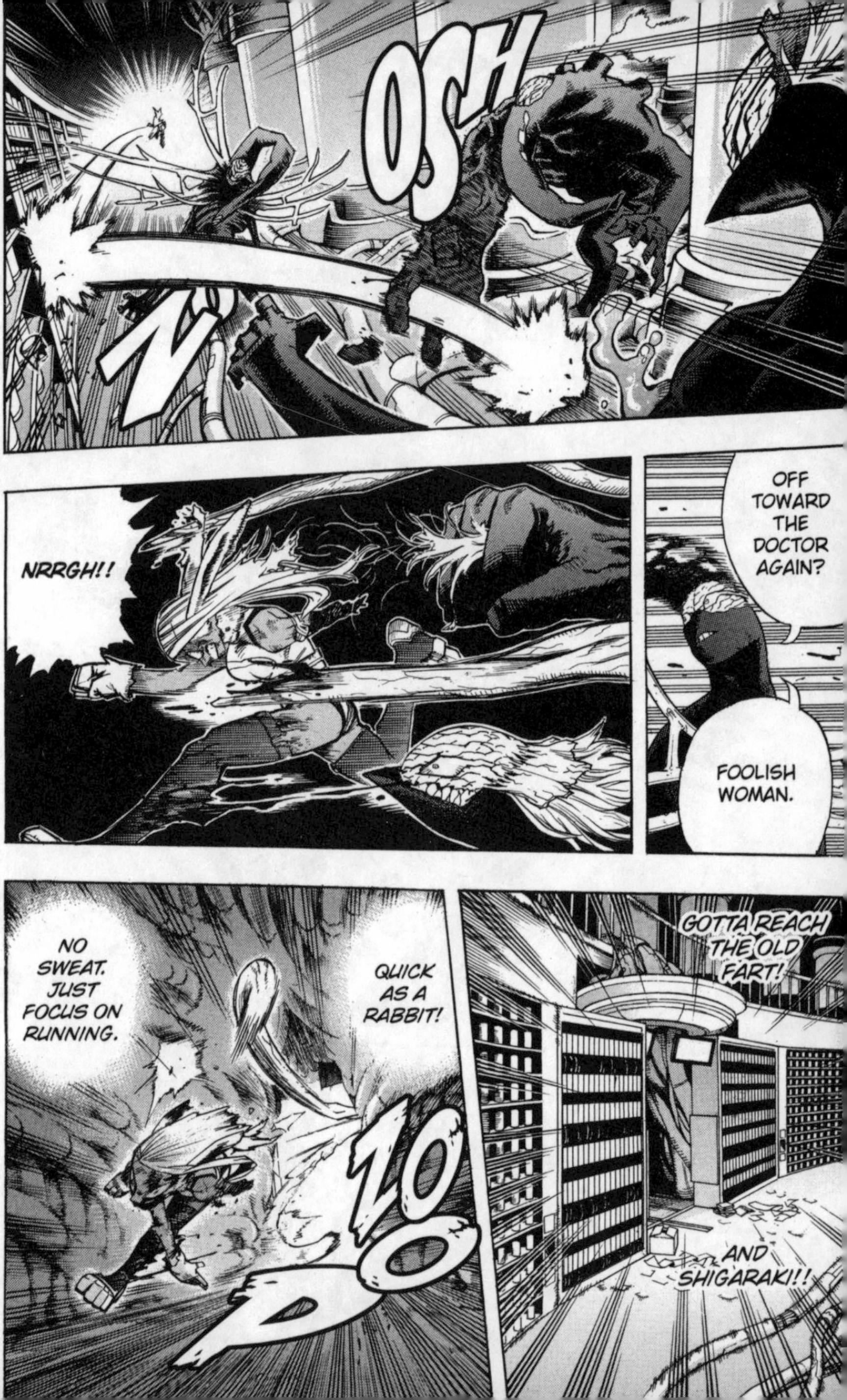
OSH
N
OFF TOWARD THE DOCTOR AGAIN?
FOOLISH WOMAN.
NRRGH!!
GOTTA REACH THE OLD FART!
AND SHIGARAKI!!
QUICK AS A RABBIT!
NO SWEAT. JUST FOCUS ON RUNNING.
ZOOP

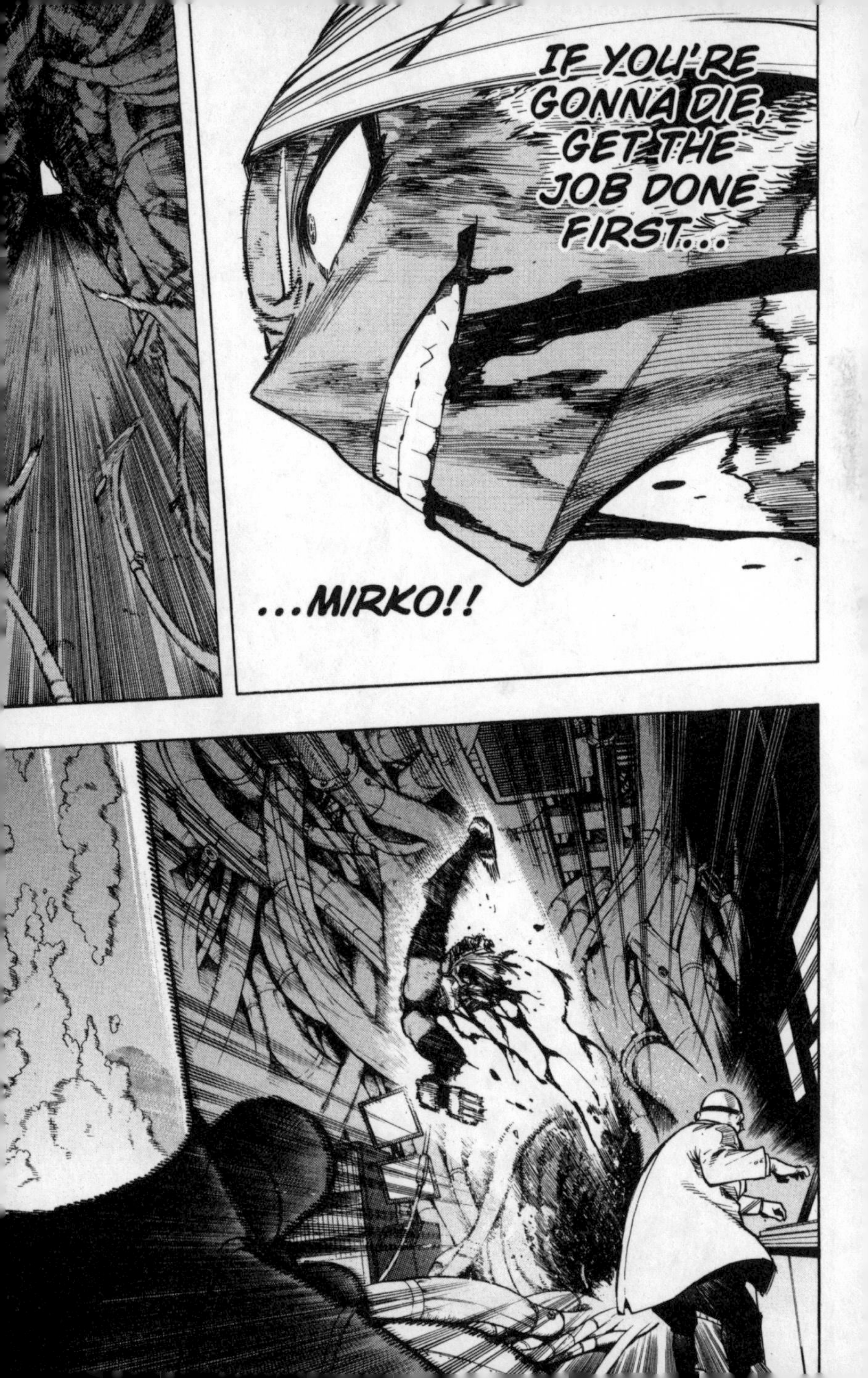
IF YOU'RE GONNA DIE, GET THE JOB DONE FIRST...
...MIRKO!!

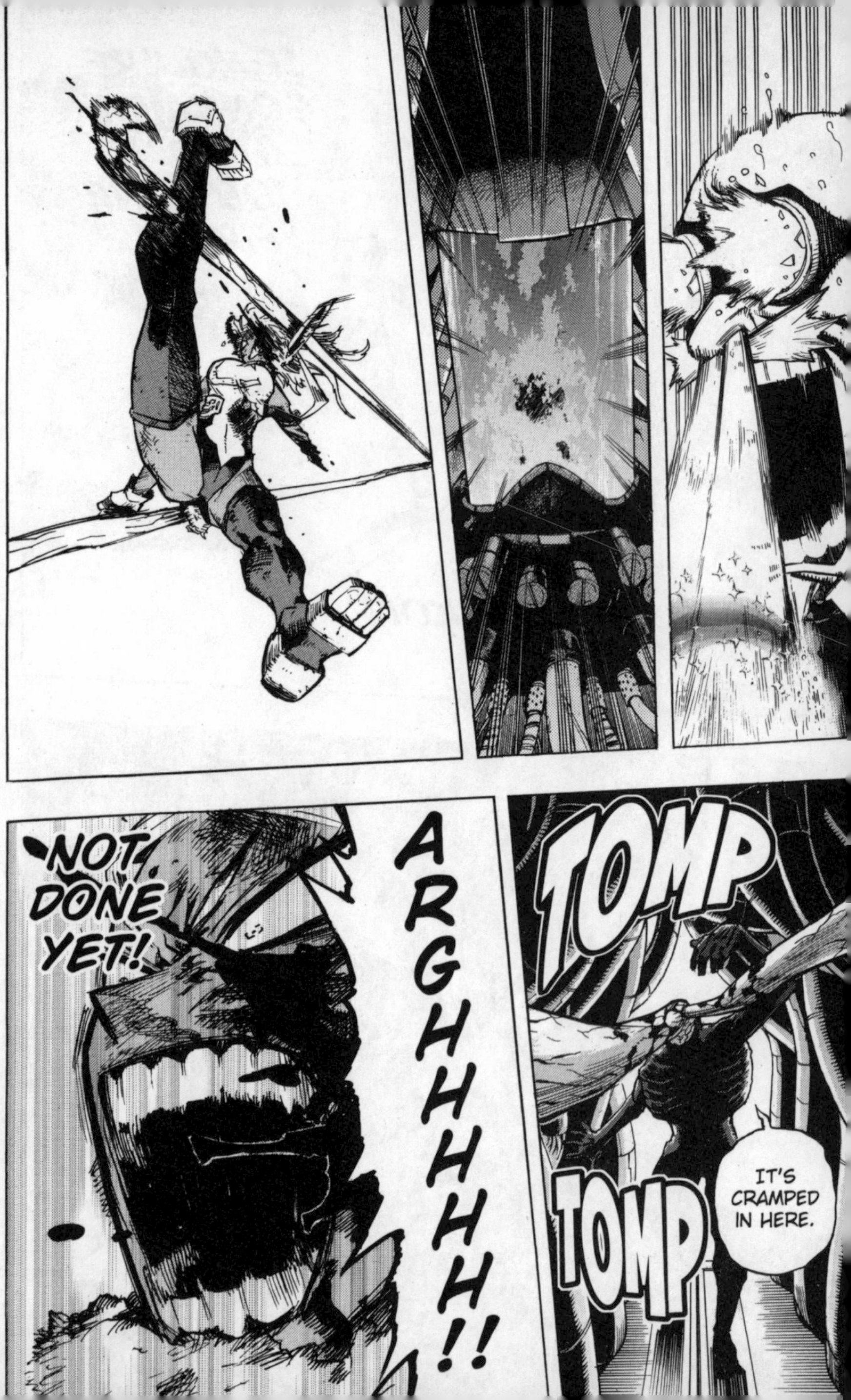
TOMP
TOMP
IT'S CRAMPED IN HERE.
ARGHHHHH!!
NOT DONE YET!

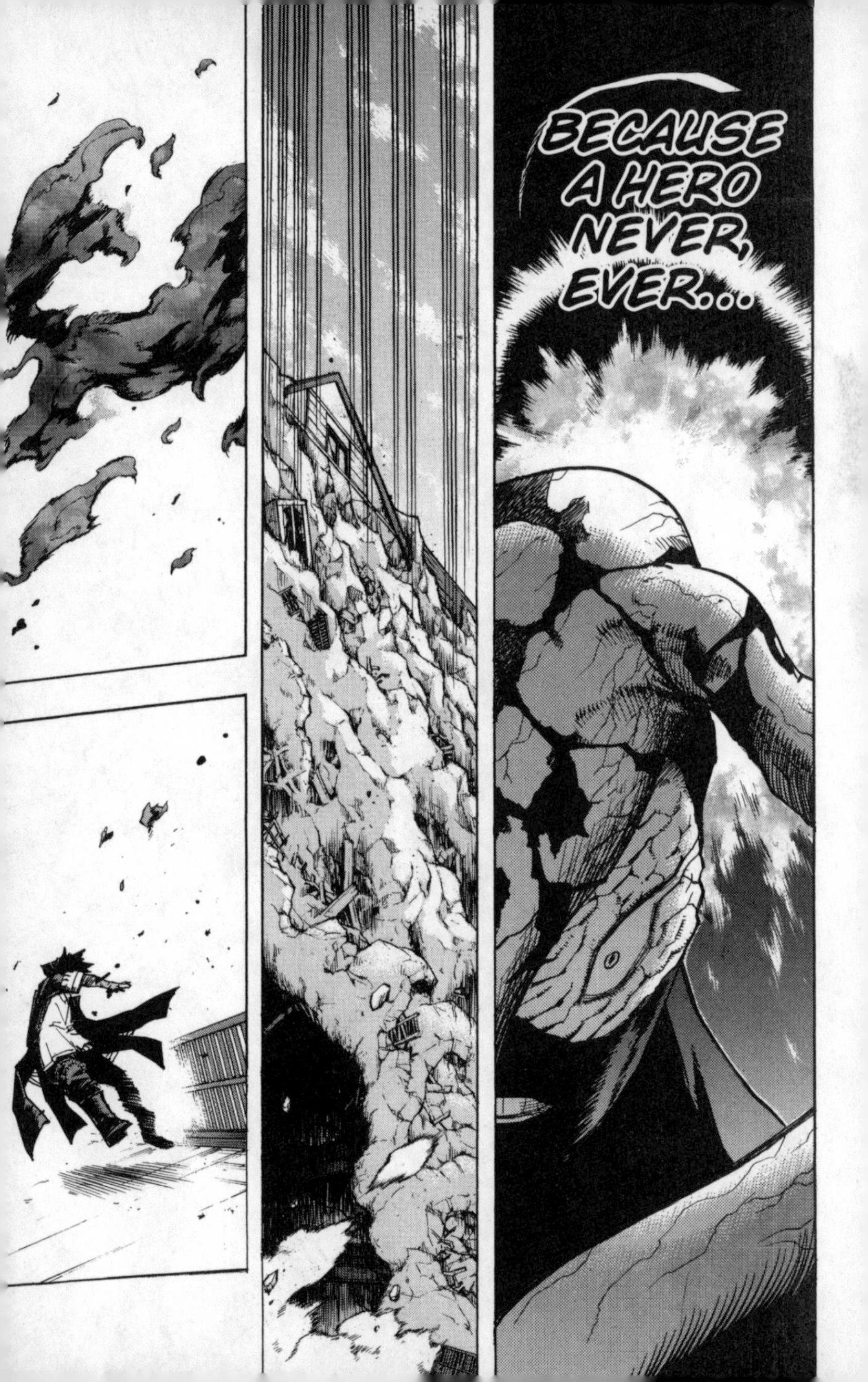
BECAUSE A HERO NEVER, EVER...

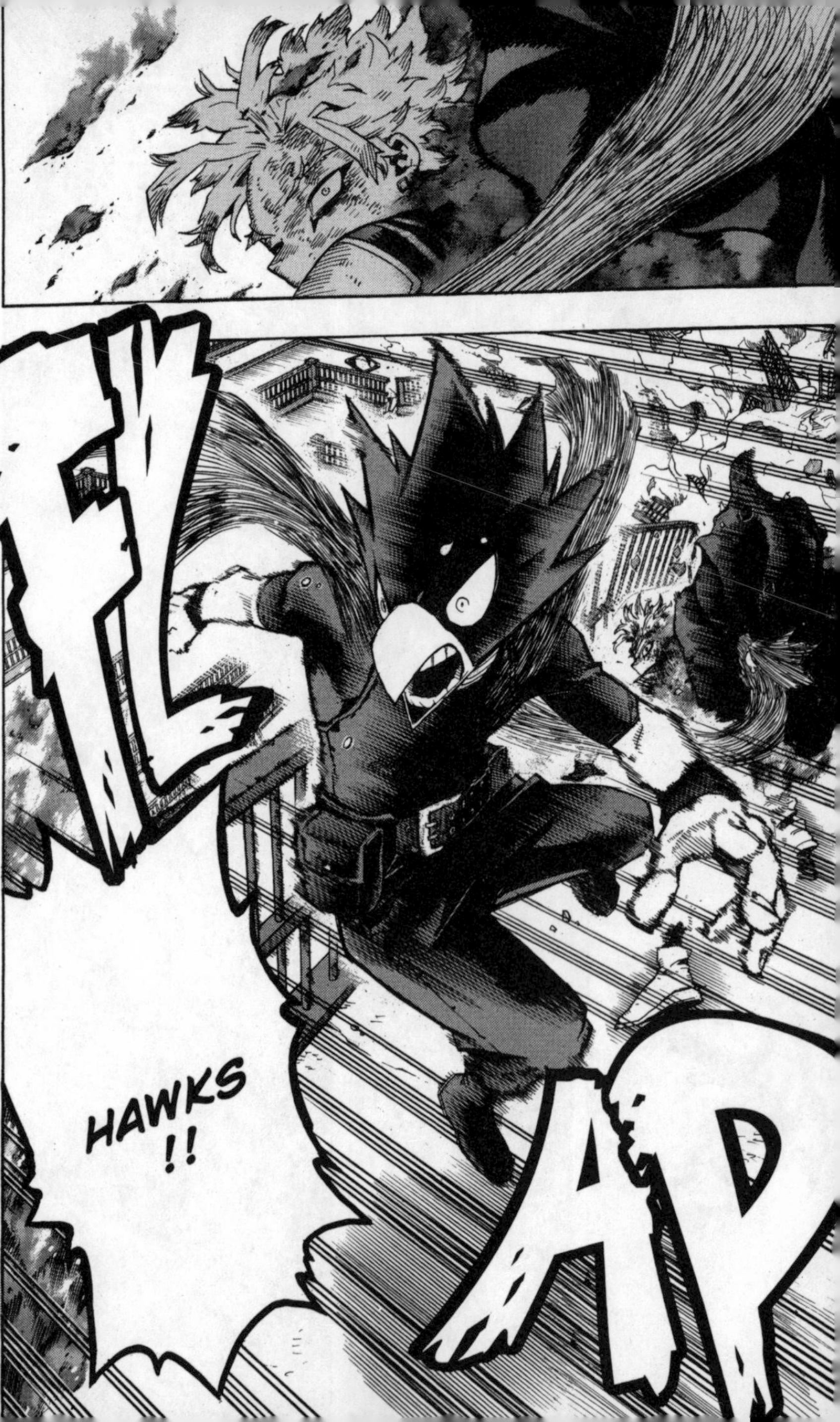
FLAP
HAWKS !!

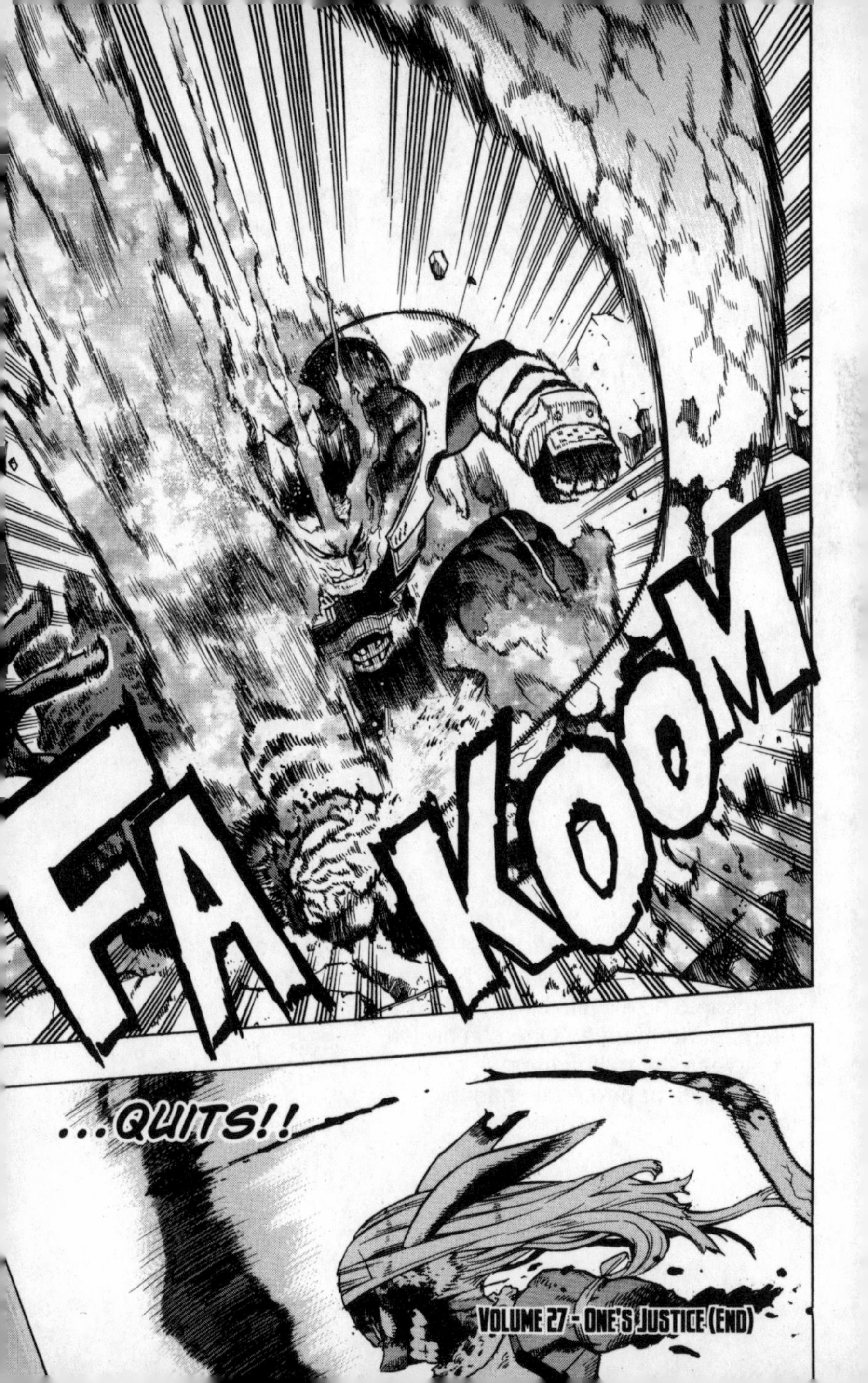
KA-KOOM
...QUITS!!
VOLUME 27 - ONE'S JUSTICE (END)

THE EARPIECE

HNKS-425M

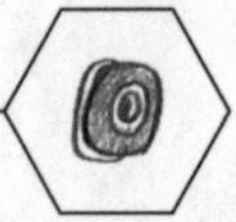

Modeling the earpiece: Moon-Viewing Mirko

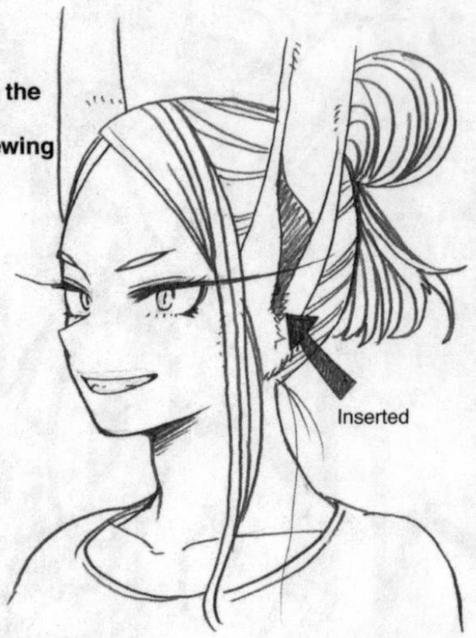
Inserted

All heroes are equipped with these micro earpieces. When someone puts a hand to their ear and speaks, that's what they're using. The earpiece stays in there, right near the ear canal, and since it isn't visible, that means no extra work to draw it!!

Mr. Skeptic (Chikazoku) 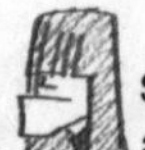 stuck a bunch of micro devices on Hawks, and these are about the same size while still boasting high performance!! One can switch between the main channel, group channels, or personal channels.

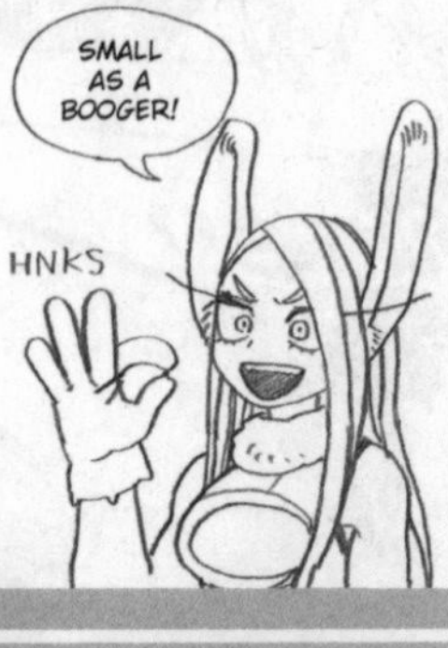
SMALL AS A BOOGER!
HNKS

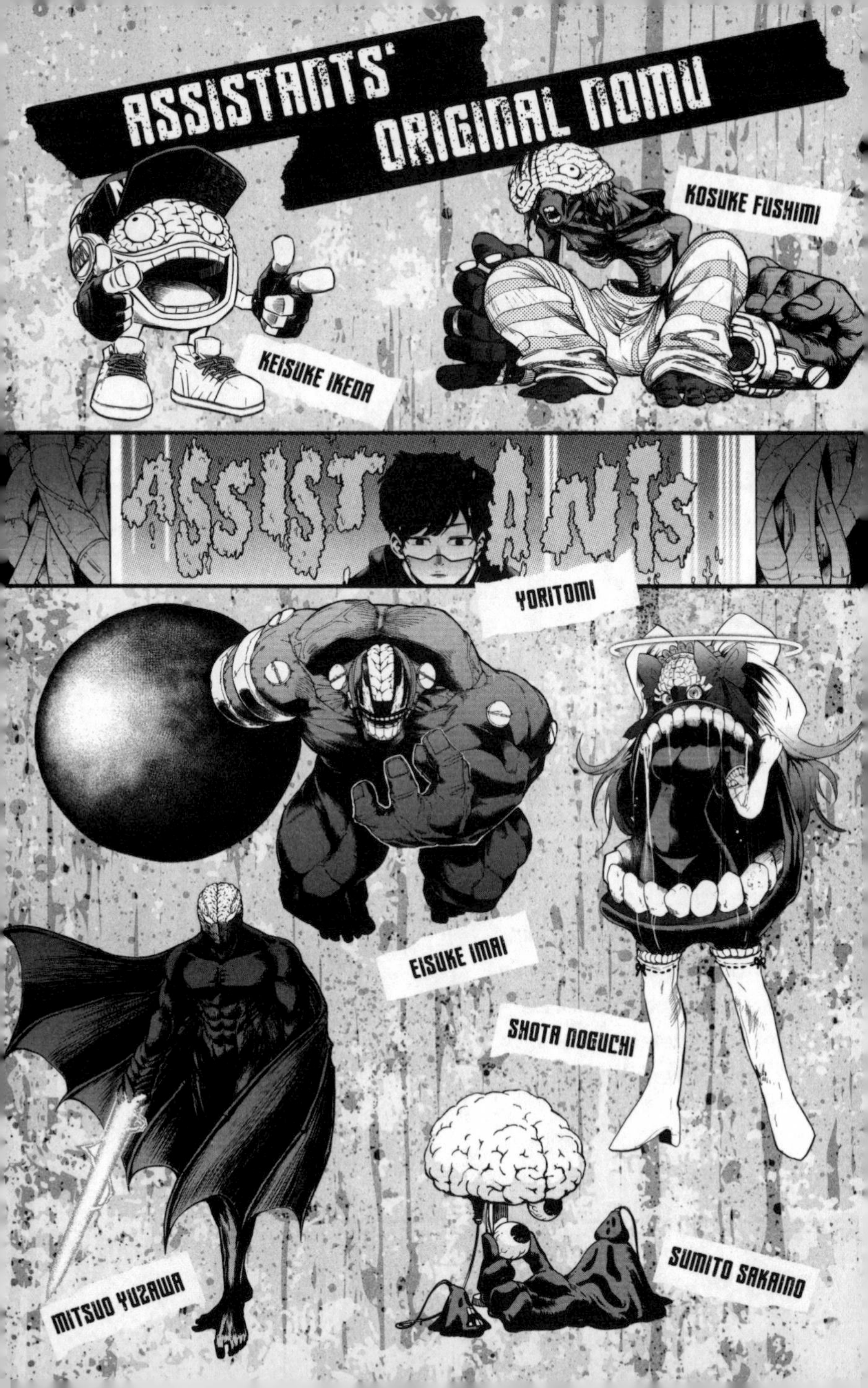
ASSISTANTS' ORIGINAL NOMU
KOSUKE FUSHIMI
KEISUKE IKEDA
ASSISTANTS
YORITOMI
SHOTA NOGUCHI
EISUKE IMAI
SUMITO SAKAINO
MITSUO YUZAWA

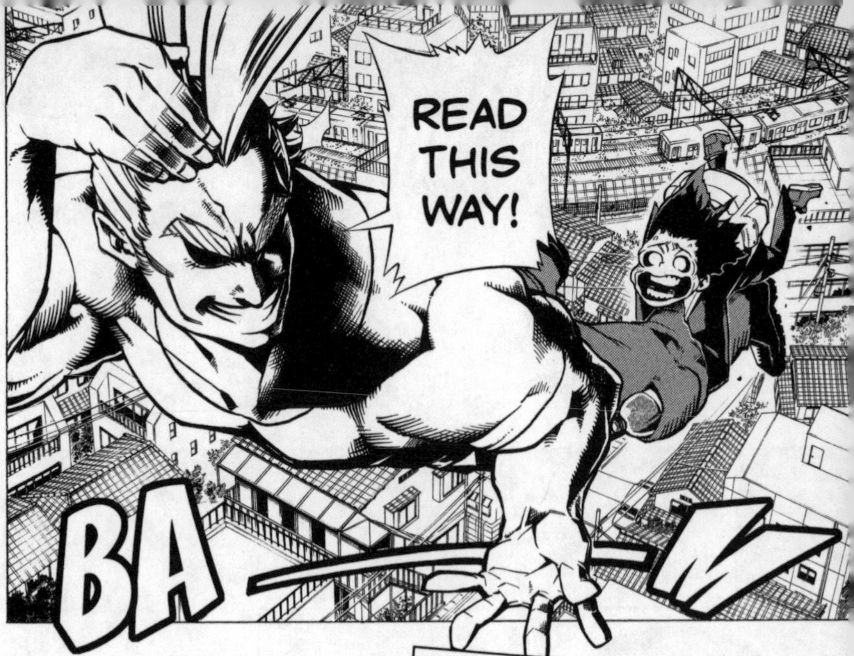
READ THIS WAY!
BA-M

MY HERO ACADEMIA

reads from right to left, starting in the upper-right corner. Japanese is read from right to left, meaning that action, sound effects and word-balloon order are completely reversed from English order.

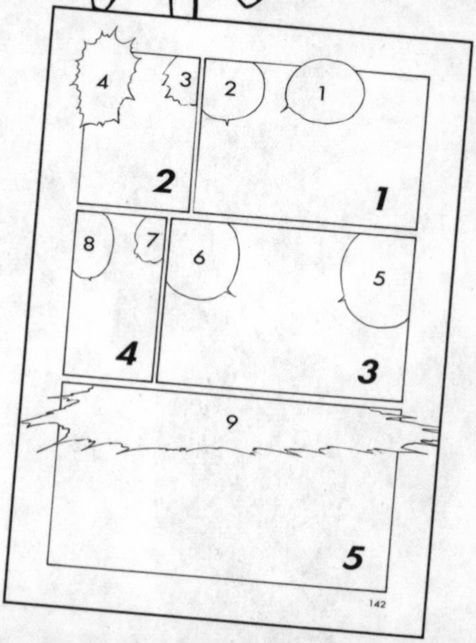
1
2
3
4
1
2
5
6
7
8
3
4
9
5
142